The Templars

For my wife Gerdien

Koert ter Veen

The Templars
Laying a legend to rest

2006 Uitgeverij Aspekt

The Templars. Laying a legend to rest
Original title: De Tempeliers. Afrekening met een legende
© Koert ter Veen
Translating: Della M. Breukelaar
© 2006 Uitgeverij ASPEKt
Amersfoortsestraat 27, 3769 AD Soesterberg, The Netherlands
info@uitgeverijaspekt.nl / http://www.uitgeverijaspekt.nl
Cover design: Peter Koch
Setting and layout: Paul Timmerman

ISBN: 90-5911-374-8

All rights reserved. No part of this publication may be reproduced in any form or by any means without written permission of the publisher.

Contents

Preface 9

I **The mother of all journeys** 13
 The preceding history 13
 The First Crusade (1095-1099) 15
 The knights 23
 The pilgrims 27
 The Kingdom of Jerusalem 28

II **The first years of the Order of the Temple** 31
 The founding of the Order 31
 Monk and soldier, is that possible? 36
 Knights of St. John or Hospitallers 38
 The descendants of Jesus 38
 The sepulchre of Jesus 42
 The Stone of Wisdom 46

III **The daily life of the Templars** 48
 The Rules 48
 The organisation 53
 The functionaries of the Order 56
 The caring of the sick 67
 The Chapter meeting 69
 Punishments 70
 The daily life of a Templar 74
 The meals 75
 The clothes of the Templars 76
 The entrance into the Order 77
 Temporary members 78
 The election of a new Grand Master 81

IV	**The period 1120-1192. Rise and fall**	*83*
	The Order of the Temple until the Second Crusade (1147)	*83*
	The Second Crusade (1147-1149)	*87*
	Noer-ad-Din: the turning point	*90*
	Saladin: the champion of the Muslims	*99*
	The battle of Hattin	*104*
	The Third Crusade (1189-1192)	*110*
	The Teutonic Knights	*114*
	The battle on the Iberian Peninsula	*115*
V	**The Templars in Europe**	*117*
	The Dutch participation in the Crusades	*117*
	Templar establishments in the Netherlands	*121*
	France	*125*
	The possessions of the Templars in the rest of Europe	*129*
	A preceptory	*136*
	The churches of the Order of the Templars	*137*
	They were not that rich	*138*
VI	**The period of 1193-1244. Anarchy sometimes pays**	*141*
	The Holy Land up to 1218	*141*
	The Fourth Crusade (1202-1204)	*144*
	The Turin Shroud	*146*
	The Fifth Crusade (1217-1221)	*148*
	The Sixth Crusade (1228-1229)	*154*
	The thirteen-thirties	*157*
VII	**The construction of the castle of Safad**	*163*
	Introduction	*163*
	De Constructione Castri Saphet	*164*
	Finally	*173*
VIII	**The period 1244-1291. The last convulsions**	*175*
	The defeat at La Forbie	*175*
	The Seventh Crusade (1248-1254)	*177*
	The Eighth Crusade (1270)	*185*
	Were the Templars and the Hospitallers enemies?	*189*
	The aftermath of the Crusades	*190*
IX	**The military role of the Order of the Templars**	*192*
	The Christian armies	*192*
	The war in the Middle East	*193*
	The *Hierarchical Statutes*	*195*

      The recrutement of the Templars   *199*
      The function of castles   *200*
      The battle for a stronghold   *202*
      The castles of the Templars   *204*
      The fleet of the Templars   *217*
      Jerusalem   *219*
      Acre   *221*

X   **The image of the Templars**   *222*
      Introduction   *222*
      The relationship between the Templars and the Muslims   *223*
      The Western monarchs   *225*
      The lower echelon   *231*
      The Popes   *231*
      The beginning of the end of the Templars   *235*

XI   **Fighting a losing battle**   *237*
      The last Grand Masters   *237*
      Who wants another Crusade?   *238*
      The Order on Cyprus   *241*
      James of Molay goes to Paris   *242*
      The inquisition   *244*
      The financial conduct of Philip IV   *245*
      An apocryphal story   *247*

XII **The End**   *248*
      The arrest, 14 September 1307 – 13 October 1307   *248*
      The first examinations, 14 October 1307 – 24 October 1307   *249*
      The examinations of the leaders,
            24 October 1307 – 26 October 1307   *251*
      The reaction of the Pope,
            27 October 1307 – 23 December 1307   *252*
      The impasse, 24 December 1307 – 26 May 1308   *253*
      The negotiations between Clement V en Philip IV,
            26 May 1308 – 11 August 1308   *254*
      The decision of the Pope, August 1308   *255*
      The charges, 12 August 1308   *257*
      The commission of eight, August 1309 – June 1311   *258*
      The defence, March 1310 – May 1310   *260*
      The defence put aside, May 1310   *262*
      The commission of eight is finished, June 1311   *263*

        The pursuits in other countries   *264*
        The end of the Order of the Temple   *271*
        The degree of truth of the accusations   *276*
        Conclusions   *280*

XIII   **The Templars are dead, long live the myths**   *283*
        Introduction   *283*
        The myths about the Templars   *284*
        The Hiram Key   *287*
        Parzival   *290*
        The Ark of Mozes   *293*

Postscript   *298*
The trial still goes on   *298*

Appendix A   *300*
Inventory of the goods from the house of Baugy   *300*
Appendix B   *304*
What James of Molay said   *304*
Appendix C   *307*
Dan Brown, *The Da Vinci Code*   *307*
Appendix D   *309*
List of Grand Masters   *309*
Illustrations   *310*

Briefly bibliography   *313*

Index   *317*

Preface

"Drink like a Templar" is still a well-known Dutch saying even though the Templars ceased to exist nearly 700 years ago. It is the first thing that comes to mind when people hear that the author of this book is interested in the Templars.

Less common, but just as persistent, are the mysterious stories about this Order. It is said to have been a mystical fellowship, surrounded by all sorts of enigmas…

The Templars were active in the 12th and 13th centuries both in the Middle East and Europe. The founding of this organisation was a direct consequence of the First Crusade: the military pilgrimage from Europe to Palestine. In 1096 thousands of Christians left for the Holy Land and they were able to capture it from the Muslims. Approximately 20 years after the taking of Jerusalem, it was in this most Christian city itself that nine knights began the Order of the Temple. They initially wanted to protect the pilgrims along the dangerous Palestinian roads.

The King of Jerusalem gave them the use of a section of his palace, above the spot where the Temple of Solomon used to be located. That is where the name of the Order originates from. Nine years later the brothers of the Temple formed the first official Roman Catholic military order; the members were monks as well as soldiers. They instantly broadened their horizons and became, in a manner of speaking, warriors for a Christian Holy Land.

After 1139 the Templars were only accountable to the Pope and they were very aware of this. It placed them in a powerful position against the Church and World leaders. Thanks to inheritances and donations, they established more than a thousand of their own monasteries in Europe, so-called preceptories.

The Templars fought the Muslims in the Holy Land for nearly 200 years. They financed their expensive operations with profits gained by exploiting their many European assets. After the fall of Acre (the last Christian bastion of the Holy Land) in 1291, the Order was abolished by the Pope in 1312 after a spectacular and long-lasting process which was instigated by King Philip IV, also known as Philip the Fair. He wanted to obtain the putative riches of the Order and therefore accused its members of heresy and sodomy.

In the centuries following the trial, a stream of publications appeared about these monk-soldiers, most of which are of a speculative nature and give the Templars an additional secretive role in the history of the world. Even today books are published about the "secrets" of the Templars; there are authors who allege that the original purpose of the Order was not to protect the pilgrims in the Holy Land. According to them they were underhandedly looking for the Holy Grail (sometimes a chalice, sometimes a stone,) or The Ark of the Covenant (first in Jerusalem and then in Ethiopia). The chalice was said to have been used by Jesus, during the Last Supper, whilst the Ark of the Convenant was being constructed by Moses to house the Stone Tablets, shortly after the departure of the Jewish people from Egypt.

Others claim to know for sure that the Order had found something that would blow Christianity out of the water. The Templars are said to have found the body of Jesus: therefore he could not have risen from the dead, let alone his ascension ever having taken place. A variation on this is that the Templars had documents in their possession about Jesus, "proving" that he was married, or had children, or that he led guerilla warriors in a rebellion against the Roman occupiers. According to others, the Order, quite differently, was intent on reconciling Islam and Christianity with each other. There is not one ounce of evidence that supports any of these claims; they are based upon half-truths, or facts taken out of context, or far-fetched explanations.

The Templars are reputed to have had secret rituals, varying from alchemy, to the worshipping of a skull. Not much is known about this because in their regulations it states, that the members were strictly forbidden to talk to others about the practices of the Order. That was completely understandable in the Middle Ages: the guilds also had an article that formulated a hefty punishment for lose-lips amongst the connected craftsman. Referring to the secrets of the Order will lead to interesting, yet endless conversations. Those who do not believe in secret rules can triumphantly claim that documents have never been found about them. Their opponents subsequently stress that they are indeed secret and then presume the most fantastic possibilities. A strong point of this last group though, is that their views have been formulated into fluently written and exciting books.

Actually there are more than enough explanations to be found about the speculations of the role of the Templars. The archives of the Order are lost, therefore there is very little factual information available, thus making it easier in itself to (re)write its history.

The trial of the Templars (1307-1312) is encompassed in peculiarities; moreover, we know of typical confessions, obtained through terrible torture. Our only information about this originates from the prosecutors, who were stimulated by the French King, Philip IV, to deal with truth imaginatively. Most of these statements however, are taken as being true by many writers.

For the rest, for someone from this time, it remains a difficult to understand and paradoxical phenomenon: clergymen, sanctioned by the Pope, brandishing a sword. Not being able to place this medieval occurrence can easily lead to the forming of myths.

Historians, who write serious books about this Order, shrug their shoulders in contempt when they see the many fictitious things written about the Templars. They are rarely drawn into the several presuppositions of the writers of the mysticism of the Templars.

The Templars were definitely a phenomonon, but above all the children of their time. Strikingly enough they were not the only monk-soldiers. In the twelfth century there were also several other religious orders with a military task. The Hospitallers (also known as the Knights of St. John or the Knights of Malta) may not have appealed to people's imagination at the time of the Crusades, but they were just as powerful. This Order, be it with an altered objective, is still in existence today. There are no strange stories circulating about the Hospitallers, with one exception. In the eighteenth century, the Scot Ramsay was the first to establish a relationship between the Crusaders and the English Freemasons. This connection was the Knight of the Hospital of St. John of Jerusalem. The Templars came into the picture shortly afterwards: by which time they had been dead for centuries and therefore unable to comment on these sorts of suggestions.

The history of the Templars can be regarded to as a jigsaw puzzle with lots of pieces missing. Many authors do their best to complete this puzzle and construct the lacking pieces themselves. Their most important tool for doing this is often their boundless imagination. Putting the facts into another perspective produces different forms, which seem to fit into the jigsaw puzzle.

For a clear understanding of the Order of the Temple, a study of the Crusades and the colonisation that followed is essential. The founding and the rapid growth had everything to do with the war between the Muslims and the Christians. This book, for these reasons, goes into detail about the events in the Holy Land. At the same time, various myths about the Templars will be exposed and disputed. A seperate appendix will also explain which falsehoods Dan Brown has written in this book, *The Da Vinci code*.

The Templars were Christian knights who fought the Muslims, enemies of the Middle Age Europeans, with fire and with sword, nothing more and nothing less. In a nutshell, that is the drift of this book.

Koert ter Veen, July 2006.

I. The mother of all journeys

THE PRECEDING HISTORY

Western Europe
Around 475 after the fall of the western part of the Roman Empire, many areas of Western Europe fell into decay. Tribes of Middle and Eastern Europe (such as Huns and Vandals) plundered their way through Western Europe, some of them permanently settling there. Little of the highly developed Roman culture and jurisdiction remained. Later the Normans went ahead and did it all over again, but this time with less ferocity. It was not until the eleventh century that the situation became relatively stable. The Church of Rome succeeded, via their connections with important dynasties, in expanding its influence enormously, during the Middle Ages. It would reach the heath of its powers in the twelfth century.

In the tenth and eleventh centuries the King's authority declined, so, on the eve of the Crusades, Western Europe mainly consisted of a number of small independent provinces. It was only in Germany where an Emperor remained, but his position largely depended on the feudal rulers of the different states in his country. The economical growth in the second half of the eleventh century was coupled with an increase in the population and a rivival of trade. These proved to be the most important conditions for the success of the First Crusade.

Byzantium
The Eastern Roman Empire, also known as Byzantium, retained a prominent position after the fall of the Western Roman Empire. Constantinople (now Istanbul), established in the beginning of the fourth century by the Roman Emperor Constantine, became an important centre that ruled over a great part of Asia Minor. Despite periods of internal division and the rise of Islam, it remained one of the most powerful Empires in the world. At the end of the

eleventh century, art, knowledge and legislation arose to a considerably higher level than in Western Europe.

The diversity in the development of West and East caused a difference in the experiencing of the Christian faith. The Greek Orthodox believers saw the Church of Rome less and less as the Mother Church and increasingly demanded an independent position. Consequently, they gradually distanced themselves from the Christians of Rome.

At the end of the eleventh century the Byzantine Empire was attacked from various sides. Egypt, Palestine and Syria were conquered in the seventh and eight century by Muslims, and then from Turkey they threatened Constantinople. The Bulgarians revolted on the northern border. It was obvious that Byzantium turned to the West for support; in spite of their differences there were still ties of friendship with the Church of Rome. There were regular negotiations taking place about Western military help in exchange for the reintegration of both religions.

Arabia

Mohammed and his successors founded an Islamic Empire during the seventh century which rapidly occupied a large portion of Byzantium. In 638 they peacefully captured Jerusalem from the Byzantines. Apart from a short interruption, this city had been in the hands of the (Eastern) Romans for more than 700 years. Despite the dominance of the Muslims most Christian and Jewish believers had freedom of choice of religion. In addition, the Christians and Jews played an important role in the Arabian court, developing many branches of knowledge. Just as in Byzantium, civilization stood at a high level in the areas that were controlled by the Muslims, incomparable with Western Europe.

At the end of the tenth century the unity of the Muslims decreased due to the lack of a strong leader. Still, in 1071 they brought a crushing defeat to the Byzantines and thereby increased the pressure on Constantinople, in such a way that the Byzantines advancement attempts expanded out to the West. In 1098, shortly before the arrival of the Crusaders in the Holy Land, the Egyptians conquered Jerusalem from the Turks. This was characteristic of the aforesaid division amongst the Muslims.

The First Crusade (1095-1099)

The appeal

During the Council of Clermont (France) in November 1095, Pope Urban II appealed for a Crusade to liberate the Holy Places in and around Palestine. Fulcher of Chartres was alleged to be present and in 1122 left a report of Urban's sermon:

> *Let hatred therefore depart from among you, let your quarrels end, let wars cease, and let all dissensions and controversies slumber. Enter upon the road to the Holy Sepulcher, wrest that land from the wicked race, and subject it to yourselves. That land which, as the Scripture says, 'floweth with milk and honey' was given by God into the power of the children of Israel. Jerusalem is the centre of the earth; the land is fruitful above all others, like another paradise of delights. This spot the Redeemer of mankind has made illustrious by his advent, has beautified by his sojourn, has consecrated by his passion, has redeemed by his death, has glorified by his burial. This royal city, however, situated at the centre of the earth, is now held captive by the enemies of Christ and is subjected, by those who do not know God, to the worship of the heathen. She seeks, therefore, and desires to be liberated and ceases not to implore you to come to her aid. From you especially she asks succour, because as we have already said, God has conferred upon you above all other Nations great glory in arms. Accordingly, undertake this journey eagerly for the remission of your sins, with the assurance of the reward of imperishable glory in the kingdom of heaven*

This appeal by the Western Church leader was a reaction to the request of the East Roman Emperor, Alexius I, to help him to defend his Empire against the threat of the Turks. Urban II had a number of other considerations for making a Christian army available. Jerusalem had to be liberated from the heathens, the Western pilgrims needed protecting, he found it necessary to strengthen the ecclesiastical power and Urban II was determined to give the knights a purposeful pastime.

Before being appointed, the Pope had been a member of the Cluny movement, a monastic order that came to prosperity in the eleventh century and propagated the pilgrimages to the Holy Land. A number of incidents in Asia Minor, where pilgrims died, were one of the main reasons for the Pope to request the Crusade. These events were moreover the effect of the unsteady

Pope Urban II calls for the holding of a Crusade at the Council of Clermont on November 1095. The illustration from 1490 is not in agreement with the chronicles because, according to them, the appeal of the Pope was done on a podium in an open field outside the Eastern entrance of the city.

political situation there, rather than the result of the persecution of other religions. From the beginning, Jews and Christians were regarded to as 'people of the Book of Books'. In the Koran, chapter 62, it is formulated thus:

> *They who believe, they who adhere to Judaism, the Christians and the Sabiërs who believe in God and the last day and who are virtuous, for them their reward is with their Lord and they have nothing to fear nor shall they be sad.*

Despite a couple of short periods of oppression and a few limitations of civil rights, many Christian and Jewish believers lived in the Islamic controlled territory. In those days Islam demonstrated more tolerance with regard to dissidents, than was shown by the Christians. No matter what, Pope Urban II considered the Muslims as heathens and therefore a threat to Christianity.

The papacy had just had a power struggle with the German Emperor; the issue being, who should name the Bishops, the Church or the Emperor (Investiture controversy). After the passing of a few years, Pope Gregory VII (the predecessor of Urban II) had what he wanted. The Church became a mighty factor which world sovereigns had to take into due consideration. Urban II made good use of this and with his appeal took charge of an international movement, thus confirming his leading position in the Church, also in the eyes of the World.

The Pope was, according to the reports of eye witnesses of his sermon, very aware of the unrest that the knights were bringing about in Western Europe. Knights were owners of fortified farms who had enough money to buy themselves a horse and armour. They received the land as a fief from their so called feudal lords. To compensate, the knights were obliged to offer their military services to their landowner. For this reason, the knight's sons received a military education from a very young age; therefore the brandishing of a sword became second nature to them. Towards the end of the eleventh century there were seldom wars in Europe and the authority of the Kings was minimal. A large number of provinces were created and these were governed by noblemen. The knights of these regional viscounts passed their time by keeping up their level of fighting strength and most of them made the country unsafe with their rapacious behaviour. The Church failed to protect the common man against these hooligans, despite various ecclesiastical disciplinary rules. The Crusade was a wonderful solution to this problem, because it enabled the knights to demonstrate their military ability elsewhere.

The fact that the request by the Pope coincided with a Church ruling, which granted the participants forgiveness for all their sins, also benefited the knights. They could redeem their sinful lives in one fell swoop: participating in the journey provided them with, as it were, an indulgence, and through that an entrance into the heavenly Jerusalem. For some landowners, such as those from North France, the wish of the Pope was a blessing too. The rich wanted to prevent the division of their possessions and therefore ensured that their estates were inherited by the eldest son, after their death. The conquering of the Holy Land gave their younger sons the chance to gain the status of landowner. At the same time, the whole of Christian Europe was convinced that the end of the world was near. It goes without saying that when Jesus returned to earth the first place he would turn to would obviously be Jerusalem: the Crusaders wanted to witness this, dead or alive.

The message from the Pope had a wonderful effect on the majority of the public. For the average man taking part in the Crusade, besides the aforementioned religious benefits, it also had economical advantages. At the end of the eleventh century the countyside was overpopulated. A number of the poor people wanted to begin a new life in Palestine.

Urban sent his Bishops, from the Council of Clermont, through Western Europe to propagate the concept of the Crusade. An international and widely spread organisation, such as the Church of Rome, was definitely the appropriate choice to pass on a message. The cry, Deus lo volt (It is Gods will), buzzed throughout the whole of Western Europe. The word of Jesus actually said:

> *Should someone want to follow me, renounce oneself and take up the cross and follow me.*

Various lay preachers took over the appeal from the Pope. The most famous was Peter of Amiens, also known as Peter the Hermit, who, according to a legend, received a divine letter with the request that he help to liberate the Holy Land. The German knight Walter Sans-Avoir, also succeeded in convincing many ordinary citizens to move to Jerusalem.

The population couldn't neglect the papal call: in that time the Church had an enormous influence on almost all aspects of society. A suitable example of this is connected with cartography. Maps from this period had one thing in common; Jerusalem was drawn in the centre. Absolutely logical because in the Bible (Ezekiel 5, verse 5) it states the following:

Thus says the Lord God: this is Jerusalem; I have set her in the centre of the nations, with countries all around her.

This reasoning stems from the influential St. Jerome who, in the fourth century, translated the Holy Bible into Latin (the Vulgate).

It was the intention of the Pope that the journey should begin on the 15th August 1096, after the harvest, under the supervision of a papal envoy. However, the propaganda of the Bishops and that of the lay preachers was an instant success. Many 'took the cross': as a sign of the pilgrim they attached a red cross to the chest. Instead of just one, at least seven armies left for Jerusalem, a journey of more than four thousand kilometres.

Historians today are of different opinions when it comes to the question of which light the First Crusade should be seen in. Was it a religious war, had the result of the papal call an economical background, was it about adventurers who only had their own interest in mind or was the Crusade the first example of a Western expansion movement? For each and every one of these views there is something to be said. In spite of all these explanations it remains odd, that so many were prepared to undertake the barren and distant (foot)journey to an unknown destination.

The seven armies

Three people's armies were the first to go on their way to the Holy Land, under the leadership of, amongst others, Peter of Amiens and Walter Sans-Avoir. They were not willing to wait for the papal force and they departed in the beginning of 1096.

After all sorts of misbehaviour (such as the massacre of a number of Jewish communities in Germany, plundering in Hungary, Constantinople and in Turkey), two people's armies were crushed by the Turks just beyond the Bosporus. A few farmers, women, children, old men and a handful of knights could not stand up to the soldiers of the Turkish Emir. The third people's army didn't get any further than the Hungarian border. The King, who out of experience had become wise, denied them passage and when the pilgrims insisted on crossing the border they were slaughtered by his army.

The four remaining armies were under the leadership of a number of important noble leaders: Hugh, Count of Vermandois, the brother of the French King from North France, the Fleming Godfrey of Bouillon and his younger brother Baldwin. Furthermore the Norman, Bohemond from South Italy, Bishop Adhémar of Le Puy and Raymond of St. Gilles, Count of Toulouse, from

An old map from the thirteenth century depicting the three well known continents: Europe (bottom left), Africa (bottom right) and Asia (top). Jerusalem is drawn in the middle conforming to a text out of the Bible.

the South of France. Adhémar of Le Puy and Raymond were in charge of the papal army. If we are to believe the chroniclers, the First Crusade had eight hundred thousand participants: knights, infantrymen and pilgrims. In reality the total would have been considerably less: sixty thousand people, of whom six thousand knights and tens of thousands of soldiers. Old people, women and children also went with them to Jerusalem. The four armies left in the period between the end of August and the end of October 1096 and in May 1097 they began their journey together from the meeting place of Constantinople, via Turkey, to the Promised Land. Due to the fact that most of the group had to walk, the journey took them more than three years. After all sorts of adventures, battles and hardships, part (present day predictions being fifteen thousand people, of which fifteen hundred were knights) of the army reached Jerusalem on the 7th of June 1099. Six weeks later on the 15th of July 1099, the Crusaders conquered this Holy City and murdered nearly all Jewish and Islamic inhabitants. The historian William of Tyre (1130-1184) described the conquest of the city as follows:

> *It was a Friday at the ninth hour. Verily, it seemed divinely ordained that the faithful who were fighting for the glory of the Saviour should have obtained the consummation of their desires at the same hour and on the very day on which the Lord had suffered in that city for the salvation of the world. It was on that day, as we read, that the first man was created and the second was delivered over to death for salvation of the first. It was fitting, therefore, that, at that very hour, those who were members of His body and imitators of Him should triumph in His name over His enemies.*

Pope Urban would never hear about the taking of the City. He died at the end of July 1099, before the message of the conquering of Jerusalem reached the West.

Eventually, three years after their departure, a number of leaders from the four original armies succeeded with their plans. Godfrey of Bouillon became the first ruler of the Kingdom of Jerusalem (between Sinai and Lebanon). His brother, Baldwin of Bouillon, became the Count of the county of Edessa (North East of Syria), Bohemond became Prince of the principality of Antioch (South East Turkey, near the Mediterranean Sea) and Bertrand, the son of Raymond of St. Gilles, conquered the county of Tripoli (North Lebanon). These four areas were named the Latin States.

The people's army of Peter of Amiens was ambushed on the way to Constantinople by Bulgarians. The pilgrims wear white clothes as sign of their purity.

During a period of two hundred years there was a continual movement of knights and pilgrims to the Middle East: including those from 1096, there are eight of these people movements known under the name Crusade. It would take until 1291 before all Western occupations in the Holy Land were reclaimed by the Muslims.

THE MOTHER OF ALL JOURNEYS

The Crusaders take Jerusalem on 15 July 1099. Of the mass slaughter that followed, the chronicler, Raymond of Aguliers says that when he wanted to visit the Temple area, he had to make his way through 'blood and bodies that reached up to my knees.'

THE KNIGHTS

In the beginning of the eleventh century France was one of the first feudal states of Europe. The French King stood at the head of this hierarchical system, upper liege of six Dukes and Counts. Each of these noblemen had their own servants at their disposal, many of whom belonged to the nobility. The lower layer of this pyramid consisted of simple knights. These employed just enough farmers and they had land to fief to support their liege. This meant that they

The two upper rows represent the Last Judgment. In the next to last drawing the Jews and the knights (armati milites) are cooked in a cauldron. A small majority were of the opinion that the knights would end up in hell. (Miniature from the end of the twelfth century).

were in a position to pay for horses and weapons, a huge expense. Due to the status that a knight possessed in the Middle Ages, the soldier-farmer thought that it was more than worth it. It suited the liege down to the ground because the waging of war was the most important objective of the feudal system.

In most feudal estates there was a difference between defensive and aggressive campaigns. Participation in the latter was short, mostly 40 days. If a feudal estate was in danger, the servants had to be ready and waiting until the threat had passed. Every region therefore had its own army with heavily armed horsemen. Officially the King sat at the top of the feudal pyramid, but in reality he was tolerated by his servants. He was often less powerful than a number of his vassals. Only the Church, for what it was worth, recognised his God given authority. The feudal system in the lower regions was anything but immobile: vassals from various feudal estates fought to gain as much ground or claims on ground as possible. The vassals of the Counts and Dukes tried to break away from the authority of the liege in order to obtain the feudal goods for themselves. If that was successful, then more often than not, they appropriated a nobility title too.

An important condition for extending the territory was the asset of a castle, because in those days it was not so simple to conquer such a stronghold. Just as later in the Holy Land, a castle was a political and military centre of power for miles around.

In Western Europe countless skirmishes were taking place, but these regional conflicts remained limited in size. The Church tried to minimise the effect of these conflicts by placing a religious ban upon the attacking of the non-military. To that end they forbad fighting on Sundays and religious holidays. These disciplinary rules had little effect and sanctioned, in a manner of speaking, the behaviour of the knights. If you forbid something in the weekend, you are surely suggesting that it is permitted during the week.

Fighting remained the main pastime of the feudal knight. He was trained from an early age to fight: wearing the heavy armour alone, demanded an excellent condition. The speciality of the knight was that he could hit a target with his spear whilst in full gallop, holding his shield in his other hand at the same time. If he demonstrated that he could do this, then he had succeeded in becoming a knight. In the eleventh century it was a simple ceremony: an experienced knight would hand over his weapons to him, he then gave him a hard slap with his arm or the flat side of the blade of his sword. Throughout his entire life the knight would practice with his weapons or fight with his neighbours. The average knight was wild, illiterate and rude; we would now call him a barbarian. He was well aware of the dogmas of Christianity, but was not impressed with the ethical issues. Nearly every medieval person believed in God, but it was an egocentric belief. The goal was to get to Heaven and that happened if he went to Mass, fasted regularly, underwent small punishments now and then and if possible, took part in a pilgrimage. If man abided by these practices completely, his daily life was of less importance. Outside of the Church the strongest ruled. The donating of money, goods and land to the church or the nearby monasteries was a prevalent way to pay for the sins. With that in mind the Pope took advantage of this by promising to give all the Crusaders forgiveness for their sins.

The Normans were the most important exporters of the French feudal system. William the Conqueror, a Norman from Normandy, occupied England in 1066 and introduced the feudal system. Countrymen of William conquered Sicily and South Italy and governed these areas in the feudal way. It was not until the twelfth century that Germany was also feudally governed.

During the Middle Ages the Church became increasingly involved in world affairs. The extensive lands of Bishops were governed by secular lords, in accordance with the feudal system. Sometimes the Bishops went to the front line in the battle, waving their sceptres. The leaders of the Church believed that they were not breaking their religious vows by doing so, since you could not spill blood with such a device.

According to Van Dale (the Dutch equivalent of the Oxford English Dictionary) knightly means: brave, honourable, chivalrous or gallant. The first knights were definitely brave, but it was not until after the fourteenth century that the other qualifications were practiced by the knights. Huizinga (2001) describes in his book, *The Waning of the Middle Ages*, an impression of the fourteenth century Western society:

> *The background of all life in the world seems black. Everywhere the flames of hatred arise and injustice reigns. Satan covers a gloomy earth with his sombre wings. In vain the militant Church battles, preachers deliver their sermons; the world remains unconverted. According to a popular belief, current towards the end of the fourteenth century, no one, since the beginning of the great Western schism, had entered Paradise.*

In the previous centuries it had been no different.

The pilgrims

From the beginning of Christianity, believers had headed towards Palestine, the biblical land. In the fourth century Emperor Constantine and his mother Helena gave this pilgrimage an extra boost. Helena had archaeological investigations carried out at places named in the Bible and marked these by building of a number of churches. With the conquering of Jerusalem in 1099, the pilgrim journeys to the Holy Land were re-stimulated.

From all the biblical geographical references, there are two that spring to mind which had the greatest appeal: Jerusalem and the Jordan. In Jerusalem, a magical reputatian for Christians, the following holy sanctuaries were popular: the spot where Jesus was arrested (the Garden of Gethsemane), the Via Dolorosa (the road to Golgotha) and Golgotha (the place where Jesus was crucified). Also the Mount of Olives (Jesus' ascension) and the Holy Sepulchre (grave of Jesus), which was founded by Helena, were attractive places for the Western pilgrims.

The Jordan is the river in which Jesus was baptised. Pilgrims bathed in it and filled bottles with water: an easy to take souvenir. From Jerusalem it was roughly thirty kilometres to the Jordan. The road ran through the savage mountains of Judea, an ideal site for ambushers. In the early years, after the conquering by the Western Europeans, the situation round and about the Holy Sanctuaries was extremely dangerous. This was mostly due to the aggressive and blood thirsty behaviour of the Franks, a collective name for the Western European colonists, during the first ten years of occupation. The inhabitants of the Middle East were used to the comings and goings of rulers; but the Western power seekers did not make themselves popular with the Muslim population because of their disdainful behaviour. The Franks occupied most of the cities of the Holy Land, whilst the Muslims controlled the countryside. According to eyewitness reports of the twelfth century, it was dangerous to leave the cities to visit the Holy Places without an armed escort: even directly under the walls of Jerusalem the life of the pilgrim was not safe. So in 1119, seven hundred unarmed pilgrims went on their way from Jerusalem to the Jordan and walked into an ambush: three hundred of them were killed and sixty were taken prisoner. An army sent by King Baldwin II arrived too late. The historian Barber (1994) presumes that this occurrence led to the founding of the Order of the Temple.

Furthermore, the pilgrims could be attacked by wild animals: lions, hyenas, leopards and bears all made the roads exceptionally dangerous. Amongst others, the Arabian history writer Usāmah (1095-1188) made many references to this. He described a Western knight who defeated four Islamic horsemen and then along the road to Antioch was attacked and eaten by a lion. Another Frank was annoyed by the fact that a leopard regularly nestled in the window of a church. Fully armed, he tried to chase away the leopard, but he was killed by the animal instead. The Muslims named the animal thereafter 'the leopard that participated in the Holy War'.

The Kingdom of Jerusalem

Actually, Bishop Adhémar of Le Puy was supposed to have become ruler of Jerusalem on behalf of the Pope, but he died on the 1st of August 1098 in the newly conquered Antioch. Godfrey of Bouillon was chosen to take his place as the ruler of the Kingdom of Jerusalem. The Fleming did not take on the title of King, but named himself Advocatus Sancti Sepulchri, the dedicated defender of the Holy Sepulchre. He probably did that as a gesture of good will to the Church: with this title he accentuated that Jerusalem would not be ruled by a worldly sovereign. Godfrey died a year later from typhoid and his brother, the Count of Edessa, succeeded him as King Baldwin I. The nephew of the brothers, another Baldwin, became the second Count of Edessa. Following the death of his uncle in 1118, he was crowned as King of Jerusalem, under the name of Baldwin II.

Both Baldwins were excellent army commanders, who extended their territory in an aggressive manner. In the period from 1100 to 1110 the Crusaders found themselves in a permanent state of war with the Muslims. Every lost battle could mean the end. An added problem was that most of the Crusaders, considered the conquering of Jerusalem the completion of their mission and returned to Europe. According to the chronicler Fulcher of Chartres, only three hundred knights and approximately one thousand infantrymen remained in the Kingdom of Jerusalem. Fulcher knew what he was talking about: he had joined King Baldwin I (as chaplain) in the First Crusade and he had established himself permanently in the Holy Land. Fortunately for the Crusaders, the Muslims were hopelessly divided and they couldn't muster up a collective army.

The colonists succeeded in conquering most cities in the Holy Land with the help of the Italian harbour cities such as, Pisa, Venice and Genoa. In nearly all cases, these conquests involved massacring the Islamic and Jewish population. Mission by word of mouth, in that time and in that area was not the done thing. The medieval person battled with the sword against the enemies of Christ. It goes without saying that the Jews belonged to these enemies; they were indeed held responsible for the death of Jesus.

The First Crusaders behaved, for the most part, as brutal adventurers, concerned only with self profit. There were also those who considered their journey as a mission from God. It was they who founded the Order of the Temple in 1120.

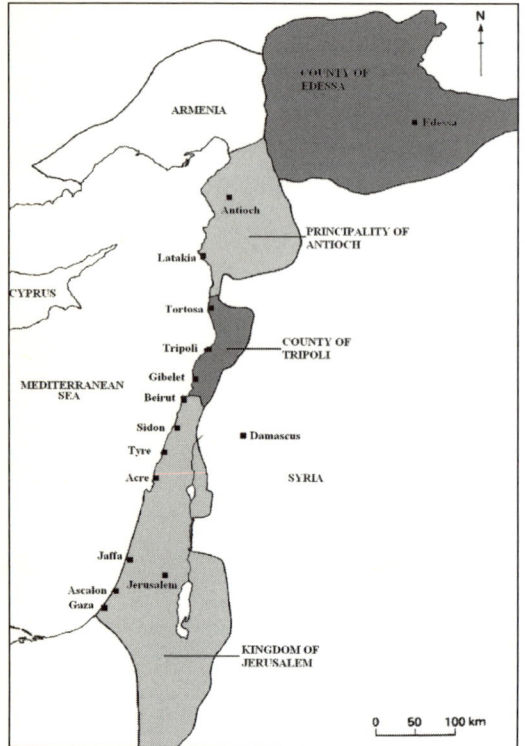 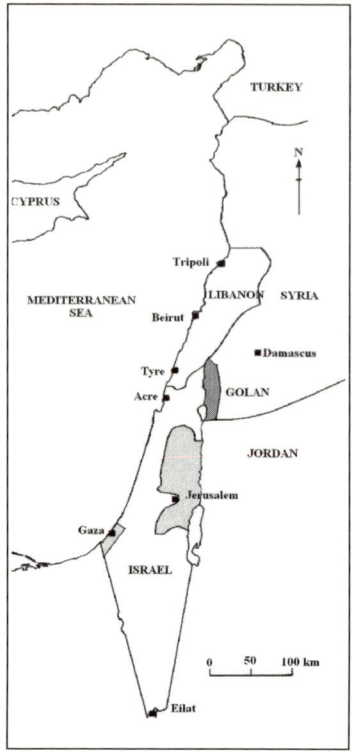

Map of the four Latin States. Around 1140 the Christians were at the peak of their power. Four years later Edessa would be conquered by the Muslims.

Map of Israel anno 2006.

II. The first years of the Order of the Temple

THE FOUNDING OF THE ORDER

The lack of safety on the roads to the biblical places was the reason for the founding of the Order of the Temple. In 1120 a number of knights took the usual monk vows at the hands of the Archbishop of Jerusalem: poverty, chastity and obedience. The knights also promised to protect the Holy Places, so they became a sort of mounted police. From that moment on they were laymen and lived like monks, but they would not be formally recognized as such. For the sake of clarity: a monk did not normally have a religious education, practically every believer could enter a monastery.

King Baldwin II gave the knights accommodation in a section of his palace, the place where once the Temple of Solomon had stood. There was nothing left of this once beautiful temple. The King lived in the al-Aqsa mosque and was about to move to the other side of the city, where he had built a new palace. Shortly thereafter, the group of knights acquired the use of the entire mosque, a number of out-buildings and the appertaining square. Due to the fact that the Crusaders had murdered the original population, there was no shortage of empty buildings.

Fulcher of Chartres, who described the history of the Kingdom of Jerusalem between 1100 and 1127, mentioned that the Franks had insufficient means to maintain the surroundings of the Temple platform. It worked out well then when the Templars offered their services. Baldwin II was in favour of the Order because the Kingdom of Jerusalem was very much in need of the extra army power.

The group quickly became known as the Order of the Temple or the Templars: after all they lived above the Temple of Solomon. The name was a perfect choice: more than any other Order, the Templars made use of the centuries old tradition of the Christian belief. The Temple of Jerusalem was in fact one of the first things that sprang to mind as the symbol of Christianity. Further, there is very little known about the beginning of the Order. The chronicler, William of Tyre, was the first to pay attention to the founding of the Templars. William was the Archbishop of Tyre, a harbour town that was conquered by the Franks in 1124. He was born in Jerusalem in approximately 1130, thus, ten years after the founding of the Templars. In 1170 William began, according to him at the request of King Amalric of the Kingdom of Jerusalem, with the writing of the history of the Crusades.

The Archbishop of Tyre is generally thought to be the best historian of his time. He considered God to be the driving force of the wheel and woe of the Kingdom of Jerusalem and he quoted many citations from the bible in his book. In his chronicle, William made different comments about the early years of the Order. The Archbishop was, in doing so, inconsistent about the exact starting date and he also did not mention from whom the idea had come. Another chronicler alleged that King Baldwin II stimulated Hugh of Payns to found the Templars, and yet another named the Archbishop of Jerusalem as the initiator.

Historians differ further in opinion over the year of the founding of the Order of the Temple. Barber (1994) thinks that it was between the 14th of January and the 13th of September 1120 (in an earlier book he mentioned 1119), whilst Demurger (1985) wavers between 1118 and 1119. Both argue that these dates are based upon the same summarised facts, but inspite of this they draw different conclusions.

Hugh of Payns (1120-1135/1136)
Historians are unanimous about the co-founder and the first leader, Hugh of Payns. Hugh belonged to the middle aristocracy and came from Champagne; Payns was on the Seine, approximately ten kilometres from Troyes, where in 1129 the council was held and where the *Primitive Rule* of the Order of the Temple was fixed. We know little more about Hugh; he had been married and he had a son (Theobald). In 1100 Hugh is mentioned for the first time in the archives. In 1104 Hugh and his feudal lord and uncle, Hugh, Count of Champagne, made their first pilgrimage. In 1114 he left again with the Count, but this time Hugh of Payns remained in the Middle East. His uncle left in 1125 for the third time to go to the Holy Land where he later joined the Order. In doing so, Hugh, Count of Champagne became a subordinate to his previous vassal. Theobald, the son of Hugh of Payns, followed in his father's footsteps and also went to Palestine. He was abbot at a monastery nearby Troyes

and in order to pay his expenses he sold, on his own initiave, a number of valuables belonging to the monastery. His monks would have been annoyed with this theft. Theobald died during the Second Crusade in 1147.

It is unclear how many knights began the Templars. William of Tyre wrote that after nine years there were still nine members. Other historians, from the second half of the twelfth century, named thirty protectors of the pilgrims. Fulcher of Chartres, who went with the First Crusade, did not mention a word about the founding and the dealings of the Templars. Some come to the conclusion that the King had commissioned the Templars for a secret mission. It is more likely, that Fulcher thought that the achievements of the Order were too few to worth mentioning. Anyway in the 1120's the Order of the Temple had already obtained its first possessions in Europe.

For example, La Motte-Palayson (France, 1124), Dowaai (Belgium, 1125), Barbonne (France, 1127) and the castle of Soure (Portugal, 1128). Barbonne was a gift from the nephew of Hugh of Champagne, who had inherited all his uncle's possessions. If the Order carried out a secret mission, they found no importance in the obtaining of these sorts of gifts. In 1127 Hugh of Payns left, with five other members, by ship to go to Europe. According to the counting of William of Tyre this meant that there were only three members who remained behind. That cannot be true; more so because the French historian Dailliez discovered the names of fifteen members of the Templars in documents that were dated from before 1127.

According to William of Tyre, Hugh left Jerusalem on the request of Baldwin II because the King needed soldiers for a campaign against Damascus. The six probably travelled in the company of a commission who were sent to ask Fulk, the Count of Anjou, to marry the oldest daughter of Baldwin II. The King did not have sons and in the Holy Land there were no suitable marriage candidates. Fulk of Anjou, who did indeed succeed Baldwin II, had already been in Jerusalem in 1120 and he had temporarily joined the Order of the Temple. From that moment on he gave the Order a yearly payment and convinced others to follow his example.

Hugh of Payns willingly complied with the request of the King. Apparently he realised that the Templars needed reinforcements from Europe: money and men. For that purpose, it was first necessary that Rome officially acknowledged the Order and thereby giving it status. Perhaps Hugh also wanted the recognition in order to obtain a religious blessing for the, so called monk-soldiers, because until then monks were explicitly forbidden to spill blood. Furthermore, in the beginning of the twelfth century knights had a bad reputation: they belonged to a class that was ferocious, proud and behaved sadistically. The first members therefore, along with approval, would have been reproached for their military plans. Hugh and his companions had the *Primitive Rule*, probably jointly made by the Archbishop of Jerusalem, with them. The members first made a propaganda campaign through Western Europe. Hugh undoubtedly spoke with the Pope and made an advertisement for the Order in France (Champagne, Anjou, Normandy), England, Scotland and Flanders. He also visited the court of Fulk, Count of Anjou. At the Council of Troyes on the 13th of January 1129, he explained the intention of the Order of the Temple and placed the *Primitive Rule* on the agenda.

That a small movement could succeed in putting forward a mission to such an important religious meeting, can only be explained from the fact that the first members had influential friends. Their sympathisers, Bernard of Clairvaux, Fulk, Count of Anjou, and Baldwin II, belonged to the highest circles of their time. By the way, until recently, it was thought that the Council of Troyes was held in 1128. The historian Hiestand, who, with a report of the journey from one of the council members, has proved that this must have been a year later. That the *Primitive Rule* itself also names 1128, is due to the fact that the people in most parts of France, at the beginning of the twelfth century, started a new year on the 25th of March.

Bernard of Clairvaux, the great stimulator of the Cistercian Order, was also present at the council. Bernard was a good friend of the earlier named Hugh of Champagne, the uncle of Hugh of Payns. He would develop into one of the most influential theologians of the twelfth century and, after his death, he was declared a saint. Bernard was involved with the alterations to the *Primitive Rule*, as set out by the council. That was noticeably characteristic of the *Primitive Rule*: the emphasis lay on the monk assignments of the Templars. The military sections would be added to later versions of the rule. A few years later, Bernard gave the Order an extra boost with his pamphlet, *De Laude Novae Militiae* (In Praise of the New Knighthood).

Hugh's European journey was a sensational success; the circumstances, which led to the large participation in the First Crusade still existed. The council spoke positively about the Order, many donated money and goods and approximately three hundred knights went with Hugh of Payns. The Templars had, without any achievements worth mentioning, acquired a fixed base in Europe. They used this for nearly two hundred years to maintain a continual stream of capital, goods and personnel in the direction of the Holy Land.

Bernard of Clairvaux had a great influence on his contemporaries. When he was nineteen and having a crisis of faith, he prayed to a wooden image of Mary and asked if she would intercede for him with the real Mary. The Holy Virgin immediately appeared, squeezed her breast and let three drops of milk drip onto the lips of Bernard.

Monk and soldier, is that possible?

For us Westerners of the 21st century it is a peculiar conception: a religious Christian order, whose members are fanatical soldiers. This was experienced differently in the Middle Ages. In the first centuries, Christians were forbidden to join the army, but that changed when the Roman Emperor Theodosius promoted the Christian doctrine to state religion in the fourth century. Later on the influential Church Father, St. Augustine (354-430), had introduced the acceptance of religious war. For him, a war was permitted, if it was necessary for defending against attackers, the reclaiming of stolen property or the protection of the unity of the Church from heretics. He thought that the worldly ruler and not the Church should handle the sword.

Urban II went a step further and developed the ideas of St. Augustine into an ecclesiastical army for a battle against the heathens in the Holy Land. His successors saw the military order as a further consequence of these thoughts. Furthermore, in the eleventh century it was not unusual for Bishops, Cardinals and even Popes to possess their own armies. They regularly behaved like a worldly power with the land lust and corruption that went hand in hand with it, and favoured their family members including eventual descendants. The difference between spiritual and military leaders was not always so great in the Middle Ages.

Eventually there were two popular phenomena in the Middle Ages: monks and knights. A military order combined both of these ideals. A few theologians judged that Christianity should be spread by the use of the Word. They pointed out that Islam had so many similarities to Christianity, that the differences could be bridged via missionaries. The majority genuinely saw the Muslims as enemies of God who tarnished the Holy Places. They deserved to die by the sword because they disturbed Gods Creation. Bernard of Clairvaux therefore wrote his pamphlet *De Laude*, in which he promised these Christian combatants a place in Gods Kingdom.

In the foreword of *De Laude* Bernard explained that he had written the pamphlet because Hugh of Payns had asked him three times to do so. From various sources it can be derived that in the twenties there were doubts from the Templars themselves about the combination of soldier and monk. Apparently Hugh needed the most influential theologian of his time to write a religious propaganda letter and support the right of the existence of the Order. It had in fact never happened before, that a monastic order pursued violent (and therewith in the nature of things sinful) activities. Bernard was explicitly referring to the new knights in order to differentiate them from the ordinary Crusaders, who were also called Militia of Christ. These consisted, according to Bernard, mainly of sinners, robbers, blasphemers, murderers and adulterers. It seems that the criminal behaviour of the Crusaders had also attracted attention in Western-Europe.

De Laude contained thirteen chapters, of which the first five are dedicated to Gods soldiers. At the same time, it was theologically well-founded as to why monks could brandish a sword. *De Laude* over-idealised the knight, it was (as explained in Chapter I) more a wish than reality. The other chapters are made up of descriptions of the most important Holy Places, including the relevant biblical story. In this way Bernard implicitly emphasised the mission of the Templars: they had to make the pilgrimage in the Holy Land easier.

It was obvious that Hugh had asked Bernard of Clairvaux for the Templars support early on. Ten years earlier Bernard had already proved himself to be a warm advocate of the idea of a Crusade. When an important monk of the Cistercian house wanted to go to the Holy Land with a number of members, Bernard wrote to let him know that the need was for 'militant knights and not for singing and whining monks.' Bernard knew what he was talking about. Before he entered the Cistercian house, at the age of 23, he was a knight for many years and that was noticeable by his use of language. When his fellow members stated that monks must only concern themselves the monastery, Bernard reacted thus:

> *Indeed the soldiers of Christ fearlessly fight the battles of their Lord, in no way concerned about the sin of slaughtering the enemy or about the danger of being killed themselves, for a death either inflicted or suffered for Christ has nothing of sin in it but merits such glory.*

The tendency of Bernard's pamphlet, *De Laude*, was more than a random indication. Still in the second half of the thirteenth century the well known theologian, Thomas Aquinas defended the monk-soldiers and he also took the view that a religious institution could also be used for military purposes. The popularity of the military order received another boost through the habitual donating of a son, to the Church, by practically every family. Because of this, the Cistercians, in the twelfth century, and the Franciscans in the thirteenth century, grew in a short space of time into important institutes. Knight's sons were used to handling weapons from a very early age and many followed the military as well as the spiritual calling. They then chose, logically, for a military order.

Knights of St. John or Hospitallers

Apart from the Templars there were also other monk-soldiers active in the Middle East. The most important were the Order of Saint Lazarus, the Order of Thomas of Acre, the Teutonic Knights and the Hospitallers. The first mentioned was especially intended for knights who were leprous; they were barely mentioned in the chronicles. The Order of Thomas was founded at the end of the twelfth century, motivated by the murder of Thomas Becket, the famous English Cardinal. It was an English order that played no significant role in the Holy Land. The Teutonic Knights, also established at the end of the twelfth century, will be referred to in chapter IV. Together with the Templars there was just one other important military order active in the Middle East; that of the Hospitallers.

Circa 1063, merchants from the Italian harbour city of Amalfi, founded a hospital for pilgrims from the West in Jerusalem. That was years before the conquering of this city by the Franks, but as already stated, the Muslims tolerated the Christians without any problems worth mentioning. The patron Saint of these carers of the sick, was John the Baptist, therefore the Order became known as the Knights of St. John. They wore a black robe with an eight pointed white cross; the symbol of the eight beatitudes from the Sermon on the Mount.

In 1113 they were recognized by the Pope as a Roman Catholic Order, with their sole purpose being the nursing of the sick and poor. After the 1230's they focused themselves more and more on fighting against the Muslims. This they did moreover, without neglecting their original activities. It was towards the end of the twelfth century when they officially received permission from the Pope for their second objective.

Undoubtedly they initiated their soldierly tasks because they were impressed by the growing popularity of the Order of the Temple. They in turn copied the international structure, especially the division in provinces, of the Hospitallers. It is more than likely that Hugh of Payns was inspired by this Order and of the opinion that it was his duty to prevent the pilgrims from being injured.

The descendants of Jesus

In their book, *The Holy Blood and the Holy Grail*, Baigent, Leigh and Lincoln claim that history should be rewritten. The Templars were founded before 1120 with the purpose of unearthing treasure from under the remains of the Temple

A Turkish emissary (with turban and a curved sword) is received by the Hospitallers.

of Solomon. They base the earlier founding date on a letter from 1114, written by the Bishop of Chartres, to Hugh of Champagne. Herein the bishop advised the Count not to join the Militia of Christ or the Evangelical Militia, because he was still married.

Perhaps the Bishop was referring to the Templars, who, at that time, could have still been in the embryonic phase. It is also possible that he had a different brotherhood in mind. There were already, immediately after the conquering of Jerusalem, other groups of soldiers active with a common background (for instance, area or language). Given the nature of the Crusade, it was logical that they called themselves Christian Soldiers. The official recognition of the Hospitallers in 1113, as a military order that cared for the sick people, would undoubtedly have brought to mind the combining of religious and knightly aims. There is genuinely not one single reason to date the founding of the Templars to much before 1120.

Apart from Baigent, there are more authors who state that the sole purpose of the Templars was the investigation of the Temple platform. They base themselves on the findings of the Brit, Wilson, who in 1894, despite strong pressure from the Muslims carried out excavations. He found a piece of a Templars' sword and a small Templars' cross in a tunnel. The only conclusion that can be drawn from this find is that, between 1120 and 1894, someone left these objects in the tunnel.

The inheritance of Jesus
According to Baigent, Jesus was as a descendant of David, the rightful worldly King of Jerusalem. Jesus was married to Mary Magdalene, who, after the crucifixion of her husband, fled to Marseille with her children. Godfrey of Bouillon descended from Jesus via the famous Merovingian Clan. Herewith, Godfrey and his descendants, at least in the opinion of Baigent, are therefore the rightful sovereigns of Jerusalem. Under the authority of the family of Godfrey, the Templars went in search of evidence under the foundations of the Temple of Solomon. It appears that they succeeded in their mission and they sent their findings to Europe; maybe (still according to Baigent) the mummy of Jesus, or his marriage certificate and/or the birth certificates of the children. Or something that was just as important. In their book they formulate as follows:

> *Through Godfrey and Baldwin of Bouillon, a "royal tradition" is said to have existed - which, because it was "founded on the Rock of Sion", equalled in status the foremost dynasties of Europe. If – as the New Testament and later*

Freemasonry maintain – the "Rock of Sion" is synonymous with Jesus, that assertion would suddenly make sense. Indeed it would be, if anything, an understatement.

Once installed on the throne of the kingdom of Jerusalem, the Merovingian dynasty could sanction and even encourage hints about its true ancestry. This would explain why the Grail romances appeared precisely when and where they did, and why they were so explicitly associated with the Knights Templar. In time, once its position in Palestine was consolidated, the "royal tradition" descended from Godfrey and Baldwin would probably have divulged its origins. The king of Jerusalem would then have taken precedence over all the monarchs of Europe, and the patriarch of Jerusalem would have supplanted the pope. Displacing Rome, Jerusalem would then have become the true capital of Christendom, and perhaps of much more than Christendom. For if Jesus were acknowledged as a mortal prophet, as a priest-king and legitimate ruler of the line of David, he might well have become acceptable to both Muslims and Jews. As king of Jerusalem, his lineal descendant would then have been in a position to implement one of the primary tenets of Templar policy – the reconciliation of Christianity with Judaism and Islam.

Historical circumstances, of course, never allowed matters to reach this point. The Frankish kingdom of Jerusalem never consolidated its position. Beleaguered on every side of Muslim armies, unstable in its own government and administration, it never attained the strength and internal security it needed to survive – still less to assert its supremacy over the crowns of Europe and the Church of Rome. The grandiose design foundered; and with the loss of the Holy Land in 1291 it collapsed completely. The Merovingians were once again without a crown. And the Knights Templar were not only redundant but also expendable.

Serious historians find that this version of world history does not ring true. It can be no other way than that the Crusaders, immediately after the conquering of Jerusalem in 1099, searched the Biblical Places. Just as Helena, the mother of Constantine, centuries earlier, they had hoped to find physical evidence of the remains of important figures from the Bible. William of Tyre wrote about the discovery of a piece of the cross of Jesus in a segregated corner of the Holy Sepulchre in 1099. Shortly afterwards it was stored above the remains of the Temple and in the years that followed taken on nearly every military action with the Christians. After the finding of the True Cross, the Crusaders carried on searching. Relics, such as those from the Holy Land, were definitely extremely popular. Something that belonged to a famous holy person would have been a wonderful stimulus for the pilgrimage to Jerusalem. Not one single chronicler, except for William of Tyre, makes mention of an extraordinary find. So therefore, nothing outstanding was found. When the plans were forged for the founding of the Order of the Temple, it was, under the Temple platform, already comparable to Swiss cheese. The Order had no reason whatsoever to dig under their building.

THE SEPULCHRE OF JESUS

The tomb of God

Since the end of the nineteenth century, the village of Rennes-le-Château, in Southern France, has been the 'Walhalla for gold diggers.' In 1885 Bérenger Saunière became priest of this poor and remote parish, where a couple of years later he made the discovery of his life. During the restoration of the altar of the old village church he found a number of wooden tubes and inside them were parchment documents. Not long after that, it turned out that the priest suddenly had an enormous fortune at his disposal. He spent large sums of money on the restoration of the church, the building of a villa and the improvement of the village's infrastructure. How he came into that money, no one knows, but the speculations about it are endless. The village of Rennes-le-Château was established long ago and the Romans, the Visigoths, the Merovingians and the Templars had all settled in the area for varying periods of time. Every one of them could have buried their riches in the surroundings of Rennes-le-Château.

Maybe the treasure that Titus stole from the Temple of Jerusalem was also hidden there. It could be that priest Saunière didn't find any gold or jewels, but discovered a huge secret that made him money. In short, there are many books about this tourist treasure hunting centre and, of course, the Templars are also connected to this mystery.

Andrews and Schellenberger treat the history of Rennes-le-Château just like Baigent, but they reach a different conclusion. In the book, *The Tomb of God*, they report on their search. They base their final theory on two documents found by Saunière. According to them, nothing more than a treasure map was hidden. It is unknown where the documents are now, but there are people who allege that they are in the possession of the Hospitallers. In the 1960's copies of the parchment were published. The documents both contained text out of the Bible, whereby the letters don't all run in a straight line. It could have been the intention of the maker(s) of the information to connect these letters together. There could also be certain signs to find, and in one document maybe even a secret message is hidden. With a pencil, a ruler and a compass, Andrews and Schellenberger constructed geometrical figures that they connect with the map of Southern France. With the aid of secret messages on several paintings (amongst others the seventeenth century painter Poussin), they determine the exact location on the treasure map of the well known cross. Close to this place are the ruins of a Templars castle which was built in such a way that the treasure could be closely observed.

According to both writers the Templars were adept in the handling of geometric instruments, a technique the Templars learned from the Muslims. The Order worked with this knowledge to make a map of Jerusalem at the end of the thirteenth century (see page 44). The drawing would have been made by or under the responsibility of the Order of the Temple. Both authors know that for sure, because at the foot of the document there are two knights painted on horseback. The knights are armed with a lance and a shield, chasing the enemy, and they are wearing white outfits, and their shields are white, furnished with a standard red cross. According to Andrews and Schellenberger, it is explainable why these knights do not resemble of the Templars. It can't be anything else, or the drawing was, for censor reasons, invisibly altered shortly after the fall of the Order of the Temple. When the geometrical tricks from the document of Saunière and from the paintings are applied in this way, then the intersection falls on the cross that marks the tomb of Jesus.

The authors have seen that the geometrical shapes correspond with the documents of Saunière. There is no longer any doubt and the conclusion is clear. The Templars had found the body of Jesus in the twelfth century and then secretly buried it in Southern France. Later they hid his old burial site and his new resting place in a map of Jerusalem. Shortly before the mass arrest of the Templars in 1307 a few initiated members managed to escape. They took their knowledge to Lotharingen where, in the fifteenth century, the secret of the Templars was incorporated into a miniature belonging to Rene of Anjou (King of Naples, Sicily and Jerusalem). Others, including the painter Poussin, would have been informed about the secret and hidden it in various paintings.

In a similar manner to Baigent and co-writers, the authors of *The Tomb of God* describe the first years of Christianity, and here the speculations are also plucked out of the sky. Priest Saunière discovered that Jesus lay buried in the area of Rennes-le-Château, and received his fortune from unknown well-wishers. The money probably came from within the highest circles of the Roman Catholic

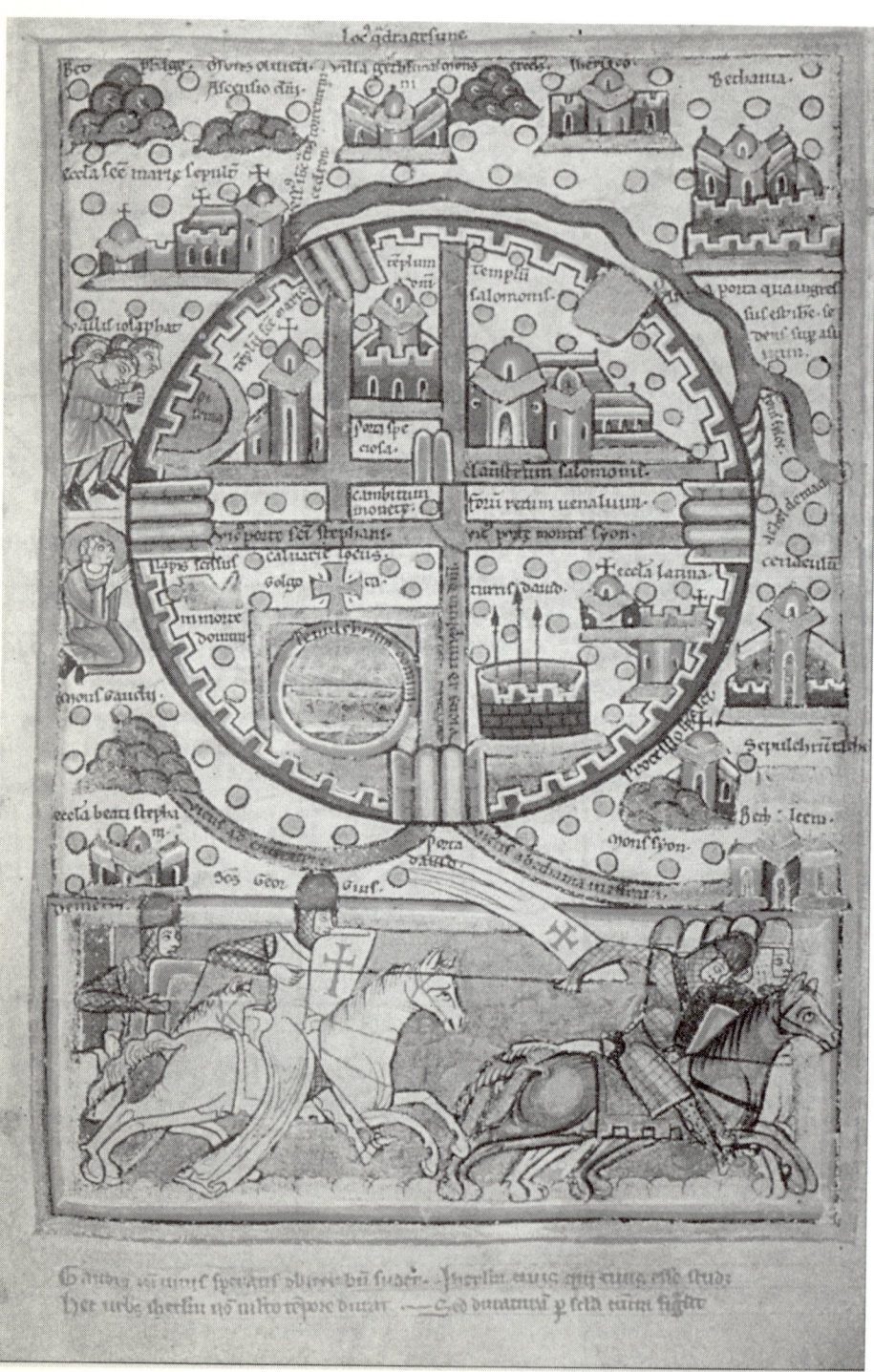

Church. It would have been a great shock indeed, if the Pope had to admit that Jesus had not risen from the dead, but that he had been buried just like any normal person.

The truth about the map of Jerusalem.
Andrews and Schellenberger gave very little information about the origin of the map of Jerusalem, which is in the possession of the Royal Dutch Library. The illustration can be found in a book called the *Collectar*, a compilation of miniatures about the Old and New Testament and several martyrs. The book was made in the Benedictine monastery of St. Bertin (North-France) in the period 1170/1180. The city is drawn as a circle with a cross inside and on the edge are the other Christian Holy Places. The dating 1170/1180 is based upon the text, the pilgrims and the fighting scenes on the drawing. It is unclear on which grounds Andrews and Schellenberger claimed that the map was officially dated somewhere in the thirteenth century.

The map does not give a real description of the city. According to William of Tyre, Jerusalem had a right-angular form; this is confirmed by all other chroniclers from before twelve hundred. Only the work of Fulcher of Chartres suggested, in no uncertain terms, that Jerusalem was circular in shape. That is, to put it mildly, peculiar: Fulcher, chronicler of Baldwin I and II, lived in Jerusalem for more than 25 years and he must have known the city like the back of his hand.

That Fulcher defined the city where he lived as being in the form of a circle is simple to explain. Jerusalem was the ideal city for the medieval man, described in the Bible, Revelation of St. John. In flowery words in chapter 21, a similar description is given about the new Jerusalem. The metaphor, so as described in the Bible, should be presented to the illiterate in a simple way. Fulcher was chaplain and joined in with the Middle Age way of thinking.

The mentioned map of Jerusalem. Saint George was martyred during the Christian persecutions in the fourth century because of his faith. He died the martyrdom nine times, but each time he came back to life. Eventually his head was chopped off and that finally killed him. In the Greek Byzantine culture, paganism was depicted as a dragon. Saint George had conquered paganism with his steadfast faith and for this reason he is pictured on icons with a dying dragon. The Crusaders did not understand anything of the symbolism of the Orthodox Church and took this occurrence literally. In the Middle Ages the French monarchy possessed a very special artefact: the sword of Saint George.

The previously mentioned illustration of Jerusalem is not unique. In the book *Geta Francorum Jerusalem Espugnantium*, by an anonymous author, a similar map (round and with a cross) was recorded for the first time. This chronicler described the Crusades from the period of 1095 to 1106. The author tells us in this book that his writings were based upon the work of Fulcher of Chartres. Because he records that Tripoli was in the hands of the Muslims, it must have been written before 1109. The map in this book had been copied at least eight times, including by the Benedictines of St. Bertin. English, French and German scientists inspected the map and not one of them discovered that it had been tampered with. It has been ruled out that the actual map of Jerusalem can be attributed to the Templars. The miniature book of St. Bertin is a collection of images, including saints. The white knight on the white horse is St. George, who pursued the Muslims. The theme appealed to the Crusaders because many of them could identify with the Holy soldiers.

Andrews and Scellenberger should have taken their time to study the literature about the maps of Jerusalem and their backgrounds.

THE STONE OF WISDOM

Besides Hancock (see chapter XIII), Baigent and co-writers, and Andrews have heard something about it, but haven't got a clue what it is. At least that is what Joh. von Buttlar surmises in his book *Die Wächter von Eden*. He also presumed that there was a secret assignment of the Templars, whom he called the 'the Secret Guardians of all time.'

Hugh of Payns, present at the conquering of Jerusalem in 1099, was impressed by the culture of the Muslims. Five years later he went back with Hugh of Champagne and collected some old Hebrew literary writings. These were later translated in Europe by a cistercian monk. In 1118 (?), Hugh of Payns obtained the al-Aqsa mosque from King Baldwin II. He and his colleagues went excavating and visited Massada and Qumran (the place where the Dead Sea Scrolls were discovered).

After this story about the first Grand Master, the author ascertained that these activities were not mentioned in any source of that time. Actually, that is a true observation; also Baigent does not admit to falsifying history. They are merely filling a gap in the past, in the same way as von Buttlar did; that is to say, they let their fantasy run away with them. The Templars found something, whereby lost knowledge became accessible to them. It is more than likely, at least that is what von Buttlar claims, that the Templars were looking for the Ark of the Covenant. If they actually found it, he doesn't know, but that they discovered the cosmic formula, for him is certain. He means by that, a strategy programme of the universe; the person that fathoms that out, thus understands the secrets of the universe, would then be the ruler of Destiny.

In retrospect it can be determined, that if the Templars had discovered the formula, that they probably would not have understood what they had found. They fought for nearly two hundred years in the Holy Land and despite their exertion and knowledge of everything, they could not prevent being driven out in 1291. Von Buttlar does not make it clear at all, why the Order of the Templars, considering the fact that it was the guardian of Destiny, was disbanded by the Pope in 1312.

The Templars were monks and soldiers, in their time a logical combination. For us Westerners that remains a peculiar phenomenon. Authors such as von Buttlar haven't got a clue, with their lack of understanding they are looking for an explanation in the mystics. The Templars were really normal people that lived in the Middle Ages. They were members of a Roman Catholic order, with the usual rules of this Church. That is what the next chapter is about.

III. The daily life of the Templars

THE RULES

The number of books about the Order of the Temple is inversely proportional to the information known to us. The fact that we know relatively nothing about these monk-soldiers is because of the few documents that are remaining from the Order itself. The archives are lost, and it is fitting with their reputation that there are all sorts of rumours circulating about the missing Templars archive. Most historians follow the argumentation of their colleague Hiestand. He claims that in 1187, directly after the fall of Jerusalem, the archive was moved to Acre. Four years later, in this harbour town, the headquarters of the Templars was established. With the fall of this last bastion of the Western Europeans, the Templars took their treasure with them to Cyprus; at least that is what a man who is known by the name the 'Templar of Tyre' writes. He participated in the last days of Acre and a couple of years later he put his experiences in writing. The Templar of Tyre was secretary to the second to last Grand Master, but was probably not a member of the Order. It could be that the archive (including proofs of ownership, covenants and rules), went to Cyprus as part of the treasure. In 1571, when the Ottomans conquered this island from Venice, the documents – still according to Hiestand – were destroyed.

There are also other presumptions as to what happened to the archive. One historian believes that it is hidden somewhere in Southern France. Whatever it is, for the person who is after the facts, there is no difference between a destroyed and a hidden archive.

As to the few documents that have remained, belong the household rules of the Templars. In the course of the twelfth and thirteenth century, six additions to the *Primitive Rule* of 1129 were made. On the basis of its experiences the Order needed new rules. There are no longer any original examples; we do have access to different copies from the fourteenth and fifteenth centuries. The domestic

affairs, the Rule, has 686 stipulations, divided into seven different documents:
1. The Primitive Rule of 1129, 76 paragraphs.
2. Conventual Life (1150), 107 articles.
3. The *Hierarchical Statutes*, also called Retrais (1165), 147 parts.
4. Penances (1165), 55 articles.
5. The Holding of Ordinary Chapters (1180), 158 sections.
6. Further Detail on Penances (1260), 113 stipulations.
7. Reception into the Order, date unknown, 30 paragraphs.

The *Primitive Rule* was fixed at the Council of Troyes in January 1129. Between 1135 and 1139 there was a French translation made which deviated on a number of points from the original Latin text. The two named dates we can determine with a degree of certainty, because the feast days mentioned in the translation were added at the council in Pisa in 1135. A Papal Bull from 1139, which gave the Templars, amongst other things, the right to name their own priests is, on the other hand, not incorporated into the French version.

The regulations from 1129 consist mainly of the rules normally used by monastery orders, supplemented with the experiences up to then. The aims are called:

> "…protect the poor, widows, orphans and churches, to defend the Holy Church…"

Compared to the six supplements this document is very religious in tone. There are constant references to statements of biblical figures such as the Apostles and the Fathers of the Church. It is noticeable that the rules of the Cistercian house of Bernard of Clairvaux stood as an example for the *Primitive Rule*. The Order of the Temple as a monk organisation was explicitly wrote about, whilst there was little attention paid to their soldierly duties. Of course that is logical in itself, because the Order then had very little fighting experience and the existing monastic orders did not play a violent role.

The military activities of the Templars are detailed in the so called *Hierarchical Statutes*, described by experts as an utmost professional military document. It deals with the functions and the authorisations of the members of the organisation, explains the manner of waging war and presents the procedure that has to be followed for the electing of a new Grand Master. It is remarkable that both of the other large military orders (Hospitallers and the Teutonic Knights), who also had a military tasks, did not know such a battle manual.

Transport ships are loaded for a Crusade. Of the vassals that are seen, there are French,

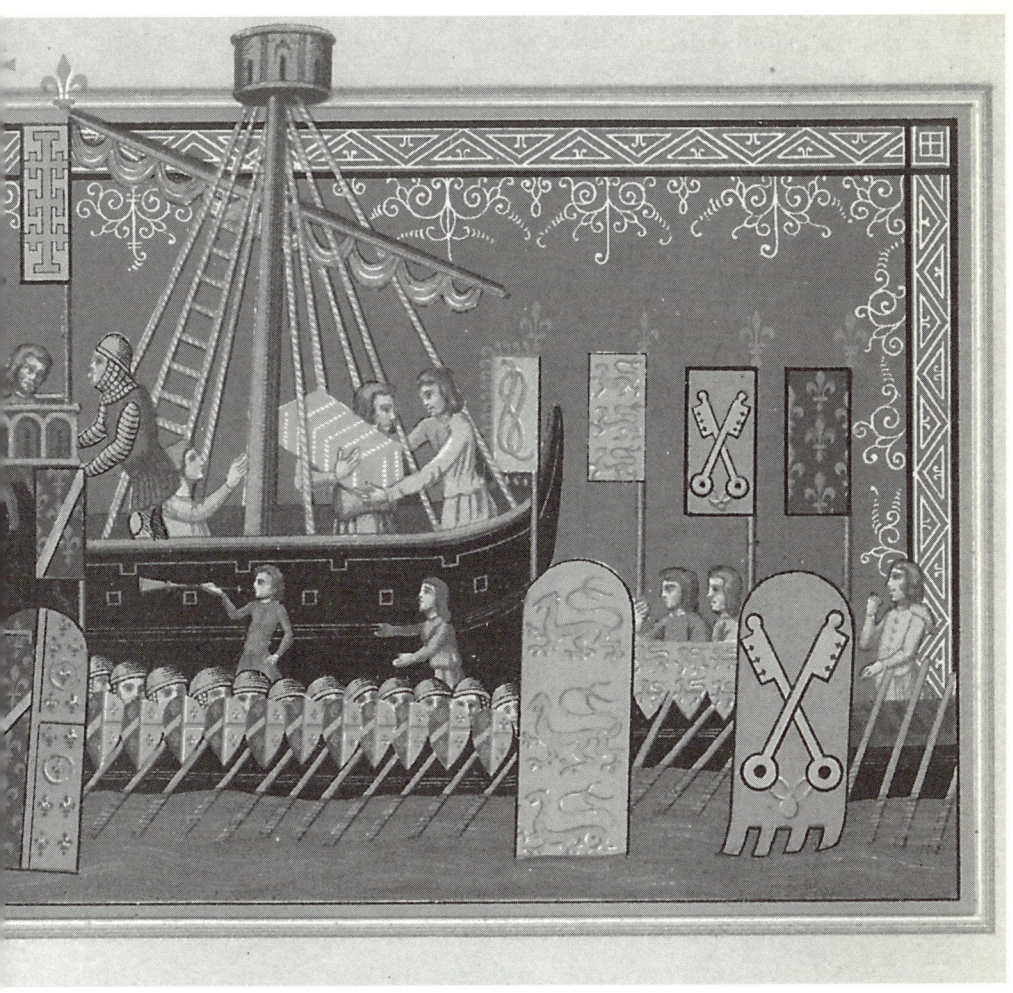

German, English and Sicilian troops amongst others. A Papal banner is also pictured

Two of the remaining documents (*Penances* and *Further Detail on Penances*) are nearly completely devoted to the internal jurisdiction; the first was written around 1165 and the second around 1260. They consist in total of 168 stipulations and the second especially, is a further extension of the earlier instructions, combined with occurrences in the Middle East. The document, *Conventual Life*, describes the pastimes and the religious customs of the members. The fifth paper deals with the procedures of the Chapter meetings and pays just as much attention to punishment. It is dated to about 1180. *Reception into the Order* is the last known part of the Rule; it is not possible to date this document, because there is no mention made to any recognized incident. It probably stems from the period after 1187, because in one of the stipulations it is suggested that Jerusalem was no longer in the hands of the Franks.

There are few examples of the Rule left, this because of the required secrecy. Only the leaders of the thirteen provinces could possess one, because according to the Rule 'publication would damage the Order.' During the trial of 1307-1312 against the Templars, this article was the reason that the inquisitors had, to suspect them of practices that could not stand the light of day, or of the existence of secret regulations and rituals. That the Templars could not discuss internal agreements in public was nothing special. The Middle Ages trades- and businessmen stood to face heavy punishment for the betrayal of their practices. Furthermore, the Hospitallers and the Teutonic Knights also had such a duty of confidentially. Because the Templars described their military strategy in the *Hierarchical Statutes* it is understandable that they did not want this to fall into the wrong hands.

Due to the fact that the archive of the Hospitallers has been kept safe, we have access to a large number of reports and decisions from the meetings of the Chapter General of this Order. In these gatherings, nuances were regularly made to the rules of the Hospitallers. It can be no other way than that the Templars continuously adjusted their rules in the same way; after the fall of Acre the Templars moved to their new headquarters on Cyprus and concentrated on piracy. They must have made rules about this, but it is unknown as to what they were. Regardless, the remaining household rules give us an outstanding impression of the functioning of the Templar, monk as well as soldier.

The organisation

Years before the Council of Troyes in 1129, the Templars received donations (money, toll rights, pieces of land, farms and such) from rich families that were true believers in the idea of the Crusade. The generous donors were convinced that by doing so they were sure of a place in Heaven. Until the beginning of the fourteenth century this remained an essential source of income for the Templars. The transportable goods went to Acre, the most important harbour town in the Kingdom of Jerusalem, via Western harbour cities such as London, La Rochelle, Marseilles and Venice. The estates on the other hand had to be exploited and that demanded a strict organisation coupled with a territorial division. The area, in which the Order was established, was divided into so called provinces. The Kingdom of Jerusalem (disappeared in 1291, with the fall of Acre), the principality of Anioch (lost in 1268) and the county of Tripoli (once again Muslim in 1289) were the three most important provinces (they also called these the Outremer).

France (including the Low Lands), England (with Eire and Scotland), Poitou (Southwest France), Aragon, Portugal, Apulia (Southern Italy and Sicily) and Hungary (joined together with the Greek possessions in the thirteenth century) formed the provinces of the Order. These seven areas, together with the three Latin States, were particularly mentioned by name in the *Hierarchical Statutes* from in and around 1165. Later, East Europe, Cyprus and the rest of Italy (Lombardy and Tuscany amongst others) also became separate provinces. All in all the Order of the Temple had at least one settlement in almost every country in Europe. They could have rightfully been called an international organisation.

Every province was divided into numerous connected proporties, so called preceptories. These were estates with a main building and different remote outbuildings. We would now call them granges. Furthermore the Templars had a base in the most important European harbour towns, where they made their money with trading activities. As to the number of

Two Templars on horseback. Probably a symbol of their vow of poverty.

preceptories, the opinions vary widely; the thirteenth century English chronicler, Matthew Paris said that there were nine thousand estates, but that seems overly exaggerated. Present day historians claim that there were between one thousand and fourteen hundred preceptories. The self same Mathew alleges that the Hospitallers had nineteen thousand estates. It is unclear how he came about this information, but this also seems strongly exaggerated.

The areas of the Templars in Europe were consequently called 'the lands from overseas'. For the Templars, Jerusalem was of course the centre of the world. Historians suspected that the Order had plagiarised the territorial structure from the Hospitallers, who had implemented such an organisation early in the twelfth century. The Statutes mention (fighting) activities in the regions of Jerusalem, Antioch and Tripoli. Only these provinces could have a commander-in-chief of the army, or at least that is according to the Rule.

In the Rule there is no special attention given to the provinces of Aragon and Portugal, which is noticeable because the Templars were militarily active on the Iberian Peninsula. On the other hand, it is also logical, because the Order directed itself more to the freeing of the Holy Land than to the battle against the Muslims.

The Order of the Temple was comparable to the traditional monastery order, or at least in peace times. The pledge of poverty, chastity and obedience were the most important elements, especially the last of the three well known monks' rules which was of great importance for the military task. In the *Hierarchical Statutes* it was precisely described how the army of the Templars should operate and how the officers were named. Every function description, from high to low, began with the number of horses that the functionary might have at his disposal. The humble Knights of Christ were apparently sensitive to status. It is curious that the horses of the higher functionaries were better fed in peace time than those of the knights and other soldiers. This difference lapsed as soon as the army left for war.

The oldest known stamp of the Templars shows two knights on one horse, but it is unclear what this represents. In the Rule it is explicitly forbidden for two brothers to ride on one horse. A knight, member of a military order or not, must have at least two horses at this personal disposal so that he could perform his duties. It is likely that the stamp symbolizes the poverty from the commencement period. It could be that the seal depicts the unity of the Order members or that the two most important founders are portrayed. In short, we have no idea.

Organisation of the Templars

Holy Land
Grand Master
Seneschal, later Grand Commander
Marshal
Draper
Turcopolier
Under Marshal
Standard Bearer
Staff
Knights, sergeants and Priests
Work force

Antioch
Commander
Marshal
Draper
Knights
Sergeants
Priests
Work force

Kingdom of Jerusalem
Commander/treasurer
Knights
Tempory members
Sergeants
Priests
Work force

Tripoli
Commander
Marshal
Draper
Knights
Sergeants
Priests
Work force

Monasteries/Castles
Commander/Castellans
Knights
Sergeants
Priests
Work force/mercenaries

Monasteries/Castles
Commander/Castellans
Knights
Sergeants
Priests
Work force/mercenaries

Monasteries/Castles
Commander/Castellans
Knights
Sergeants
Priests
Work force/mercenaries

1. The Kingdom of Jerusalem did not have a Marshal or a Draper, because the headquarter was established there.
2. In the Holy Land there were preceptories (monasteries or farms) as well as castles.

Countries overseas
Visitor
Staff

England	North France	Portugal	Poitou	Apulia
Commander	Commander	Commander	Commander	Commander

Monasteries	Monasteries	Monasteries	Monasteries	Monasteries
Commander	Commander	Commander	Commander	Commander
Knights	Knights	Knights	Knights	Knights
Sergeants	Sergeants	Sergeants	Sergeants	Sergeants
Priests	Priests	Priests	Priests	Priests
Work force	Work force	Work force	Work force	Work force

1. During the twelfth century, the function of Visitor was established; he took care of the communication between the headquarters and the provinces. Although the Rule does not mention anything about his authorisation, it can be no other way or he was the substitute Grand Master in the countries overseas.
2. At first there were seven provinces outside the Holy Land: North France, England, Poitou, Aragon, Portugal, Apulia and Hungary. Later, East Europe, Cyprus and North Italy were added. The Templars had between one thousand and fourteen hundred preceptories in the countries abroad.
3. In Portugal and Aragon, the Order of the Temple possessed a few dozen castles. In addition, they had a unknown number of strongholds in Greece and East Europe at their disposal.

There is also the following text on the stamp: Sigillum Militum Christi (stamp of the Soldiers of Christ).

THE FUNCTIONARIES OF THE ORDER

Central in the household rules are the procedures in the Holy Land. Herein, there is little attention paid to the functions and the assets in overseas lands, this whilst most possessions and members were to be found in Europe. In Chapters V and X of this book, there will be a deeper insight into the influence of the Templars in their 'colonies.'

Grand Master

The Grand Master was the highest leader and he stayed in Jerusalem until 1187 and then in Acre (1191-1291) and later on Cyprus (1291-1307). These moves were forced by the Muslims: Jerusalem was re-conquered in 1187 and in 1291 they drove the Franks out of Acre. All the members were supposed to be absolutely obedient to the Grand Master. At the same time he had to explain certain decisions to the meeting (the Chapter General) of the headquarters. So he needed to have the consent of this official body for the appointment of the Seneschal (his substitute), the Marshall (the army commander), the Draper and the Masters of the province. Furthermore, the Chapter had to agree to the sale of the land, taking over of castles, the waging of war and the making of peace.

Everything that was transported from the European provinces, via the harbour town of Acre, to the headquarters, was held separately. Next the Grand Master inspected these products and handed the money and the possessions, over to the bursar (the treasurer) and the horses to the Marshall. He had the authorisation to give an amount of one hundred bezants (Byzantine gold coins) and possessions to important relations. That of course had to be deliberated with his advisors. The Grand Master could loan, to third parties, the sum of up to one thousand bezants (in 1165 one could buy approximately 10 horses with this amount). But for this he had to have the permission of a number of important members of the Order. For a higher amount he needed the agreement of an even greater number of Templars. Given the fact that the Order of the Temple operated more and more as a banker during its existence, this was not an empty stipulation.

The Grand Master regularly inspected all castles, farms and other houses; if necessary he would set things right. The Visitor did the same in overseas lands.

If the Grand Master left his province, he could name 'the Commander of the Kingdom of Jerusalem or any other brother' as his replacement.

The Grand Master was also the figurehead of the Templars to the less fortunate people. Every day that he was in the headquarters, five poor people would receive the same food as the Chapter in his honour. On Maundy Thursday the leader would wash the feet of thirteen (this number because of Jesus and the twelve disciples) poor people and every one of them received a new shirt, trousers, two loaves of bread, some money and a pair of shoes. If he was at a place where he could not do this, he did it at the first possible opportunity.

The Grand Master had a number of special privileges. It was strictly forbidden for the other members to have money or possessions, but the leader had a safe. Because he was one of the most important men in the Kingdom of Jerusalem, the Grand Master regularly received gifts, which he could put in his own safe or which he could give away. The Grand Master was the only person with a room of his own, where he could receive important visitors. If he was to eat his food in the community dining room with the other members, only the Grand Master had the privilege of distributing the food in special circumstances, the leader would then get a few extra portions that he could give to punished members. The household of the Grand Master comprised of twelve people, not necessarily all members of the Order, included in these were, a cleric, a secretary, a squire, a local interpreter, a cook, a blacksmith and two important knights. The two knights were the direct advisors to the Grand Master. The blacksmith was needed because the entourage of the leader had at least thirty horses. In war times he could choose between six and ten knights as body guards. The last Grand Master James of Molay, this we know from the trial documents of 1307-1312, had even more personnel. One servant saw to the harnessing of his animals, one took care of the household duties and two servants guarded his room.

The position of the highest leader was clearly changed after the Council of Troyes, so after the fixing of the *Primitive Rule*. According to the *Primitive Rule* the Grand Master was practically an absolute autocrat:

> *For as soon as something is commanded by the Master or by him to whom the Master has given the authority, it should be done without delay as though Christ himself had commanded it.*

In the period following the council the organisation became too large for this sort of authoritarian leadership. According to the *Hierarchical Statutes* from tens of years later, in many situations the Grand Master had to first discuss things with different important brothers of the Chapter General. The further growth of the Order in the twelfth century led to a need to create a new function: the Visitor. He would represent the Grand Master as controller of the overseas areas in Europe. The authorities of this functionary are however not described in the Rule.

Seneschal
This authority was the replacement of the Grand Master. In the *Hierarchical Statutes*, the battle document of the Order, very little attention is paid to this function. In peace time he carried the banner of the Order of the Temple, this was a two-pointed, oblong streamer, with two horizontal colours: white above and black underneath. The banner functioned as a status symbol for the bearer and on the battlefield it was the sign of the gathering place for the warriors. The company of the Seneschal was noticeably smaller than that of his boss: eight men and twelve horses. At the end of the twelfth century this function disappeared and was replaced by the Grand Commander. The holder of this position was at the same time substitute of the Grand Master, Commander of the Kingdom of Jerusalem and leader of the election to a new Grand Master.

Marshal
The Marshal was the commander-in-chief of the army and therefore he had all the soldiers, weapons and horses under his command during war time. Tripoli and Antioch were the only provinces that also had a Marshal. Only in situations where it concerned the whole Order, were they subordinate to the Marshal of the Kingdom of Jerusalem. The commander-in-chief did not have to consult with any advisory body whatsoever, but he always remained answerable to the Grand Master. His entourage was purely military, four soldiers and seven horses.

Draper
The Draper provided the brothers with clothes and bedding; for this he employed a number of tailors. He had to ensure that the members were clothed and shaven according to the rules and wherever necessary he had to address them about this. The Templars were obligated to have the same hairstyle as monks of a common clerical order. Paragraph 21 describes it as follows:

> *And the Draper should ensure that the brothers are so well tonsured that they may be examined from the front and from behind; and we command you to*

firmly adhere to this same conduct with respect to beards and moustaches, so that no excess may be noted on their bodies.

After the Grand Master and the Marshal, the Draper was, according to the Rule the third functionary in the hierarchy. He was named by the Grand Master, provided that the Chapter from the Kingdom of Jerusalem gave their permission. The entourage of the Draper consisted of two squires and four horses.

Turcopolier

The Turcopoles were natives, from Christian ancestry or not: these soldiers formed the mercenaries of the Order. They were called Turcopoles because they fought in the same way as the Turks, on horseback with bow and arrow. William of Tyre called the Turcopoles the lightly armed knights of the cavalry. They were, it goes without saying, lower in rank than the knights, but stood higher in the hierarchy than the sergeants (the non-knightly members). Two knights were, according to the Rule, worth as much as three Turcopoles and two Turcopoles as much as three sergeants. They ate, together with the punished knights, at a separate table.

The commanding officer of the Turcopoles was the leader of the mercenaries and in times of war, of the sergeants too. From the text of the Rule it shows that he was a member of the Order, probably a knight. If an alarm was sounded, he waited for the orders from the Marshal and in certain circumstances he sent a number of Turcopoles out on reconnaissance. If necessary he could take ten knights with him, but if the Commander of the Knights was present, then he was in command of the patrol. The Turcopolier had five horses, four for the battle and a parade horse.

Under Marshal

The Under Marshal was responsible for the forage and the armour of the soldiers. The tradesmen that were involved in the war, such as the saddle makers and the armourers, were the subordinates of the Under Marshal. If the Marshal was absent, the Standard Bearer fell under his command. He had nothing to say over the knights, not even in war time; possibly it was a staff function. The Under Marshal was named by the Marshal. He had the use of two horses.

Standard Bearer

All squires were under the command of the Standard Bearer (also Confanonier), a sergeant. Squires were not members; they took care of the horses and supported the knights on the battlefield. The Order employed one thousand squires continuously. The Standard Bearer recruited these workers, took their oaths and informed them of the Order rules. He also informed the squires about the punishment measures for misconduct: confinement, flogging or dismissal. After these employees had served for the agreed time, he paid them their wages. If the army was marching, the Standard Bearer rode up front, whilst the Turcopolier carried the banner. On this black and white banner was written: Non nobis, Domine! Non nobis, sed nomini Tuo da gloriam! (Give us not, Oh Lord, not our, but your name the honour!) The Standard Bearer was named by the Marshal; he could have two horses.

Commander of the Kingdom of Jerusalem
The Commander of the Kingdom of Jerusalem was also the bursar (the treasurer) of the Order. All transportable possessions had to be given to him after they had been checked by the Grand Master. He registered them and locked them in the treasure room. His administration could be examined by the Grand Master or every group of important members. The spoils of war, (such as pack animals, goods, livestock and slaves) that were captured in the Kingdom of Jerusalem, went to the bursar. The horses and weapons were handed over to the Marshal.

The towns, buildings, castles and brothers in the Kingdom of Jerusalem fell under the command of these Commander. That was also the case for the ships and the dockyards of the Templar district in Acre. His entourage was made up of eight men, including a translator and a cleric/secretary and eight horses. In the Rule it is registered that the Draper belonged to his following. This suggests a subordinate position of the Draper in relation to the bursar, even though the Rule says that the Draper, after the Grand Master and the Marshal is the third in rank.

Commander of the city of Jerusalem
This functionary was responsible for the original task of the Templars. The Commander of the city of Jerusalem could bring ten knights into action for the protection of the pilgrims going to the river Jordan. In this contingent of knights were added a number of sergeants, squires, archers and servants. The Rule gave them explicit permission to invite pilgrims into their tent and to care for persons who were in need. Normally it was forbidden for any member to take strange men, let alone women, into their tent. The pieces of the True

Cross, which were guarded day and night by ten knights fell under the care of this Commander.

The spoils of war that he captured 'on the other side of the river Jordan' were shared with the Commander of the Kingdom of Jerusalem; but the spoils from this side of the river 'he could keep entirely.' All worldly knights that had found themselves in Jerusalem and temporarily 'given themselves to the Order' slept in the monastery and rode under his banner. If the Grand Master was absent, the Commander of the Kingdom carried out the orders over these temporary members. His household consisted of four soldiers, a native secretary/translator and seven horses.

Commanders of the provinces of Tripoli and Antioch
The heads of the provinces were responsible for all possessions and men in their area. They had to provide the castles with crew, food, iron, building materials and weapons for defence. A Marshal, a Draper and the Castellans could be appointed and fired by them. This could only be done with the permission of the General Chapter of their territory. Every day that they spent in the monastery in their area three poor people were treated to the same food as the convent. If the Commander of Antioch went to neighbouring Armenia, he could take a cleric and a chapel with him. This special tent was needed because, the Armenian religious rituals deviated from the Latin. The Commanders were accompanied by four soldiers, a cleric and thirteen horses.

Masters of the Western provinces
The tasks of these Templars were not explicitly mentioned in the Rule. The battle in the Middle East, where the central governing body was situated, was the most important. The Masters of an area were named by the Grand Master, who consulted a number of high placed leaders from the Kingdom of Jerusalem. It was forbidden for the provincial leaders to come to the East, unless the Grand Master or his replacement requested it. This occurred every couple of years, whereby they had to give account of the exploitation of their estates.

Their role was essential for the operations in the Middle East. Thanks to the proceeds of the preceptories the Templars were insured of a gigantic influx of money, food, horses, weapons and building materials for the castles. A non lesser important task was the recruiting of new soldiers. Despite the fact that practically the whole knight army of the Order of the Temple was destroyed a number of times, the Masters succeeded time and time again in getting the necessary reinforcements.

The title of the function of Master of the province was not always so clear; the terms Grand Master, minister, proceptor and procurator also show up in the Western documents.

Commanders of the knights
The Commanders of the knights fell, in the absence of the Marshal, under the Master of the concerned province. They were officers, who also could carry the banner of the Order, which was of course seen as a great honour. When the Marshal and the Master of the province were absent, they could hold a Chapter meeting.

Commander of a house
These could be knights as well as sergeants: in the last instance if there wasn't a knight in the monastery. He was responsible for the managing of the possessions, even though there is not much mentioned about it in the Rule. For the building of a house, the Commander needed the explicit permission of the Master of the province or the Grand Master. The renovating of existing buildings appertained to his competency. The status of this leader was determined by the possessing of two squires and four horses. If the Commander was a sergeant however, then he had just one squire and one horse.

The number of Templars that lived in a preceptory varied greatly. London and Paris had large settlements, but most of the preceptories in the West housed approximately four members, knights and/or sergeants. Important castles in the Middle East had dozens of soldiers.

Castellans
If the army was on manoeuvres and the Castellans were ordered to go with them, then these Commanders fell under the command of the Commander of the Knights. Just as with the Hospitaller Order, these were not high ranking functionaries. This is due to the fact that the Castellan, even if he was a knight, could only have two horses and one squire.

During the twelfth century and, particularly in the thirteenth century, the number of castles owned by the Templars in the Middle East had increased. The colonists were not in a position to raise the exploitation charges or the crew for their castles and they yielded these, out of necessity, over to the military orders.

Knights and sergeants
The organisation had different sorts of male members: knights (fratres milites,

frères chevaliers), sergeants (frères serjans), workmen (frères de métier) and clerics (frères chapelains). One could only become a Templar knight if his father had passed to become a knight. Illegitimate sons of a knight, even if they were a knight, were not recognized as such by the Order. They never rose further than frère serjans. A soldier had only to be a 'free man' to become a member. The *Primitive Rule* from 1129 advised not to let children into the Order. However this was usual in other monasteries, the Rule of the Templars says that it was better to wait until the child was old enough to handle the weapons 'with might.' From the chronicles it seems moreover, that not all the preceptories abided by this advice.

A knight did not only enjoy more prestige, he also had more privileges than the sergeant: more horses, a better armament and more food. The knights wore a white and the sergeants a brown or black robe, both having a red cross on the back and the left shoulder. The difference between knight and sergeant had everything to do with the social gap that existed in the Middle Ages between both sections of the population. Sergeants couldn't actually be promoted to knight, however this did happen a couple of times. According to the *Hierarchical Statute* the Grand Master could bestow a knighthood on a person who carried his shield and lance, but that could not happen too often.

The sergeants who were armed, had to be just as disciplined themselves as the knight. The ones with a supporting function had the right to leave the battlefield without permission, for example if they thought that the battle was lost or if they were wounded. Five sergeants from the Holy Land were higher in prestige than their classmates: the Under Marshal, the Standard Bearer, the cook of the Jerusalem convent, the blacksmith and the Admiral of Acre. They had two horses and one squire. If one of the five was to be named as Commander of a monastery, then their second horse would be given to the Marshal. The brothers, knights and sergeants, were supposed to obey their superiors unconditionally. They couldn't take a bath, ingest medicine, let themselves be bled, enter a town or let their horse gallop without the permission of their Commander.

The knight had at his disposal, three horses (a parade horse or mule, a pack horse and a steed) and one squire; in times of plenty he received an extra steed and a squire. It is unclear on which grounds the knight had the use of a parade horse rather than a mule. A parade horse was more expensive, whilst the mule also gave the knight a certain status. From the time of Solomon until the Babylonian exile of the Jews the Davidic Kings always rode on mules to their coronation. The sergeants, except for the five functionaries, never had more than one horse.

Knights were heavily armed men: a coat of mail, iron stockings, a helmet, a sword, a shield, a lance, a Turkish battle club, iron shoes, a dagger, a bread knife and a pen knife all belonged to the standard equipment of the knight. A coat of mail was a jacket made out of metal rings that also protected the neck and the head. The equipment of a knight weighed nearly fifty kilos.

The sergeants were less heavily armed; it was not permitted for them to wear a coat of mail. In war time the knights formed an elite troop, whilst the sergeants supported the attack of the knights. The weapons and the battle methods of the Christians barely changed during their presence in the Middle East. The Western European way of fighting remained their starting point. In the Middle East it was extremely hot, which rather impeded the use of their heavy equipment. The continuous stream of armed pilgrims prohibited adaptations on this point for the Christian militaries, this in contrast to the Muslims.

It is unclear how many soldiers the Templars had available; some maintain that, from the second half of the twelfth century until the end of the thirteenth century, six hundred knights and two thousand sergeants continually rode around the Middle East. Now and then, a few thousand more mercenaries were added; a considerably large battle force for its time. The mercenaries of the Templars were a mixture of Turcopoles and Westerners. Many colonists and newcomers could only afford to live in one way: hire themselves out as a soldier.

For their own members alone, the Templars needed more than four thousand steeds, a gigantic number, all the more, because during small and large battles these animals fell in large numbers. The Muslims knew the weak spot of their enemy and directed their arrows at the horses of the knights. A knight without a horse was in effect the same as a tank without petrol. The horses were expensive to keep; they ate six times as much as a person and needed, even in the Western European climate, 25 litres of water in one day alone. An additional problem was that practically all the fresh horses had to be imported from Europe. The Arabian horses, because of their light build, were not suitable for the Western cavalryman with his heavy pack.

Priests

The priests of the Templars, who had mostly no military background, followed the same initiation procedure as the other members. They wore a closed brown frock, could wear gloves and had to shave off their beard. They received the best clothes (but not white!) from the Chapter and during dining they sat next to the Grand Master. The food was first served to the priests. The members could exclusively confess to their own priests, who could give them absolution for most sins. The Rule says with some pride, that their priests, in that respect, were more powerful than an Archbishop.

The Order of the Temple received, from Pope Innocent II in 1139, the right to name their own priests and that made them independent from the normal clergy. Innocent was a friend and follower of Bernard of Clairvaux and was once a monk in his monastery. Bernard stayed loyal to his favorites. The Order of the Temple, at the same time, received the right to build and maintain their own churches. The Bull *Omne datum optimum* motivated this privilege as follows: it is dangerous that the Order members could be confronted with sinners and people that have contact with women. That is the same as the text of the *Primitive Rule*, paragraph 70 and 71:

> *On Sisters*
> *The company of women is a dangerous thing, for by it the old devil has led many from the straight path to Paradise. Henceforth, let no ladies be admitted as sisters into the house of the Temple; that is why, very dear brothers, henceforth it is not fitting to follow this custom, that the flower of chastity is always maintained among you.*
>
> *Let Them Not Have Familiarity with Women*
> *We believe it to be a dangerous thing for any religious to look too much upon the face of a woman. For this reason none of you may presume to kiss a woman, be it widow, young girl, mother, sister, aunt or any other; and henceforth the Knighthood of Jesus Christ should avoid at all costs the embraces of women, by which men have perished many times, so that they may remain eternally before the face of God with a pure conscience and sure life.*

From the chronicles it seems that the Order of the Temple regularly opened their churches for normal folk, therefore, also women. This was due to the offertories and donations to the relics, a nice source of income. This difference between theory and practice was, for a Roman Catholic organisation, nothing special.

The Hospitallers were less afraid of the opposite sex. They had female members from the start; mainly in separate monasteries, but there were preceptories with a mixed composition. It goes without saying that the Hospitallers ladies were not involved in warfare.

The Templars fell, thanks to the Bull *Omne datum optimum*, directly under the Pope. In 1154, thus fifteen years later, the Hospitallers also received such a free position. In a couple of circumstances, such as the killing of a Christian and the act of simony, the Templars priest could not give absolution. The term simony, the buying or selling of an ecclesiastical function, comes from the Bible. Simon Magnus offered the Apostles money if they would teach him how he could have the Holy Ghost bless people by the laying on of hands. Simony, and the murder of a Christian had, to be punished by the Bishop of the implicated area.

Nearly every preceptory had its own priest, the smaller ones shared one. Other than Franciscans and Dominicans, very few clerics of the Templars made a career in the regular ecclesiastical hierarchy. In hindsight, explicable, because they were not seen as the most important functionary in the Order of the Temple and therefore, not fulfilling a prominent role. The Rule did allow the promotion of priests (article 434).

> *But when it happens that any chaplain brother is elected archbishop or bishop of any church, he may wear a white mantle; but before he wears it he should ask both the Master and the convent very humbly and devoutly that they grant him the habit of a knight brother, and they should grant it to him with good will and voluntarily for love of the dignity which he has attained and so that the great honour comes to the Order.*

Infirmarer

In the *Primitive Rule* quite a lot of attention was paid to this function. That is logical because the Templars in the Middle East, from the start, practiced a dangerous profession. The Infirmarer, also a member of the Order, had to be able to judge whether a brother had to be admitted into the sick bay. The provincial Master or the Grand Master had the authorisation to call in a doctor or not. Next to the Grand Master and the Draper, the Infirmarer is the only functionary that is mentioned in the *Primitive Rule*.

Craftsman brothers

There were various members without a direct military duty. In the Rule there is mention made of craftsmen brothers who worked in saddleries, smithies and farms. Besides this, the Order employed cooks and, for the (re)building of castles, various handicraftsmen.

Supporting personnel

There were large numbers of hired workers, such as Turcopoles, as soldiers, interpreters, squires and farm servants. The Order continuously employed thousands of squires and farm servants. They had after all, somewhere between a thousand and fourteen hundred preceptories, which were mainly aimed at agriculture and livestock. From the documents of the trial it becomes clear that on some preceptories, female personnel were working.

THE CARING OF THE SICK

The Templars had, in contrast to the Teutonic Knights and the Hospitallers, only a military purpose. These other Orders administered, conforming to their statutes, hospitals for pilgrims, whilst the caring of the sick of the Templars was mainly limited to their own members. The nursing did not only take place in the Middle East. The preceptory, Denney in Cambridgeshire, England, in parts still existing, was intended for sick and pensioned members. The Order bought it in 1170 from another monastic order, because the monastery buildings were extremely suitable for a sick bay. The Templars also had their own hospital in Eagle (Lincolnshire). It was donated to the Order in the 1130's by the English King Stephen (1135-1154). The Templars possessed a special hospital in the county of Tripoli, where the poor were furnished with 'bed, warmth and water.'

After consulting with a number of important members the Grand Master could send the sick members to the lands overseas so that they could recuperate. The *Primitive Rule* calls for great attention for the sick brothers and referred to the Sermon on the Mount: 'I was sick and thy visited me.' For this care the members should inherit the Kingdom of Heaven.

In Western Europe and therewith the Crusader towns, the medical knowledge, in the Middle Ages, was on a questionably low level. Barbers took care of letting blood and, in a manner of speaking, acted like butchers in the treatment of wounds. The Arabian historian Usāmah gives a striking example of the latter, by telling how the Franks in about 1150, had a leg wound treated. An Arabian healer was asked for advice, he was convinced that the administering of medicine would heal the wound, but he was not believed. A Frank knight removed the whole leg with the strike of an axe, after which the patient died almost immediately. Usāmah was witness to this incident and he stated that the Arabian doctors were considerably better than the, in his eyes, barbaric Franks.

The Infirmarer was not much more than a male nurse. Members who could not bear the food from the Chapter, or were not capable of visiting the chapel, were admitted to the sick bay. The nurse decided if blood had to be drained (blood letting) and if it was necessary to cut the hair of the patient. For the administering of medicine, the cutting of wounds and the trimming of a beard, he had to have the permission of the Grand Master or the Master of the Province. They arranged, if desired, for the attendance of a doctor. The sick ate in the sick bay, where they in principle received different food than the rest of the Chapter.

Lentils, beans, beef, trout, goats' meat, mutton, veal and eel could not be served at the sick table, 'except if this was eaten at the monastery.' This is on the whole peculiar; apparently the Templars were not completely up to speed with the affairs of medical science. We know of an eating prescription from the twelfth century from the famous medical University of Salerno, close to Naples. Therein, it states that, the eating of pears and apples, milk and cheese and meat causes 'bad blood and depression; it is foolish to give this to the sick.' The eating of cheese was by the way forbidden for the Templars who were sick. The expressed assumption by some, that the Templars were exceptional surgeons, is not supported by stipulations in the Rule.

If the Grand Master wanted to eat with the sick, the Infirmarer ensured that he was given ample portions so that he could distribute them. The Grand Master was the only member of the Order who did not go to the sick bay, but was nursed in his own room.

The Commander of a preceptory had to provide the Infirmarer with everything that he needed. The Infirmarer was in charge of the cellar, the large kitchen, the oven, the pig sty, the chicken coop and the garden. If the Commander did not permit this, he had to give the Infirmarer money for the necessary shopping to be done. Ultimately, the Master of the province was responsible for the care of the sick members.

The sick could not go to the church, but that did not excuse them from their obligation of saying nine Our Father's every hour. During matins this was thirteen times. At the vespers the 'Our Father' prayer was said nine times. The priest took the confessions of the sick and if necessary gave the last rites. If a brother passed to the other side, Mass would be held for him and all the brothers would have to say a hundred extra Our Fathers for seven days. A poor person would receive meat and wine for forty days in remembrance of the dead brother.

Two articles concern the leprous members; the Rule states that Templars who have the leprosy sickness have to join the Order of Saint Lazarus. Leprosy was a collective name for all sorts of ailments, including leprosy; most of the sick were nevertheless able to fight. The Order of the Lazerites was founded in the 1130's in the Middle East. They received a papal blessing in 1255, many years after the other Orders. In the chronicles from the Middle Ages, the Order is barely mentioned. It was a small Order, as proven from the donation given by Pope Alexander IV. He gave, in about 1257, two hundred 'marks' to the Order of Saint Lazarus, ten thousand to the Templars and two thousand to the Hospitallers.

The Chapter meeting

Every Sunday the preceptories held a Chapter meeting; according to paragraph 385 of their rules this only had to happen if there were four or more brothers present at the preceptory. By entering the Chapter hall the knights and sergeants (others were not allowed to be present) made a cross and took off their cap, unless they were bald. After having said an Our Father, they could all sit down. The Commander would then request them to stand up, say a prayer, whereafter the brothers would say another Our Father.

If there was a cleric present, he prayed as well. After, one by one, the brothers had to confess their sins, standing, humble and with their cap on their head. In the absence of the sinner, the brothers considered the seriousness of the sin and together set the severity of punishment. Those who forgot to confess a sin were gently reminded about it. If he did not react to this, his co-members had to explain the sin of the brother concerned to the Chapter. It was not possible to appeal against the punishment and it had to be unconditionally and obediently carried out. During the trial in the years 1307-1312 the Order was accused of letting the Commanders forgive the sins of the Templars as well as the priest. The procedure during the Chapter meetings could have led to this misunderstanding.

After the public confession the daily affairs of the preceptories were on the agenda. These Chapter meetings also took place at a provincial level, but then only once a year. In France this took place in June, on the holy day of John the Baptist. The Chapter General was always held in the headquarters on the initiative of the Grand Master.

Punishments

When reading the Rule one could not escape the impression that the organisation contained so many sinners. At least 225 of the 686 stipulations deal with the theme punishment, whereby it has to be noted that many of the articles appear more than twice. In the *Primitive Rule* of 1129, three of the 76 articles are dedicated to this subject, whilst the part *Penances*, from about 1160, counts 43 penalty clauses. The segment, *The Holding of Ordinary Chapters*, from circa 1187, has 67. *Further Detail on Penances*, from around 1260, covers 112 descriptions of infringements and the consequences.

The worst thing that could happen to a Templar was expulsion from the brotherhood. This happened if a member was found guilty of simony, the passing on of affairs of the Chapter, the killing of a Christian, theft, conspiracy, deflecting to the Muslims, heresy, cowardly behaviour on the battlefield and lying about his ancestry. In a number of cases flogging and solitary confinement in one of the dungeons of the Templars castles was to be added.

Simony was the buying of an ecclesiastical function, in this case the membership of the Order. The Rule gives a touching example of some important brothers who, together with many tears and in great sadness of heart, confessed to the Grand Master that they had bought themselves into the Order. A diplomatic mission to Rome made sure that the Pope himself gave the men absolution. After having renewed the initiation rituals, they became members again. One of them went on to be Grand Master, probably Reginold of Vichiers (1244-1247).

Apparently the conception of simony was so vague that this sin could pass you by without it even being realized. In that regard there are enough known examples of men who donated their goods and chattels to the Templars in order to become a member. The previous consultation about the membership could later burden the conscience. For the Templars it was difficult to purely get on with the phenomenon of simony. After all they were dependent on donations from rich well doers and they would sometimes ask for compensation. That varied from the reciting of Mass to membership of the Order.

If a knight or sergeant killed a Christian (man or woman), he was expelled from the brotherhood. In Antioch three members murdered a number of merchants, admitted the crime to their Chapter and gave as an excuse that the devil had driven them to it. They were not only set out of the Order, but above all publicly flogged in Antioch, Tripoli, Tyre and Acre. That happened to the shouting of the words 'Look at the law that the Order applies to evil men.' The message was clear: the name and fame of the Order was at stake. The three members were sentenced to life imprisonment and passed their last days in a cell at Château Pèlerin. This Templars' castle (also called 'Athlit) was situated just south of Acre. Of course the killing of Muslims was permitted: the Rule implicitly says that this was not a sin. Bernard of Clairvaux formulated the Christian standpoint about the Muslims in his *De Laude* as follows: 'Or the belief or the confessors must be destroyed.'

The concept of theft was conceived broadly; the leaving of a monastery in a way other than by the main entrance fell under this and led to preclusion. When a brother died and gold or silver was found between his possessions without ever acknowledging this during his life, his body was then fed to the dogs. If the funeral had already taken place, the men dug up the body and still gave it to the dogs.

The administrating of justice was not always simple; a brother who worked in a blacksmiths on a settlement of the Order of the Temple, wanted to leave the organisation and stayed overnight in a village of the Teutonic Knights. There were, at that time, a lot of Muslims (it would have been during a cease fire). He regretted what he had done and the following day went back to his monastery and confessed his deed to the brothers. He was nevertheless not expelled from the Order, because he had spent the night in a Christian house.

Sodomy fell under heresy and is graphically described in the Rule. It is mentioned for the first time in the document, *The Holding of Ordinary Chapters*, from around 1187. It says there that

> *a brother is tainted with the filthy, stinking sin of sodomy, which is so filthy and so stinking and so repugnant that it should not be named.*

In 1260 it was describe differently:

> *If a brother does anything against nature and against the law of Our Lord, he will be expelled from the house,*

followed by an example (article 572 and 573). In Château Pèlerin there were three brothers who practiced perverted sins and caressed each other at night. The ones who caught them redhanded blabbed 'it', weighed down by this, to the Grand Master. The three were arrested, they were deprived of their robes and they were put in irons. Brother Lucas managed to escape and went over to the Muslims, the second sinner was killed during his escape attempt and the third went to prison for a long time. During the trial against the Order of the Temple in 1307, sodomy was one of the 127 accusations, but only three stipulations of the Rule deal with this theme. Sodomy undoubtedly occurred in all (ecclesiastical) ranks and classes. There is no reason to presume that it was any different with the Templars. Anyway it was a mortal sin based on the wide spread misunderstanding that Sodom and Gomorra were destroyed because the male inhabitants were supposed to have had 'unnatural' intercourse with each other. In the first centuries of Christianity the destruction of these cities was attributed to the fact that the inhabitants of Sodom had not treated both the angels of God hospitably (see Genesis 19). In the sixth century the East Roman Emperor Justinian introduced the present meaning. His position was weakened by a number of staggered natural disasters and he wanted some political opponents out of the way. The Emperor could do that by comparing the destruction of Sodom, to declare these disasters as being Gods punishment for the deeds of his opponents, whom he accused of sodomy.

Not everyone was honest about his ancestry. A Frenchman became a knight, but when he arrived in the Middle East his countrymen recognized him as someone whose father was not a knight. His white robe was taken away from him and he received a brown frock. The one who had introduced him was found to have acted in good faith and was not punished.

Cowardly behaviour was a special offence. In the Catalan version of the Rule the example is about the Baghras Castle, which was situated in the north of the principality of Antioch. The garrison had left the castle, in 1268, because it was of the impression that it could no longer withstand the Muslims. In fact the Templars did that after the Grand Master had admitted that further resistance was futile. Because they had not received formal permission to leave the castle, they were summoned before the Chapter. After a lengthy deliberation the perpetrators were not thrown out of the Order, however this was the usual punishment for their desertion. They were sentenced though, because they had omitted to destroy the castle and they had to yield their robes for a year and a day.

Disobedience, lying, contact with a woman, mutual arguments, the killing of a slave or a horse, and hunting, are a few examples from a series of 31 infringements. For these offences a member could lose his white or brown robe for a time, ranging from a couple of days to a maximum of a year and a day. He then had to turn in his horses and armour, to live on bread and water for three days a week and to perform slave duties. Flogging and prison sentences were often added to this and the law breaker could never carry the banner or take part in the choosing of a new Grand Master. The sinner could therefore forget promotion within the Order. Thus, the Commander of Acre went on a raid in Muslim territory and fell into an ambush. A number of knights, sergeants and mercenaries died there. Because he had not asked for permission before taking action, his white robe was taken from him and the Commander was put in irons.

Sometimes the Order of the Temple was inclined to be forgiving; a brother that had underhandedly spent the night with a woman and 'had his way with her' was sentenced to the temporary loss of his robe, but because he had an outstanding reputation, he was forgiven and handed back his robe.

Horses were very important to the Templars. Anyone who was at fault of killing, injuring or losing a horse, had his robe taken away. The Rule gives a nice example of this (article 606):

> *It happened on Cyprus that a rich man had sent his horse which was sick to our house; and when it was cured, the commander rode it out and found a hare and chased after it, and the horse fell and was so wounded that it died of that wound. And the brother came to Acre and pleaded for mercy in Chapter General, and the brothers sentenced him to lose his habit; and there were some who thought to give it back, for they said that the horse did not belong to the house, and others said that that did not matter, for they had to heal the horse at the house and now it was dead: so one should not bring harm to another. And the brother lost his habit and some said that he could indeed have put in irons because of the loss which was so great.*

In the *Primitive Rule* it is explicitly mentioned that the members cannot become a godfather, but not everyone abided by that. In 1251 a son of the French King, Louis IX, was born on the Templars complex of Château Pèlerin and the then Grand Master became godfather to the boy. For the Order, it would have brought grist to their mill.

Members, who had committed their sins overseas, were sent to the Middle East for their punishment to be determined. It is questionable as to whether the Templars who slipped up in the Holy Land lost their robes for a year. Extra fighters were badly needed, and dying for the Holy ideal was the best way to get forgiveness for sins.

With the reading of the articles about the discipline, one gets the idea that the Order came down strongly on erroneous members. The imposing and reducing of punishments was a democratic matter and always had to be decided by a group of members at a Chapter meeting. Even the Grand Master did not have the authority to come to this kind of decisions on his own.

The daily life of a Templar

The theme of the life of the Order members was the serving of God and the obedience of his commandments. As far as that is concerned they followed most of the usual monk vows. The ritual of matins, prime, terce, sext, nones, vespers and compline (the monastery hours) were done by each and everyone. It was not necessary if they were ill, or if they had to take care of the horses or the armour. In war time the military activities took preference over the religious pastimes, but even then the men tried to live their monastical lives as much as possible. Sixty Our Fathers had to be said daily, thirty for the dead, so that they would go to paradise, and the other thirty to inhibit the living from sinning. There was little talking, not only during the meal. In any case, it was better if they stayed silent, so as to insure that they didn't come out with any sinful talk. After the compline, the Order members checked the horses and armour in silence and then went to bed. To prevent the delegates from the underworld annoying the brothers they lit a small lamp in the sleeping hall.

On the holy days of the twelve Apostles, just like the Templars comrades in arms of the Lord, men would fast; along side these days there were also approximately ten days a year of fasting. Maundy Thursday was a special day for the Templars: every monastery had to make sure that the feet of thirteen poor people were washed on this day. The Rule warned that they had to ensure that the poor did not have any infectious diseases. After the foot washing the poor received two loaves of bread, a new pair of shoes and some money.

In the Rule there is nothing mentioned about training with horses and weapons. It is further suggested that participation in a knight tournament was forbidden. It goes without saying that the knights and the sergeants (the sergeants to a limited extent) had enjoyed a military upbringing, but it is hardly imaginable that the soldiers didn't regularly train. The carrying out of, for example, an assault, demanded a disciplined performance and therefore practice. From documents it shows that the important preceptory Templecombe in Somerset, of which parts of the main building and the church are still in tact, was used as a recruiting- and exercise centre for the English branch of the Templars. They received it in 1185 from a descendant of William the Conqueror. There are in the stipulations warnings about the damaging of weapons by trying them out, with the punishment being a temporary loss of the robe.

The game 'marelles' (it is unclear what is meant by this) was allowed, but chess and backgammon were explicitly forbidden; in those days chess was a game whereby you could gamble. Reading was permitted, but only a few were literate. James of Molay, the last Grand Master, said himself that he could not read. As was normal in the Middle Ages, only the priest of the Order would have been literate.

The visiting of a town, a house, a garden or a farm without permission was not allowed. Hunting, a popular pastime of knights, was not permitted except the hunting of lions.

THE MEALS

The wearing of the robe during duties and mealtimes was compulsory. Knights and sergeants ate after each other and in absolute silence. The *Primitive Rule* says that the brothers, because of the shortage of cups, must eat together. Which, at the same time had the advantage, according to the Rule, that men got to know each other better and prevented them from fasting.

Soldiers in fact had to be well nourished, if they were to carry out their appertaining duties. Eating implements and serviettes were usually shared, except by the Grand Master and the priests: they had their own goblets.

During meals the Bible would be read, so that the silence could be easily brought to order; it is questionable as to who understood any of it. In the Middle Ages knowledge of Latin was indeed not common. Paragraph 23, thus from the *Primitive Rule*, describes how to behave during the meal.

> *In the palace* [the al-Aqsa mosque], *or what should rather be called the refectory, they should eat together. But if you are in need of anything because you are not accustomed to the signs used by other men of religion, quitly and privately you should ask for what you need at table, with all humility and submission. For the apostle said: Manduca panem tuum cum silentio. That is to say: "Eat your bread in silence". And the psalmist: Posui ori meo custodiam. That is to say: "I held my tongue". That is: "I thought my tongue would fail me". That is: "I held my tongue so that I should speak no ill".*

Besides on the fixed days of fasting, men ate meat three times a week. They believed that meat would awaken the sexual drive and that was not the intention. With fish, that was not the case, because in the Middle Ages, they thought that the breeding of fish did not take place with a sexual deed. The Templars went for it anyhow: goats, meat, beef, mutton, veal, trout and eel were, according to the Rule, regularly on the menu. The meal consisted further of vegetables, bread and wine and was served two or three times a day. Solomon was of the opinion that wine corrupted the wise, so the Rule prescribes that excess use of alcohol was forbidden. There are no known documents from where it can be proved that they did not uphold this rule. Besides, the author has come across just one example of public drunkenness, but this incident was concerning the Hospitallers. (see page 241).

Friends of the Templars were allowed to eat with them, but at a separate table. Punished Order members had to always sit on the floor to consume their meal. They could wear their robe and had to use this as a table cloth. In the Rule it states that they could chase away cats and dogs, but it was not always simple. An anonymous pilgrim described that he had seen that a punished brother was not succeeding in chasing away hungry dogs. The Rule was not always consequent, because in another part members who were punished had to eat with the Turcopoles.

The clothes of the Templars

William of Tyre wrote that the members of the Christian Militia, he meant the Templars, wore lay clothing in the beginning, cast offs from sympathisers of the poor brothers of Christ. The *Primitive Rule* of 1129 brought in a uniform dress code: white for knights and brown or black for sergeants. White is, so as the Rule says the sign of purity and chastity. It signalled that the knight had said goodbye to the dark life in order to serve his creator.

In 1147, during the preparations for the departure of the Second Crusade, the Pope gave the Templars permission to wear a broad armed cross, representing the suffering of Jesus. It was coloured red because of the blood spilt by Christ and was a sign of martyrdom. The cross was attached on the back, above the left shoulder, and above the heart. Further finery, what ever it was, was out of the question and the clothes had to be worn without pride. The Draper saw to all of this. If a brother, due to his ego or arrogance, wanted to have better clothes, then according to the Rule, he received the ugliest example. The old clothes mostly went to the poor. Because of to the extreme heat in the East, during the period from Easter to All Saints Day (out of compassion and not as a right) a linen shirt was provided for those who wished.

Entrance into the Order

New members were admitted through the weekly Chapter meeting of the preceptories, in the East and in the West. In the absence of the forthcoming member the brothers spoke about the candidate. When there were no protests, two or three members talked in a room nearby the Chapter hall with the future member. They pointed out the dangers and the ordeals of his new life. They also asked him if he was single, was a free man, was healthy and if there were no creditors. If he fulfilled these demands and he continued to say that he would unconditionally serve the Order, they then reported this to the Chapter. Thereafter the candidate member would enter into the meeting and the chairman would remind him of the life he would lead, because 'what you see is that we have beautiful horses and wonderful armour, good food and drink and our fine clothes,' but the reality was different: from being your own boss, you became a slave and life became suffering. With a sergeant something was added, namely, that he had to carry out the menial tasks, such as in the bakery, the mills, with the camels or in the pig-sty. The Rule continues then with (article 662 and 663):

> *Now decide, good gentle brother, if you could tolerate all these hardships. And if he says: "Yes, I will tolerate them all if God pleases", the Master or the one who takes his place should say, "Good brother, you should not request the company of the house in order to have domains or riches, nor in order to have physical ease or honour. But you should request for three reasons: one, to put aside and leave behind the sin of this world; the other, to do the work of Our Lord; the third is in order to be poor and do penance in this world, that is for the salvation of the soul; and such should be the thought by which you ask it".*

The candidate disappeared to think about his wish, returned to the meeting and the chairman interrogated him again. He asked him if he was married, a member of another Order, without debts, in good health or if he had paid entrance money.

A sergeant was asked if he was single and a knight if he was the son of a knight through a legal marriage. Finally the vows of obedience, chastity and poverty were taken and the robe was placed on his shoulders. With this, the Templars had a new member.

The other house rules were reeled off to him by the Chairman. If there was not a knight present in the preceptory, then one came from a nearby settlement to lead the admittance procedure. From documents of the trial against the Order of the Temple, it shows that this procedure was still prevalent in 1298 or 1299. One of the questioned members told that he was admitted in such a way by the Commander of France in a Chapter meeting in Cahors.

The French translation of the *Primitive Rule* deviated in two places from the Latin version. In the first years of the Order there was a probationary period, but the French document did not mention it. Besides that, according to the original text, it was explicitly forbidden that the members associate with excommunicated men. According to the French document the Templars could recruit excommunicates who, before becoming members, had first to receive absolution from a Bishop. The excommunicated were knights who were cursed by the Church because of their rapacious behaviour; they were certainly no Saints. Due to the fact that this article is written in the French *Primitive Rule*, the conclusion could be made that it was not exceptional that knights were excommunicated. Evidently the original rules were a barrier that was too great for the fast growth of the Order.

Temporary members

From the outset it was possible for knights to become a temporary member of the Order, so called frates ad terminum. They had to get themselves a horse and armour and to hire a squire. The price of the horse was fixed and noted down. Everything that the knight, his squire and horse needed was furnished by the monastery. If the horse died during action, he received another. During this period he was a full member of the Templars. If his time was up, the knight would receive a half of the value of the horse in cash from the Order of the Temple. The temporary members reported mostly in the Middle East. During the period 1099 to 1291 there was a continuous stream of groups of armed pilgrims who went to the Holy Land. They were from the same area or vassals of a lord who went on pilgrimage. There were also individuals who had to do a penance, imposed by the Church, or simply wanted to serve the Holy Land. They mostly joined the Templars for a certain period of time, because this

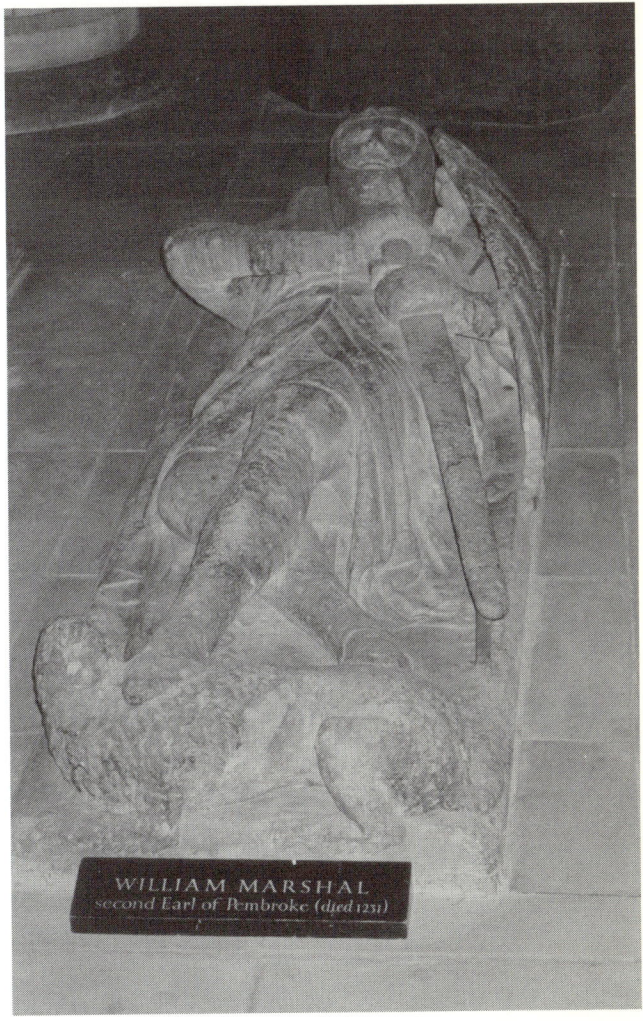

The tombstone of William Marshal in the Templars Church in London.

organisation gave their mission an extra God serving character. Another advantage was that they could become road wise in otherwise, absolutely strange surroundings. Furthermore; there would have been many knights who could no longer pay for their abode. Apparently there were temporary members who left the Order before their time was over. Pope Innocent III gave out a Bull at the beginning of the thirteenth century wherein he fixed the penalty for this sort of infringement.

It was not unusual that knights promised to become members of the Order in the future. A perfect example of this is William Marshal, one of the most important men in England in the period 1180-1219. He was named the 'best knight in the world', because he had won nearly every knight tournament in France and England in his younger years. Williams' grandfather was Marshal of the English Royal Household, thus responsible for the military duty that the vassals owed to the crown. He was put in charge of supervising the spending of the money, that was destined for war. His nickname became his family name.

William was the most important servant of Henry the Younger, son of King Henry II, who promised that he would make a pilgrimage to Jerusalem as soon as he could. On his deathbed he passed this promise over to William in order to 'pay off his debt to God.' On the whole, the breaking of a promise to go on a pilgrimage in that period was classed as a mortal sin. From 1185-1187, William was in Syria and he was deeply impressed by the activities of the Templars. He wanted to join them, but he postponed his entrance until he felt his death nearing. William returned to England, married, had ten children and became a member of the Templars on his deathbed in 1219. He received his clothes from the Commander of London and was buried in the London Temple. His gravestone can still be seen there.

Towards the end of the twelfth century many of the nobility entered in this manner. Their forefathers also did the same, but then with the Benedictine Order for example. Alongside this it was usual that the knights who had committed a crime in the West were sentenced to making a pilgrimage to the Holy Land. They then had to take up their duties in one of the Orders for a certain time. Historians guess that the Order of the Temple consisted of about seven thousand knights, sergeants and priests in the thirteenth century. The number of temporary members and subordinates were multiples of this.

Around the Western preceptories associations of 'friends of the Templars' arose. The members of these carried on leading a citizen life and regularly made donations to the Order. Some became members on their deathbed and others were satisfied with a burial in the cemetery of the Templars. This phenomenon was also usual practice in other monasteries in the Middle Ages. We have a list of the donors from the Templars complex of Reims. The Order kept track of this from circa 1160 to 1307, in total 42 pages. The French King Philip II August, a Countess, a Count, an Archbishop, a Bishop and 34 other clerics were mentioned herein. Fifteen Grand Masters and eleven other Templars also appeared on the list, 67 of the nearly two hundred non members of the Order were of the female sex. The Templars from Reims were kept very busy. They had to commemorate 223 people yearly, on 154 different days in their prayers. This was a frequent condition for the giving of a donation to the Templars. The Archbishop of Reims donated a hundred year old church upon his death in the

1160's. This in goodwill for the 'saving of his soul and those of his parents'; he wanted them to pray for him on his dying day.

THE ELECTION OF A NEW GRAND MASTER

In the event that the Grand Master died there was a comprehensive procedure to elect a successor. During seven days the brothers who were in Jerusalem had to say two hundred Our Fathers. At the same time hundreds of poor were provided with a lunch and supper. All brothers from the overseas lands had to eat bread and water on three Fridays: given the distance, that happened a few months after the death of the highest leader. The Marshal organized a Chapter, in which the Grand Commander would be named. He functioned as Grand Master until a new leader was chosen.

All Masters of the Province were warned to be present at the headquarters on the day of the election. They could bring as many members with them as they liked. In practice that was not always so easy because it took a long time for a message to get to the West. The Election Day was decided by the Marshal, the Grand Commander and the leaders of the three provinces in the Middle East. All of the members present at the Chapter took part in the election.

First "two worthy men of the house", who mutually determined who the leader of the election should be, were named. They chose two brothers from those present, next the four named two more and this made a total of eight. When there were twelve members named in this way, they choose a Chaplain together. The total of thirteen had a symbolic meaning: Jesus had, after all, twelve Apostles.

From the twelve there had to be eight knights and four sergeants, whereby, for the sake of peace, a representative from as many provinces as possible was demanded. Whilst the thirteen were in conclave the rest prayed to God in order that a good choice could be made. The commission would first see if a knight from the Middle East was suitable for the function; if this was not the case, then they looked for someone from 'the overseas lands.'

When the commission was divided, the Chairman of the ballot office went to the Chapter to ask those present to pray for unity, hereafter the thirteen continued deliberations until some one was pronounced. If his name was called, the new Grand Master was cheered by the brothers present. Whilst the clergy sung the Te Deum, he was led to the altar. He was then offered to God as the true one.

The procedure was a well kept secret, but it was rumoured about. A knight alleged that James of Molay became Grand Master because of deceit. James, the last highest leader, was named Grand Commander whilst he stated that he did not want to become Grand Master. When the men wanted to call Hugh of Pairaud, the Visitor of the overseas areas, to the highest function, James interfered. He declared the Grand Commander was actually the leader of the Order and that is how it happened.

In total there were 22 Grand Masters named in the period between 1120 and 1312, of which at least seven on the instigation of a secular ruler. Richard I in 1191 and Louis IX in 1250 expressly interfered with the choosing of a new leader. Amalric, King of Jerusalem and contemporary of the historian William of Tyre, seems to have nominated two Grand Masters. The Templars were pragmatic enough to keep an eye on the friendship of the leaders of the world.

Also in the naming of other functionaries, rulers endorsed and used their influence. The King of Spanish Aragon brought forward candidates for the function of Master of their province in 1290 and 1307. In both instances the Templars refused these men, but they made sure that the one who was eventually named had the approval of the King.

Two Grand Masters stepped out of their functions early. Everard des Barres became Grand Master in 1149 on the request of Louis VII. He returned to the monastery of Clairvaux for unknown reasons in 1152, where he died in 1174 or 1176. Philip of Nablus, the only Grand Master that was born in the Middle East, left the order at the same time. He became Diplomat of the Kingdom of Jerusalem and died during his first mission on his way to Constantinople.

Just five leaders were non French: Philip of Nablus, Gerard of Ridefort, Odo of Saint-Amand-les Eaux (Flemings), Arnold of Torroja (Spain) and Thomas Bérard (Italy or England). Six Grand Masters came from the overseas lands, without ever having been in the Middle East earlier. At least six Grand Masters died on the battle field or in prison and one, the last, burnt at the stake.

We know little further about the background of most of the Grand Masters of the Order. As far as it is known, the overall majority reached the function of provincial Master, before becoming the most important man.

IV. The period 1120-1192.
Rise and fall

THE ORDER OF THE TEMPLE UNTIL THE SECOND CRUSADE (1147)

The first Crusaders conquered Antioch, Jerusalem and various other places, in what we now call Israel, Lebanon, Turkey and Syria. They realised that in order to keep hold of these possessions, then the supplies from Western Europe were of the utmost importance. Therefore they succeeded in quickly getting the most important harbour towns under their control.

Syria was a strip of fertile land between the Mediterranean Sea and the desert, which linked Egypt and the countries around Baghdad. (see the map on page 30). The Crusaders never succeeded in conquering Eastern Syria and therefore failed to break this link. It remained simple for the leaders of Baghdad and Cairo to maintain contact with each other. Islamatic trade convoys and armies could reach both Capital cities, undisturbed, via Damascus. The Franks had in fact never carried out an explicit strategy to possess the East of Syria. The co-operation of the four so called Latin States was therefore far from ideal. The county of Tripoli was intermittently a vassal state of the Kingdom of Jerusalem, and the county of Edessa was likewise, for a short period, subordinate to the Kingdom. The King of Jerusalem however had little to say about the principality of Antioch. In practice the Latin States all operated apart and one only came to help the other in dire need. Once, two Christian armies, both complemented by Islamite combatants, were even fighting each other.

The area conquered by the Westerners was above all as leaky as a sieve. Armies from the North East of Syria and Egypt regularly crossed through the Christian lands without the Franks being able to prevent it. The colonists were namely Lord and Master of most of the cities, but they had too few soldiers to keep the countryside under the thumb. The politics of the King of Jerusalem was therefore aimed at sowing the seeds of doubt between the Muslims that surrounded them. They were fortunate that the Shiites were in power in Egypt.

A fresco with the picture of a Templar leaving Jerusalem.

This Muslim sect was considered, by most other Muslims (especially the Sunnites), as a heretic movement. Furthermore the Kingdom of Jerusalem had entered into an alliance with Damascus.

In the first thirty years after the conquering of Jerusalem in 1099, the Franks had the most successes, helped by the dissension and the mutual distrust of the majority of the Islamic leaders. They were afraid that if they entered into battle with the Franks, their neighbours would take the opportunity to extend their area. It was also a lucky circumstance that the inheritances of deceased, powerful leaders were fought over by their (numerous) sons.

So as explained in the second chapter, the Order of the Temple was founded in Jerusalem, but they had their base in Europe for their later position of power in the Middle East. The founder of the Order, Hugh of Payns, managed to interest many parts of Europe in the movement and during 1129 went with approximately three hundred knights, to Jerusalem. They probably travelled in the company of Fulk of Anjou, who succeeded Baldwin II as King of the Kingdom of Jerusalem in 1131.

Most of the newly arrived Templars did not survive their first battle; at the siege of Damascus in 1129, many lost their lives. In 1139, the Templars made a bad impression when a large number of them died in an ambush at Hebron. That was their own fault, because they behaved recklessly in their hunt for spoils of war. Both incidents are recorded by William of Tyre. According to another source, the Franks suffered severe losses in 1137, in a battle against the Muslim leader Zengi, and only eighteen Templars had a lucky escape.

The chronicles up to the period of 1148 report little further about any special fighting activities of the Templars. We do know that in the remaining writings about the Crusader states, in this period, only eleven names of Templars appear, whilst in Western documents up to 1148, there are 210 references made to a member of the Order. Here, the loss of the Templars archives and those of the Crusader states are felt, because such a discrepancy does not seem logical. More so because Alfonso-Jordan, the son of one of the leaders of the First Crusade, Raymond, Count of Toulouse, wrote praise fully about the Order. He stated that they had gained a mighty position in the Kingdom of Jerusalem, the principality of Antioch and the county of Tripoli.

Robert of Craon (1137-1149)

It is unclear when the first Grand Master Hugh of Payns died, 24th of May 1136 or 1137; the cause of his death is also unknown. He was succeeded by the Frenchman Robert of Craon in 1137. Robert also appears under the name of Burgundy, belonging to the high nobility. He is mentioned for the first time in 1093 in a charter, together with his father and two older brothers. Robert had been an employee of Fulk, count of Anjou since 1113. After an argument with a rival, they were after the favours of the same rich young lady, he left for the Middle East and around 1126, he became a member of the Templars. The destiny of a third son from the aristocracy was, at that time, clear. In his younger years he fought as a warrior for a high nobleman. In his later years he tried to marry a rich woman and if that didn't work he would mostly become a member of a monastic order. As Seneschal in 1132, Robert was in Europe on a propaganda trip. In 1138 and 1139 he was back in the West, but now as leader of the Order: the Templars' hinterland was always mobilised. Given the long existing relationship with King Fulk, he would have had an influence on the appointing of Robert.

Hugh of Payns managed in creating a great reputation for the order in Europe and Robert of Craon took care of getting the organisation on its' feet. He appears to have been an excellent administrator and an outstanding diplomat. During his leadership the *Primitive Rule* was translated from Latin to French. It was one of the first documents that appeared in French and it made the Order accessible to new members. Robert convinced Pope Innocent II to publish a Papal Bull in 1139 *(Omne datum optimum)*, wherein a large number of rights of the Order were set. The Templars were, from that moment on, only answerable to the Pope and they could set their own statutes. Undoubtedly Bernard of Clairvaux, who was friendly with the Pope, had stimulated Innocent II into giving the Order of the Temple an independent position.

The Order was popular from the outset in France. It is very likely that Robert, during his stay in Europe, spoke to Louis VII. The French King donated two mills and a number of buildings, in the harbour town of La Rochelle, to the Order in 1139. At the same time they received the right to freely (so without tax levies) export goods from France to the Holy Land.

William of Tyre was, according to his chronicle, very impressed by the second Grand Master and called Robert of Craon God-fearing and an exceptional knight of impeccable behaviour. The chronicler studied, according to him, between 1146 and 1165 in Europe. Due to the fact that William was about sixteen when he left the Holy Land, he would have received this information second hand.

About 1136, the Templars to the North of Antioch received the command of five castles, of which Baghras was the most important. They had to defend this part of the principality against the Muslims, but undoubtedly also against the Armenians and the Byzantines. The Templars controlled this area, not only in a military sense, but they also could use it as a colony.

At the end of the 1130's the Byzantine Emperor, John II, interfered with the Eastern border of his Empire. The First Crusaders had promised his father to bring the conquered area under the control of the East Roman Empire. He came demanding his rightful ownership, beginning with Antioch.

The city was besieged by him, where after a treaty that didn't affect the existing relationship, was arranged. The Emperor furthermore guaranteed that he helped the Christians in their conflict against the Muslims. In 1138, a contingency of Templars was added to his army without producing much of an effect on the campaign thereafter.

In 1142, John II re-appeared in the principality of Antioch; he stayed at the Templar castle in Baghras. The Emperor sent a diplomatic mission to King

Fulk with the request for permission to visit the Holy Places. Besides this, the Byzantine Emperor wanted to discuss the joint struggle against the Muslims. The King did not trust John. He was afraid that the Emperor was intending to re-conquer the Latin States and sent a delegation to Baghras, including an important Templar.

The negotiations gave no result. A year later the Emperor died from blood poisoning due to the neglecting of a wound sustained during a hunting party. His death liberated the Muslims from a dangerous opponent.

In about 1149 the Kingdom of Jerusalem had a castle built in the former ruin city of Gaza, South of the Egyptian city of Ascalon. The stronghold was the last part of a ring of fortifications around this city, so that Egypt could only reach Ascalon by crossing the sea. When the castle was ready, the Templars were given the task of equipping it with soldiers.

With this they were the rulers of the large surroundings. It was the first castle (at least according to remaining documents) of the Templars in the Kingdom of Jerusalem. Even William of Tyre, known as no supporter of the Templars, encouraged this gift and dedicated a line to the brave attitude of the Templars. Due to the continuing military actions of the Order, the grip of Ascalon on the area became considerably smaller. The gift from the King was a clear sign on the wall: apparently the Kingdom of Jerusalem had insufficient money and manpower available for the exploitation of the castle.

From other possessions of this period we know nothing, but there had to have been more. In the 1130's King Fulk constantly provided the Hospitallers with various fortified establishments. It can be no other way, than he also made his friends the Templars responsible for the defence of his Kingdom.

THE SECOND CRUSADE (1147-1149)

After 1130, the co-operation between the Muslims grew under the leadership of Zengi, in succession, his son Noer-ad-Din and Saladin. Zengi conquered the county of Edessa in 1144 which led to great consternation in Western Europe. Bernard of Clairvaux, the great supporter of the Order of the Temple, journeyed through France and Germany to call the people up to take part in the Second Crusade. Bernard was afraid that the fall of Edessa would lead to an Islamic re-conquering of Jerusalem and he warned the Western Europeans as follows:

The French King, Louis VII takes the cross in the presence of the high clergy. To the left of Louis stands Bernard of Clairvaux.

THE PERIOD 1120-1192. RISE AND FALL

What are you doing, you mighty men of valour? What are you doing, you servants of the cross? Will you throw to the dogs that which is most holy? Will you cast pearls before swine?

The King of France, Louis VII, and the German Emperor, Conrad III, took up the cross. Pope Eugenius III was definitly unhappy with the behaviour of Bernard of Clairvaux. Because of the experiences from the First Crusade, he wanted there to be only one leader. Eugenius was, for this reason, angry with Bernard, because he had taken it upon himself to preach the Crusade in Germany and won over the German Emperor.

With the Second Crusade in 1148, the Templars allowed themselves be seen as an emphatic military concern. A year earlier, on the 27th April, 130 Templars held a meeting in Paris, probably to discuss their taking part in the Second Crusade with the army of the French King Louis VII. The Pope, Louis VII, and a number of high clerical functionaries were present: the Order was unmistakeably taken seriously. They probably received permission whilst there, from the Pope to furnish their frocks with a red cross. Everard des Barres, Master of the province of France since 1143, was the leader of the contingent of knights and became an important advisor to the French King. He was a member of the trio that negiotated with the Byzantine Emperor over the conditions for the passage of the French troops. During the journey through Asia Minor the army was constantly besieged by the Turks. Thanks to the heroic and disciplined performance of the Templars, the French succeeded in reaching the Holy Land. Odo of Deuil, who as the chronicler of Louis VII, participated in the Crusade, was full of praise about the role of the Templars. When the French King eventually arrived in Antioch, he called upon Everard des Barres to borrow a gigantic sum of money from the Order of the Temple. The King would later write that he was able to proceed his Crusade, thanks to the Order of the Temple. His loan nearly bankrupted the Order. The Templars were also very friendly with the German Emperor Conrad III; he stayed at the Templars house of Jerusalem.

The leaders of the Crusade, Louis VII, Conrad III and Baldwin III (successor to Fulk), consulted near Acre about the choice of the object of attack. Grand Master Robert of Craon was present at this meeting, but we do not know what his contribution was. Instead of undermining the position of Noer-ad-Din, at that time the uncontested leader of the Muslims, the collective army entered into the battle against Damascus. The colonists had made a peace treaty a few years previously with the ruler of this city. The new arrivals found that Damascus sounded better for the home front in the West than the name of an unknown Muslim. The Christian army did not succeed in conquering Damascus, they broke the siege and returned empty handed to their countries. The Second Crusade had not improved the position of the colonists.

Of course it was wrong to attack a friendly city. It would not be the last time that the colonists and the Crusaders judged the Holy Land differently. The colonists realised that for self preservation, compromises had to be made with the enemy. Crusaders came to the Middle East to fight the heathens and they found this pragmatic attitude hard to understand. There was also the fact that the colonists were adapted to the climate, the customs of life and the culture of the Middle East. Also in this regard there was a gap between colonists and the new arrivals. The Crusaders did not understand that the Franks, out of self preservation, had to adapt to the Eastern practices and situations. The Crusaders would have been surprised by the freedom of religion in the Holy Land. Jacobites, Nestorians, Orthodox, Jews, etc, lived alongside each other without any problems worth naming. Originally the newcomers were not used to that: in Europe there were regularly Crusades held against dissidents.

What the cause of the defeat under the walls of Damascus was, according to a German chronicler from the twelfth century, was the rumour that the Order of the Temple was bribed by the Muslims. The Templars would have enticed the remaining leaders with a payment of lots of gold so that they would withdraw. Others write that the siege of Damascus failed because of betrayal, but they did not name the Templars. According to William of Tyre, the Barons of the Holy Land were responsible, but he wouldn't name them so as not to burden their families. Modern historians attach no value to the accusations against the Order. They presume that the criticism has more to do with the strong growing position of the Order of the Temple.

NOER-AD-DIN: THE TURNING POINT

In 1146 Zengi was murdered by his servant and he was succeeded by his son, Noer-ad-Din. He applied the unabridged policy of his father and he further broadened the co-operation between the Muslims. In 1154, Noer-ad-Din succeeded in winning Damascus for them. The three remaining Latin States were now closed in on two sides by Noer-ad-Din. Egypt formed no tentative threat, because the Shiites were still in charge. For them there was hardly a difference between Sunnites and Christians. The fourth border, the coastal

THE PERIOD 1120-1192. RISE AND FALL

The deliberation of Acre and the subsequent attack on Damascus. This illustration is out of the book of William of Tyre.

strip, was the safest. The Italian cities, allies of the Christians, were Lord and Master of the Mediterranean Sea (see map on page 30).

Everard des Barres (1150-1152)
Robert of Craon died on the 13th January 1149, shortly after the siege of Damascus. Everard des Barres became the new Grand Master, undoubtedly after the intervention of the French King. He originated from middle nobility and he was also a younger son. In the forties, Des Barres fought on the Iberian Peninsula against the Moors. As previously mentioned, he then became Master of the province France. Everard left in 1149 together with Louis VII to go to

France. He was chosen as Grand Master somewhere between the 13th January 1149 (the date of Craons death), and the 3rd April 1149 (the date of the Kings departure). The Seneschal, Andrew of Montbard, superseded Everard in Jerusalem.

Andrew wrote a letter to his boss in that same year, with the question as to whether Everard could come to Jerusalem. He let it be known that the Order had a shortage of knights, sergeants and money. It was not an exaggerated request. Shortly before, the army of the Templars had been decimated again. That was because Noer-ad-Din besieged Antioch and the Order had made 120 knights and a thousand sergeants available to the relief army of Baldwin III. Although, Noer-ad-Din had to suspend his attempt to conquer the city, few of the Order survived this expedition.

Everard did indeed come to the Holy Land, because he and Andrew of Montbard were, according to a deed, present in 1152 during a ceremonial event in Tortosa (now Tartus). The Order received a part of Tortosa and the right to renovate the castle there, from the Bishop of this city. It was, after Chastel-Blanc, the second castle that the Order had received in the county of Tripoli. Everard, more than likely, arranged reinforcements, because in 1153 the Templars played a significant role in the conquering of the Egyptian harbour town of Ascalon. In the autumn of 1152 Everard, for reasons unknown, resigned his position and became a Cistercian monk in the monastery of Clairvaux. There he died in 1174 or 1176. His resignation would not have been without a struggle; it was after all, according to the Papal Bull of 1139, forbidden to leave the Order. There is no other possibility than he discussed this with the Pope and Bernard of Clairvaux.

Bernard of Tremelay (1152-1153)
The Frenchman Bernard of Tremelay succeeded Everard des Barres. He originated from a family with connections to the French court. When he became a member of the Order, is unknown. He probably came along with the Second Crusade to Jerusalem. William of Tyre wrote that Andrew of Montbard, the Seneschal, was passed over because he had taken sides with the mother of Baldwin III. She was the regent of her son and she didn't want to hand over this position when he became of age. Baldwin III did eventually become King, and shortly after he donated a piece of land to the Templars via the Bishop of Tortosa, upon which they built a famous castle. In order to defend his Southern border, in 1153, Baldwin III marched to the harbour town of Ascalon, which was still in the hands of the Egyptians. The Order of the Temple made a poor

impression there, according to many, and they were given the blame for it a long time.

William of Tyre gave an account of how the Franks did their utmost to conquer the city with the use of a large wooden tower. The defenders set this on fire during the night of the 15th August, but the wind turned and the fire caused a breach in the wall. The besieged, who awoken because of the noise, engirdled their weapons and hurried to the hole. Due to the fact that the Templars were responsible for that part of the wall, Bernard of Tremelay was on the spot in a flash. He prevented, together with about forty members, the other Franks from entering, and went into the city. All the knights died and the following day their bodies hung, to the horror of the besiegers, on the walls of Ascalon. Shortly thereafter the city fell though, despite the fact that (still according to William of Tyre) the Franks were so de-motivated that they wanted to retreat. The Hospitallers managed to convince the other colonists to carry on with the battle. William was merciless in his analysis: the Templars wanted to keep the spoils for themselves and their egoism nearly led to the collapse of the venture.

Some historians doubt the grade of truth in this negative story about the Order. They think the Templars, in their enthusiasm, were the first in and that the residents managed to close the breach so that no outside help could enter. It hardly seems likely that the Grand Master thought that he could conquer a city with so few knights.

There is another version about the role of the Templars and the conquering of Ascalon. The chronicler of the Benedictine abbey of Egmond in Western Frisia (North East of Amsterdam) said that the Templars behaved rather passively during the siege of Ascalon. For several years they raided regularly the Egyptian convoys that supplied the city and they were afraid that this lucrative source of income would cease. When they realized that the other Christians were complaining about their attitude, they were ashamed and attacked the city at dawn. They killed a large number of Muslims and all Templars died in this fight. The chronicler would have heard this from the Crusaders from Norway, who took part in the siege of the city.

Andrew of Montbard (1153-1156)

Anyhow, Bernard of Tremelay had to pay for his behaviour in Ascalon with death and now Andrew of Montbard, up to that point Seneschal, was chosen. Bernard of Clairvaux, with whom Andrew regularly corresponded, was his full uncle. Andrew had three older brothers and was born around 1103. After his entrance into the Order, in 1129, he journeyed to the Holy Land. He had an excellent network of high ranking French acquaintances; King Baldwin was no longer angry with Andrew for having supported his mother. Andrew was the first Grand Master who was as one of the family of the royal court, which became clear from the fact that his name was often cited as first witness on royal decrees.

So as said, William of Tyre did not like the Templars and he gave another example of their 'commercial' tradings. Shortly after the fall of Ascalon a Christian army overtook an Egyptian company in Sinai. Due to the fact that the Order of the Temple formed the greatest part of the Christian battle power, they received the most spoils, including the right to take an important Egyptian hostage. For sixty thousand dinars these warrior was bought free.

That was a lot of money: approximately fifteen years later the Templars built the castle Jacob's Fort for eighty thousand dinars. This indicated that the Egyptians wanted to pay willingly for the release of those taken hostage. William wrote that the prisoner was at the point of converting to the Christian belief, with this it is suggested the Order of the Temple were led by financial gains rather than by impulse to Christianize the Muslims.

William of Tyre had a negative judgement of all military orders; he thought that they were operating too independently of the regular clergy. He was worried about the fact that they were getting more and more assets in the Middle East. That was at the cost of the Church contributions, because these were now flowing in the funds of the military orders. The Templars were, according to him, a heroic and respectable organisation from the start, but lost their humble effect after a good beginning.

The Order was, so he complained, successful in withdrawing from the autority of the Archbishop of Jerusalem. He made no secret of this, for him, unwanted situation and in his book he depicted the Templars, four times, in a poor light. Moreover William made six positive comments about them. So he wrote that there

> *was no area in the Christian world, that did not yield a portion of it's riches to the Templars.*

Bertrand of Blancfort (1156-1169)
On the 17th January 1156 Andrew of Montbard died and he was succeeded by Bertrand of Blancfort. He came from the South of France, but we know nothing further about his background. If Bertrand fulfilled a function in the Order

and, when and what that was, is not known. Under his governing which lasted thirteen years, two important additions appear in the *Primitive Rule* of 1129: The *Hierarchical Statute* and *Penances*.

Baigent names, in the book *The Holy Blood and the Holy Grail*, Bertrand the fourth [sic] Grand Master. They allege (also unrightfully) that the Grand Master came from the area where the Cathars were active. On these grounds Baigent presumes that there was a relationship between the Cathars and the Templars. In our remaining documents there is not one shred of proof to be found. William of Tyre, who knew Bertrand personally, found him to be a 'religious and God fearing man.' If William had heard just one rumour about the heretical behaviour of the Order, he would have certainly made it known: the Archbishop of Tyre was indeed a declared opponent of the Order.

Bertrand was barely in this function for a year when he, in June of the year 1157 together with 87 co-members, was taken prisoner by the Muslims. The Templars had joined the army of King Baldwin III in order to relieve the city of Banyas, which was under siege by Noer-ad-Din. The action was a success, but on the return journey they fell into an ambush and a great number of brothers lost their lives. The King could barely escape to Safad. This castle became the property of the Templars in 1166. Pope Hadrian IV wrote about this attack, that the Order of the Temple had to be held accountable for saving of the King. Two years later Bertrand was, after the intervention of the Byzantine Emperor, released by Noer-ad-Din. He was traded for the brother of the famous chronicler Usāmah, who was taken prisoner in 1153 by the Templars near Ascalon. On the whole 1157 was a bad year for the Templars. In April many members lost their lives, when a convoy that they protected along with the Hospitallers, was raided by Muslims.

Noer-ad-Din sometimes suffered a defeat. At the end of 1163 he had put up his tents in the area of Tripoli, when a number of pilgrims arrived in this city. Under the leadership of the Templar Gilbert of Lacey, from English birth, they raided Noer-ad-Din and inflicted a crushing defeat upon him. He barely managed to escape. Gilbert of Lacey belonged to the high nobility and according to William of Tyre, was an experienced warrior and was Commander of the Templars from the district of Tripoli. Perhaps Gilbert was the Marshal of this province.

Baldwin III was succeeded by his brother Amalric after his death. In the years 1163 to 1168 King Amalric led four campaigns to Egypt. This country had recently become politically unstable and King Amalric realised that the rich Egypt, strategically and economically, was of vital interest to the Franks. It threatened to unite with the other Muslim states and on the other hand, could become a dependency for the Franks. Amalric was thwarted by Saladin, a vassal of Noer-ad-Din, when he attempted to conquer Egypt. Saladin eventually managed to conquer Egypt for his leader.

The Templars took part in the campaigns of 1164 and 1167. During the last campaign a delegation of Amalric, including an important member of the Order, entered into a treaty with the Egyptian ruler, which was, for the Franks, extremely beneficial. In October 1168 though, Amalric waged war against Egypt again, even though the Templars and William of Tyre found that a violation of the treaty. The Grand Master of the Hospitallers had another point of view and convinced the King to incorporate Egypt. The Hospitallers were nearly bankrupt and the leader hoped that their Order could seize a sizeable portion of the spoils. The Templars were not the only ones who constantly needed money. William of Tyre suggested that the Templars did not want to take

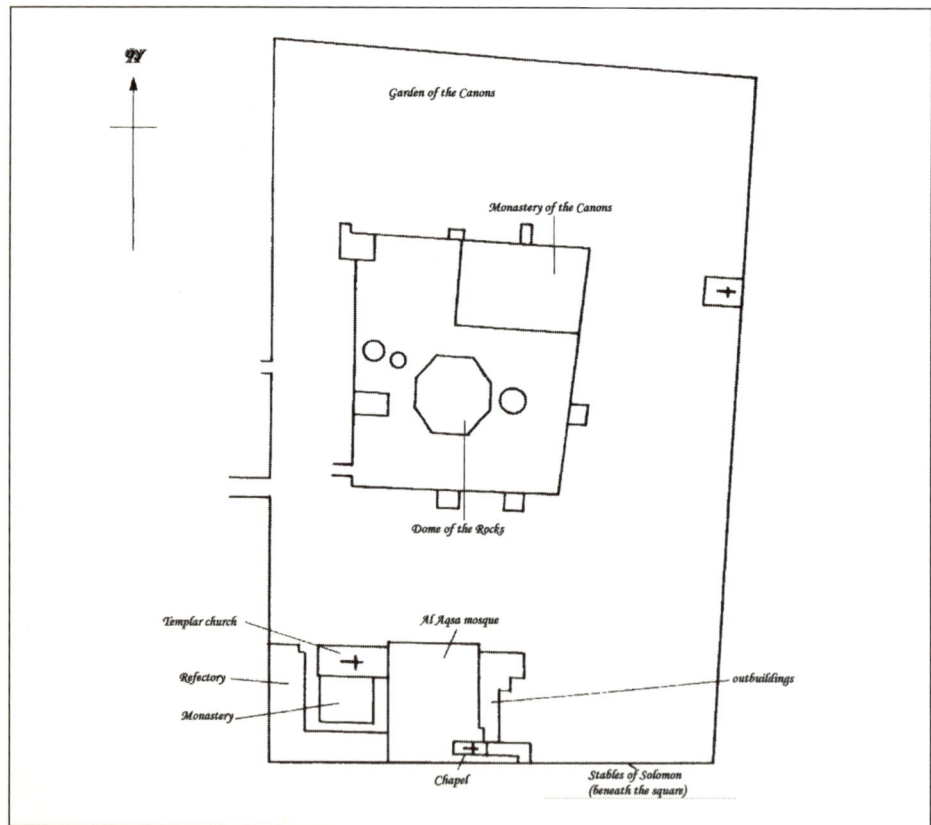

The Temple platform in Jerusalem.

part in a campaign that a rival Order was proposing. Probably the Templars realised that they could not afford a double fronted war. Whilst the main body of the Order was active in 1164 in Egypt, sixty knights and an unknown number of sergeants perished in a battle between the armies of the principality of Antioch and Noer-ad-Din and only seven knights managed to escape.

The Egyptian undertaking of Amalric was not a success and Egypt came under the definite control of Noer-ad-Din. It must have saddened King Amalric when the Templars did not go along on his last campaign. He wrote to the French King Louis VII, namely that 'if we can achieve something, then it is thanks to the Templars.'

The fact that the Order of the Temple could independently decide if they took part in the Egyptian campaign of Amalric, was an indication of the growing weakness of the Latin States. It was the first time the Templars had refused to work with the plans of the King of Jerusalem. From the third quarter of the twelfth century, the Order of the Temple was a state within the state. The dissension amongst the Christians came at the wrong moment, because the unity amongst the Muslims was strongly on the increase.

Philip of Nablus (1169-1170)
Philip of Nablus was the only Grand Master that was born and raised in the Holy Land. After Bertrand of Blancfort had died on the 2nd January 1169, Philip was chosen as the seventh Grand Master. Before Philip became a member at the age of about 45, in 1166, he was one of the leading Barons in the Kingdom. He took part in the deliberations in 1148, when it was decided to attack Damascus and he was also present in 1153 at the conquering of Ascalon. The new Grand Master was an important advisor to King Baldwin III and his successor Amalric. Shortly after the death of his wife 'Philip embraced the religious life,' as William of Tyre formulated it. Upon his entry he donated large pieces of land on which the Order later built the castle Ahamant (Amman). With this the Templars could settle in the Eastern part of the Kingdom of Jerusalem, to the other side of the Jordan. A year after his appointment, Philip, for unknown reasons, returned to his duties for King Amalric. On his first assignment (he led a diplomatic mission to Constantinople), the once Grand Master died.

Odo of Saint-Amand-les Eaux (1170-1179)
Philip of Nablus was succeeded by Odo of Saint-Amand-les Eaux, again someone from within the immediate circle of King Amalric. Odo originally

came from Flanders, but was not related to the co-founder of the Order of the Temple, Archambaud of Saint Armand. In the 1150's he had spent nearly two years in an Islamic prison as the leader of the army of the Kingdom of Jerusalem. That was at the same time as the then Grand Master of the Templars, Bertrand of Blancfort. Odo was a member for less than a year when he was called to the highest function of the Order. Amalric is said to have interfered with the appointing of this Grand Master.

William of Tyre wrote about a number of conflicts between the Order of the Temple and King Amalric. In 1166 an 'impenetrable' fort on the river Jordan (it is unclear which castle the chronicler meant) was surrounded by Muslims. King Amalric sent a rescue army, but before they arrived the Templars garrison had abandoned the castle. Amalric was so angry about this surrender, that he immediately had twelve of the knights from the fort hung.

In 1173 there was an even more serious incident when Amalric violently arrested a member of the Templars. The King negotiated with the Assassins, a Shiite sect from the mountains of Lebanon in the centre of the Christian territory. This was a suicide commando unit under the leadership of 'the old man of the mountains.' The sect members used hash when carrying out their suicide attacks; hence the name Assassins. The French term for 'murderer' (assassin) comes from the name of this grouping.

The sect had already had a lot of Sunnite Muslims murdered and Amalric wanted to enter into a pact with them. Noer-ad-Din was a Sunnite and therefore a mutual enemy. William wrote that the Assassins were prepared to convert to the Christian faith. The negotiator of the Assassins was, under royal protection, on the way to his leader with the propositions of Amalric. He was waylaid by the Templars in the surroundings of Tripoli and murdered.

Amalric reacted furiously and demanded that the Grand Master handed over the perpetrator to him. Odo refused, because he thought that the Order had the right to handle the matter themselves, but he was forced to obey Amalric by the royal army. The sudden death of Amalric in 1174 (he was only 38 years old) prevented that the affair brought to a head. This episode is typical of the independent position of the Order of the Temple. Even a previous subject of the King was prepared to defy the wish of the most powerful man in the Kingdom.

It is unclear why the Templars killed the representative of the Assassins. The Order received a large payment from these Muslims as 'protection money' and it was more than likely that they were scared that this arrangement would be over if there was a co-operation between the Franks and the Assassins. William of Tyre therefore suggested that there were financial considerations for the behaviour of the Order. Another chronicler, Walter Map also described the incident and alleged that the Templars were afraid that there would be peace with the Muslims. That would put this military organisation out of work.

Saladin: the champion of the Muslims

A couple of months before Amalric died, Noer-ad-Din had passed away. The Muslim leader was just about to start a military action against Saladin, who as regent in Egypt threatened to go off independently. Subsequently, it took Saladin a number of years to fight his way to becoming leader of the Muslims and it would have pleased him that the Kingdom of Jerusalem was divided. Whilst the unity of the Muslims grew, the discord within the Franks just became greater. The death of Amalric was beneficial for the Templars, but for the Kingdom of Jerusalem it was a downright disaster. Amalric was the last King of Jerusalem who had enough power to align the various factions. All the following successors to the throne were confronted with great conflicts between the most important leaders in the Kingdom of Jerusalem. The son of Amalric, Baldwin IV, suffered from leprosy, but the right of inheritance usually preceded the question as to whether one was physically able to function as King. Baldwin IV was only thirteen and Raymond III, Count of Tripoli, acted as regent.

At the same time there were two parties which fanatically opposed each other. The local Barons, Raymond and the Hospitallers wanted the position of the Latin States to continue along the diplomatic way. Newcomers from the West and the Templars formed a militant and aggressive part of the power, prepared for risky adventures. Increasingly, the Templars began interfering in the politics of the Kingdom of Jerusalem. It couldn't be any other way: they had after all, along with the Hospitallers, become the largest land owners, possessed the most castles and played an essential role in every battle. Also, the Order of the Temple was involved in practically every diplomatic mission of the Latin States.

William of Tyre realised that the Kingdom of Jerusalem was in great danger. Towards the end of his book he gave three reasons why the enemy could act so powerfully against the Christians. The First Crusaders were God fearing men, whilst their great-grand children neglected the commandments of God. Furthermore, the Archbishop lamented over the fact that his contemporaries were not experienced warriors and that they gloried in passivity. Finally, he was greatly concerned about the growing unity of the Muslims.

After the battle of Hattin, Saladin receives the King of Jerusalem, Guy of Lusignan.

In 1177, Saladin made the first attempt to conquer Jerusalem from Egypt. The Order of the Temple called all available members to fortify their castle in Gaza. They were afraid that this stronghold would be the first target, but Saladin headed directly towards Jerusalem. Baldwin IV, meanwhile crowned King, sent a messenger to Gaza and the Templars came to his help. The army of Saladin was 26 thousand men strong and Baldwin IV had only 375 knights at his disposal, of which 80 were Templars. Saladin suffered a crushing defeat and he had a narrow escape. According to a chronicler, the courage of Grand Master Odo of Saint-Armand-les-Eaux assured the victory.

It had happened before, a small army defeating a greater power and in this case there is also a logical explanation. The army of Saladin was scattered about, unorganised and busy plundering, when they were surprised by the Franks. This disciplined army managed to make the confusion even greater and delivered Saladin with the greatest defeat of his career. Very few Muslims survived this battle; the ones that managed to escape, threw their weapons away and they were robbed and murdered by Bedouins in the Sinai desert. It was unpleasant for the image of Saladin, but not a total disaster. Egypt was rich enough, had money and men, so Saladin could afford this kind of defeat.

On the other side of the Jordan, Baldwin IV built the stronghold of Jacob's Fort and donated the castle to the Templars. It was for Saladin a thorn in his side and when the King was not prepared to dismantle it for payment, he wanted to destroy it himself. In June 1179 he tried for the first time, without success. In August of the same year he succeeded; the garrison commander and a large number of Templars were killed and Saladin took seven hundred men prisoner.

In 1179 the Order was ready for a new Grand Master again. Odo of Saint Amand-les-Eaux was taken prisoner because of an inconsiderate action nearby the Jordan, where once again many members were slain. It was the intention that Odo would be traded for an Emir taken prisoner by the Franks, but the Grand Master was too proud to cooperate. He could not imagine that the Emir was as worthy as he was. A year later he died in a prison in Damascus. According to an Arabian source, his body was traded for a Muslim prisoner of war. William of Tyre knew Odo personally and held strong views about the Grand Master:

> ...a wicked man, haughty and arrogant, in whose nostrils dwelt the spirit of fury, one who neither feared God nor revered man. Many people laid at his door the loss and never-dying shame of his disaster. It is said that within the year he died a captive in a squalid prison, mourned by no one.

Some historians are surprised by the sharp tone of William and ask themselves if his analysis of Odo was an expression of his repulsion for the Templars.

Saladin, in the meantime, carried on with his attacks on Christian areas. In 1180 he plundered the surroundings of Tripoli. He could do this undisturbed because the Templars and the Hospitallers would not leave their fortifications for fear of a siege. It was again a sign of the lack of leadership by the Christians and the independent position of the military orders.

Arnold of Torroja (1179-1184)

The ninth Grand Master was Arnold of Torroja, a Spanish Baron. His family was related to the royal house of Aragon and provided the Spanish Templars with many donations. In 1163 he appeared for the first time as a Templar in a Spanish charter and from 1166 he was Master of the province of Spain. In this capacity he belonged to the most important advisors to the King of Aragon. Arnold had no experience in the Middle East and came to the Holy Land a year after his election. His late arrival was probably due to the fact that there was a cease fire valid from 1180 to 1182 between Saladin and the Kingdom of Jerusalem. The choice of Arnold was obvious: the Order needed an outsider in the turbulent years of the Kingdom. It seemed an intelligent move, because according to the chronicles Arnold was a diplomat, who filled an intermediary role between the various factions.

Meanwhile, the Kingdom of Jerusalem had a new King again: the six year old Baldwin V, a nephew of Baldwin IV. He died three years later and was succeeded by Guy of Lusignan, the second husband of the mother of Baldwin V. This ascension to the throne did not conform to the will of Baldwin IV. In it was written that if his nephew should die at a young age, Raymond III should carry out the regency. The Pope and the rulers of Germany, France and England then had to decide who the new King of Jerusalem should be. William of Tyre could no longer have anything to do with all of this. He died in 1185 in Rome, shortly after being removed as Archbishop. He was probably the victim of the dissension in the Kingdom. All the interchanges of the crown since the death of Amalric were coupled with squabbles and the forming of various power blocks. High ranking people such as William were no longer sure of the term of their function. The Kingdom was teetering on the edge of a civil war.

In the meantime Saladin carried on with the uniting of the Muslims. In 1183 he completed the Islamic encirclement of the Latin States with the conquering of Aleppo. Only the Mediterranean Sea remained a safe border for the Franks. Saladin united the Muslims by calling for a Holy War (jihad) against the heathen occupiers. He was a modest man, popular with the Muslims and, also in the eyes of the Franks, a great statesman.

Gerard of Ridefort (1184-1189)

Arnold of Torroja made a journey to Europe, on the request of Baldwin IV, to search for military support for the Holy Land. He died on the 30th September 1184 in Verona, Italy. The Templars named Gerard of Ridefort as their tenth Grand Master. He was well known as a braggart, loudmouth and an adventurer, with the nick name of 'the wandering knight.' In that regard he was like one of his predecessors, Odo of Saint-Amand-les-Eaux. It was understandable that the Order chose for a militant leader. The colonists regularly closed an armistice with Saladin, which most of the newly arrived members could not understand. Gerard, a Fleming, came to Tripoli in 1173. He was, at first, a subject of Raymond III, Count of Tripoli. His lord promised him a marriage to a rich heiress and to donate an estate, but at the first opportunity Raymond gave the young lady to another candidate for financial reasons. The daughter of the deceased Lord of Botron did not marry Gerard of Ridefort, but a rich Italian merchant. He was prepared to pay the weight of the girl in gold. Raymond was in desperate need of this money to pay his debts to Saladin and the Hospitallers. According to a chronicler, Gerard was furious with this and he hated his feudal lord from that moment on. He then went into service for King Baldwin III and in 1179 he was the royal Marshal. Shortly thereafter, Gerard of Ridefort joined the Templars and by 1183 he had risen to Seneschal of the Kingdom of Jerusalem. At the end of 1184 or the beginning of 1185, he became Grand Master of the Order. Just as his predecessors, he had, due to his last citizen function, easy access to the royal house.

Raymond III functioned in the meantime as regent of Baldwin V; during his rule, he entrusted the Templars and the Hospitallers with the management of the castles of the Kingdom of Jerusalem. In 1186 both Grand Masters, together with the Archbishop of Jerusalem, received the keys to the depository of the royal jewels. Both functions point out the powerful position of the Orders.

Raymond was removed by Guy of Lusignan, with the support of Gerard of Ridefort. Guy was the step father of King Baldwin V who died in 1186. He started a relationship in 1180, without the permission of King Baldwin IV, with his sister. When Baldwin discovered this, he wanted to kill Guy. The Order of the Temple asked him to spare his life and the marriage still went ahead. The Grand Master would have said to that, that the crowning of Guy was a nice compensation for missing out on the Botron feud.

Grand Master Ridefort subsequently pushed Guy into violently forcing Raymond to acknowledge him. Raymond closed a pact with Saladin as a reaction to this. A diplomatic mission, including the Grand Masters of the Templars and the Hospitallers, had the instruction to agree a peace treaty with Raymond and they spent the night in the Templars castle, La Fèvre. The son of Saladin asked Raymond permission to travel through the territory of the county of Tripoli. Raymond could hardly refuse. His defending against the King was after all his friendship treaty with Saladin. He did send a messenger to the diplomatic mission to inform them. It would have touched on a sore spot for Gerard of Ridefort. He immediately called in the help of the nearby castle Caco, also that of the Order of the Temple, and went looking for the Muslims. The army of Gerard was made up of 140 knights, of which 90 were members of the Order. It is probable that there were also a couple of hundred sergeants, for chroniclers only counted the knights and kept quiet about the number of soldiers, on or off horseback. At the springs of Cresson in the region of Nazareth, Ridefort and his companions discovered the Egyptian army of approximately seven thousand soldiers. The Marshal of the Templars and the Grand Master of the Hospitallers tried to convince Gerard to turn back, but he accused them of being cowards and gave the signal for the attack.

Ridefort was a fanatical and adventurous Muslim opposer and would have thought about the biblical figure, Gideon. Many centuries earlier, with three hundred men and Gods help, Gideon managed to defeat a large army. This time it went differently: Gerard of Ridefort and two members of the Order were the only ones to escape. The others were killed or taken prisoner; at a crucial moment, the Templars lost a Marshal and the Hospitallers a Grand Master. It turned out to be an omen of the battle of Hattin, two months later.

The battle of Hattin

Shortly after the battle of Cresson, Saladin entered the Kingdom of Jerusalem with an army of twenty thousand men and besieged Tiberias. The Christians gathered together at the watery Saforia. It was one of the largest armies that the Christians had put together so far. Approximately twelve hundred heavily armed knights, between three and four thousand mounted soldiers, a few thousand infantry men and a huge number of Turcopoles with their bows and arrows, a total of about twenty thousand men. There were about three hundred Templars present. The Order of the Temple paid the wages of more than four thousand

THE PERIOD 1120-1192. RISE AND FALL

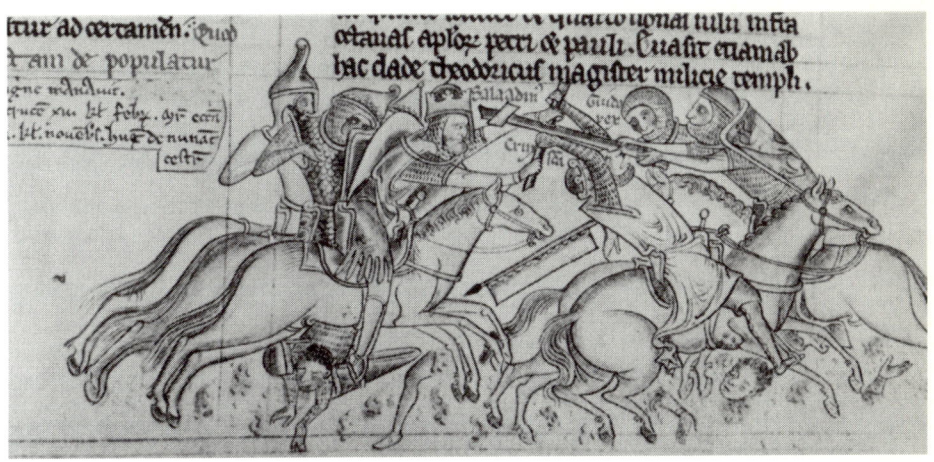

The battle of Hattin; illustration from the chronicle of Matthew Paris.

mercenaries, but not from their own pockets. The English King, Henry II, involved in the murder of Thomas Becket, had sworn the Crusader promise and afterwards placed a fortune under the supervision of the Order of the Temple. Even though Henry II had explicitly ordered that that the chests could only be opened when he was in Jerusalem, Ridefort used some of the money. Also in another regard the Order benefited from the murder of Thomas Becket. A number of the perpetrators had to serve, for a period of fourteen years, the Order of the Temple and fight in the Holy Land, according to a decree from the Pope.

The message that Saladin threatened to conquer Tiberias led to a war deliberation of all the military leaders. Raymond, who in the meantime had reconciled with King Guy, was in favour of a wait and see approach, despite the fact that his wife was staying in the threatened city. He pointed out to the other leaders that there was no water avaible on the journey to Tiberias.

In the twelfth century it was the usual strategy of the Latin States: keep a field army up your sleeve, gamble that the fortified places can withhold a siege and wait for an opportune moment for the battle. Frank army leaders realised that a confrontation with the Muslims, because of the uncertain outcome, should be avoided as much as possible. The Latin States were in fact dependant upon one, and not more than one field army. If that was lost, the enemy would have a free game. The Muslims always had the advantage that they could simply raise a new army.

The proposal of Raymond made all the more sense, because Saladin sometimes had trouble in holding his army together for long periods of time. His force was mostly made up of farmers who could fight. It happened regularly that they did not want to leave any of their possessions unattended for too long and they weakened the army of Saladin with their departure.

The deliberation did indeed decide on a passive strategy, but in the evening Gerard of Ridefort and Guy of Lusignan spoke in private. Gerard called Raymond a traitor and strongly insisted on the King to set out to Tiberias the next day. The ruler was convinced by his friend and gave the order to break camp the next day and to go to battle with the Muslims. Despite the insistence of the other leaders to reconsider his decision, Guy stuck to his guns and the army went on its way.

The decision of the King, at the insistence of Gerard of Ridefort, was later (then and now) heavily criticised, but the King faced a difficult dilemma. Four years previously, when he was regent of the Kingdom of Jerusalem, he had faced a similar situation and evaded the battle with Saladin. Some of the colonists had then accused him of cowardice and the leaders of the Kingdom later stripped him of his regency for this reason. The fact that shortly thereafter, Saladin had to stop his campaign was irrelevant for his opponents. Above all the King did not trust Raymond. He had in fact just made an agreement with Saladin, was his opponent for years and besides that, proposed a strategy that cost him his high position four years ago. The King should not have, despite all this, listened to the Grand Master of the Order of the Temple. He knew that Gerard of Ridefort hated Raymond and above all that the Templar was too impetuous.

As the recent chosen King, Guy wanted to perform an act, but it became a torture; it was the middle of summer and the mobile Muslims soon bombarded the Franks line. The back ranks of the Christian army were formed by the Templars and they had a hard time. As usual, the Muslims wanted to break the connection of the lines in order to then destroy the separated army. Because the military orders had disciplined soldiers available, they generally formed the front and rear of the Christian army. Half way to Tiberias the Franks set up camp and waited for the following day, without water for the horses or the men. The springs in the area were guarded by the army of Saladin.

The battle of Hattin took place under grave circumstances for the Christian army: unfavourable territory for making their charges, no water and a poor moral. The result was according. Saladin gained an overwhelming victory and took at least fifteen thousand prisoners. Raymond was one of the few members

THE PERIOD 1120-1192. RISE AND FALL

Saladin.

which managed to break through the line of the Muslims. A chronicler claimed the troops of Saladin let him escape. All 230 surviving Templars, apart from the Grand Master, were ritually beheaded. We have an eye witness report from an Arabian chronicler Imad-ad-Din.

Muslim soldiers who had captured a member of the Templars or the Hospitallers received fifty dinars from Saladin because, these 'were more warlike than all the other Franks.' Saladin, and with him most Muslims, held strong views about the Hospitallers and the Templars. He wanted the world rid of the impure military orders, and named them the enemies of his religion. Imad-ad-Din was impressed with the fighting power and the courage of the Templars.

The life of Gerard of Ridefort was spared by Saladin, reputedly, at the request of Guy. It could be, more than likely, that Saladin's most important consideration was the possibility that the Order of the Temple would appoint a much better leader after the death of Gerard. Most of the other prisoners were freed after the payment of a ransom. Saladin was often accommodating to the common knight and the other Christians. The Muslims had no further problems in conquering most of the possessions of the Christians. Nearly all garrisons had obeyed the calling of King Guy of Lusignan, to gather at Saforia. The cities and castles were minimally occupied because of this.

Saladin crowned his victories a couple of months later, when he conquered the city of Jerusalem in October. He was very aware of the massacre that the First Crusaders had inflicted in 1099. Still, he did not choose for the Christian method. All residents could buy themselves free for a small price, but many poor could not pay this. With difficulty, the military orders were prepared to save a number of paupers from slavery. Archbishop Heraclius dug in his heels. He did not have one single penny over for the poor; he loaded all his money and goods on to mules and left Jerusalem. Heraclius was known to the Templars, for in 1185 he had consecrated the Templars church in London. Saladin and a number of Emirs bought freedom for a large number of Christians with money from their own pocket. Again, Saladin let it be seen that he was not such a heathen as the Christians wanted to make believe.

The Muslims immediately recovered their holy buildings after the conquering of Jerusalem. Ibn al-Athir described it thus:

> *The Templars had added a building to the West side of the al-Aqsa mosque, with granary, lavatories and other supplies: with this they had made the mosque a part of their buildings complex. The territory was returned to its original state. The Sultan ordered that the mosque and the Dome from the Rocks be disconnected from all the filth, and thus it happened.*

They did this expeditiously, because a week later Saladin was present for the first prayer service in the mosque. The Muslims had done their work well. There was not a single trace left of the presence of the Order.

Saladin then journeyed to the North, plundered Tortosa, but did not manage to conquer the castle from the Templars. He broke off the siege and went on his way to Antioch. The five Templars castles in the surrounding area of this city all fell into his hands. His conquering of the largest castle, Darbsak, was described by the chronicler Ibn Shahhad. The Muslims managed to quickly make a breach in the structure, but the Templars formed a human barricade. The battle lasted fourteen days, where after an agreement was reached. The Templars could leave unarmed; alongside the leaving of provisions in castle, they paid a high ransom afterwards. Ibn Shahhad described his amazement at the latter, because this would never have happened before.

From the Kingdom of Jerusalem, there was only the city of Tyre still in the hands of the Christians. The principality of Antioch consisted only of the city and a castle of the Hospitallers. The county of Tripoli had become even smaller; the city, three castles of the Templars and one of the Hospitallers were still in the hands of the Christians.

There were only a few Templars that managed to escape from the battle of Hattin. One of them was brother Terricus, who was now the highest ranking. The Marshal was killed in May, the Seneschal lost his life in Hattin and the Grand Master was a prisoner. Terricus was Grand Commander of the Order and came from the same region as Gerard. He sent two letters to Western Europe, one shortly after the battle of Hattin and one in January 1188. He stated that the calamities were Gods punishments for their sins, a usual explanation of the Christians for a defeat. He wrote that directly after the battle of Hattin, 230 brothers were beheaded. The True Cross was captured by Saladin, Acre had fallen and the heathens now stood at the gates of Tyre.

Thanks to the coincidental arrival of Conrad of Montferrat, this city withstood the siege of the Muslims. That also happened because a fleet of, amongst others, ships of the Templars, had defeated an Islamic armada. According to Terricus, Saladin was so angry about this defeat that he burnt the remaining Muslim ships and cut off the tail and ears of his horse.

In September 1187, Gerard of Ridefort was released in exchange for the surrender of the Templars castle in Gaza. The biographer of Saint Louis, would later write that the Templars had sworn an oath on their holy relics, never to surrender the castle to free whoever. Probably the actions of Gerard of Ridefort led to this promise.

The Grand Master guaranteed the Muslim leader that he would no longer fight against him, but he didn't hold to it. A promise to a Muslim, thus heathens, was for most of the Franks without meaning. Saladin later let the King go; undoubtedly to sow dissension through the remaining Christians. Gerard of Ridefort fell in action, together with the new Marshal, in October 1189, nearby Acre. Guy of Lusignan, freed in the summer of 1188, wanted to raise his image by re-conquering the city and the Grand Master was of course, on his side. This attempt failed and his death released the Order of the Temple from its reckless leader.

The Third Crusade (1189-1192)

The fall of Jerusalem hit the West like a bomb shell. Again, the Christian lands were up in arms and everywhere a Crusade was arranged. No less then three rulers headed towards the threatened territory: they formed the Third Crusade. In England and France a tax measure was implemented the 'Tenth of Saladin.' The Templars were very helpful in the collecting of this, although one of them was caught when he wanted to put the proceeds in his own pocket. The English King forgave him, but the thief was severely punished by the Order of the Temple.

The German Emperor, Frederick Barbarossa, came over land. He drowned in June 1190 in a river in Asia Minor. The sudden death of the mighty ruler made many German noblemen decide to return home. A modest remainder of his gigantic army began on the journey and part of them joined a new order: the Teutonic Knights (see page 114).

King Richard I (nicknamed Lion Heart) of England and King Philip II August of France, had to first end a reciprocal war before they could set off for the Middle East. Richard hated sailing and went over land to South Italy. On Sicily he joined his army, which had made the trip totally by boat. Pope Clement III, the propagandist of the Third Crusade, invited Richard to visit him in Rome. The King refused the request with the comment that he didn't feel like it, because in the Papal court there was nothing more to see than greed and corruption.

The French King, Philip II August, arrived in Tyre in April 1191 and Richard took a month longer; both came by ship. Richard had conquered the island of Cyprus from the Byzantine Emperor shortly before his arrival in Tyre. He was aided in this by a large group of Templars. His advisors dissuaded him from keeping it and Richard sold Cyprus for stacks of money to the Templars. Despite the fact that the Order had suffered large financial losses since 1187, they could still make a large down payment to him. Saladin had inflicted a heavy blow on the Order, but money, horses, weapons, food and men flooded out of Europe to the Holy Land. It was amazing how quickly the Order of the Temple, despite the many recent setbacks, found itself in the foremost rank again. This happened due to the fact that they were in a powerful position in the overseas territories. The fact that Saladin had massacred the Order of the Temple after the battle of Hattin made them pre-eminently martyrs of Christianity. They would have exploited that in their propaganda.

The Templars didn't manage to hold on to Cyprus. A small garrison of approximately a hundred Templars (whereof fourteen knights) controlled the island, but that got out of hand. According to a chronicler, the Templars treated the people of Cyprus in the same manner as they were used to treating those on the mainland. They demanded high taxes and maintained order on the island with the use of violence. For centuries the Cypriots were familiar with the friendly rule of the East Roman Empire and they devised a plot to murder all the Templars. Arnold Bouchart, the leader of the contingent of Templars, found out about it and withdrew with his men back to their castle in Nicosia. The castle was surrounded and the Templars didn't seem to have a snowball's chance in hell: few soldiers, no outside help and scarcely any provisions. Bouchart decided that he would prefer to fall in action than to starve as a coward. With a reckless sortie he surprised the besiegers completely and massacred them. Bouchart withdrew thereafter to Acre and convinced the Grand Master that it would be better if they left the island. The Order realised without a doubt, that many soldiers were needed to control such a large island, relinquished Cyprus and gave it back to the English King. After all, the work terrain of the Templars was on the mainland. Looking back, that was an unwise decision. The island was rich and fertile and could have been an exceptional retreat base for the Holy Land. Both of the other Orders managed, more than a century later, to found their own states: the Hospitallers on Rhodes and the Teutonic Knights to the East of what is now Germany. It made these colleagues of the Templars considerably less vulnerable.

A year later, Richard sold the island on the advice of the Templars, to their friend Guy of Lusignan. Shortly before he was dethroned as King of Jerusalem by the local Barons. The Order of the Temple did keep a number of castles and parts of the most important cities on Cyprus.

Richard and Philip conquered Acre a month after their arrival, despite the fact that Saladin had invested all of his fighting power in order to keep the city. Here also, the Templars were involved, with the bringing into action of their own catapult. That Acre fell, was an unusual feat, because it rarely occurred that a besieging army could take a city whilst the army itself was surrounded. Richard took his temporary residence in the house of the Order of the Temple.

Robert of Sablé (1191-1193)

Robert of Sablé was in the meantime chosen as Grand Master, in June 1191. That there were two years between the death of Gerard of Ridefort and the voting of a new Grand Master was undoubtedly because of the uncertain situation in the Middle East. With the naming of Robert there would have surely been a royal intervention. The Grand Master was after all a fellow worker of Richards and just shortly before his appointment he became a member of the Templars. Robert was one of the admirals of the fleet which brought Richard's army to the Holy Land. Robert of Sablé was related to the family of Robert of Craon, the second Grand Master, and he belonged to the high French nobility. Because he lived in the English part of France, he was a vassal of Richard. Despite this he was also appreciated by the French. A minstrel sang of him as a distinguished, brave and friendly man. Before his departure to the East, he gave large pieces of land to four monasteries.

The English King relied heavily on the Order of the Temple during his whole Crusade. Only once did they let him down. Conrad of Montferrat, supported by Richard, no longer acknowledged Guy of Lusignan as the King of Jerusalem. In the discussion that followed, the Templars took the side of their friend Lusignan, but in vain.

A dual between Richard the Lion Heart and Saladin. The English King impacts the helmet of the battle between a Christian knight and a Muslim.

THE PERIOD 1120-1192. RISE AND FALL

Philip II August returned to France at the end of July, a few weeks after the conquering of Acre; he gave his spoils of war to the Templars and the Hospitallers. Richard stayed because he wanted to re-conquer Jerusalem. He travelled along the coast to get to Jaffa, hindered by the army of Saladin. The King chose for the costal route in order to keep in contact with the fleet and thus with his supplies. Besides, doing so Richard ensured that Saladin could not attack him from all sides. Just as on the day before the battle of Hattin, the Muslims bombarded the lines and the Templars formed the rear. At Arsuf it came to a clash, but this did not deliver a victor. The result raised the moral of the Crusaders, because Saladin did not gain the final victory. The Muslim leader could not prevent Richard reaching Jaffa. From here, Richard wanted to go to Jerusalem, but the colonists and even the Templars advised him not to conquer the city. It would, according to them, be a temporary affair because it would not take long before a large part of the army returned to Europe. Those

head of his enemy and he appears to resemble the devil. According to others, the image depicts the

who remained would therefore not be able to retain Jerusalem. The Templars undoubtedly remembered the recent results of their last reckless leader. Richard decided not to proceed with trying to get his army to the Holy City, forced by these circumstances.

Saladin and Richard had both had it with the war and, after arduous negotiations sealed a 5 year cease fire, in September 1192. All significant parties had to promise Richard that they would respect the agreement. The internal difficulties in the Holy Land were structural by nature, so it was necessary that the leaders took some sort of oath.

Shortly afterwards Richard headed to England on a boat belonging to the Order, under the guidance of a number of Templar knights. He would have said that they should bring him, as if he was a Templar, to his country. However, because he suffered a shipwreck he had to travel through enemy territory, dressed like a Templar. In Austria Richard was recognised and taken prisoner by Leopold, Duke of Austria. Directly after the fall of Acre, Richard had prevented the banners of this Crusader from waving on the wall. Leopold had remembered this insult and as a result of his imprisonment, Richard did not reach his motherland until a few years later.

The Third Crusade did not fulfil the high expectations, but it did ensure that the Franks had the whole of the coastal area back in their possession. The Christians could maintain this for nearly a century because the Muslims had fallen back into dissension after the death of Saladin.

The Teutonic Knights

The third important Order, that was active in the Middle East, from the end of the twelfth century, was the Teutonic Knights. This originated in 1190 from a hospital (the German Hospital of Saint Mary of Jerusalem) that was established during the siege of Acre by the German merchants, for their countrymen. A separate sick bay was necessary because the Templars and the Hospitallers spoke French. This made the confessions or the anointing of the last rites too complicated for the Germans.

In 1198 the Pope gave permission for the transformation into an Order via a Bull. The rules of the Hospitallers were used for the care of the sick and the poor and those of the Templars for waging war. Just like the Hospitallers, they had a dual purpose: charity and fighting. The members of this Order wore a white robe with a black cross; the Templars protested in vain to various Popes about the white robe. According to the *Primitive Rule*, the Templars in fact had the exclusive rights to wear the white clothing. The Teutonic Knights had considerably less possessions than the two other large Orders. During the thirteenth century they moved their field of activity to the East of Europe. After the fall of Acre in 1291 they concentrated completely on the Christianisation of the population there.

The battle on the Iberian peninsula

In the beginning of the eighth century, the Muslims conquered what is now Spain and Portugal. In 732 Charles Martel defeated the Arabs at the French city of Poitiers and prevented them from entering further into Europe. In the eleventh century a modest part of the Iberian Peninsula was in the hands of the Christians. In this period various Popes began, supported by the Cluny monastery, with their appeal to wage a Holy War against the Moors in this part of Europe. This was with little success, because of the amount of participants as well as the achievements. The appeal from Pope Urban II in 1095 concerned the Middle East, but in the slipstream, the Christian Kings profited from the Muslims with this declaration of war.

The Templars were gifted at least 42 donations in the period between 1128 and 1136 in Portugal and Spain. In 1128 the Order received their first castle from the Countess of Portuguese Soure. The Count of Barcelona, Raymond Berenguer III, gave them the border castle Grayana and on his deathbed in 1131 he became a member of the Order. He died in that year in the settlement of the Templars in Barcelona. His son went a step further when he transferred no fewer than six front castles in 1143. Further, Berenguer IV paid Raymond all the costs for ten Templars during his life. It is worth noting that in the will of the King of Navarre and Aragon, he bequeated his Kingdoms to three international organisations from the Holy Land, of which the Templars were one. When the King died in 1134, his heirs did not want to honour this gift, but the Templars received an important role in the Reconquista. This was formerly set in a charter of 1136, in which it was also agreed that the Templars could keep 20 percent of all the areas, which were, together with others, conquered from the Muslims.

The Templars played a fairly insignificant role in the conquering of the Peninsula. The leaders from the various Christian Kingdoms were too powerful. They applied divide and rule tactics and established their own military orders in the second half of the twelfth century. Furthermore, the priority of the Order lay in the Middle East, where, over the course of time, they had received an unassailable position. Most Templars that were active in Spain and Portugal were natives. The Portuguese unit went so far, that in 1146 they had already become a national Portuguese Order and from the beginning of 1169 their income was solely used for the war in Portugal. Then they received one third of all the territories which lay south of the river Tagus that had been conquered from the Moors, on the condition that the proceeds were invested in the battle for freedom.

In the Spanish Kingdoms of Navarre and Aragon around 1200, the Templars possessed more than 35 castles and forty preceptories. In some Spanish principalities the Order of the Temple competed with the national military orders that the Kings had established. When the battle front removed more and more from the most important castles, it was apparent that the regard of the Spanish Templars for the Reconquista was minimal, so in 1250 a Papal Bull was needed, wherein the Order of the Temple was ordered to fight against the Moors.

Half way through the twelfth century, little more that half of the Peninsula was in Christian hands. It would take until the end of the fifteenth century before the last bastion of the Muslims, Granada, was conquered by the Spanish King.

V. The Templars in Europe

The Dutch participation in the Crusades

At the end of the eleventh century, the Netherlands consisted of four, more or less independent areas, whereof the borders were liable to drastic changes. The county of Holland bordered the coastal area from Vlaardingen (near Rotterdam) up to the island of Texel. The present day provinces of Utrecht, Overijssel, Drenthe and the city of Groningen were governed by the Bishop from the diocese of Utrecht. The church leader was also the secular ruler and was not loath to use his sword in order to secure his own rights. Western Frisia, Frisia and the countryside of Groningen had a large number of farmers' republics. The county of Gelre originated during the twelfth century. Just like the county of Holland, Gelre expanded its territory considerably during the following decades, at the expense of the diocese of Utrecht. Compared to the mighty Flanders, which played a pivotal role in the Crusades from the beginning, the Northern territories were not greatly represented. Their golden age would come in later centuries.

The appeal of Pope Urban II in 1095, resounded through to the North of Europe. The higher lords of Holland were not touched by the Pope's address. They were under the influence of the Germans and they had not forgotten the pilgrimage to Canossa of their emperor (1077). A large number of their subjects joined the army of Godfrey of Bouillon. They were practically all farmers and farmhands. Holland had recently been ravaged by floods and crop failures and that made the country folk restless. They saw these natural disasters as a sign that the end of the world was nearing. Frisian farmers journeyed with the peoples' army of Peter of Amiens. Then, it was abnormal practice that befalls of the riffraff were mentioned in detail in the chronicles. However, it is clear that very few of the commoners survived the First Crusade.

In 1139 we come across the name of a high Dutch nobleman for the first time: Count Dirk VI of Holland, feudal lord of Kennemerland, Rijnland and the estuary areas of the rivers Maas and Merwede. He and his wife and a number of knights made a pilgrimage to Jerusalem. Dirk didn't do this in the wake of the Crusade organised by the Church. He belonged to a large group of Europeans who journey to the Holy Land on their own initiative between 1099 and 1291. At the request of the King of Jerusalem, Fulk, the Count helped him with a successful action beyond the river Jordan. The Pope was very grateful to Dirk and rewarded him with the separation of the abbeys of Egmond and Rijnsburg (which were situated in his territory) from the Utrecht's Church. The monasteries fell under the direct responsibility of the Holy Chair from that moment on.

Bernard of Clairvaux was, so as earlier disclosed, the great stimulator of the Second Crusade. In January 1147 he preached a number of times in Maastricht. According to the chronicler of the Rolduc monastery, no less then 10 percent of the population of the duchy of Limburg took the cross. The nobility of Holland again failed to turn up. They gave preference to the Crusade against the heretical Wenden then living in the present day Mecklenburg, Germany. In this manner they could obtain important Church blessings, just as the other pilgrims, but nearby and with less danger. Comparatively few knights journeyed from Holland to the South East; they joined an English contingent, so they could proceed to the Holy Land by ship. This army conquered Lisbon from the Moors, for the Portuguese on their way to the Holy Land. The soldiers were richly rewarded for this.

In 1184, Count Floris III, son of Dirk VI, made a pilgrimage to Jerusalem and he was again involved in the Third Crusade. Together with his son Willem, he travelled with the army of the German Emperor, Frederick Barbarossa; they took the overland route. Otto I, Count of Gelre, chose another way; he went to South Italy on horseback and sailed from Brindisi to Acre. Frisians and Flemings went together by ship and after having first fought in Portugal, they navigated from there to the Holy Land. Dutch and Flemings left from Walcheren (Zeeland) and received reinforcements in South England from other Frisian seamen. Count Floris III accomplished some diplomatic missions for the German Emperor. He died in 1190 in Antioch. His son Willem travelled through to Acre where he met his 'countrymen' from Gelre, Frisia and Holland.

During the siege of Antioch (1190) Rudolf van Seppenrode, Viscount of Groningen died: he was one of the few high placed leaders from the North who took part in the pilgrimage. After the fall of Acre, the French and English

Crusaders divided the loot. Out of protest, practically the whole contingent from Holland and Frisia went home. The brother of Willem, had in the meantime taken over the government of his father and Willem had to be satisfied with a part of Frisia; a couple of years later he succeeded his recently deceased brother as the Count of Holland.

A number of Northern Netherlanders took part in the Fifth Crusade (1217-1221). Oliver of Paderborn, a teacher in Cologne, propagandized the battle against the Muslims in Frisia and Groningen. He was in Dokkum in June 1214, where a thousand people were in remembrance of Boniface (English by birth), who was murdered 460 years earlier. Oliver had experience in the preaching of the Crusade, because he called for the participation in the punishment expedition against the Cathars in South France in 1207, at the request of Pope Innocent III. The people of Frisia and Groningen departed in 1217 by ship to go to the Middle East. Bishop Otto II, the leader of the Utrecht's contingent, went overland and joined the army of the Hungarian King, Andrew II. The Bishop did not take part in the battle and limited himself to the reconstructing of deteriotated fortifications.

Count Willem I went, about twenty years after his first pilgrimage, to the Holy Land for the second time. Due to the fact that he had participated in a French expedition against England, which was forbidden by the Pope, he was threatened with a Papal ecclesiastical ban. Willem therefore had little choice. In 1217 he left from Vlaardingen with a fleet of 212 ships. In South England he mixed with a fleet of eighty Frisian vessels which had recently sailed out from the Lauwerszee. Oliver of Paderborn was a member of the North Netherlands contingent and wrote a chronicle about his experiences: *Historian Damiatina*. Count Willem had supreme command over the whole fleet, but this did not stay in tact for long. Once again the men from Holland went via Lisbon. Here, the Christians could still use all the support that they could get. The people from Frisia and Groningen refused to help the Portuguese because they wanted to go directly to the Holy Land. They chose Rome as a stopover and there they were received by the Pope. In 1218 the Northern Netherlanders arrived in Acre. Count Willem I helped the Portuguese with the conquering of the city of Alcazar and arrived in Acre six months later.

The collective army of the Crusaders journeyed to the Egyptian harbour city of Damietta which was conquered in 1219. The warriors from Frisia, Groningen and Holland fulfilled a notable role. They apparently felt like a fish in water in the marshy surroundings of this city, especially a young Frisian, Hayo of Wolvega, who distinguished himself by destroying a defence tower. He killed the enemy Standard Bearer with a flail (!). Just as with the previous Crusade, the men from Frisia, Groningen and Holland received next to nothing of the spoils and at the end of 1218, most of the Northerners went home. Count Willem left Damietta in 1219 and on his return journey he visited Frederick II in Sicily.

Oliver of Paderborn again called for participation in a Crusade, the sixth, in the years 1224-1226. He handed over a letter to the Frisians from Frederick II, in which he praised them for their part in the conquering of Damietta and he called for the avenging of their dead friends. Pope Honorius III wrote a similar letter and let it be known that the Frisian participation would be very much appreciated. In 1227 a fleet sailed out of Borkum, but only a portion of the boats arrived in Jaffa. Most ships sank without survivors due to a storm. The remaining Northerners returned home shortly thereafter, having achieved nothing. During the Sixth Crusade, a diplomatic success for the German Emperor Frederick II, there was very little fighting.

In the period 1230 to 1261 many Northerners (from high to low) participated in a Crusade. The aim of these four different Crusades nevertheless always lay in Germany. The Pope wanted to deal with a number of heretical movements there. In 1247 many men from Zeeland, Holland and Frisia joined the Crusade of Count Willem II of Holland. He journeyed to Aachen, where he was crowned as the Roman King of the German Empire. Due to his conflicts with Frederick, the Pope wanted an anti-king.

In 1269 a Crusade was preached again in Frisia and Groningen. On this occasion it was an abbot from Dokkum who called for the participation in the journey of Louis IX. He only wanted soldiers to go and set as a demand that they had sufficient money and provisions. It was explicitly forbidden for women to join them, because on the previous journeys they were motivated by the devil to commit lewd proceedings. Fifteen boats left from Frisia to go to Marseille, but Louis had departed in the meantime. The Crusaders followed him to Tunis. It turned out that the French King had died there, on the beach and that his brother, Charles had made peace with the Emir. They wanted to fight the enemies of Christianity anyhow, so they sailed on to Acre, only to discover that the Franks had followed the example of Charles. Their participation in the Eighth Crusade had not been of any importance.

Compared to the Flemings, the men from Holland, Frisia and Groningen played a modest role in the Crusades, especially the nobility who were hardly interested in the Holy Land, undoubtedly because they were orientated on the events in East Europe. Furthermore, there were three where the Germans took part, without succes. The Second and Third Crusades went, as we have already seen, very poorly for the German Emperors, Conrad and Frederick Barbarossa. Frederick II scored an incredible result with the Sixth Crusade, but not everyone considered this as a succes. Thanks to his negotiations, Jerusalem was again under the occupation of the Franks in 1229. Diplomacy was definitely not acceptable and honourable for the average knight. On top of that, in the eyes of the Church, Frederick II was a disputed figure. Due to the scant zest of the noblemen from Holland in particular, and the disappointments of the Frisian, the Templars had very few possessions in Northern Netherland.

TEMPLAR ESTABLISHMENTS IN THE NETHERLANDS

Legends
Just as in the other countries, all sorts of stories about the possessions of the Templars appeared in the Netherlands in the sixteenth and seventeenth centuries. The historian Streefland suggested that this great interest in the Templars and their downfall had to do with religious motives. Protestant historians wanted to use the nasty course during the trial against the Templars in their conflict with the Roman Catholic Church. In the *Monasticon Batavum* of 1941-1942 there is an enumeration given of 24 settlements of the Templars in what we now call the Netherlands. The places named are based on tradition and in nearly all cases are lacking medieval sources. A characteristic example is the supposed Templars house in Zierikzee. A German encyclopaedia from the eighteenth century reports the following occurrences there.

> *In 1312* [1307 is meant] *the justiciary received a stamped letter that had to be opened at midnight on a certain day. The letter contained an order that had to be carried out immediately. The justiciary did so, they arrested all Templars and killed them without due trial and process. Only two of them survived the attack because they had spent the night in a brothel.*

The encyclopaedia based this on a history book that was written a century before by a Protestant theologian who originated from the Netherlands. The truth was really different. In 1274, in Zierikzee, a small mendicant order of the "Ekster brothers" was abolished. The Dominican Order bought the monastery from them. Later writings report that the Dominicans had bought a building from an Order which had vanished around the fourteenth century. Even later, historians deduced from this, that it must have been the Order of the Temple;

they had in fact been abolished at that time. Thereafter, there are vivid details added, such as the visit to the whores whom two knights had saved the lives of. From thorough research in the archives, there is not one single piece of evidence of a Templar establishment in Zierikzee.

For Haarlem it was similar. In the *Monasticon* it is stated that the monastery of the Templars was established in 1311, but that is impossible. The persecution of the Templars had already been in progress for four years. Perhaps people had seen the monastery of the Order of Saint Lazarus and considered it to be a Templar complex. This monastery was transferred to the Hospitallers in 1379. Due to the fact that this happened at the beginning of the fourteenth century along with the transfer of the possessions of the Templars to the Hospitallers, this misunderstanding is easy to declare.

In Limburg, including Maastricht, there would have been three establishments of the Templars. The archivist Ramakers has determined that the traditions don't match with the facts. The Templars do not appear in the deeds or wills in Maastricht. From an inventory list from the diocese of Liège in 1313, wherein it is written which of the Templars possessions were transferred to the Hospitallers, Netherlands Limburg is absent. In a similar way, nearly all the records from the *Monasticon* fall away one by one.

The one and only
The Templars only had a preceptory in Alphen, North-Brabant, called Ter Brake. This monastery originated in 1144, when the Baronet of Breda donated various estates to the Order of the Temple. Over a period of time, the Templars received possessions in Turnhout, Oosterhout, Rixtel and Heesbeen. It could be that Oosterhout was an independent preceptory, but the sources are very vague about it. The *Monasticon* believes, wrongfully so, that Rixtel was an independent establishment, which undoubtedly comes about because the Templars possessed buildings with considerable estates in Rixtel (and Heesbeen). There is nothing left of all the buildings; the last one, the monastery in Alphen, was demolished in the middle of the nineteenth century.

Streefland has researched the archive material of the preceptory in Alphen. He gives a clarified analysis of the revenues from this Templars complex. Gerard van Duffel donated all his possessions to the Templars in 1187, comprising of estates, forests and vassals. As compensation they had to pay him a life annuity of three marks. In 1212 the Order of the Temple was gifted with a farm and estates in the surroundings of Turnhout from Duke Hendrik I. Two years later they received all of the possessions in Rixtel, including the patronage rights to

An evangelical book shop is now established in the previous house of the 'ekster' brothers and the Dominicans on the Meelstraat in Zierikzee (near to the old Town Hall).

A plaque that is mounted on the building where the evangelical book shop is situated.

the church of the Count of Megen, Willem, and his son Dirk. In 1289 the Commander of the preceptory rented all the assets in Rixtel and Heesbeen to a resident of 's-Hertogenbosch. It concerned farms, cultivated fields, ground rights and buildings, but not the patronage rights to the church of Rixtel. The serfs had to pay taxes to the preceptory of Ter Brake. The Templars received 24 denarii's, a huge sum of money, from this citizen of 's Hertogenbosch.

The dispute between the Templars and the Premonstratensian monastery, Tongerlo, is described in a deed from 1236. The monastery owned a farm and the adjoining estates, over which the Templars had rights too. A commission of three people was named, including one Templar, who had to deliver a binding recommendation. The dispute was about grounds that were surrounded by dykes and were in cultivation. The compensation was decided on the worth of the land before and after the reclamation of the Premonstratensianers. The arbitrators decided that the monastery near Tongerlo had to pay the Templars, four sesters of rye, four sesters of oats and three Cologne shillings. In a later deed from 1245 it was determined that if the monks wanted to develop more land then they had to have the permission from the Master of the province of France. In the above mentioned deed from 1289, there was definitely no mention of a French interference, but that the Commander of Ter Brake was responsible. Apparently, between 1245 and 1289, the Order had re-organised the say over the Northern possessions.

In Alphen and Oosterhout, the Templars had other sources of income. They received one third, respectively one quarter, of the rights on waste land there. This meant that the Templars received ground rent from the one who made the land available for agriculture. It could be referring to the areas that were the property of the Baronet of Breda. The Templars shared the proceeds from the lower jurisdiction with him. The Order received from the fines of up to one hundred solidi, a quarter in Oosterhout, and a third in Alphen. They received nothing of the proceeds from the higher punishments. In their own area they could keep the fines of up to a hundred solidi, but they got nothing from the higher amounts.

The Templars possessed several other rights in Oosterhout: the tenths (the ecclesiastical tax on the proceeds from the land) and the right to keep a bull and a goat. The Lord of Oosterhout was not permitted to build a windmill, church or castle in the parish of Oosterhout. The Order possessed a windmill, forest and waste grounds in Alphen as well as in Oosterhout. In Alphen, the Premonstratensian monks from Tongerlo collected the tenths.

After the statement of Clement V, in 1312, in which he abolished the

Templars, practically all the possessions of the Templars were transferred to the Hospitallers. An inventory was made of the possession of the Order of the Temple in Brabant during their demise. From the documents it turns out that the estates were quite unkempt; after the mass arrest of the Templars at the end of 1307, the farms were undoubtedly neglected. From the previous, it appears that there were a large variety of methods of payment available in this small area. The English King, Edgar carried out unification of the monetary system around 973, so in England noticeably less money sorts appeared centuries earlier than on the Continent.

Compared with both of the other Orders, the Templars had very little possessions in the Netherlands. It is logical the Teutonic knights were larger in the Netherlands than the Templars because in the Middle Ages Holland was very much under the German influence. The large distinction between the Hospitallers, who had establishments in at least eight cities, is more difficult to explain. The difference between both Orders was that the Hospitallers still carried out social tasks, but in other countries this did not lead to such an unbalanced division.

France

A book with a complete survey of all the French possessions of the Templars does not exist. In fact that is peculiar, because most of the publications about the Templars are written in French. The historian Dailliez, counted, without further information, a total of 1167. Barber finds this too high: according to him there were between 870 and 970 preceptories in Europe, including Cyprus. In the following there will be a summary of the possessions in the most important French provinces.

Paris

In the second quarter of the twelfth century, the Templars received their first possessions in Paris. There is not a stone to be found of the church, the monastery and the other buildings, all encircled by a wall. During the nineteenth century it was flattened to the ground. The name of the quarter, the Temple, is a reminder of this location. The French King, Louis VII gave the Parisian unit of the Order of the Temple, estates, money and various toll rights in 1143. Presumably the Parisian Templars house was established five years previously. The first building of the Templars, Vieux Temple, already existed in 1146. It was situated in the swampy part of the right bank of the Seine, where the Templars possessed a harbour. Around the Vieux Temple there was a large district which accorded with the Temple quarter from the present day Paris. The church, rebuilt in the course of the thirteenth century, had a round dome with a diameter of nearly twenty metres. The church itself measured a length of forty metres and was nine metres wide. On the Templars terrain there were two small churches: the "magna capella" where new members were accepted and the "parva capella", where they took the habit.

The donjon of the complex, built at the end of the thirteenth century, was a rectangular building whereby the outside measurements amounted to eight by fourteen metres. The walls were more than a metre thick. On two of the four corners there was a round tower that was ten metres high. The donjon, in total 35 metres high, had two storeys with a pyramid shaped grain loft and a cellar which was surrounded by a moat. Besides, the Templars complex had an extra smaller tower, called the tower of Cèsar, built at the end of the twelfth century. Both fortifications were probably meant to protect the valuables of the Order and those of the non-members. In addition to these houses, the complex also had many monastery buildings, stables, guest houses, a hospital and various gardens. Matthew Paris further mentioned an extremely large hall, where the English King, Henry III, gave a party for his French colleague in 1254. In total it was nearly 61 thousand square metres in size (about ten football pitches) and was completely enclosed by a wall, metres high, in which there were fourteen watch towers. Directly outside the walls, the Templars possessed even more large pieces of land, on which they built houses and two windmills.

After the abolition of the Order of the Temple in 1312, the possessions went to the Hospitallers. For nearly five hundred years this Order possessed the complex and during this time they made many changes. The last French King, Louis XVI, was held prisoner with his family in the donjon of the complex for a couple of months. In 1792 he was taken from this place to the location of his execution. In chapter XII it will be described how the French Royalty, at the beginning of the fourteenth century, ensured the abolition of the Order of the Temple; Louis XVI passed his last days in a former Templars house and it could be seen as a form of 'long term justice.'

Burgundy and Champagne

These provinces are situated in the East of France, with Champagne to the North of Burgundy. The geographical denotation of these areas was not always as clear in the general chronicles from the twelfth and thirteenth century.

Further, there are a limited number of documents available. This puts us again in a position where an exact picture of the possessions of the Templars cannot be formed.

Champagne was the birth place of the Templars. The first Grand Master, Hugh of Payns, was born there and Andrew of Montbard also grew up in Champagne. The most important monastery of Bernard of Clairvaux was situated there. Troyes was the city where, in 1129, the council was held, which was of great importance to the Templars. The *Primitive Rule* of the Order was set there.

The Templars apparently possessed 22 preceptories in both provinces, twenty less than the Hospitallers. From the remaining 250 interrogations from the process (see chapter XII) there were approximately 150 of the Templars who came from Burgundy and Champagne. Due to the fact that in October 1307, about two thousand members of the Order were arrested in France, these few reports say more about the manner in which these archives from the trial are kept, than the significance of these provinces. The important monastery of the city of Payns originated between 1128 and 1130, as a gift from the Count of Champagne to the First Grand Master. Many donations followed before long. The gift from the Lord of the estate of Grancey, Odo, is a shining example. His father donated part of his property to the Templars before 1150. Odo followed his fathers' example and at an old age he became a member of the Order in 1185. He was admitted to the preceptory of Bures, where he died in 1197. It is unlikely that Odo had ever been to the Middle East. His grandchildren were invited to his funeral by the Commander of his monastery, after which they confirmed the donation of their forefather.

Hugh of Bourbonne gave a piece of land as security to the Templars in 1191, undoubtedly to pay for his Crusade. During the siege of Acre in 1191 he transferred this to them. This was a regularly occurring manner of acquiring property by the Templars.

Nice

In 1308 the possessions of the Templars in the area of Nice were confiscated. With the aid of a notary deed, the historian Durbec (1954) made a summary hereof. The problem with this is that the documents are not consistent in the defining of goods and rights. Just as unclear is also, if and in what degree the Order was the owner of the goods. In many instances the deeds could have explained that the Order had the rights to a portion of the income from the farms without the Order actually having possessed them. In the concerned area, Alpes-Maritimes, there were about forty places where the Order possessed rights. Alpes-Maritimes formed a rectangle, with sides of roughly forty by 25 kilometres. There were presumed to be eight preceptories in the area of Nice. Those of Biot had a farm, a large estate (287 seterées that were sown in the winter of 1307/1308), a vineyard (80 fosserées) and a meadow (60 souchoirées). In Grasse the Order was the owner of a monastery building, a church, a smithy, a vineyard, a garden, a meadow and three spread out pieces of land. In the village of Gaude, the Order possessed an estate and also a wasteland terrain. The Templars could claim rights to more than seven hundred assets in the concerning area.

For the most part these possessions were in the form of vineyards, meadows and farming land, a couple of fig tree orchards, some windmills and a furnace. These rights were very diverse in nature: a permanent gift, a percentage of the income, covees and products such as wine, cheese and oats. In a number of documents a combination of rights appeared. All together it ensured that the Order of the Temple had a suitably large, yet crumbled source of income in this area.

In this part of Southern France there were over six hundred people who, in one way or another, had a relationship with the Templars. Approximately one third rented a piece of land from them and about four hundred farmhands (men and women) worked on the estates. A portion of the first group was also bound to another feudal lord. The above mentioned registration from 1308 was limited to that time: we know very little about the history of the possessions.

Provence
Champagne was the province where the most important founder of the Order of the Temple came from. The first donations were made in the Provence and hence the first preceptory established. On the 1st July 1124, therefore five years before the Council of Troyes, William of Poitiers donated a part of the income from the church of Saint-Barthèlemy in La Motte-Palayson to the 'poor knights of Christ.' Further expansion mostly occurred because Raymond Berenguer III (see page 115) was not only Count of Barcelona, but also Count of Provence and Toulouse. He was involved in the struggle with the Moors and therefore understood the aims of the Templars. These possessions fell under the province of Aragon until 1143. Furthermore, many knights from the area took part in the First Crusade. They would have also given generously to the Templars. The Order had about 45 monasteries in an area of approximately 190 by 150 kilometres, spread over more than sixty places. We know this from the remaining

2200 deeds and other documents. Again, we have very little knowledge about the exact size of the preceptories. Those of Marseille, Aix-en-Provence, Orange, Avingon and Saint-Gilles belonged to the most important.

THE POSSESSIONS OF THE TEMPLARS IN THE REST OF EUROPE

Flanders
The Southern Netherlanders played a central role during the Crusades from the outset. Godfrey of Bouillon and his brother were the founders of the Royal dynasty in the Holy Land. Baldwin IX, Count of Flanders and of Hainault, became the first Latin Emperor of the newly conquered Byzantium in 1204. He was one of the most important leaders of the Fourth Crusade. A year later, Baldwin was succeeded by his brother Henry, a very capable ruler. From the nine founders who were named in the *Primitive Rule*, two are definitely from Flanders: Archambaud of Saint-Armand and Godfrey of Sint-Omars. Maybe Payen of Mont Didier was also a Fleming. Flanders generated two Grand Masters of the Order of the Temple, Odo Saint-Amand-les-Eaux (1170-1179) and Gerard of Ridefort (1184-1189). They belonged to the most aggressive leaders that the Order ever knew and both died in a battle with the Muslims.

Oste of Sint-Omaars, maybe a brother of Godfrey of Sint-Omaars, became a member of the Templars in Jerusalem in 1137. Together with his father he provided the Templars with many donations which led to the founding of the preceptory in Slijpe. Oste became the first Master of the province of Flandriae. He was the confidant of the English Kings Steven and Henry II. Thanks to this friendship, he was later promoted to Master of the province of Anglia. Oste was also active in the Holy Land, Catalonia and France. By royal order issued by the French King, Louis VII, Oste of Sint-Omaars managed three French castles together with two colleagues. The castles of Gisors, Neuchâtel and Néaufle formed a part of the dowry of Louis' daughter. He handed them, in spite of the agreement, prematurely, over to Henry II, where after the three members had to flee to England in 1160.

Eustachius Canis (half way through the twelfth century) came from the area of Bruges and was a financial expert. Whilst he stayed in the Middle East he was consulted by the Pope and Louis VII about their financial matters. The Pope called Canis 'mon fils' and the French King described him as 'son ami et serviteur.' Later Eustachius became Master of the province of France and founder of the banking activities of the preceptory in Paris. In the beginning of the fourteenth century we come across Flemish Templars again. They allowed themselves to be transported to Paris so that they could defend the Order against the accusations of the French King, Philip IV. What became of him further is not mentioned in the chronicles.

The first donations in Flanders date from around 1125, before the Council of Troyes. Numerous gifts followed and before 1171, probably 1140, there was a separate province, Flandriae. Not in one single document do we find evidence of the correct founding date of a preceptory. The first gifts were accepted by the Master of Flandriae. Only when the functionary of a certain preceptory is named in the documents, are we sure of the existence of one. Veurne and Atrecht were the first Templars houses; both dating from before 1142. In the diocese of Doornik the Templars possessed seven independent preceptories: Saint-Léger, Corbrieus, Slijpe, Ruiselede, La Haie, Bruges and Ghent. This information comes from a deed in which these monasteries are assessed for an ecclesiastical tax. La Haie, Bruges and Ghent consisted of commercial centres and storage places, the remaining monasteries were situated in the countryside. The possessions were spread throughout the whole diocese, just as in Alphen, without them being separate preceptories. Probably in the other dioceses (Terwaan and Kamerijk), preceptories of equal size were established. All in all, the Templars would have had about thirty large monasteries in Flanders.

The Flemish Templars did not build any round churches. They presumably had one castle, which was situated in Roesbrugge-Haringe. In Veurne, Slijpe, Cobrieux and Ruiselede, they were farmers. The English Templars transported their wool to their monastery in Ieper, where many weavers, shearers and fullers lived in the preceptory. The yearly Templars' market in Ieper was famous everywhere for its cloth industry amongst other things.

England

The Templars received their first preceptory, in about 1135, as a gift from members of the Royal Family. At the end of the thirteenth century there were about forty monasteries. From approximately 1150, England, Scotland and Eire formed together as one province, with its own provincial Master. Given the close relationship with the royal house, the English sovereignty would have had an influence on the naming of this functionary.

The headquarters of the province of Anglia were of course established in London. During the first years it was in Holborn, on the site where the station of High Holborn is now. The foundations of the building can still be seen. Around 1155, the Templars sold this complex to the Bishop of London. The

Order then moved to the bank of the Thames, between Fleet Street and the river. In 1185 a large church there was consecrated by Archbishop Heraclius of Jerusalem. The Order further possessed various small chapels, two large houses, windmills, ponds, smithies, a wharf and harbour facilities there. On the bank of the river Thames was a piece of land of six hectares, Fickettscroft, probably a military practice area of the Templars. The headquarters were regularly used for royal and religious meetings. The English parliament occasionally gathered there and the Bishops of England held a least nine councils during the period 1256 to 1299. It was obviously a nice place to be. Archbishops from Spain and Germany, papal representatives and foreign diplomats very frequently stayed there. The London Temple functioned at the same time as the financial centre of the English branch of the Order. The Kings and the nobility made use of the various banking facilities of the Templars. They lent and kept money, jewels and important papers. The knights of the Templars collected many ecclesiastical and secular taxes from out of London; these were then locked in the safes of the New Temple. It is unclear if the Templars always took interest into account and in which manner they were paid for their services. Anyway, as compensation they received goodwill, gifts and exemption from taxes.

The Templars regularly carried out diplomatic missions for the English King. During their missions they visited Austria, France and Italy with all sorts of messages for the Kings and the Pope. They were advisors to the English royal house. Aymmeric of Saint Maurer, the English provincial Master from 1200-1218, was one of the most important preparers of the Magna Charta (1215). During the signing of this document, he stood next to King John.

In 1185, the Master of the province of England made a summary of the possessions of the Order. About 150 years later, the Hospitallers inventoried which goods they had received after the abolition of the Order of the Temple. With the use of these lists we can form a good impression of the wealth of the Templars.

In Yorkshire there were ten preceptories and various estates of equal importance. To the South of these (in the county of Lincolnshire) there were five monasteries. Four of these five belonged to the richest in England. The monastery Temple Brurer was situated, in the first instance, in an uncultivated area. A few years later the Templars owned various churches, at least one market, extensive building grounds and fields. To the North of these counties, the Templars did not have any preceptories, but did have various possessions.

Bristol was the financial centre for the four counties in the South West of England. There were two hospitals, where the old and sick knights were taken care of, in the province of England: one in Lincolnshire and one on the Island of Ely, Cambridgeshire. When the sheriff of the King arrived to arrest the brothers in 1308, they came across eleven men. Eight were old, two were middle aged and sick and one was mentally ill. The Templars belonged to the most important land owners in England where the size of their preceptories varied from a few, to four hundred hectares.

In Eire they had thirteen monasteries with the associated domains, 21 churches and large forests, building land and meadows. Scotland had four preceptories and Wales only one. The Order used these lands for the cultivating of grain, oats, rye and barley. They were also cattle farmers and cared for numerous horses, sheep, cows and pigs on their farms. The sheep they used for wool, which was sold to the Flemish cloth industry. On the basis of these contracts, it is calculated that they owned tens of thousands of sheep. In the whole of England, in total they utilized at least 81 mills; a lucrative activity because forced sourcing was usual. Trade in the Middle Ages mainly took place via market stalls. The owner of the right to hold a market earned plenty of money. The Templars owned such a privilege in at least thirteen cities.

Alongside the proceeds from these agricultural products, the Templars had other sources of income. They received money and materials for the building of churches, mills and other structures. They were allowed to fell between two and seven oak trees a year from the royal forest. King Henry II gave them a section of the river so that they could run their mills using the flow of water. The Templars did not have to pay the tolls on bridges and main roads, or the tax on the market. Neither the import, nor the export of goods, such as wine and wool, were taxed.

On their own land, they were totally economically and juridically independent from the secular and the ecclesiastical leaders. Conflicts with the Order could only be handled by the King or the highest legal body. All these rights were valid for both the preceptories and the leaseholders of the Templars' grounds. These buildings were earmarked with a cross so that everyone could clearly see that there was 'nothing to collect' at this house. Evidently, this was misused, so King Edward I passed a law in 1285, in which heavy punishments were given for unrightfully using this symbol. It is questionable as to whether the Templars had as many possessions in England as the other religious orders. Benedictines, Augustine's, Cistercians and Hospitallers probably owned more land (Parker, 1963).

Italy

From 1138, when the Order received its first gift of the surroundings of Lucca, the Templars built an extensive network in Tuscany. They then established themselves in Siena (1148), again in Lucca (1157) and Pisa (1163). In the thirteenth century, in addition to these were Colle di Baggiano (between Pisa and Pistoria), Florence, San Gimignano, Arrezo, Piacenza, Vignale, Grosseto, Montelopio and Frosini. Frosini was a small place which was situated in a very prosperous part of Italy. The Commander had extensive staff at his disposal. It was a financial centre, where the Order also owned a large hospital. Most of the monasteries were situated on the important pilgrimage roads to Rome and the harbour cities along the Adriatic Coast. The latter being important because many Westerners sailed from there to go to the Middle East. It goes without saying that the pilgrims were given shelter; this rendering of services was a supplement to the continuation of the protection of the believers on the roads in the Holy Land.

Apulia (South Italy) and Lombardy, which at that time stretched from North Italy to Rome, each had their own provincial Master, whilst Sicily had a similar functionary from 1282. There were two Templars' monasteries in Rome, furthermore the Templars were established in practically all the large cities in

Most churches of the Templars were rectangular. So is the San Bevignate in Perugia.

Italy. In the documents covering these locations, in nearly every single instance, the appertaining churches are named. On Sicily the Order possessed dozens of preceptories and furthermore mills, fishing rights, toll places, vineyards, olive trees and cultivated land. Charles of Anjou made use of the financial expertise of the Templars. Thanks to him, the Templars could transport many goods from South Italy to the Middle East during the last decades of the thirteenth century. We have no specifics about how many members of the Order there were in Italy, but when the number of possessions are taken into consideration, there must have been more than a hundred.

Hungary, Croatia, Slovenia and Dalmatia
In the *Hierarchical Statute* from around 1165, Hungary was named as a separate province. This only occurred if a territory had a large number of possessions, so there must have been more than is now known. The province comprised of preceptories situated in Hungary, Croatia, Slovenia and Dalmatia.

In 1169 the Templars owned a monastery in Varna, on the Black Sea, and they had managed an estate in Golgonissa since 1175. The Order was anyway established in Pula, Triëst and Ljubljana. They had a castle in Vrana, on the Adriatic Coast. In 1219 the Templars accepted various donations from King Andrew of Hungary, whilst two years earlier they had received the castle at Clissa. Around 1250, all the Hungarian possessions were confiscated by the son of Andrew. He did so after the land had suffered immensly from the plundering of the Mongolians. Moreover these measures applied to all religious orders.

Greece
In 1204 the French and Italian Crusaders conquered Constantinople and large parts of the former East Roman empire. The first Emperor, Baldwin, was short of knights. Obviously he appealed to the Order. He named the Templars as advisors and just like his vassals, he gave the Order many gifts. He made the Order, according to a letter from Pope Innocent III, responsible for the small Asiatic harbour town of Adalia, which had been conquered by the Muslims in March 1207. The remaining possessions of the Order are also known from the letters of Pope Innocent III. The Order settled in Thebes, Thessalonica, Lamia, Ravennika and on the Island of Evvoia, the Peninsula of Khalkidhikí; a place to the North East of Athens and on the peninsula to the West of Athens. The Templars founded a preceptory here in a former Greek Orthodox monastery, whilst they built a castle in the cities of Lamia and Ravennika. In 1209 and the years following, everything except their preceptory in Thebes was reclaimed by

Emperor Henry of Constantinople, for unknown reasons. The city of Ravennika was demolished at this time and was never re-built.

The Templars were definitely not mourning the loss of their Greek possessions. After the conquering of Constantinople, the Franks also marched into Greece in order to control the rest of the country. It was a constant battle, because they had a different manner of governing than the Greeks, and irreconcilable differences with the Greek Orthodox religion. This civil war prevented a profitable exploitation of the land.

East and Central Europe
In 1167 the Templars received their first possessions in Germany, in the surroundings of Munich. This becomes clear from a charter, which is co-signed by the Master of Lombardy (North Italy). In around 1210, they possessed German land to the East of the river Elbe, for the first time. The preceptories established here, were situated to the South of Berlin: Templehof, Marienfelde, Mariendorf and Rixdorf. In 1208 the Bishop of Halberstadt and the Visitor, regulated a transaction together concerning ground exchange with the Templars. It is evident that they were established there some time ago. The Templars also owned preceptories in Trier, Koblenz, Bonn and Cologne.

It would take until 1227 before a Master of the province of Germany first appeared in the deeds. This province boundaried Eastern Europe, including Austria. The Slavic monarch Henry I of Lower Silesia (surroundings of Breslau), Odonicz of Poland and Barmin of Pommeren (to the East of Gdansk), all acknowledged the significance of the Order for the colonisation of the countries. They gifted the Templars with large areas on both sides of the river Oder to the North of Frankfurt. In 1227, in Ohlau, in the region of Breslau, they were granted the tenths. In 1242, in Jamolz, the Order received an estate from a donor because some members had saved his life during the battle with the Mongolians. Duke Bolesaw of Poland also thought of the Templars; in 1239 he donated lands close to Skuszewo (in the vicinity of the river Bug), Orzechowo (on the river Narew, nearby Warschau) and near the city of Plock to the Order. The Templars also had preceptories near Wroctaw (Mala Olesnica) and on the Baltic Sea (Wielka Weis).

The Templars were established in Lukow for a short while, before 1257, on the Eastern border of Poland. It was surely situated a long distance from Paris and Jerusalem. They served, in this part of the world, as protectors of the Christian borders against the Eastern heathendom, but they did not need to fight. The Templars had to attract colonists and found villages and cities. The small monasteries could hardly permit themselves to build castles, only a couple of stone towers offered some sort of protection. When the Mongolians invaded Poland in 1241, the Templars could also not offer any resistance. A number of unprotected hamlets and two of the strongest towers were trampled over and destroyed by the Mongolians. That is what the Master of the province of France wrote to the French King. Henry II of Lower Silesia waged war against the Mongolians. On April 9th 1241, a battle took place near Legnica, West of Breslau. The Templars lost three knights, two sergeants and five hundred mercenaries. A few days later, there was once again a battle with the Mongolians in Hungary. Many Templars lost their lives, but King Bela IV escaped. The Mongolians did not march forward because their leader had died in the Far East. Their general wanted to interfere with the succession. The intruders withdrew and that saved the German border cities from further destruction.

The Templars returned to their properties and continued their peaceful colonisation. They only possessed a few castles to the East of the river Wista. In 1295, at the request of the Templars, King Adolf of Nassau also instituted all freedoms and privileges for the brothers and also the possessions in the areas of Poland, Pommeren, Krakow en Slavia.

A PRECEPTORY

The Templars exploited approximately a thousand preceptories in the overseas areas. They had very few castles in the West and the majority of them were in Spain and Portugal. The most significant monasteries, such as London, Paris and La Rochelle, were surrounded by walls. On the European pilgrimage routes and in the harbour cities in the direction of the Holy Land especially, they founded preceptories, intended also for the recruiting of new members. The average preceptory consisted of a farm yard with a chapel, and sheds or small buildings scattered here and there over the land. The Order often owned a mill or a furnace which ensured extra income and of course they tried to order the area efficiently and to maximise the utilisation of the land with the use of exchange or acquisition of ground. Depending on the region, they kept themselves busy with all aspects of farming life. Sheep were kept in England, wine was made in France and olives were cultivated in Italy. A number of French monasteries were involved in the breeding of horses. The Order employed a few dozen farmhands in all preceptories. It was only in Spain, Portugal, Sicily and the Middle East where slaves worked for them.

There were not any knights present on most Western preceptories and the smaller communities shared a priest. If new members joined the Order, they were admitted by a knight; from the documents of the trial it is evident that the provincial Master was regularly the chairman of the reception meeting. Weapons were available to a very small degree, so it is shown from the inventories of the French possessions in 1307 (see the appendix). This is obvious; the battle took place in the Middle East. From the same investigation it was revealed that in the monasteries were few liquid assets available. The preceptories had to provide for themselves and the profits were regularly relinquished to the headquarters.

THE CHURCHES OF THE ORDER OF THE TEMPLE

It is obvious that all preceptories of the Templars (large or small, castle or farm) had a prayer room which was set up in a building, such as in all castles, or it stood very near the preceptory. The latter situation was of course preferred, because then the common people could visit the chapel. The more souls that went to church, the more income there was for the exploitation of the houses of God. The Templars owned a large collection of relics; ultimately, they had first choice. Thanks to these, they made their church more attractive to the Western believer, who showed their appreciation by filling the relevant offertory bags. The Order regularly used their relics in order to interest the West in the Holy Land. In 1247, the Templars church in London received a bottle containing the blood of Jesus. The authenticity of this blood was guaranteed by the Archbishop of Jerusalem and other ecclesiastical leaders of the Holy Land.

The Order had 22 churches in central Italy. Their church in Perugia, from around 1260, was named after a local Saint, Bevignate. They chose this name for a good reason. Bevignate was the patron saint of the so called flagellant brothers. The San Bevignate, Templar church of Perugia, was an attractive pilgrimage spot for this popular section of the Church of Rome.

A great number of papal bulls were dedicated to the difference of opinion between normal clergy and the Templars and their churches. The subject of discussion was never related to religious matters, but was of a financial nature. Along side this the Templars controlled many parish churches, apart from the chapel in their monasteries. They quite often received the parish churches from a Bishop: apparently the Roman Catholic Church could not care for the spiritual needs in every area of the countryside.

In contrast to what was thought in esoteric circles, their architecture is not based upon a certain number theory combined with a circular pattern. The Templars did indeed have round churches, but not as the norm nor in large numbers. Helena, the mother of Constantine, founded the Holy Sepulchre in the fourth century, on the supposed spot of Jesus' short-lived earthly resting place. This church was round, conforming to a century's old tradition. Just as the cross, the circle was a recognised religious symbol, which was often used as a building principle by the Romans and Greeks for instance. It was obvious that the mother of the Christian Emperor Constantine was familiar with this tradition. Other Christian architects (the builders of San Vitale in Ravenna and the Palace Chapel in Aachen) chose to follow in the footsteps of Helena with this building style. The Palace Chapel, an example for many eleventh century builders, was constructed at the beginning of the ninth century during the reign of Charlemagne. Art historians presume that it was an imitation of the circular form of the San Vitale from the sixth century.

Most churches that the Templars built were, on the other hand, rectangular, therefore rather simple buildings and without unusual numerology. This was also the same for their churches in the overseas areas and in the Holy Land. There is absolutely no evidence of a typical architecture of the Templars.

They were not that rich

In general the idea that the Order of the Temple was extremely rich predominates. From the chronicles, it is evident that contemporaries of the Templars also thought the same, but it is doubtful if their income offset their enormous costs. The visible wealth of the Templars was mainly the possession of land and buildings, therefore immovable goods. The proceeds from these should have been extremely high; however, the practicing of agriculture from time to time was not always lucrative. Crop failure, adverse weather and sickness made the agricultural workings in the Middle Ages a riskier sector than it is in our time.

There are authors (i.e. Knight and Lomas) who declare that the fast growth of the Order of the Temple was because the Templars had found the treasure of Solomons Temple. Indeed, up until 1947 it was unclear what had happened to the valuables from the Jewish Temple in Jerusalem after the destruction in the year 70. A portion of this was shown to the public by Titus during a triumph parade through Rome. The discovery of the Dead Sea Scrolls at Qumran, in particular the Copper Roll, hereafter gives a decisive answer.

The Copper Roll records a summary of 61 places where gold, silver and

Temple implements are hidden. It cannot be any other way, than that the valuables originate from the Temple of Jerusalem, which was built around the beginning of our era by Herod. The Temple treasures were undoubtedly hidden by the Jews just before the destruction. In his book *The Treasure of the Copper Scroll* (1960) the scientist Allegro attempts to describe the contents and the meaning of the Copper Roll. Allegro is very clear about his translation from the Hebrew text:

> *It will be appreciated, therefore, that any translation of the copper scroll at this stage must be considered as provisional. There are often so many alternatives to the reading of a particular word, each dependent upon the true interpretation of another, itself perhaps resting on one or two other indeterminates, that, failing the discovery of new evidence, the rendering can be only a succession of possibilities.*

To emphasise this, Allegro provides his translation of the 61 hiding places with more than three hundred notes.

An added problem is that the indication of the locations is ultimately vague. For example, article seven of column II:

> *In the cavity of the Old House of Tribute, in the Platform of the Chain: sixty five bars of gold.*

Presumably, only 24 of the places indicated are associated to the immediate surroundings of the Temple. The Roman General (and later Emperor) Titus demolished the city in 70, so this portion of the treasure is unfindable. Most of the other locations are in the large surroundings of Jerusalem. Neither the Ark of the Covenant nor the Stone Tablets, or the seven armed candlesticks are mentioned in any way. Allegro guessed the total worth to be approximately eleven hundred kilo's of silver and about four hundred kilo's of gold; present day value of about 2 million British pounds. If the Order of the Temple had already found part of the valuables then it did not make them much richer. Nowadays the long maintaining of an army would in fact cost multiples of two million pounds.

The Order needed a large annual income. The maintenance of a knight (transport, armament, horses, food and supporting personnel) was extremely expensive. An estimation is given in chapter IX; for keeping a knight operational in 1260 approximately fifteen hundred hectares of agricultural land was necessary. Above all, the costs of the horses of a knight were tremendously high. From out of a thousand preceptories of an average size of three hundred hectare, the Order of the Temple could place two hundred knights in the field from these sources of income. These men desperately needed the gifts and the tax income from the West, especially since they were supporting a few dozen large and small castles in the Middle East.

In chapter VII, on the basis of the data of an eye witness report, it will describe what had to be spent annually for the exploitation of the castle of Safad. Château Pèlerin and the castles of Beaufort and Tortosa were of a comparable size. The ransom for an imprisoned Templar in the second half of the thirteenth century, almost undoubtedly cost more money than the Templars received for ransoming a Muslim. They were forced onto the defensive. The conclusion is clear: people saw the wealth of the Templars, but did not realise that they had high costs.

The Hospitallers and the Cistercian Order had more land and monasteries than the Templars. The remarkable thing is that these organisations were not well known for their wealth. Over the last seven hundred years there have been barely any legends made around these Orders. The sudden and peculiar end to the Templars appeals to the imagination and makes the Order of the Temple legendary, indeed literally.

VI. The period of 1193-1244.
Anarchy sometimes pays

THE HOLY LAND UP TO 1218

In the North of the Christian territory between 1198 and 1216 a struggle for power took place between Leo, the ruler of Christian Armenia, and the leaders of Antioch. The Hospitallers supported Leo and the Templars were on the side of Antioch. The Templars wanted, per se, to regain castle of Baghras including the surrounding area. The castle was conquered in 1188 by Saladin and Leo had managed to occupy it shortly thereafter. The Templars were supported by Pope Innocent III, who had banished Leo due to his behaviour during the conflict with the Templars. This quarrel, which cost many members their lives, did not end until 1216. The Order gained back the castle of Baghras in that year. It was immediately fortified. Due to this, the Templars once again became the independent rulers of the overall region. They wanted to expand this area and fought the Muslims of the domain of Aleppo to that end.

In the county of Tripoli the tension was also mounting between both Orders. It was in 1179 that the Templars and the Hospitallers made peace in this region. As a consequence the defeat at the battle of Hattin, which minimized the Christian landlords, both Orders had almost become the single rulers of the surroundings of the city of Tripoli, these agreements were almost impossible to keep. In 1198 there was a conference held between both Grand Masters in order to re-settle the rights to the territory. Brother Terricus was sent to Rome to submit the result to the Pope for his approval. Terricus had survived the battle of Hattin and informed the West of the catastrophic consequences of the defeat. For most of the thirteenth century, the Templars and the Hospitallers were Lord and Master of the provinces of Tripoli and Antioch. They were practically the only ones in this area who continued the war against the Muslims.

Gilbert Erail (1194-1200)

In 1191, Acre became the new capital city of the Kingdom of Jerusalem. As a result of this, the headquarters of the Templars were established in this harbour city. Grand Master Robert of Sablé, the protégé of King Richard, died after a short rule of two years, on the 23rd September 1193. Gilbert Erail became the twelfth Grand Master a year later. His background is unclear; he came from Aragon or Provence. Gilbert already had a long career behind him in the Order. In Jerusalem he was the substitute of the Master in 1183 and he held the function of Master of the provinces of Provence and Spain between 1185 and 1190. He then became the Visitor and therefore responsible for the overseas provinces. Despite being appointed to Grand Master, Gilbert remained in the West. In the years 1196-1197, he received possessions in various European countries. This we know, because the Grand Master signed the relevant transfer deeds. He first arrived in Acre in 1198. Gilbert remained in the Holy Land thereafter; thus he was witness to the transfer of a number of possessions from the wealthy monastery of 'St. Maria in the Vale of Josephat', to the Order of the Temple.

Gilbert Erail was present at a council in the Templars complex of this city, where the Teutonic Knights were officially accepted as a military order in March 1198. After the Third Crusade, there were many German knights remaining in the Holy Land. Up until then the Germans were members of both of the large Orders, but the language barrier was obviously a problem, especially during the ministering of the last sacraments when the dying German knights did not always know what was happening. The Germans, not yet used to the political situation in the Middle East, found that above all, both of the other Orders were too nice towards the Muslims. They had no interest in armistices, but in war. The Teutonic Knights rapidly made themselves all too unpopular because their members were combative, rough and extravagant. In Acre, for this reason, the Germans were not tolerated and the people directed them towards an army camp outside the city.

Evidently the peace on the front did not go unnoticed in the West either, because Pope Innocent III wrote a letter to the most important leaders of the Middle East in 1199. He complained that the Westerners did not want to go on a Crusade because the Christian leaders had agreed to a cease fire with the Muslims. The Grand Masters of the Templars and the Hospitallers also received such a letter. On another level there were also problems with the Church. As William of Tyre had already described in his book, the Orders regularly held discussions with the bishops about the payment of the Church taxes, the tenths.

In 1196 the Pope had to intervene when the Templars did not honour the agreements with the monks of the Holy Sepulcher.

Around the same time, the brothers had a difference of opinion with the Bishop of Tiberias about their income from his territory. Pope Innocent III appointed a commission, under the leadership of the Archbishop of Jerusalem who resided in Acre. The Bishop of Sidon (Saida), also a member of this commission, did not agree with the outcome. When the Order appealed to this, the Grand Master was excommunicated by him. The Pope overruled this because, so he declared, the Order fell under the responsibility of the Holy Chair.

Philip of Plessis (1201-1209)
Gilbert Erail died on the 12th December 1200 and Philip of Plessis, again a Frenchman, became the new leader of the Order a year later. He descended from an unknown family. Philip had been in the Holy Land since the Third Crusade, but as yet was not a Templar. In order to pay for his Crusade he wanted to sell his possessions to a monastery. When the abbot did not agree to the asking price, his brother bought his belongings. He then donated these to the monastery in order to save the soul of Philip. Somewhere in the nineties Philip became a member of the Templars, but we do not hear of him again until he is in his capacity as Grand Master.

The residents of the Holy Land were heavily afflicted by an earthquake. Large parts of Acre, Tyre and Tripoli were destroyed. The Templars quarter in Acre remained unharmed, whilst the castle Chastel-Blanc of the Templars was badly damaged. As a result of the earthquake, at the beginning of summer, bubonic plague broke out among the people and animals. The Muslims could not profit from this chaos, because their cities were also stricken with desease.

Innocent III (pontificate from 1198-1216) supported the Templars wherever possible. He handed out about fifty bulls, in which he described and set the rights of the Order. They could have their own burial sites and had the right to build churches on land donated to them. He warned ecclesiastical and secular leaders that the members and their belongings had to be respected and he condemned a number of bishops who had forced the Templars into fighting against other Christians and had put members of the Order in irons. The important bull of 1139 *(Omne datum Optimum)*, which gave the Order numerous privileges, was sanctioned by him on a number of occasions. Thanks to his influence, the Templars were in a position to recover from the disasters of ten years earlier.

He also reprimanded the Order on a number of occasions: in 1207 he wrote to the Grand Master Plessis to say that he was angry about the number of complaints that had reached him and he accused the Order of being too proud. In this same letter, the Pope complained about the ease in which the Order took on new members. According to the Pope, there were too many scum mixed in, which made it too easy for them to profit from the privileges of a Christian. The Order was probably desperate for extra knights and therefore not so fussy about the antecedents of the new members.

The Pope remained active in interfering in the Order. The Templars were annoyed with the fact that the Teutonic Knights wore a white robe. They were of the opinion, in accordance with their statues approved by the Council of Troyes, that they had the exclusive right to it. This once again led to fighting. As earlier described, the knights of the Teutonic Order had a black cross on their white cloth. In 1210, the Templars handed in their appeal to Innocent III and the Pope forbad the Germans from wearing a white cloth. A year later, the archbishop came to a compromise with both Orders, with the result being that the Germans could again wear white. Despite this the Templars continued to complain; Pope Gregory IX put an end to the dispute in 1230. He forbad the Templars from molesting the members of the Teutonic Knights any longer because of their white cloth. These were restless times for the Order, but hardly due to the war activities with the Muslims.

THE FOURTH CRUSADE (1202-1204)

Pope Innocent III called, just as his predecessors, for the holding of a new Crusade and the West reacted positively. It was the fourth and the most scandalous in history. The original aim was Egypt, because that country had, in the meantime, become the strongest Muslim state. Due to the fact that it had become too dangerous to travel over land, the leaders of this journey spoke with the Venetians and it was agreed that the Italians would take care of the transport. The Muslims, unlike the situation during the First Crusade, were now Lord and Master of, the present day, Turkey. Furthermore, sailing across the Mediterranean Sea had in the meantime developed to such an extent that the ship had become a conventional means of transport. When a large army (approximately ten thousand warriors) assembled in the summer of 1202 in Venice, there proved to be too little money to pay for the passage. The Venetians would nevertheless take care of the transport, but with the agreement that the army conquered Zara first.

This city on the Adriatic Sea had just been taken from Venice by the Hungarian King. The Pope was consulted about the new target and he refused to give permission for this action: the Hungarian King was after all a fellow Christian. Innocent really had no control of the forthcoming events.

The Venetians had their way. After the conquering of Zara, a large sector of the army left for Constantinople. The son of the removed Emperor had asked the leaders of the Fourth Crusade for help and Venice, in particular, was willingly prepared to help him. They were very interested in the trade from Constantinople, but not enthusiastic about the journey to Egypt. Venice had in the meantime, extensive economic ties with this country. The Emperor's son and claimant to the throne, promised the Crusaders a large sum of money and an extra army for the journey to Egypt. He indeed became the new Emperor, thanks to the effort of the Western army, but he was not able to keep his promises. The Crusaders decided to force the Emperor to pay them. Therefore, in 1204, Constantinople was conquered, massacred and plundered by the Westerners. The soldiers were paid by being allowed to run riot in the city for three days. Even the Arabian chroniclers spoke of the scandalous behaviour of the Christians amongst themselves. Geoffroy of Villehardouin was extremely proud of the Western accomplishment:

> *The rest of the army, scattered throughout the city, also gained much booty; so much, indeed, that no one could estimate its amount or its value. It included gold and silver, table-services and precious stones, satin and silk, mantles of squirrel fur, ermine and miniver, and every choicest thing to be found on this earth. Geoffroy of Villehardouin here declares that, to his knowledge, so much booty had never been gained in any city since the creation of the world.*

The European part of the Byzantine Empire (the present day Greece) was shared between the leaders of the Fourth Crusader thereafter. The Byzantine authorities fled over the Bosporus. In 1261, Constantinople was finally back in the hands of the Byzantines. The aggressive behaviour of the Western Christians did not help the relationship between the Roman Catholic and the Orthodox Church.

No monk-soldiers took part in this Crusade. The Templars did however receive a number of possessions in the present day Greece, during the thirteenth century. The Fourth Crusade had an extremely negative effect on the Latin States. Many European adventurers preferred to travel to the prior Byzantium to claim an area there, rather than help the Latin States. Only the Templars, the

Hospitallers and the Teutonic Knights remained concentrated on the Middle East. The fall of Constantinople in 1204 ensured that the Holy Land became more and more dependant on the growth of the military orders. In the long term, the Fourth Crusade had even greater damaging consequences for Europe. The Byzantine Empire was extremely weakened by the conflict between the European and the East Roman Christians. Therefore it no longer formed a threat to the Muslims. In 1453, Constantinople fell in to the hands of the Turks; from then on called Istanbul. The Muslims now had a bridgehead for their battle against Europe.

The Turin Shroud

Various writers are of the opinion that the Templars played an important role in the history of the so called Turin Shroud. This is a cloth of about four and a half metres by one metre, in which the body of Jesus was wrapped after his crucifixion. On the shroud is a face and the front and back of a body of a man (thus Jesus) is visible. In October 1988 it was determined by various laboratories that the cloth originated from the fourteenth century. In their book, *Das Jesus Komplott*, Kersten and Gruber claim that the Vatican had this scientific examination falsified. The Roman Catholic Church should have done that, because it appears, from analysis, that a living person was once wrapped in the cloth. The story of Kersten and Gruber is mostly speculation and it is typical of the way that one involves the Templars in all sorts of vague history.

The cloth would have been brought to Edessa immediately after the crucifixion of Jesus. In the tenth century it came into the possession of Constantinople. This city is famous for its' large quantities of relics. There are indeed chroniclers who record one or another shroud of Christ in an inventory. Immediately after the fall of Constantinople in 1204, the Templars would have taken possession of the cloth via a ruse. The cloth would have been, according to the authors, an essential relic of the Templars. The shroud disappears completely from history after 1204 and suddenly reappears again in 1357. It was then exhibited in a church in the area of Troyes. It now hangs, after various wanderings, in Turin.

Kersten and Gruber base their findings, with regard to the role of the Templars, on the following facts:
1. after the fall of Constantinople, the Templar Baroche, Master of the province of Lombardy arrived in the city. In the meantime, Count Baldwin IX of

Flanders and Hainault was crowned Emperor Baldwin I of the new Empire. Baroche was asked to inform the Pope of the recent developments in the former East Roman Empire. Innocent III wrote this in a letter of November 1204, in which he confirmed that Baroche had handed over various valuables from Constantinople to him. He did not mention a word about the shroud. The Order received, along with many other things, a piece of the True Cross and two icons of the Emperor;
2. after their mass arrest in 1307, the Templars were tortured in a terrible manner in France. The inquisition was convinced in advance that the Templars worshipped an idol likening a head. A few members admitted that they had worshiped something, but the confessions were ambiguous: a cat, a lion, one head, two heads and a skull;
3. Geoffroy of Charney, Master of the province of Normandy, was one of those imprisoned Templars. He confessed to worshipping a head with four feet (two on the side of the face and two behind), amongst other things. According to both authors, this had to have been the shroud. In 1314, he withdrew all his confessions and as a consequence of this, died by being burned at the stake;
4. in 1312, the Order of the Temple was abolished by the Pope;
5. the widow of Geoffroi of Charny (Charny is on the Cote d'Or, far from Normandy) found the cloth between the belongings of her husband, after which she held an exhibition in the church that her husband had founded. Nobody knew how it had come to be in the possession of Geoffroi;
6. due to the different writing styles of names in the Middle Ages, it could be true that both Geoffroi's actually had the same surname. There is absolutely no proven (family) connection between both of the noblemen.

On the grounds of this information, Kersten and Gruber explain how Templar Baroche was robbed by pirates from Genoa. That was arranged, in order for the spoils to be divided between Genoa and the Templars. In the remaining preserved documents of the plundered items, there is actually no mention of a cloth. That is logical, because Baroche and Baldwin would have arranged for the transfer of the cloth to the Pope be kept secret! The Templars smuggled the shroud with the help of Genoa and would have worshipped it for the next hundred years as a relic: underhandedly and only in limited circles. Just before the mass arrest of the French Templars, Geoffroy of Charney would have handed the cloth over to a family member in order to keep it from the hands of the French King. Fifty years later, it was found by a relation of Geoffroy.

These sorts of stories, which are two a penny, call for more questions, rather than giving an explanation as to how the shroud came to be in France. It is indeed more logical to hypothesize that the cloth could have been stolen by a French knight. There were enough of them walking around in Constantinople. The thief could have taken the cloth to France, felt guilty and hidden it. It could have lain there in oblivion until, in 1357, it reappeared in a dusty attic. Obviously, handy explanations do not sell as well as mystical stories. (Picknett and Prince suggest, in their book *Turin Shroud: In Whose Image*, another theory: the Turin Shroud is a five hundred year old photograph from no-one other than Leonardo da Vinci.)

THE FIFTH CRUSADE (1217-1221)

In 1209, a five year cease fire with the Muslims had ended and most Christian leaders wanted to extend it. Philip of Plessis, the Grand Master of the Templars, was the only one against extension and he managed to convince the others to come around to his way of thinking. The new King of Jerusalem, John of Brienne, would shortly come from Europe to Acre and, according to Philip, could have difficulty in being obligated to this agreement. John was approached by the King of France, to marry the princess. In the same year the Templars and a number of vassals of the King went to Damietta by ship, but it was not much more than a plundering trip. In 1212, an agreement was reached with the Muslims to a 5 year treaty. At the same time, John sent a letter to the Pope, in which he asked for a new Crusade. This had to begin as soon as the duration of the agreement was over.

William of Chartres (1210-1219)
William of Chartres was the successor to Philip of Plessis, who died on the 12th November 1209. William descended from a French family with close ties to the Order of the Temple. Shortly before 1193 he joined the Templars and quickly became Commander of the castle of Chastel-Blanc.

Around 1212, in Europe, there were a number of Crusades called for. The first was aimed against the Moors on the Iberian Peninsula and it was a great success. The second was called for in order to bring the Cathars to their senses.

The only ones to profit from this last Crusade were the French monarchy, which considerably strengthened their position in South France. Just as usual, the Pope promised forgiveness of all sins to those taking part. The Templars were not involved in the Crusade against the Cathars. That was not because, as hypothesized, they had a special bond with the Cathars: the Templars were only interested in the Middle East.

In the same period, in 1212, a Crusade occurred. A French shepherd boy (Stephen) received a letter from Jesus via a pilgrim, which he had to hand over to the French King. Despite the fact that the King had dissuaded Stephen from going on a Crusade, Stephen went to the South with a large number of children. At the same time, groups of children from other parts of Europe went on a Crusade, many thousands in total. The enthusiasm of the children was explicable: in the first ten years of the thirteenth century there was a lot of propaganda, made by the Church, for the various Crusades. The children believed the messengers unconditionally. They thought that the adults had made a mess of it and they were convinced that their belief in God would kill his enemies. Eventually a large part of the children's army came to Marseille, where, according to tradition, two merchants had made a number of ships available. That was evidently not charity, but big business: they offered their passengers for sale at the Arabian slave market. This pilgrimage was definitely not supporting the Christians in the Middle East and caused the concept of Crusade more harm than good.

Nevertheless, Pope Innocent remained ambitious; he wanted to bring the Crusade to a happy ending, at any price. In 1213 he wrote to the Western leaders that he would hold a council in 1215, in order to discuss the conquering of Jerusalem again. Based on the grounds of experience with the Fourth Crusade, this had to be under the leadership of a papal ambassador. He wrote many letters on this subject and saw to it that an important role was put aside for the ordinary people. They had to hold two processions a month in the parish: one by men and one by women. Everyone had to pray for the liberation of the Holy Sepulchre. In order to finance the new Crusade an ecclesiastical tax was implemented; as usual the military orders played a central role in the collection of this. In France, the Paris Temple took care of the receipt of the French payments. Innocent was optimistic about the outcome of his second Crusade. It was after all, nearly 666 years ago when Mohamed was born. The Bible was very clear about this Antichrist: the Beast would be destroyed after this period. (Revelations 13:18)

In the years between 1217 and 1221 a number of Christian armies trickled into the Middle East. They had answered the papal calling; together they formed the Fifth Crusade. Just as with the First Crusade, no important rulers from Western Europe took part. King Andrew II of Hungary went, accompanied by the Count of Austria, as the first. Andrew gathered his army in

1217 in the harbour city of Split, where he was received with great respect. Out of gratitude, the King wanted to gift to the city the neighbouring castle, Clissa. The city refused this purely out of fear of the responsibilities that would come along with it and the King then gave the stronghold to the Templars. Andrew was kindly disposed towards the Order of the Temple. Before his departure he determined that the Master of the Hungarian Templars would receive the regency of Croatia and Dalmatia should he not return.

According to various chroniclers, the East Europeans formed an army of twenty thousand knights in total and two hundred thousand foot soldiers. That is probably over exaggerated, but even 10 percent of this tally was an army with which one could do something.

Grand Master William of Chartres wrote to the Pope in that same year, that the gathered military forces wanted to attack Damascus and he asked for more troops and provisions. Syria was afflicted shortly before by the failed harvest and it was difficult to feed the many Crusaders. Regardless, a portion of the army still journeyed in the direction of Damascus, but they did not reach any further than the Jordan. Many bathed in this Holy River and visited the nearby religious places. Because there was no definite leader (Andrew had remained in the comfort of Acre), the army returned to the encampment at Acre. Shortly afterwards, the King of Hungary turned around and went back to his own country. He had not taken part in the military actions, but for him the journey was purposeful. The Hungarians had in fact captured a number of unique relics: a wine decanter which was used at the wedding of Cana and the skull of the biblical martyr, Stephen. The Crusade was therefore a Western European concern again.

With the coming of new Crusaders, they chose for another object of attack. The target became Egypt, which was conceived as being the key to the re-conquering of Jerusalem. Saladin had finally won the battle of Hattin, thanks to the wealth of this land. For the believers, another biblical argument erupted: Jesus had lived there in his younger years. In the meanwhile, the Templars began, with the help of the Western Crusaders, with the building of Château Pèlerin between Haifa and Caesarea. The Teutonic Knights helped just as much with the construction of this colossal castle. Evidently the Templars had made peace with them again.

In April 1218, an army arrived from the Low Lands (including Holland, Frisia and Groningen) and Germany. Some of these had helped the Portuguese King with the conquering of Lisbon from the Moors. A month later the men navigated via Château Pèlerin, where provisions were stored, to the Egyptian harbour city of Damietta in six days. William of Chartres had been sick for a while and died here on the 26th August 1219.

Peter of Montaigu (1220-1232)

In 1220, Peter of Montaigu, originating from Auvergne, France, was named as Grand Master for the first time. It is presumed that his brother had been the leader of the Hospitallers since 1207. Peter had already been a member of the Order for a few years, first as Master of the provinces of Provence and Spain, later as the Visitor of the overseas areas.

After a siege of around a year, the city of Damietta fell, in 1219, into the hands of the Crusader army. An eye witness had been full of praise for the role of the Templars and he wrote that the use of their ships and their pontoons in the morasses around Damietta were of decisive significance. Directly after the conquering of Damietta, the Templars plundered the nearby city of Burlus. They took a hundred camels and many hostages, horses, mules, oxen, goats, clothes and household goods with them. The Templars did not only make their living out of the overseas areas, but for sure out of the Middle East too. Other than in the time of Amalric, fifty years earlier, the Templars attached great importance on the conquering of Egypt.

The Egyptians did not enjoy fighting with the Christians. Nine months before the fall of Damietta, the Egyptian Sultan had offered Jerusalem in trade for the withdrawal from Egypt. The sultan also offered a thirty year armistice. Cardinal Pelagius, the papal emissary and leader of the Crusade, declined this offer. Pelagius was an arrogant man who was sure that God was on his side: according to him, the Fifth Crusade was not a military, but a religious expedition. He was supported in his standpoint by the Hospitallers, the Templars and the Italian city-states. Most of the other leaders of the Franks did not share his vision, because the purpose of the Crusade would indeed be achieved. Six months later the sultan repeated his proposal, and Pelagius was again opposed. The clergy, the Templars, the Hospitallers and the Italians were again his only supporters. Around the same time, Francis of Assisi, the founder of the Franciscan Order, went to visit the sultan. He explained the faults of the Islamic belief and to the surprise of the Crusaders, he survived this journey. He definitely did not succeed in converting the Muslim leader. A month later, the sultan made his request for the land trading again, but without result. The fact that Trans-Jordania was not part of the proposal would weaken the position of Jerusalem. The Templars especially, were interested in this area; they held a strong position there before 1187.

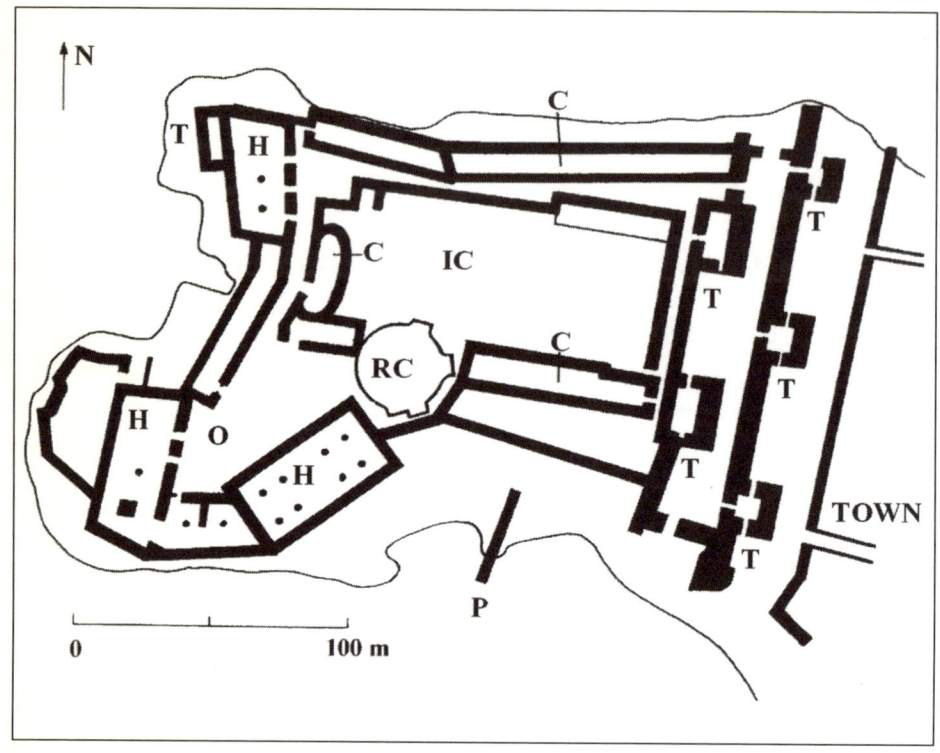

IC = Inner courtyard
P = Pier
C = Cellar
O = Ovens
RC = Round church
T = Tower
H = Hall

The ruins of the Pilgrims castle ('Athlit).

The castle is surrounded by the sea on three sides.

Because most soldiers in and around Damietta remained, the leader of Damascus threatened the Kingdom of Jerusalem and he attacked Château Pèlerin. Peter of Montaigu and a section of the Templars received permission from Pelagius to relieve this newly built castle. In September 1220, he was in Acre and from there he sent a letter to the West, in which he described the situation. After the conquering of Damietta there were a lot of new Crusaders, enough to defend the Holy Land and Damietta. In the meantime, he disagreed with the conception of Pelagius, that there were enough soldiers to move further into Egypt. They waited a long time for the expected arrival of the army of the German Emperor, Frederick. If this did not arrive quickly, the whole expedition would have to be cancelled, according to Montaigu.

In June 1221 the Egyptian Sultan again offered a trade between Damietta and Jerusalem and this time nearly everyone was in agreement with Pelagius. The army leadership was sure that the arrival from Frederick II was nearby, but he sent, despite his promise, an unpretentious army. Nevertheless, in the summer of 1221 all the leaders decided to advance to Cairo. It went utterly wrong. In a letter from September 1221, from the Grand Master of the Templars, we can read what happend. In a short space of time approximately ten thousand men deserted. On top of which, the Muslims destroyed a number of dykes, which in turn isolated the Christian army. The leaders had to surrender. They could attain freedom if they gave Damietta back to the Egyptians. Peter of Montaigu and the Grand Master of the Teutonic Knights stood at the head of the mission of those who had to explain to the occupiers of Damietta, and that was not easy. There were new Crusaders that had arrived in Damietta, who had the usual Western arrogance. The Venetians offered, just like the new comers, to resist the handing over of the city; they raided the possessions of the Templars and wanted to occupy the city. When Peter and his associates threatened to surrender Acre to the Muslims, people changed their opinions. Eventually, a cease fire of eight years was agreed.

Once again a Crusade had amounted to nothing; many contemporaries blame the German Emperor, who did not live up to his promises. James of Vitry, Bishop of Acre, from 1216 to 1228, had a totally different analysis: the native Christians hated the Franks and would have given preference to a Muslim rule. The colonists led a lazy, luxurious and immoral existence and were totally Eastenised. The clergy was corrupt, greedy and consisted mainly of intrigants. Only the military orders behaved themselves commendably. According to James, the Franks had no desire for the Fifth Crusade. They had known peaceful times and enjoyed their luxurious lives since the death of Saladin and wanted to keep it that way. James regarded the Templars highly; he described them as follows:

> *Lions in war, mild as lambs at home; in the field fierce knights, in church like hermits or monks; unyielding and savage to the enemies of Christ, benevolent and mild to Christians.*

The vision of James of Vitry was testimony that the colonists and the Westerners had absolutely no understanding of each other. The militairy orders found themselves in a melting pot of concerns and expectations. They were mighty and independent, but did not succeed in controlling the situation.

The Sixth Crusade (1228-1229)

The leaders of the Holy Land were, despite their negative experiences, still after the support of Frederick II. In 1223, they decided to marry him to the 11 year old heiress of the King of Jerusalem. It was the first time that they had not turned to France for a suitable candidate. The marriage did indeed occur in 1225, and it made Frederick II the regent of the Kingdom of Jerusalem. He was the most powerful ruler of his time, Emperor of the Holy Roman Empire, King of Sicily and large parts of Italy. Frederick II was an extraordinary man: he spoke six languages fluently (including Arabic) and was interested in mathematics, Islam and philosophy. But he also had bad qualities: cruel, self centered, untrustworthy in friendship and unforgiving of his enemies. The Templars would soon discover this.

In 1215, at his coronation in Aachen, he had already taken the cross. He repeated this promise in 1220 shortly after the fall of Damietta and again in 1223. This happened in Italy in the presence of the Grand Masters of the military orders. The preachers journeyed afresh through Western Europe, but the leaders of the high nobility of England and France did not respond to this calling. Both countries were buckling with internal conflicts and therefore had no interest.

In 1227, Frederick departed, but he became ill: he sent an army in advance and he remained behind in Sicily. The Pope immediately banished him thereafter. Frederick II took no notice of this and in 1228 the monarch finally arrived in Acre. He was received with mixed feelings there. The German Emporor in the meantime, was known as a dictatorial ruler, whilst the leaders of the Holy Land had anarchistic tendencies. On top of this, the bishops, the Hospitallers and the Templars had just received a letter from the Pope: they were not allowed to have any contact with the excommunicated Emperor. This was also the case for the Teutonic Knights, but their Grand Master happened to be a good friend of the Emperor. For this reason, these knights were the only ones who supported the Emperor.

Frederick II demanded that the Templars handed over Château Pèlerin to him. He went there with an army, but the Order closed the gates. They were powerful enough to withstand the Emperor. Despite the fact that Frederick had comparatively few soldiers at his disposal, his Crusade delivered excellent results. The Emperor got along well with the Egyptian Sultan, with whom he had already negotiated since 1226. When these discussions began to proceed with difficulty, Frederick departed with his army, to demonstrate his weapons, along the coast.

The Templars and Hospitallers followed him first, a day later. They did after all answer to the Pope and he was still not pleased with the German Emperor. The monarch pressed both Orders to join his lines. The demonstration helped, because Jerusalem, Bethlehem and Nazareth were handed over to him without any resistance. The cities were in contact with the coast via corridors. A cease fire of ten years, five months and forty days was agreed, but Antioch and Tripoli fell outside of the treaty.

The possessions of the Templars (and the Hospitallers) were attacked by the Muslims with the permission of Frederick II. The castles concerned were Castel-Blanc and Tortosa in the county of Tripoli. It was forbidden for the Order to fortify their castles. Undoubtedly, Frederick II was angry with the lack of co-operation from these knights. The Templars had to overcome yet another disappointment.

The Temple platform in Jerusalem, their earlier domain, remained in the possession of the Muslims; although unarmed Christian pilgrims were permitted to visit this place. The Archbishop of Jerusalem, who still had his seat in Acre, was against the agreement. For him, the essence of a Crusade was the flowing of the blood of the heathens and not the closing of a deal that recognised the rights of the Muslims in the 'Christian' city of Jerusalem. The Order of the Temple agreed with him: after all, these hoodlums could not fight against the Muslims from out of the Kingdom of Jerusalem, for ten years.

The Western chronicler, Matthew Paris, reported that the Hospitallers and the Templars were out to murder the German Emperor. They tipped a Muslim leader about an ideal place for an ambush, but the Sultan warned Frederick. The discord between the Templars and Frederick II was an open secret. An Arabic chronicler (Sibt Ibn al-Jawzi) deems to have known that Frederick was afraid that the Templars threatened his life. Pope Gregory IX sent a letter to the Templars, the Hospitallers and the Sultan of Egypt at the beginning of 1229, with the request that the Emperor be taken prisoner and executed. At least that is what Bartholomew of Neocastro ascertains, who recorded the exact text of the letter in his chronicle *Historia Sicula*. It seems unthinkable that the Pope stated that he wanted Frederick murdered and that he would have put this in black and white.

Frederick was moreover, unaware of the heinous plans of the knight Orders. In letters to Henry III (1229) and Richard of Cornwall (1239), he describes the events in the Holy Land. In these letters he makes no reference to the military orders making an attempt on his life. Barber, who describes these incidents, suspected that the rumours about this fitted into the propaganda war, which coincided with the argument between the Pope and the knight Orders on one side, and Frederick II on the other.

Frederick crowned himself King of Jerusalem in the Holy Sepulchre and returned to Acre. There the archbishop, with the support of the Templars, was busy rounding up troops. The ecclesiastical leader wanted to deprive the Emperor of the rule over Jerusalem. Frederick immediately took measures and surrounded the possessions of the Templars in Acre. Together with the Pisans, the Emperor put his artillery into action.

There were few defenders, but the Templars had help from the Genoans and the local barons. Frederick had to stop his siege because of their superior number and fled to the Hospitallers. It did not advance all out, because Frederick was forced to quickly go to Sicily. A papal army under the leadership of John of Brienne, Frederick's predecessor as King of Jerusalem and son-in-law, was on the brink of capturing his possessions in South Italy. Thanks to this attack by John, a full out war between the Templars and the German Emperor was averted.

Frederick left a strong garrison behind in Acre and gave the Teutonic Knights large pieces of land in the surroundings of Acre; the latter in order to thwart the Templars. He left in a hurry to go to the area threatened by John and thereafter made peace with the Pope. He carried on his feud with the Hospitallers and the Templars in Sicily. He confiscated all the possessions of these military orders and took the leaders prisoner.

A letter from Pope Gregory IX from 1231, in which he ordered the Emperor to leave the Sicilian possessions of the Templars and the Hospitallers alone, had no effect. When Frederick was again ecclesiastically banished in 1239, the same Pope gave one of the reasons as being that Frederick had still not returned the possessions of the Orders. It was not until 1250, after the death of Frederick, that the Templars received all their possession in Sicily back.

The Sixth Crusade was the most exceptional one in history. Despite counteraction from the leaders of the Church and most of the other Franks, Frederick II succeeded in realising the objectives of the Church without bloodshed: the recapturing of Jerusalem.

The thirteen thirties

Frederick II assured continual unrest in the Holy Land. He appointed a representative (bailli, comparable with the English sheriff), who had a large army at his disposal, supposedly to defend Palestine. However, the bailli first tried to occupy Acre and when that did not work, he established himself in Tyre. It was in 1243 when the Franks succeeded in driving the imperial troops out of this city. The Westerners therefore remained mutually divided and the Templars fantically joined in.

The Pope wrote a letter to the Grand Master in 1231, in which he passed on a number of complaints from Frederick II. The Templars did not pay attention to the orders of the bailli and with their provocations, threatened the newly closed peace treaty with the Muslims.

Armand of Périgord (1232-1244)

On 28th January 1232 Peter of Montaigu died. He was succeeded by the Frenchman Armand of Périgord, the Master of Sicily. Just as is the case with other Grand Masters, his name appeared in the documents and chronicles in many variations: Peregort, Pierregort, Pierre Gort, Harmant of Guort, Pieregor, Pierefort and Peragors. Even though there are no indications, it is possible that his appointment was indirectly influenced by Frederick II. Perhaps the Order hoped that they could impress the Emperor by choosing an acquaintance of his. However, the policy of the new Grand Master was supported by the majority of the local barons and these were anti-Frederick.

A comparatively peaceful period began; the sultans of Damascus and Cairo remained enemies and paid more attention to each other than to the Christians. It was only in the Far East where two nomad tribes were causing agitation: the Mongolians and the Turks. The Mongolians began a march towards the West at the beginning of the thirteenth century under the leadership of Genghis Khan. At the peak of their power they controlled a huge empire: from Korea to Poland and from Tonkin to the Mediterranean Sea. The Khorezmian Turks were pushed to the West by the Mongolians, but would later assert themselves again in the Holy Land. In a letter from the Pope from 1231, it appears that the Christians, including the Grand Masters of the military orders, were fully aware of the danger from the East.

In the 1230's there were no alterations in the size of the territory of the Latin States. This era was characterised by repeated plundering trips back and forth. The Templars and the Hospitallers regularly worked together for this purpose.

Frederick II depicted on a manual, written by him, about falconers.

The Assassins (see Chapter IV), in 1231, were forced by the armies of the Templars and Hospitallers to continue to pay their yearly contributions to the Hospitallers. Both military orders closed an agreement in 1233 with regard to the harbour city of Gibelet (Jabala) and two years later they set aside their differences over the exploitation of the mills on the river to the South of Acre. In 1233 the Templars assisted the Hospitallers, who wanted to force the Sultan of Hamah to remit his yearly payment to the Hospitallers. The two military orders plundered the territory of the Sultan for eight whole days, until he was prepared to pay the 'protection money.'

In 1236 the Templars raided a group of shepherds, subjects from the city of Aleppo, and they captured a gigantic booty. The Muslims from Aleppo, supported by Damascus, were out for revenge and besieged the Templars castle of Baghras. Bohemond V, the Prince of Antioch, managed to buckle the stronghold and made peace with the Muslims. The Templars did not take any notice of this treaty and a year later re-conquered the castle of Darbsak, which was situated in the principality of Antioch. This had been in their possession from 1135 to 1188. The joy of this was short lived because Aleppo sent a large army after them. The Templars were warned, but they were convinced of their own capabilities. They were nevertheless totally defeated; at least a hundred Templars were killed. The Order of the Temple then closed a long duration peace treaty with the ruler of the Muslim city. The Pope agreed to this pact and paid a large portion of the ransom money for the imprisoned Templars.

In 1237 the Templars suffered another great defeat. A line of 120 Templars sought revenge on the plunderers in their territory between Château Pèlerin and Acre. Despite the warning from the Count of Jaffa, who knew that there were a lot of Muslims in the area, they went ahead with the conflict. Only nine members and the Grand Master survived the battle. The Templars remained an important power factor despite this fiasco; the overseas areas could always deliver new men every time.

In the period 1229-1241, approximately 70 percent of the area of Caesarea was occupied by the Church and the military orders. The Order of the Temple was the greatest landowner there and they possessed more than a quarter of this region.

In 1239 it was once again time for a new Crusade, because the treaty between Frederick and the Muslims was coming to end. The Pope sent messengers throughout England and France. Once again, the Kings were not interested. A large group of noblemen departed from out of France under the leadership of Theobald of Champagne, the King of Navarre. The Grand Master of the Templars described the situation on the eve of this pilgrimage as follows:

The Sultan of Egypt was a coward and had an argument with the Sultan of Hamah in the North of Syria. The ruler of the Kerak waged war on the Sultan of Damascus.

There was a meeting in Acre about the object of the attack and of course the Grand Masters of the military orders took part in this deliberation. There were, given the internal quarrels between the Muslims, many reasons for a diplomatic offensive, but the Crusaders had come to fight and had no intention of following the 'bad' example of Frederick II. Theobald ultimately decided to move towards Gaza, to fortify the Southern border and thereafter to conquer Damascus. On the way to Ascalon, Peter, Count of Bretagne and a Crusader, discovered that a convoy in the valley of the Jordan of Kerak was on its way to Damascus. He did not hesitate and went there to look for the succes. He returned with a huge booty and this made Henry, the Count of Bar, jealous. He thought that the Egyptian army near Gaza, consisted of only a thousand men and he wanted to show what he was worth. Henry had his information from a spy of the Templars. He wanted to slyly leave the army camp, but shortly before his leaving he was discovered. Henry had sworn an oath that he would obey Theobald, but Theobald had insufficient power to stop him. Despite warnings from the Franks, the Count of Bar left to go to the South. It turned into a disaster; the Egyptian army was much larger than expected and very few managed to return to the main body of the military force. The most important cause of this defeat was, according to a report of the conflict, the inexperience of the Crusaders. The Muslims gradually discovered how they could best fight the Franks. Newcomers from Europe did not have the foggiest idea about the Eastern circumstances and fighting methods and that cost many their lives.

Theobald wanted to pursue the Egyptians, but the Templars and the Hospitallers were able to convince him that this had no purpose. This advice would also have been given out of self importance: the colonists and the military orders would benefit more from the defending of their positions than with a risky attack on the Muslims. In the meantime, the Emir of Kerak had taken revenge for the action of Peter, Count of Bretagne. He attacked Jerusalem, destroyed the defence functions and then left to return to Kerak.

The raid on the convoy and the battle at Gaza were typical of the lack off leadership of the Franks in the Middle East. Only a mighty King was in a position to be able to keep the army on a tight rein. An additional complication also remained between the competence of the colonists and the Crusaders. They wanted to tell the home front of their great exploits and in the West, a diplomatic victory hardly gave anything to boast. Violence was still a characteristic of knightly behaviour. After the defeat at Gaza it was still decided to negotiate with the enemy. The delegation was under the leadership of the Templars. They concluded peace with the ruler of Damascus, Ismail. The result was advantageous; the Templars were given back the remains of the castle of Safad and the stronghold of Beaufort was once again in the hands of the colonists. This did not happen without problems. Ismail had to force the garrison to give Beaufort back to the Christians. The Franks, as compensation, had to restrain the ruler of Egypt.

Thanks to the efforts of the Bishop of Marseille, the Templars were able to rebuild their castle of Safad. He had to, according to a document from the middle of the thirteenth century, convince the sick Grand Master of the benefits of this. This history will be described in Chapter VII. The Templars now possessed five large castles (Safad, Château Pèlerin, Baghras, Chastel-Blanc and Tortosa) and a few dozen smaller ones. The maintenance and the manning of these must have cost them a fortune. The Hospitallers were sad to see the success of the Templars. Approximately ten years earlier they had, on account of the German Emperor, concluded a mass alliance with their rivals/colleagues. But this went too far for the Hospitallers. Therefore, they negotiated independently with the Sultan of Egypt and achieved just as much of an exceptional result. Ascalon and Galilee were again under the rule of the Franks and those Crusaders taken prisoner at the battle of Gaza were released. Theobald went, to the fury of the colonists, in agreement with this treaty, which led to a complex situation. Theobald became so unpopular with the local barons that after a pilgrimage to Jerusalem he returned to France at full speed.

A couple of weeks after his departure, Richard Plantagenet, the Count of Cornwall and the brother-in-law of Frederick II, arrived in Acre. He was extremely disgruntled with the dissension that he encountered. The Hospitallers and the Templars had nearly caused a civil war with their mutual arguments. The Templars were supported by nearly all the local barons and the Hospitallers wanted to join with the bailli of Frederick, who still occupied Tyre. The conflict between both of the largest military orders had everything to do with their different ideas about the policy of Frederick II. He was friendly with the Egyptian Sultan and the Templars consequently chose for Damascus. Richard, cousin of King Richard I, sorted everything out. He closed a new treaty with Damascus and Cairo and even managed to get extra pieces of land with this deal. Only the Templars were against the agreement with Egypt, but it was understandable that Richard did not listen to them. The colonists were after all, too weak and too divided to allow themselves to enter into a war with the Muslims.

The Holy Land was now nearly as large as it was in 1150, when it was at the peak of its power (see map on page 30/162). The Grand Master of the Order of the Temple described the results of the activities of Theobald and Richard as Gods' miracle. There could be no other explanation, because the Christians (colonists and newcomers) disagreed with each other on all fronts. For the rest, there were various assemblies constantly threatening each others lives. In this regard, the three military orders did not get left behind. The Hospitallers and the Templars were on the brink of war with each other and on top of this, the Hospitallers were of the opinion that the Teutonic Knights should become members of their Order. Finally, the Templars and the Teutonic Knights had problems with each other. The Templars drove the Germans out of Acre in 1241; they saw this Order as an extension of the German Emperor. In 1243, the Templars and the Teutonic Knights concluded peace again.

It was not only the military orders that made trouble; the representatives of Frederick II also ensured armed unrest. On top of this, the Italian city-states increasingly began to dispute each others commercial rights. Genoa was supported in this conflict by the Hospitallers, whilst the Templars and the Teutonic Knights were behind Venice. Pisa stayed neutral in this conflict. The anarchy would only increase during the thirteenth century.

According to the official list, in the period 1095-1291, there were eight Crusades, whereby the one of Theobald and Richard is not taken into account.

The pilgrimage of these leaders actually had a fantastic result. It would not stay that way for long, because after the departure of Richard Plantagenet, the ones remaining fell back into their old wicked ways.

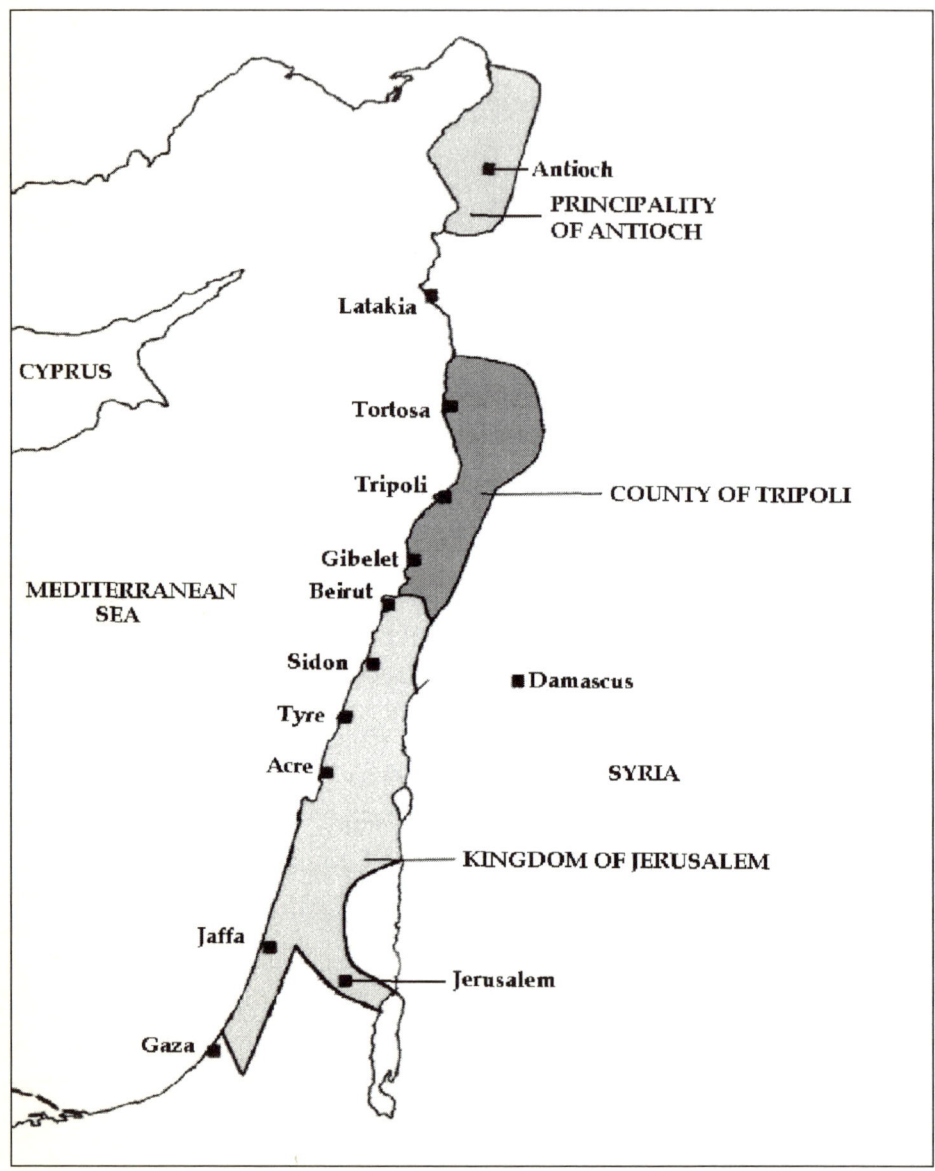

The Christian territories before the battle of La Forbie (1244).

VII. The construction of the castle of Safad

INTRODUCTION

Around 1166 the Templars acquired the castle of Safad, near to the lake of Tiberias. It was 850 metres above the level of the lake and Safad gave them the control over the westerly shore, the lake of Tiberias and the road from Damascus to Acre. With this, the Templars became an important power factor in the area of Galilee (see map on page 207). In 1189 Saladin captured the castle and it remained in the hands of the Muslims until 1240. Thanks to the Crusade of Theobald of Champagne in 1239, the Templars could again occupy the ruined castle.

The pamphlet, *De Constructione Castri Saphet*, describes the rebuilding of the castle of Safad by the Templars from 1240. The story centres on Benoît d'Alignan, Bishop of Marseille from 1229-1267. Benoît visited the Holy Land twice, in the periods of 1239-1242 and 1260-1262. It appears from the story that he took the initiative to rebuild the castle.

There are two copies of the pamphlet, one in Paris from the fourteenth century and an undated manuscript in Turin. Both belong to a collection of texts about the Crusades, including the *Histori Occidentalis* of James of Vitry. The pamphlet was written by an anonymous author between 1260 and 1266. It tells of the second visit of Benoît to Safad, but omits the conquering by the Muslims in 1266. The anonymous author may have written it to commemorate the work of the bishop. It seems more likely that it was a propaganda leaflet of the Templars, intended to raise money for the battle against the Muslims.

The religious impact of the story suggests that it could have been used for the sermons in the Western churches. The emphasis lies namely on the high construction costs of the castle and on the importance of Safad to the Christians. The last Chapter describes a number of well know Holy Places for Christians. In that regard, the document has similarities to *De Laude* by Bernard of Clairvaux.

Whatever the motivation of the author was, the pamphlet narrates one of the best accounts of the construction of a medieval castle. At the same time it gives a fine insight into the penmanship of that time: the writer continually refers to God and the Bible. It is clear that the author considers the Muslims to be non believers and enemies of Christianity. The original piece exists of long sentences and is therefore difficult to follow. For the sake of readability, the author has written the original piece in a somewhat reader friendly version, without ignoring the divine inspiration.

DE CONSTRUCTIONE CASTRI SAPHET

It is our firm and steadfast intention to be always zealous in those things that are to the honour of God. We will continually and mainly be faithful to those whom we see that glorify and spread the Faith and the Church. It is our intention to save souls and to promote the support of the Holy Land. It is for these reasons that we intend, accurately and principally, to establish the how, why and when of the construction of the castle of Safad.

Why, when and how the building of the castle of Safad was begun
A great Christian army arrived in the Holy Land [in 1239]; it wanted to help the Christians in the battle against the non believers. The participants were the King of Navarre and the Count of Champagne, the Duke of Burgundy, the Count of England, the Count of Nevers and Forez, the Count of Montfort, the Count of Bar, the Count of Macon and numerous other counts and barons. The army numbered more than fifteen hundred fully armed knights. In addition to these, there were those who were insufficiently armed and an almost uncountable number of crossbowmen and footmen that had travelled with them. They arrived in Jaffa and Ascalon and discussed their plans of attack the Muslims.

In the meantime some noblemen, who had faith in their own strength, left the army by night. They did that against the advice of the Templars, the Hospitallers and other ecclesiastical and secular leaders of the country. Because they did not give glory to God, to whom victory belongs, they were shamefully defeated. After all, they strived after their own honour. Many of them were taken prisoner or killed and the army was driven back to Jaffa in great confusion. There it was decided to rebuild the castle of Safad. The survivors wanted to lighten and ease the disaster and were of the opinion that they could do no better work in the entire country. In order for the Grand Master of the Templars to begin on the construction, they promised to give him a sum of seven thousand marks. The army would stay at Safad for two months so that the castle could be built more safely and easily.

But, when they returned to sandy Acre they forgot their promises. They did not set to work, nor did they begin to build. When an armistice was made with the Sultan of Damascus, the King and the great army returned to their country. The Bishop of Marseille, named Benoît went, with the permission of the Sultan, on a pilgrimage to the monastery of St. Mary of Saidnaya [30 km north of Damascus]. While he was waiting for some days in Damascus, as commanded by the Sultan, many people constantly asked him if Safad was to be rebuilt. When he wanted to know why they approached him so frequently, they answered that with the rebuilding of the Castle of Safad, the gates to Damascus would be closed.

Therefore, when the bishop returned from Damascus, he carefully observed the land surrounding Safad. He did not see any fortresses apart from Subeibe, which was occupied by the nephew of the Sultan. When he reached Safad, he saw a heap of stones but not any building. This, where there had once stood an impressive and famous castle. He was received with great happiness by brother Rainhardus of Caro, who was at that time the castellan there. But the Templars had nothing on which to lay their head, except for the garbelaris [cloaks of wool and linen]. These were carried by the servants during the day and at night used as bedding for their masters.

The bishop carefully inquired about the surroundings of the castle. He asked why the Muslims were so scared of Safad being rebuilt. He perceived that if the castle was rebuilt, the area could be defended and protected. It would serve as shield against the Muslims for the Christians as far as Acre. Safad would be a strong and tremendous base for attack and it offered the possibility to hold plundering raids in the land of the Muslims as far as Damascus. Due to the building of the castle, the Sultan would lose lots of money, estates and the services of the men to those who ruled the castle. The Sultan would also lose in his own land villages, agricultural products, pastures and other renders. The Muslims did not dare to farm the land out of fear of the castle. As a result of this, the land of the Sultan would become desert-like and worthless. In addition to this, the Sultan was obliged to incur great expenses. In order to defend Damascus and the surrounding area, he had to employ many soldiers. In short, he found from various sides that there was no stronghold in that area that was of detriment to the Muslims. The fortress would not only help the Christians, but help to spread Christianity at the same time.

When the bishop heard this and similar other opinions, he went to Acre and visited the Grand Master of the Templars. The Grand Master, Armand of Périgord [1232-1244], lay sick in bed and asked the bishop what he had seen and heard in Damascus. Benoît told him about what was important to him. Namely, how he had seen and heard that the Muslims were fearful and trembling. They wanted reassurance from him about the building of the castle of Safad. With that, he began to forcefully persuade the Grand Master to rebuild the castle of Safad. If they would expend all their strength on the castle, this could be built during the time of truce. But the Grand Master sighed: 'Lord Bishop, it is not easy to build Safad. Did not you yourself hear what the King of Navarre, the Duke of Burgundy and the counts and barons of the army promised? They would help with the building of the castle so that it could be built faster and safer. They would stay there for two months and give us seven thousand marks. In the end they did not pay a single penny for the building and you are saying that we should build the castle without the help of anyone?'

The bishop said, 'Grand Master, stay resting in your bed and give your good will and support to the brothers. I have faith in the Lord and say that you will do more from your bed than a whole army with a multitude of men and an abundance of their riches.' Since the bishop persisted, the great men who were there said, 'Lord Bishop, you have said what seems good to you and the Grand Master will take counsel and respond to you.' After the bishop had left the Grand Master, he called the senior members of the council together and told them what he had said to the Grand Master. The bishop convinced them and they answered that he should return the following day and place his proposal before the council.

How the bishop of Marseilles persuaded the Grand Master of the Templars and his council to build the castle of Safad

The following day the bishop came to the Grand Master and asked him to call his council together. He wanted to speak to them about something that he found important. When they were gathered, the bishop said the following to them: 'Lords, I understand that your Order was first begun by holy knights. They dedicated themselves totally to the protection of the Christians and the attacking of the Muslims. Since they did this with determination and faithfulness, the Lord has exalted you. Your Order is favoured by the Holy Chair and by kings and princes. Today your Order is greatly celebrated and renowned by God and humanity. It seems to me that you should now follow the example of these holy knights. When I was in Damascus, I understood from many people that there is nothing that the Muslims fear so much as the building of Safad. They said that with the building of the castle, the gates of Damascus would be closed. We have ourselves inspected the site and we have come to the following conclusion: there is no better place in this land to build a castle. Safad would protect Christianity like no other and at the same time combat the unfaithfulness of the Muslims. Therefore, I ask, advise and demand, as your faithful friend, that you rebuild the castle. I am mindful of the honour of God, the saving of souls and the promotion of your Order. You deserve, as faithful servants of God and devoted and strong knights, to look back at the example of your first holy knights. They founded your Order and you and yours should follow the example of your founders, and you must offer to make the same sacrifices. Safad will always remain a threat to the infidels and a defender of the faithful. I however, do not have enough money for you to do this work. But, if you will build it, I offer myself to make a pilgrimage to Safad. However, if you do not want to, I will preach to the pilgrims. I will go there with them and use the rubble for building. After all, there is a large pile of stones there and I will build a wall of dry stones. With this, the Christians will be protected against the attacks of the Muslims.'

When the Grand Master heard this, he laughingly replied: 'You are clearly determined what should be done!' and the bishop replied: 'May you and yours take good deliberation and may the Lord be with you.' And then he withdrew from their midst. The Lord however, directed their council and they unanimously decided that the castle should be rebuilt immediately. There was in fact a truce with the Sultan of Damascus and if that expired, the building could easily be delayed.

The joy at the building of the castle at Safad
When they had decided that Safad should be rebuilt, there was great joy in the house of the Templars, in the city of Acre and among the people of the Holy Land. Without delay, an impressive body of knights, sergeants, archers and other armed men were chosen. Pack animals to carry the weapons, provisions and other necessary materials were also made available. Granaries, cellars, treasuries and other offices were generously and happily opened. A great number of workmen and slaves with the necessary tools and materials were sent to Safad. The land rejoiced at their arrival and the true Christianity of the Holy Land was exalted.

The Bishop of Marseilles himself came with all the pilgrims he could bring. He pitched his tent on the site of the synagogue of the Jews and the mosque of the Muslims. With this, he made it clear that the castle of Safad would be rebuilt to weaken the faithlessness of the infidels and to strengthen and defend the faith of Our Lord Jesus Christ. When all the necessary preparations to begin with such glorious work were ready, Mass was celebrated. The bishop came and gave a short sermon to encourage the devotion of those present and begged for the mercy of the Holy Spirit. With a blessing and due solemnity, he laid the first stone in the honour of Our Lord and the exaltation of the Christian faith. On the stone he displayed a silver gilt jar full of money to support subsequent work. This was done in the year of Our Lord 1240, on the 11th of December.

How a well of fresh water was found within the castle of Safad
There was a lack of water near the site and this had to be brought from afar by pack animals, with a lot of trouble and at great expense. The bishop, therefore, sought for several days for small springs with which a cistern could be filled. An old Muslim said to the servant of the bishop: 'If your lord gives me a tunic, I will show him a spring of fresh water within the castle.' When he had promised him the tunic the old man indicated to the source, under the ruins of the towers and walls and many piles of stones. When they asked him for a clear sign, he said that they would find a sword and a helmet in the mouth of the well. And so it was. After this discovery, they worked more determinedly and energetically. Eventually they found an excellent stream of water and in great abundance for the whole castle. The bishop stayed in Safad until the building of the castle was firmly established and it could defend itself against the enemies of the faith.

When he returned home, he gave the castle to the Templars as if they were his favourite son. He also left all his tack, tents and furnishings behind. After he had given a blessing, he entrusted the control, the progress of the work and the workmen to Our Lord Jesus Christ. The building was, after all, begun to honour the Son of God and it was dedicated to his name.

The wonderful construction of the castle of Safad.
On October 4th 1260, the same bishop returned to the Holy Land for the second time, this time to support it against the Mongolians. When he visited Safad he discovered that, between one journey and the other, lots had happened. That was thanks to the grace and providence of God, and the energy and influence of the brothers of the Temple. The castle was diligently, miraculously and beautifully built; the exquisite and excellent construction seemed to have been made, not by the hands of men, but by the almighty God himself.

The following will make this fully understandable and somewhat clearer. The castle of Safad is situated almost half way between Acre and Damascus, in Upper Galilee. It is built on a spur of a mountain, completely surrounded by mountains and hills, sheer precipices, crags and rocks. It is inaccessible from most directions and impregnable because of the difficulties, hardship and narrowness of the roads. In the direction of Damascus it is boundaried by the river Jordan and the Lake of Genasereth [also known as the Sea of Galilee and the Sea of Tiberias]; they are like natural fortifications at a distance. There are however, both inner and outer walls, wonderful manmade fortifications and buildings to be admired.

It is not easy to convey in writing or speech how many fine buildings there are there; the beautiful and numerous defences and fortifications, surrounded by ditches. From the rocks the ditches measure seven cannas [a good fifteen metres, one canna is 2.2 metres long] in depth; the breadth of the ditch is six cannas. An inside wall: twenty cannas high and a canna and a half thick at the top!

As for the outer walls and trenches, the measurements are: ten cannas in height and a circumference of 375 cannas. There are many underground tunnels between the outer wall and the inner ditch with underground chambers round the whole castle. What casemates, called *fortie cooperte*, which are above the ditches and underneath the outer wall! The archers could defend the ditches and things near and far, with great precision. They are not able to be seen from the outside, therefore they are safe and no other protection is necessary. What towers and battlements; there are seven towers, each 22 cannas in height and ten cannas in breadth!

The walls of the towers are two cannas thick at the top. What a number of offices for all necessities! What a number, size and variety of construction of crossbows, arrows, machines and every sort of weapon! What effort and amount of expense in making them! What numbers of guards every day, what number of the garrison of armed men are needed to defend the castle and to withstand the enemy! How many workmen with different trades and what expense are made for them daily! Is it not suitable to pass such a famous, magnificent and necessary work in silence? They are done for the honour of God and the exaltation of the Christian name; also to destroy the infidels and build up the faithful. The castle of Safad is like a calling to the believers: it encourages the devotion and compassion of the faithful.

The massive daily expenses for guarding the castle of Safad
We will detail the expenses which the house of the Temple made for building.

Saint George slays the dragon, a metaphor for the conquering of the heathens

We do that for the honour of Our Lord Jesus Christ and to show the strength and the immense need of the holy knights of the Order of the Temple. We will kindle the devotion and the courage of the Christian faith towards the Order and the castle. We have asked for the amount of the expenses and carefully enquired of the senior men of the land and the senior leaders of the Templars. In the first two and a half years, the Templars spent on building the castle of Safad, in addition to the revenues and income of the castle itself, 1100 thousand bezants. The annual costs after this period were more or less forty thousand bezants. Every day provisions are given to at least seventeen hundred men; in time of war, that is 2200. There are fifty knights needed for the daily staffing of the castle, thirty sergeants and fifty Turcopoles with their horses and weapons. On top of this, there are three hundred crossbowmen present.

For the works and other offices, 820 men and finally there are also four hundred slaves for various duties. Every year there are more than twelve thousand mule-loads of barley and corn, apart from the other victuals. In addition the castle requires other necessities which are not easy to account for.

The excellence of the castle of Safad
We would like to demonstrate that the building of the castle was not useless, burdensome, dispensable and insufficient. Above all, it is a suitable habitat, because it has a temperate and healthy climate. The area is rich in gardens, vines, trees and grass; it is pleasant and friendly, rich and abundant in fertility and variety of fruit. Figs, pomegranates, almonds and olives grow and flourish there. God bless it with rain from the sky and richness from the soil and an abundance of corn, vines, oil, pulses, herbs and choice fruits. There is plenty of milk and honey and there are enough pastures to feed the animals. There are glades and enough trees and wood for the lime-kilns in which to cook the food. From out of springs and large cisterns there flows enough water for the animals to drink and to irrigate the plants. Not only outside the castle, but even inside there is fresh water a plenty. There are twelve water mills outside the castle and many more that are driven by animals or the wind. So as demanded, there are more than enough ovens. The castle also provides for all the requirements of the nobility; there are various ways to hunt. Many sorts of fish were available in large amounts, in the river Jordan, the Lake of Genasereth, the Sea of Galilee and the Great Sea. Other fish, fresh or salt water could be bought daily from other places.

Amongst the other excellent features which the castle of Safad has, it is notable that it can be defended by a few men. Many can be protected in the castle and it can only be besieged by a very large army. Such a great army would not have supplies for long. It would not be able to find food or water. The enemy could also not come too close to the castle at the same time. If they scattered over various places, they could not help each other.

The usefulness of the castle and the surrounding places which are attached to it

You can realise how useful and necessary the castle is to the whole Christian land and that it, above all, can bring destruction to the infidels. From experience, we know that before the building of Safad, Muslims, Bedouins, Khorezmians and Turks used to make raids to Acre and other lands of the Christians. By building the castle of Safad, a bulwark and obstacle was placed. They did not dare to go from the river Jordan to Acre, except in great numbers. Now the loaded pack animals and carts could safely use the roads between Acre and Safad. Agricultural lands could be worked freely. On the other hand, the land between the Jordan and Damascus remained uncultivated; it resembles a desert. This was out of the fear of the castle of Safad, because raids and depredations could be carried out as far as Damascus. The Templars won many miraculous victories against the enemies of the Faith. These are not so easy to recount, because a thick book could be written about them.

However, it should not be forgotten that below the castle of Safad, in the direction of Acre, there is a town or large village where a market is held. It has numerous inhabitants and can be protected and defended from the castle. Above all, the castle of Safad has more than 260 casals in its district. In these casals, which are called *ville* in French, there are more than ten thousand men with bows and arrows. In addition, there are many others from whom it is possible to collect large sums of money. That money can be divided between the castle of Safad, other Orders, barons and knights to whom the casals belong. Before the building of Safad, nothing could be collected from these men, nor would it be collected today if the castle had not been built. Everything before this time would have been subject to the Sultan and the other Muslims.

When considering its usefulness, the most important thing of all should not be omitted. It is now possible to preach the faith of Our Lord Jesus Christ freely and make an end to the blasphemies of Mohammed. In our sermons we can now publicly destroy and disprove the Islamic doctrine, something that could not be done before the building of Safad. The Muslims no longer presume, as they did before, to proclaim the blasphemies of Mohammed against the faith of Our Lord Jesus Christ. Famous places in the district of Safad can now be visited. Places such as: the well of Joseph, where he was sold by his brothers; the city of Capernaum (in the area of Zebulon and Naphiti), where Our Lord Jesus Christ lived and began his preaching and performed his many miracles. Capernaum, where Peter paid the tribute of a stater found in the mouth of a fish, for himself and the Lord Jesus Christ.

Capernaum is also where Matthew sat at the toll house when he was taken to become an apostle. Likewise nearby, on a mountain towards Tiberias, is the place where Our Lord fed five thousand men. He did that with five loaves of bread and twelve fish. The apostles gathered the twelve baskets with the pieces left over afterwards.

Nearby is the place where Jesus showed himself to his disciples and ate with them. This can be read in the Gospel, which is read on the fourth Sunday after Easter. It is the place that is commonly known as the Table of the Lord; there is now a church and a solemn pilgrimage. Also nearby, by the Sea of Tiberias, is the village called Bethsaida, where Peter and Andrew, Philip and James the Less were born and where Christ chose Peter and Andrew and the two sons of Zebedee to be Apostles. Again near there, by the Sea of Tiberias towards the city of the same name, is the place called Magdalon, where it is said Mary Magdalene was born. Places even more holy are in the same area: such as Nazareth, Mount Tabor, Cana of Galilee and many others. These can be visited freely and in safety because of the castle of Safad being built.

Because of this, it can be seen how much harm was caused to the infidel Muslims and how they are humiliated. With the building and the existence of the castle of Safad, Christianity grew and expanded. All this was done to confound, to weaken and to hold back the infidels, but also to expand, multiply and to comfort the faithful; to honour Our Lord Jesus Christ and the exaltation of the church of the Lord God. Amen.

Finally

The Muslims were just as aware of the importance of the castle of Safad; the Egyptian chronicler Ibn-al-Furat named it 'an obstruction in the throat of Syria and a blockade in the chest of Islam.' There was a seed of truth in that, but it was somewhat exaggerated. A border castle can never withstand a great enemy army. According to Ibn-al-Furat, thousands of Muslim slaves worked on the building of the castle. When they saw that there were less than two hundred Christians present, they plotted a rebellion. The Sultan of Damascus, Ismail, found out about this and drew the Templars' attention to it. They had carried out the negotiations with Damascus on behalf of the Franks shortly before this. Undoubtedly, the Sultan stood in good stead with the Templars, even more so since they had opened a bank in Damascus. Ismail had at that moment, because of the conflict in Egypt, great importance in the maintaining of peace with the Christians. After the warning from their friend, the Templars killed all slaves.

The anonymous writer claims that the Templars had taken many miraculous victories from the Muslims. That is a poetic exaggeration, because in the period of 1240 to 1266, the Christians suffered one defeat after another. They could only keep going because of the passive behaviour of the Muslims. In 1261 this came to an end, when Sultan Baybars became the undisputed leader of the Muslims.

In 1266, Baybars, an Egyptian Sultan, tried to conquer the castle on a number of occasions. It finally fell later in the same year because of betrayal. The castle was used thereafter as a local governing centre, until an earthquake levelled it to the ground in 1837. In a later chapter we will come back to this.

VIII. The period of 1244-1291. The last convulsions

The defeat at La Forbie

In 1241, Robert Plantagenet left the Holy Land and directly thereafter the internal conflicts began again. The Templars no longer wished to recognise the treaty with Egypt and in 1242 plundered Hebron. The Emir of Kerak therefore closed the road to Jerusalem and the pilgrims and merchants were obligated to pay toll. Six months later the Templars attacked Nablus (in the Bible called Sichem) and destroyed it. On this occasion they murdered many of the residents there, including a large number of Christian natives. The report of this victory was spread far and wide in Europe by the Templars. A fresco in the Bevignate church in Perugia, Italy, still recollects this heroic behaviour.

In the meantime, the relationship between the Templars and the Teutonic Knights had improved greatly. Together they had helped with the fortification of the city of Jaffa. The Grand Master of the Teutonic Knights resigned his position in 1244, due to financial maladministration, and he and a number of his fellow members wanted to join the Templars. Even though the Pope had given permission for this, the Order of the Temple refused to take on the Germans as members. Evidently they feared a new conflict with the Teutonic Knights, with whom they had just closed a treaty.

In Acre the quarrels between the Hospitallers and the Templars continued. Not one single leader could restrain the powerful military orders. The representative of the German Emperor Frederick II, the bailli, was still occupying Tyre and he thought that he could profit from this unrest and plotted a conspiracy. The bailli wanted to conquer Acre together with the Hospitallers, but that failed. The local barons then left for Tyre where they succeeded in driving the Germans and the Hospitallers out of the city. This defeat of the Hospitallers inspired the Templars to negotiate with the Sultan of Damascus. This led to the Templars once again being Lord and Master of the Temple platform in 1243.

Grand Master Armand of Périgord, wrote to the Master of England at the end of 1243 about this fine success and let it be known that the Order was busy fortifying Jerusalem.

Immediately after this, war broke out between Damascus and Egypt. The Order of the Temple convinced the other Christian leaders to take the side of Damascus. The Franks would receive a part of Egypt if they, together with their allies, defeated the Egyptians. Even though the Hospitallers did not approve of this, they were still solidary and they made their army available. It would have been better if the Franks had not concerned themselves with the dissension amongst the Muslims, but the Templars were on the whole not diplomats, but primarily hooligans and the knights of the Kingdom could not be inactive. Cairo sought support from the earlier mentioned Khorezmian Turks, who moved towards Jerusalem in the summer of 1244. Because Jerusalem could no longer be defended against a Muslim attack since the battle of Hattin, all warlike men had gone to Acre. The Franks presumed that if they had defeated the Egyptians, the city could be easily reconquered. Nevertheless, in 1244 Jerusalem was definitely lost for the Christians.

In the meantime a large army gathered at Acre, including 345 Templars, under the leadership of their Grand Master, Armand of Périgord. The Christian army consisted of approximately two thousand knights and ten thousand infantrymen. The leaders of Damascus and Kerak were also present with their warriors. Together they set off to Gaza and a war deliberation was held in the area of La Forbie. The ruler of Damascus was an advocate of waiting, but they still decided to attack the Egyptian army. It was a huge defeat, comparable to the one at Hattin in 1187. Reputedly, 312 Templars fell in action; only 33 Templars managed to escape to Ascalon, which was now controlled by the Hospitallers. The Marshal died, and the Grand Master, at least according to most sources, also perished.

All the results of diplomacy from the previous years were annulled in one go. Only the coastal cities and the large castles inland could still be defended. It could have been a great deal worse but the Muslims, different than during the time of Saladin, were divided. For that reason they could not advance towards the Christian possessions. At the end of 1244 it would have been an easy task for the Muslims to drive the Franks out of the Middle East. The battle at La Forbie took place in October 1244 and it would not be until the following year that new reinforcements could again arrive. Therefore, for half a year there were very few Christian soldiers available. In a letter to his brother-in-law, Richard Plantagenet, Frederick II left no doubts existing as to who he held responsible for

THE PERIOD OF 1244-1291. THE LAST CONVULSIONS

the fiasco. The Order of the Temple had turned the Franks against the Sultan of Egypt, with whom Frederick was on good terms. They had received the rulers of Damascus and Kerak in their houses and entertained them in a lavish way. The Order of the Temple had indeed backed the wrong horse. Matthew Paris was the only historian who alleged that the Grand Master of the Templars was taken prisoner at La Forbie. He wrote that the Templars wanted to buy their Grand Master free in 1246, but that the Sultan of Egypt had refused. If this is true, the Grand Master died whilst incarcerated and the election for a new leader only took place after 1246.

Richard of Bures (1244-1247)

According to the historian Bulst-Thiele (1974), after the battle at La Forbie, the Order chose Richard of Bures as the successor to Armand of Périgord. Richard signed a treaty between the Hospitallers and the Prince of Antioch, as castellan of Chastel-Blanc, in 1241. There is nothing further known about him. Richard does not appear in the list of the 22 Grand Masters which was composed by Barber. Because the titles of the higher functionaries were not always simple, the number of leaders of the Order is a debatable question. People of the seventeenth century reckon that the Templars had nearly forty Grand Masters. Most historians conclude that in fact there were 22 in total.

William of Sonnac (1247-1250)

William of Sonnac was elected the new Grand Master in about 1247. He probably came from the region of the French Saunhac-Belcastel. In 1224 he was the Commander of a monastery at Poitiers and fulfilled the function of Master of the province of Aquitaine from 1236 to 1246. Even Matthew Paris, who wrote critically about the Order, was satisfied with this choice. He called William intelligent, prudent and an experienced knight. William had met King Louis IX on a number of occasions and directly after his electing he journeyed to the Holy Land.

THE SEVENTH CRUSADE (1248-1254)

Once again, help came from Western Europe and this time it was from a King, Louis IX. He was the most important monarch of his time: powerful, rich and popular amongst the Christians. On this occasion the omens were extremely favourable: one leader, nearly all fellow countrymen and an outstanding organisation. There were special disciplinary rules established. So a knight, who was caught in an improper situation, was given the following options: either abandon his horse and weapons and leave the camp dishonourably, or be led around the camp in his vest by a cord around his neck. The prostitute, with whom he was caught, held the rope.

Luckily for Louis, the Muslims were still arguing about the inheritance of Saladin. In the East the Mongolians stood before the gateways of Baghdad and that also prevented a united collaboration between the Islamic states. All of this was of no benefit.

On his sick bed in 1244, Louis promised that if God should make him better, he would take up the cross. It could be that the defeat of the Franks at La Forbie had given him an extra stimulus. Louis stayed in the Middle East for about six years. He was loved in France so much that he could easily allow himself this long absence. In 1248 the King sailed to Cyprus with his army, where he was waylaid by the troops of the colonists and the military orders. The Grand Master of the Templars was also there and directly after his arrival he informed Louis of the treaty that he had made with Damascus. The French King, who was knowledgeable about the conflicts between the Christians, hauled the Grand Master over the coals. William of Sonnac had to revoke the treaty. Louis contacted the Mongolian leaders, because he knew that they had sympathy for the Christian faith. Louis thought that they should convert to Christianity and the Mongolian chief wanted the French King to be his vassal. The negotiations lasted until 1253, but without results.

In the spring of 1249 Louis sailed to Damietta, which surrendered without any problems. The Crusaders stayed there for nearly six months, waiting for extra reinforcements from France. It became a considerable army of approximately twenty thousand men. In the meantime, Louis and his advisors deliberated over the possible strategies: conquering Alexandria, the other important harbour city of Egypt or take Cairo. In the first case, the King could swap both cities for large parts of the Holy Land. Conquering Cairo could shatter the power of Egypt and provide a base of operation for an attack on the North.

The Egyptians greatly feared the Christian army. The Sultan of Cairo proposed, just as his father had done thirty years earlier, to swap Damietta for Jerusalem. The French King refused to enter into this: he did not wish to negotiate with a pagan. Louis decided to go to the South and suffered a great defeat near Mansurah (about sixty kilometres South of Damietta). A part of his army was under the leadership of his brother and, along with the English

THE PERIOD OF 1244-1291. THE LAST CONVULSIONS

Saint Louis lands on the coast by Damietta.

contingent, accounted for an important part of the knights of the Templars. They defeated an Egyptian army and stormed into Mansurah. The Templars refused to attack the city at first: it was against the order of the King and the cavalry was unusable in the narrow streets of the city. Out of fear of being made to look like cowards, the Templars ended up going with them. They were right and the army was butchered. The brother of the King, a large number of knights and 285 Templars lost their lives, only five Templars managed to escape.

Louis realised that there was nothing else to do other than return to Damietta, but just as during the Fifth Crusade, that was easier said than done. The remainder of the Christian army was surrounded and had to surrender. Only fourteen members of the military orders survived the conflict, including three Templars. Grand Master William of Sonnac fell in battle on the 11th February 1250. A couple of months later it was agreed that Damietta should be evacuated and that Louis had to pay eight hundred thousand bezants as ransom money. Half of this, a little less than the yearly income of the King, had to be paid in advance. It was a large amount, but Louis could easily afford it. Part of the ransom he borrowed from the Templars, but this did not occur without problems. The Templars had a fortune stashed in one of their ships, loaned from the pilgrims. They would only offer the money from this deposit if they were threatened with brute force. It happened in this manner, so the Order could maintain its trustworthiness as bankers. John of Joinville described the facts of the matter as follows:

> *I told the king it would be a good thing if he sent for the Commander and the Marshal of the Temple – the Master being dead – and asked them to lend him the thirty thousand livres still needed to obtain his brother's release. So the king sent to fetch the Templars, and instructed me to tell him them what he wanted. After I had spoken to them brother Étienne d'Otricourt, the Commander of the Temple, gave me their reply. "My lord of Joinville," he said, "this advice you have given the king is neither good nor reasonable. For you know that all money placed on our charge is left with us on condition of our swearing never to hand it over except to those who entrusted it to us." On this many hard and insulting words passed between us.*
> *While we were thus disputing brother Reginald of Vichiers, who was Marshal of the Temple, intervened to say: "Your Majesty, let us call a halt to this quarrel between the Commander and my lord of Joinville. For indeed, as our Commander says, we could not advance any of this money without breaking*

our oath. But as to what your seneschal advises, namely to take the money if we will not lend it, I find nothing surprising in such a suggestion and you must do as you think best. Anyhow, if you take what is ours here in Egypt, we have so much of what is yours in Acre that you can easily give us adequate compensation.

Reginald of Vichiers (1250-1256)

Louis left to go to Acre in May 1250 and remained in the Holy Land for four years. He lodged in a house of the Templars. Reginald of Vichiers, originally from Champagne, was chosen to be Grand Master of the Templars in the same month. We know from the chronicler Joinville that this happened with the support of the French King. Reginald, Master of France between 1241 and 1248, was well known to the King. He had negotiated with Marseilles over the passage of the Crusaders on behalf of Louis. Reginald knew the Middle East, because he was the Commander of Acre in 1240. The Order promoted him to Marshal on Cyprus in 1249. He was taken prisoner at the same time as Louis IX and lodged in the same residence. The previously quoted John of Joinville wrote that he was deeply impressed by his courteous manner towards him.

Louis had only a small army at his disposal which, in spite of this, formed a threat to the Muslims. Damascus and Egypt continued with their civil war and the balance could be tipped with the friendship of the Franks, so both Sultans sought contact with Louis. Damascus offered them Jerusalem and the Egyptians promised to release the imprisoned Christians and a gift of half of the ransom money.

Reginald of Vichiers carried on with the independent strategy of his predecessor. In 1252 he sent his Marshal, Hugh of Jouy, to Damascus, where he entered into an advantageous treaty for the Templars. Hugh, together with a representative of the Sultan, returned to Acre, because the treaty needed royal approval. Louis reacted furiously; the obstinate Order frustrated his negotiations with the Muslims. All Templars, including the Grand Master, had to walk barefoot through the camp in view of the entire army. The Grand Master was ordered to explain to the representative of the Sultan that the treaty would not take place. Subsequently all knights had to kneel before the King and they had to formally hand over all possessions to the King. The Marshal was banished from the Middle East on the order of Louis and he left to go to Spain. There, Hugh made it to the Master of the province of Aragon. The Templars would have felt terribly humiliated.

This event did not disturb the relationship between the Grand Master and

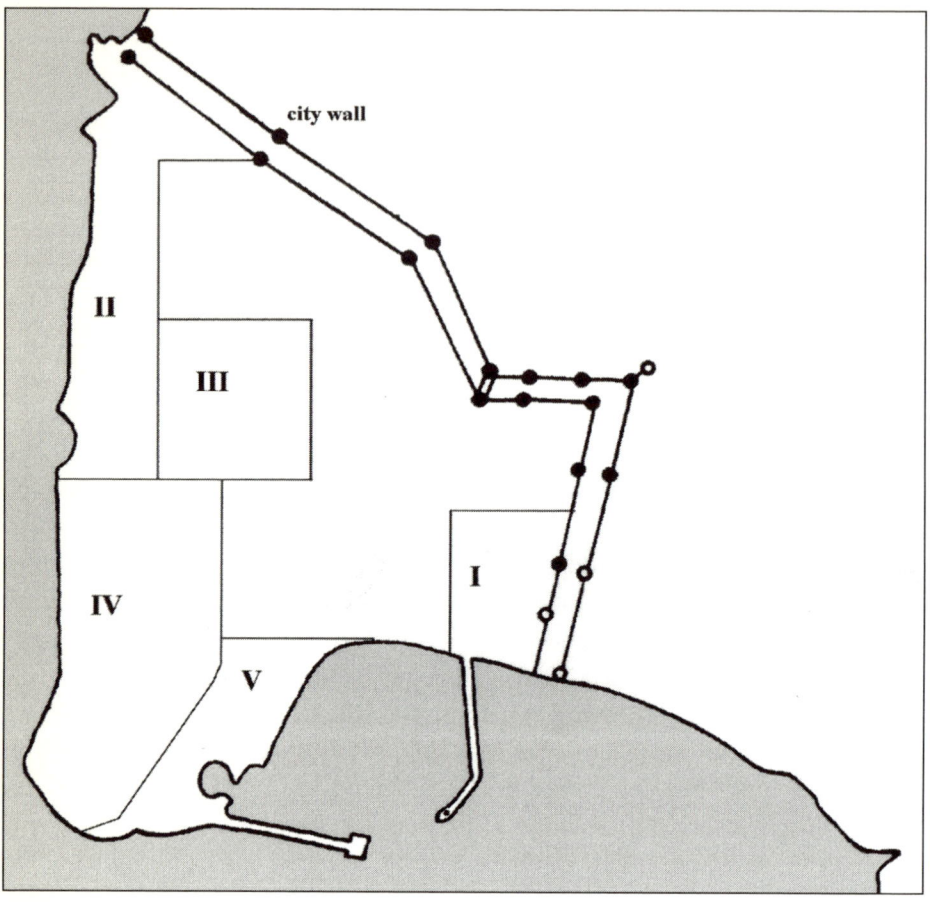

Quarter I = Venice
II = Hospitallers
III = Genua
IV = Templars
V = Pisa

the French King in the least. Shortly thereafter the son of the King was born in the Templars castle of Château Pèlerin and Reginald became his godfather. Due to their interest in Trans-Jordania, the Templars were in favour of a treaty with Damascus, but Louis chose for Egypt. The remainder of the ransom, four hundred thousand bezants, was given to him and many Christians were released. Louis hoped to profit even more from the disagreements between the Muslim rulers, but they made peace in 1252. In the meantime, thanks to the effort of the French King, the coastal cities of Acre, Caesarea, Haifa, Jaffa and Sidon were strengthened. In April 1254 Louis IX returned to France by sea; the captain of the ship was a Templar.

Louis was regarded as a God fearing man, but despite this he never managed to occupy Jerusalem. Their was a growing body of public opinion in Europe, which doubted Gods' will for the conquering of Jerusalem, increased due to the failures of Louis.

Thomas Bérard (1256-1273)

Reginald was Grand Master for six years; he died in action during a battle South of Jaffa in 1256. We know very little of the background of his successor, Thomas Bérard, the nineteenth Grand Master. He originated from either Italy, or England. Immediately after his appointment, a trade war broke out in Acre between Venice and Genoa. Complete districts of Acre were destroyed: a chronicler sighed that it looked like the city had been devastated by a Muslim army. The Hospitallers chose the side of Genoa and the Templars and the Teutonic Knights supported Venice. It was characteristic of the complex situation and the anarchy of the thirteenth century in the Holy Land. The Orders could have chosen for a combined intermediary role, but they all wanted to profit from the conflict between the Italians. They behaved themselves moreover as passive and limited themselves to lending a helping hand to their Italian allies.

The war lasted for five years and only because of the threat of the Mongolians prevented the Muslims from profiting from this conflict. In 1258 the three leaders of the Orders made a treaty, in which they promised to maintain peace in the areas of Jerusalem, Cyprus, Antioch and Tripoli. The secular and ecclesiastical leaders in the Holy Land also signed this pact. The leaders of the three Orders had to support each other in recurrent situations. The costs incurred would have been reimbursed by the Order, to those who gave help. East Europe was considered to be the exclusive hunting grounds of the Teutonic Knights. The Hospitallers promised to stop with their attempts to incorporate the Teutonic Knights. It was in 1275 when the Pope first gave his blessing to the triple party agreement. In 1261, thanks to the continual intervention of the Pope, Pisa, Venice and Genoa finally signed a treaty. The Christians felt threatened by the Mongolians, who were on the brink of invading North Syria. Thomas Bérard wrote a letter to the provincial Master, in which he described the misery. There were only three castles in the Kingdom of Jerusalem which were able to withstand a Mongolian attack, including two of the Order of the Temple. He was probably referring to Safad, Château Pèlerin and Montfort of the Teutonic Knights. The three Orders sent representatives to Spain (Templars), France (Hospitallers) and Germany (Teutonic Knights). They desperately needed money in order to organise their defences.

In 1260, the Egyptian Sultan Baybars defeated the Mongolians and a year later the Franks tried to take advantage of the occurred confusion. A large army of five thousand men plundered the area of the Sea of Galilee. The Templars from the garrisons of Acre, Safad, Château Pèlerin and Beaufort also took part. Most of them did not survive the raid and the later Grand Masters, William of Beaujeu and Theobald Gaudin, were taken prisoner; they were released for a large ransom. The Marshal of the Templars, Stephen of Sissey, was the only high official to escape. The Grand Master held the Marshal responsible for the defeat, stripped him of his robe and sent him to the Pope for condemnation. Although Stephen protested against this, Urban IV and his successor Clement IV wanted to make use of their rights. Clement IV forgave Stephen for his sins in 1265 and the Order readmitted him as a member. A few years later Stephen of Sissey was appointed Master of South Italy.

In 1263 Baybars offered a truce and a general exchange of prisoners, and again the Hospitallers and the Templars behaved arrogantly. The Orders did not agree, because they could not do without their Muslim slaves; there were too many skilled workers amongst them. Baybars, in the meanwhile leader of Damascus and Cairo, therefore carried on with the conflict and proved to be a worthy successor to Saladin. One castle after another fell into his hands between 1265 and 1271 and Baybars could attack these fortifications undisturbed. There were so few Christian knights available that the Franks were not capable of mustering together a relief army. The colonists were already happy with the fact that they could suitably staff the castles. Baybars did not succeed in conquering Château Pèlerin, but that did not discourage him. He had enough soldiers and the technical ability, of no other, to conquer most of the other castles.

In 1266 the Templars' castle of Safad fell because of the betrayal of a Syrian member of the Order of the Temple. Baybars tried to destroy the castle on the 7th, 13th and 19th of July, but he failed. He subsequently promised the native defenders complete amnesty and the Templars could not prevent them from leaving the castle. The Templars sent their member, Sergeant Leon, to Baybars to negotiate a safe withdrawal. He returned with the message from Baybars that the garrison could go to Acre if they surrendered. When the Templars opened the gates, they were all slaughtered. Baybars was of the same opinion as Saladin when it came to the Templars and had no mercy for them. Leon, a Syrian, returned to the Muslim faith after his betrayal. Two years later the Templars also lost Beaufort; Baybars used 26 ballistic weapons and that was far too many.

Just as at the end of the twelfth century, the Franks did not possess much more now than a few coastal cities. Antioch fell in 1268 and at the same time that meant the end of the presence of the Templars in the North. They left their castles in this area without a fuss. The population of Antioch was treated barbarically by the Muslims and even the Arabian chroniclers reacted with shock. In 1270 Baybars stood before the walls of the castle of Castel-Blanc, and after a fanatical resistance, the Templars were allowed to leave unarmed. This time Baybars kept to his word.

THE EIGHTH CRUSADE (1270)

Louis remained involved in the Holy Land from France and he sent large sums of money there. In 1266 he decided to once again undertake a Crusade and this time he wanted to go to Tunisia. It is unclear as to why he chose for this Muslim state; he probably wanted to use this as a base of operation for a journey to Egypt. It could be that his brother Charles of Anjou convinced him of this risky action. Charles had in the meantime become the King of Sicily and still had a bone to pick with the leaders of Tunis. No armies from the Holy Land took part. Historians guess the total number of soldiers was ten thousand. The Eighth Crusade ended as soon as it had begun and became a total disaster. Louis died immediately after landing, a couple of hours before the arrival of his brother Charles of Anjou. His death was mourned by many; Louis was declared a Saint in 1297.

Charles made a trade agreement with the Sultan of Tunisia and left again to go to Sicily. The Crown Prince of England, Edward, arrived when the treaty was signed. He discovered, to his rage, that he could not fight. He sailed with an army of about a thousand men to the Holy Land, but not much more than a cease fire with Baybars was reached. Baybars wanted to concentrate on the Mongolians amassed in the North and he was afraid that a total defeat of the Franks would cause yet another Crusade. He especially feared Charles of Anjou; wrongfully so, because the King of Sicily intended to conquer Constantinople. For the Muslims this break, above all, meant that they would fully profit from the trading activities of the Christian harbour cities.

William of Beaujeu (1273-1291)

On the 25th March 1273 Thomas Bérard died and he was succeeded by the 40 year old William of Beaujeu, Master of Sicily and South Italy. He was a participant in the Seventh Crusade and became a member of the Order in 1253. William was family of the French monarchy and that benefited the Order. Charles of Anjou was very interested in the countries surrounding the Mediterranean Sea. At the height of his power he was King of Sicily, South Italy and Albania; his cousin was King of France and his son-in-law King of Hungary. Even though William was related to the monarchy, he did not quickly make a career in the Order. In 1268 William was castellan of Beaufort, in 1271 Commander of Tripoli and next Master of South Italy.

Two years after his appointing to the highest function, William left to go to the Middle East. At the request of the Pope, he first of all visited the courts of France, England, Flanders and Aragon in order to call for a new Crusade. In 1274, William was also present at the Council of Lyon. He sat next to the Pope and was one of the most prominent participants there. The Order of the Temple had easy access to the highest secular and ecclesiastical circles. The council spoke about a new Crusade, but the spirit of this phenomenon had disappeared long ago. Later councils also had the reconquering of Jerusalem on the agenda, but this only was strong within the clergy. The Kings, noblemen and the common people had seen too many failures and did not have faith in it any more. At the Council of Lyon a discussion was held about a fusing of the military orders for the first time. The Spanish Kings moved against this, because they were afraid of losing the influence over their own Orders. In addition, they feared that only one strong military order would arise.

In September 1275 William landed in Acre, laden with many gifts from the sovereigns whom he had visited. Charles of Anjou bought the Kingdom of Jerusalem in 1277 and his representative moved into the house of the Temple in Acre. This laid the golden egg for the Order; because the Templars received money and provisions from Charles of Anjou. The internal wrangles between the Christian leaders continued. The King of Cyprus (a descendant of the Western knight Guy of Lusignan) did not approve of the kingship of Charles and twice tried to conquer Acre. The Templars played a significant role in the failure of this endeavour. The ruler of Cyprus therefore dismantled a Templars castle on his island and confiscated two Templar houses. The Order then brought in the Pope to get these possessions back, but this eventually occurred after the death of the monarch in 1284.

Between 1277 and 1282, the Templars and the Prince of Tripoli opposed each other, on land and at sea. It was an argument between the bishops of Tripoli and Tortosa which had got out of hand, characteristic of the reciprocal behaviour of the Christians. The Order of the Temple chose to side with the Roman Catholic Bishop of Tripoli, who had problems with the fact that the Greek Orthodox Bishop of Tortosa might gain the power over Tripoli. It cost dozens of Templars their lives. Internal conflicts remained in the forefront. In 1287, for example, Pisa and Genoa fought a battle at sea off the coast of Acre. Subsequently, the ships from Genoa blocked the whole coast and were only prepared to move the blockade after the intervention of the Grand Masters of the Templars and the Hospitallers.

After the pilgrimage of the Crown Prince Edward, in 1271, the Franks had very little trouble from the Muslims. In 1281 and 1283 there were new truces between Acre and the Egyptian Sultan, Kalavun. The treaty should be valid for ten years, ten months, ten days and ten hours. With the death of Charles of Anjou in 1285, all the potential threats disappeared and Kalavun decided to finish the work of Baybars. The places that were not named in the treaty with Acre were successfully conquered. In the meantime, between 1285 and 1289, there were various Mongolian delegations visiting Europe. They were received by the Pope, the English and the French Kings. The Mongolians suggested that they could fight the Muslims collectively. They made concrete proposals for a simultaneous attack, but they did not get much more than friendly declarations of sympathy.

In February 1289 Kalavun wanted to move on to Tripoli. William of Beaujeu knew al-Fakhri, an emir in the Egyptian army, who sold the plans of Kalavun to William. He immediately warned Tripoli, but no-one believed him. The war between the Templars and Tripoli was then over, but the inhabitants of Tripoli did not trust the Grand Master. William sent a regiment of Templars, under the leadership of the Marshal of the Order, to help, but to no avail. A couple of months later, Tripoli and the surrounding area fell into the hands of the Muslims. The male population was murdered, the women and children were traded at the slave market and the city was demolished. The brothers of the Templars' house in Tripoli all perished.

Tripoli had been in Christian hands for almost two hundred years. The fall of this city led to unrest in Western Europe, but the most important Kings were busy with their own concerns. Shortly after the fall of Tripoli, Kalavun and Acre again signed a treaty for ten years, ten months and ten days, so ten hours shorter that the previous one. Acre was still an important transit harbour for the Muslims. They also appreciated the banking activities of the Templars. As long as the city behaved appropriately, it could stay in the hands of the Christians with the permission of Kalavun.

Despite the hopeless situation of the Christians, money, goods and personnel carried on coming to Acre. The summer of 1290 saw a boom in the trade in Acre, whereby many Islamic merchants were in the city. In August 1290 twenty ships arrived in Acre, laden with soldiers from North Italy. They were adventurers out for spoils; to their grave disappointment they could not fight because of the cease fire. Out of boredom and irritation, the Italians caused a riot in Acre, in which many Muslims were killed. Kalavun had had enough and he demanded compensation. William of Beaujeu suggested to let all the imprisoned Muslims go and to hand over the instigators of the rebellion to Kalavun. It did not matter to him if the Italians were sentenced to death by a Christian or Islamic court. Again the leaders of Acre did not listen to him and the Franks told the Sultan that they were newcomers and did not understand the law.

Kalavun immediately began with preparations for a large attack on Acre. William was informed about this by his spy, al-Fakhri, but the leaders of Acre did not take William seriously. The discord between the Christians had become too large for this. William of Beaujeu sent a diplomatic mission to Cairo on his own initiative. Kalavun was prepared to spare the city if every inhabitant would pay him a Venetian penny. When William brought this proposal to the attention of the city leaders, he was greeted with howls of derision. The rulers made him out to be a traitor and William could barely save his skin. Kalavun died in November 1290, but his son immediately carried on with the work of his father. A new Christian diplomatic mission, including a number of Templars, was immediately taken prisoner and executed.

In 1291, the Muslims stood before the gates of Acre. According to some Arabian documents, the army consisted of sixty thousands cavalrymen and a hundred and sixty thousand foot soldiers. This was probably overly exaggerated, but it was definitely a multiple of the total defenders of Acre. The city numbered roughly forty thousand inhabitants, approximately one thousand knights and fourteen thousand infantrymen.

The battle of Acre was the last military action of the Templars and they distinguished themselves in a tremendous way. William of Beaujeu departed this life at 60 years of age, on the 18th May, on the battlefield. A spear struck him under the armpit, a weak spot in the knights' armour. The Grand Master was carried inside his palace on a shield and died the same evening. The members burried him in front of the altar of the Templars' church.

The Temple stronghold was the only remaining building that was still in the hands of the Christians; it was full of refugee's. The Marshal of the Templars agreed with the Muslims to surrender themselves in return for protection. When the gates opened, the Muslims began to plunder and molest women and children. The Templars immediately shut the gates and the battle continued. That night, Theobald Gaudin left the Templars haven with the portable assets of the Order and sailed to Sidon. The members of a diplomatic mission, who were sent to the Muslims to restore the treaty, were directly beheaded. Ten days later the bastion of the Templars fell and all the survivors were killed. There were three hundred Templars who perished in the siege.

Some historians are of the opinion that Philip IV pursued the Order of the Temple sixteen years later, because of its friendly relations with the Muslims. The events during the last years of their presence in the Holy Land, give no support to these suggestions whatsoever. Acre was flattened to the ground; the Muslims wanted to hinder the Europeans from easily returning.

The Templars still had three properties: Sidon, Tortosa and Château Pèlerin. The remaining knights chose Theobald Gaudin as Grand Master at Sidon, probably because he was the oldest. Theobald had already been fighting for more than thirty years in the East as Commander and Turcopolier. A month later, a large army left to go to Sidon and the Templars entrenched themselves in their castle in the city. It lay a hundred metres from the coast in the harbour and was only accessible via a small bridge. Theobald went to Cyprus to get reinforcements, but he did not return. The defenders received a message from Cyprus that they would not get help, and on the 14th July they abandoned their castle. Tortosa was evacuated by them and on the 14th August 1291, the Templars departed from Château Pèlerin. The Muslims destroyed the entire coastal area thereafter: cities, vineyards and castles. They wanted to impede a new Western attack, but their fears were ungrounded. The West was no longer interested in risky adventures.

Were the Templars and the Hospitallers enemies?

By far, the Templars and the Hospitallers were the largest military orders in the Holy Land. The relationship between these monk-soldiers was not always optimal. This first became apparent in the 1160's, when the Hospitallers had participated in the last Egyptian expedition of King Amalric. The Order of the Temple could permit itself to ignore the request of the King. Twenty years later they again found themselves in different camps. The Templars supported King

Guy of Lusignan, while the Hospitallers had chosen to favour the denounced regent, Raymond III. In the same period, both orders were arguing about the division of their possessions in Tripoli. At the beginning of the thirteenth century, in Antioch, there was unrest when the King of Armenia wanted to take advantage of a weak heir to the throne. Again, both Orders were not able to follow a combined strategy. It was only in 1218 when they succeeded in preserving the peace in the North of the Holy Land.

The situation in the Kingdom of Jerusalem was more critical. When Frederick II interfered with the Middle East, the Hospitallers and the Templars formed a united front. Both offered resistance to the German Emperor, who in the meantime was declared persona non grata by the Pope. After Frederick II was once again mercifully accepted by the Church, the Templars maintained there stance towards the German Emperor. The Hospitallers on the other hand, altered their opinion and supported Frederick II from 1234 onwards. This difference of opinions led to various squabbles; both Orders were practically on the brink of war with each other. In 1258 they managed to burry the hatchet when they closed a treaty with the Teutonic Knights.

On a majority of occasions the Templars and the Hospitallers strived side by side. When the anarchy in the Christian camp began to grow, during the thirteenth century, a very complicated situation arose in the Holy Land. Both Orders were colleagues and rivals at the same time and they did not always succeed in permitting their joint concerns to flow in harmony. Even though the Templars gave charities to the poor, and attention to the weal and woe of the pilgrims was high in importance, they were, first and foremost, a military organisation. The Hospitallers were also responsible for the poor and sick. It was then also logical that the Order of the Temple had a much more militant character. This difference in culture between both Orders was expressed in their policies. But, the conclusion can be no other way than that both Orders felt jointly responsible for the defending of the Holy Land.

The aftermath of the Crusades

The Crusades marked a fracture in the development of the Muslim states and the West. At the time of the Western occupation, the Arabian world was intellectually and materially regarded as the most progressive in the world. After 1300 the centre undeniably shifted to the West. The renaissance ensured Europe of a cultural, scientific and social revolution. Seamanship coupled with exploration became a Western concern. The forerunners of the decline of the Muslim world were already visible in the tenth century. The political and religious unity in the Arabian world crumbled more and more from that time on. The Crusades stimulated an already existing process. Saladin and Baybars succeeded, with their excellent leadership, to delay this decline.

The attitude of Islam, in relation to other religions, has fundamentally altered because of the Crusades. Before the year 1100 the Muslims were tolerant of the Jews and Christians. The violent actions of the Franks upset this attitude into one of hate against dissentients. The native Christians first noticed this after the departure of the last of the Westerners. They were heavily blamed for the barbaric behaviour of their fellow believers. The present-day hostile behaviour of the Muslim people against the West is, to a certain degree, traceable to the misbehaviour of the Christians in the twelfth and thirteenth century.

IX. The military role of the Order of the Temple

THE CRISTIAN ARMIES

The leaders of the Christian areas in the Middle East realised, that the military orders fulfilled an important role in the defending of the Holy Land. This was mainly because the Kingdom of Jerusalem, the principality of Antioch and the county of Tripoli had a permanent shortage of colonists and therefore soldiers.

Clear figures are lacking from the available chronicles, but the three Latin States presumably had their own army of approximately twelve hundred knights. The Hospitallers and the Templars could each throw around six hundred knights into the fray. The Templars had about three hundred knights at their disposal in the Kingdom of Jerusalem; just as many as in operation in Tripoli and Antioch.

The number of six hundred Templars can be determined on the basis of the chronicles covering the various important battles. During the conflicts at Cresson and Hattin in 1187, about four hundred Templars were active. In 1244 approximately 350 Templars participated in the battle at La Forbie (near Gaza). Around three hundred Order members fell in battle during the Seventh Crusade of 1248. Given the fact that in each of the dozens of castles belonging to the Templars, a garrison had to stay behind, it is likely that the amount of six hundred Templars is correct.

The knights formed the cavalry of the army and were the pivotal part of the medieval Western army. They could also not do without infantry, which protected the knights and their horses against the actions of the Muslims. That happened for example in the battle of Hattin; one of the causes of the defeat of the Christians, was that the foot soldiers fled in panic. The horses lost their protection, because of this they were killed in large numbers and that rendered the knights powerless. With their heavy armour of roughly fifty kilo's, they were too cumbersome to be able to fight on their feet with the less heavily armoured opponent. In addition to the knights, in the Christian states there were more or less three times as many warriors to call upon, some infantrymen and some on horseback. On its own, this was not enough to offer resistance to the Islamic supremacy; hence, the rulers of the states and the orders employed the services of mercenaries in times of need. These soldiers belonged to the native population and were not always so trustworthy: on occasion these hired soldiers would disappear during the battle because, as an afterthought, they did not want to fight against their fellow believers. These locals, called Turcopoles, were mainly infantrymen and a small few rode a horse, armed with a bow and arrow. The Christian army was, on more than one occasion, supplemented by pilgrims. These visitors, wether or not armed, nearly all returned to their own countries after a trip to the Holy Places.

Westerners were not really used to the climatological circumstances in the Middle East. The 'men in the iron suits', as an Arabian source named the knights, in particular, had a lot of problems with the dryness and the heat. In addition to that, the battle methods of the Muslims, were some what different to that of the Europeans. The Muslim horsemen were less heavily armed and very manoeuvrable due to their swift horses. The Turks units especially, consisted of experienced warriors and, with their agility, formed a formidable opponent for the Crusaders.

After about 1150, the military orders were an important factor in the Christian army. They had disciplined and well trained hooligans at their disposal, who were permanently available. Their bravery was described in many Arabian and Western chronicles; they thought that the fighting power of these soldiers was better than that of the other troops. The important military position of the Templars and the Hospitallers became even more obvious in the number of fortified places that they controlled. The majority of the castles in the Latin States were manned by monk-soldiers. After the battle of Hattin, practically all castles were in their possession. This occurred because the military orders were the only ones who had the enormous financial means available, which were needed to attain the strongholds.

THE WAR IN THE MIDDLE EAST

The history of the Western occupation of the Holy Land is one of continual warfare. Even in the periods of cease fire, squirmishes were taking place, on one side the local barons or the Orders, and on the other the Islamic rulers. Similarly

Christians (visible on the flags, German, French and Flemish) in a fight against the Muslims.

in Western Europe, the waging of war was also quite often a regional occurrence. If a large-scale Muslim attack took place, the defence tactics of the leaders were concentrated on the fortified places, the cities as well as the castles. Whenever they were threatened, the colonists mustered up a large field army. The Christian troops gathered together at a central location. Obviously this occurred in areas where water and food were in supply. After all, the army of the colonists amounted to a few thousand horses and these were useless without plenty of fodder.

Subsequently the scouts were then sent out and if one discovered what the target of the Muslim army was, the other Latin States were called in to help, if it was necessary. In recurrent circumstances, the gathered army would depart and go to the fortress being threatened by the Muslims. This sort of march did not go without a hiccup. The manoeuvrability of the Turks in particular, placed them in a position where they could frustrate a Christian column. They constantly attacked in waves and in small groups, fired their arrows and then quickly retreated. The flanks and the rear of the advancing army found this especially difficult to endure.

The Muslims were determined to split the Christian army and subsequently butcher the separated stragglers. Therefore it was essential that the lines of the Christian army remained intact. Because of their experience and discipline, the knights of the Hospitallers and the Templars were posted at the most vulnerable locations.

The Franks hoped to impress and dispel the intruders with such a march. They preferred to avoid a conflict, because they could not afford to lose an army. It often turned out that these passive battle tactics were sufficient to cause the intruders to retreat. Should it still amount to combat, then the Franks were extremely dependant on the mounted troops in order to gain victory. The army was then positioned in battle order, where the knights (and the horses) were protected by a row of foot soldiers, armed with bows and arrows and spears. The knights were divided into groups of mostly five or six men; on more often than one occasion there were between a hundred and 150 so called eskaders. These were probably split into four sub-armies: the left- and right flank, the middle and the reserve battalion.

The latter section was under the command of the commander in chief. There were more of these, such as during the Second Crusade, but on the whole, the Franks realised that there could be one, and only one leader. The army leader gave the signal to charge and used the reserves to support the main attack. The Order of the Temple knew precisely how to apply the battle methods and they placed their knowledge in writing.

The Hierarchical Statutes

In the *Hierarchical Statutes* from about 1165, it is written in which manner the army of the Templars operated. It is regarded to by experts as a unique document, the first military manual of its kind. It was based upon the personal experiences of the Templars and not upon classical documents.

How the Brothers should make Camp
Before a battle commenced, the knights and the sergeants from the preceptories and castles were called to gather together. A certain amount of the garrison remained behind in order to defend the possessions of the Templars. The others

took their squires, horses and equipment with them and built up an encampment at the agreed site. The Standard Bearer began with the pitching of two tents: the chapel- and the cooking tent, hereafter the brothers received the order to place their tents around the chapel.

Only the Grand Master, the Marshal and the Master of the province did not have to wait for such an order. When the tents were pitched, the chapel was opened for the members. They could not enter any further than the middle section of the chapel tent, so as not to disturb the priest on duty. It was expressly forbidden to wander too far from the camp, because one should always be able to hear a possible alarm. The squires were sent out to collect water and fire wood.

The knight kept his armour close by and one squire stayed near to him, in case they had to go into battle. If the alarm was given, the knights in the vicinity of the alert grabbed their spear and shield and left the threatened area. They all gathered at the chapel to take the orders from the Marshal. If the alarm was sounded outside the camp, nobody left the camp, 'not even for a lion or a wild beast' (article 155). When it was peaceful, the normal services were taken in the chapel tent. The Templars were, after all, religious soldiers.

How the Brothers form the Line of March
The Marshall gave the order to break camp and that also happened in phases. After the tents were taken down, the soldiers waited until the Marshal gave them permission to mount their horses (steed, mule or parade horse). After the order to mount was given, the brothers had to first of all ensure that none of their equipment had been left behind. They all then calmly and silently looked for the eskader; the squires were required to follow their master. As soon as the Templars had taken their position in the army, the squires rode off in front of them. If two brothers wanted to talk to each other, the one who rode in front had to drop back. The retaking of his original position took place downwind, in order to prevent the circulating dust from disturbing the lines.

The army regularly travelled at night, mostly to primes, the third religious service. Should the knight not be able to find his place again in the dark, then he had to follow in the path of another eskader until it became light. In peaceful areas, the horses could drink at a spring, provided that the discipline was not disturbed. In enemy territories this only occurred if the Standard Bearer gave his permission. If an alarm was given during a ride, the knights who were near to the alert swapped horses and mounted their steed.

They held their battle shield and spear in position and awaited the orders of the Marshall. The others rode to the Marshall to find out what they had to do. Self initiative was absolutely forbidden.

How the Brothers should go in a Squadron

Before the battle with the Muslims broke out, the army was formed into a number of groups, mostly existing of five or six knights. In front of the knight, mounted on his steed, was his squire with the battle lance of his master, whilst behind him was another squire holding the second steed by the bit. At the commencement of battle the remaining squires were drafted into eskaders by the Standard Bearer. No one could leave the lines other than with explicit permission. Only, thus the Rule, if a Christian warrior was in danger and the consciousness of the knight told him that he could help him, may the knight assist the Christian. Should a knight leave the formation for one reason or another, he was stripped of everything, apart from his robe. Thereafter, pending his condemnation, he had to return to the camp on foot. Walking, for a knight, was a humiliating activity; after all, he saw himself as a mounted warrior.

In practice, it proved to be necessary to maintain the formation; in the twelfth century many battles were lost by the Franks, because the Turks succeeded in separating the Western army. The isolated units were then successfully surrounded and destroyed. Disciplinary behaviour was a difficult task for most knights. The knight was an individualist, convinced of the fact that he was man enough to defend himself against the hit-and-run attacks of the enemy. From the chronicles it appears that the army leaders were very aware of the arrogant character of their knights. In 1115, Roger, Prince of the principality of Antioch, rode on a fast horse through his camp with an unsheathed sword. In this manner he forced his knights not to react to the provocations of the Turks.

When the Marshal takes up the Banner to Charge

Before the attack, the Marshal took the banner from the Under Marshal and commissioned a maximum of ten knights to defend the banner to the best of their abilities. A Commander of the knights wound an extra banner around his lance and was entrusted with defending the flapping and convoluted banner. He remained in the vicinity of the Marshal and unfolded the rolled up banner when the first one was damaged or no longer visible. He was strictly forbidden to use the lance as a weapon during the conflict. The banner was a thing of great importance to the Order: it was the sign of the fighting power of the army and the loss of it was comparable to acknowledging defeat. The Grand Master, or his substitute, then gave one or more units the signal to attack. When the Order of the Temple formed part of the Christian army, it waited until the commander in chief present wanted to go into action.

A storming compact mass of iron clad horses, mounted with armoured knights brandishing a lance as a thrusting weapon, brought the enemy army in grave confusion. Behind the attackers, the warriors, un-mounted and mounted, were ready to optimally profit from the chaos, which this type of charge brought about. The squires held the reserve horses by the bridle so that the knight could quickly return to action if his horse had fallen. The Turcopoles on their fast horses were mainly armed with bows and arrows and therefore increased the panic within the enemy camp. The effect of a charge was moreover extremely dependant on timing, the maintaining of the formation, the circumstances of the terrain and the manoeuvrability of the enemy line.

The Templar had to to remain close to the banner of his eskader. If he could not do so because the enemies had obstructed the path, he joined in with the first other Christian banner. As soon as it was possible he returned to his own pennant. He could not leave his eskader, not even if he was wounded. In this case, he had to first ask permission; if he was mortally wounded, he sent another brother. The Templar only had the right to leave the battlefield without

A Templar makes a charge.

permission and return to his garrison, if the Christian banners had all disappeared. Should he do this beforehand, he was definitely thrown out of the Order.

In the beginning, the Muslims were not accustomed to the Western manner of fighting and even though they were later prepared, they desperately feared an assault from the Franks. The Muslims altered their usual strategy during the twelfth century. They did this in order to better anticipate the Christian fighting techniques. The Franks armies were a lot less flexible in this regard, because the army consisted mostly of Crusaders. The newcomers, who fought mostly one battle in the Holy Land, were less inclined to alter their European combat techniques. A striking example of this was seen during the battle of Gaza in 1239. A Crusaders army wanted to, in spite of the advice of the colonists and the military orders, attack an Egyptian army. The army left the main body and struck the camp in a dune like area, not exactly ideal for making a charge. The army was surrounded and because there were not any guards on duty, the leaders dicovered their dangerous situation when it was too late. The Westerners were forced into a charge, because they ran out of arrows. The Muslims had to flee, but they did this with tact. The knights gave their enemies an undisciplined chase, and therefore lost their formation and the battle. The Muslims had taken into account that the newcomers would carry on for too long with their charge and because of this, they were victorious.

THE RECRUITMENT OF THE TEMPLARS

The Order of the Temple recruited their members from all parts of Western Europe, but most of them came from France. There are also no decisive numbers available about this, but it is obvious. Approximately three quarters of the Western preceptories were in this country. Historians base their foundations on the data from the trial, which proceeded in the fourteenth century (see Chapter XII). Of the 75 brothers who were then arrested in Cyprus, forty came from France. Besides, most of the Grand Masters came from this country. They often came from families of the lower to middle-class aristocracy. The common members were mostly from the lower class. It meant that adult men could become knights if they descended from a knight. Illegitimate sons of knightly lineage, as previously mentioned, never rose any higher than sergeant. The majority of the members remained in the preceptories of the overseas areas, thus in Western Europe. Actually that was logical: the Order had about a thousand preceptories in that area. There were noticeably more sergeants than knights and again, the numbers from the trial give this indication. The background information from 193 of the members taken prisoners in France was registered: 177 were sergeants and sixteen knights. On Cyprus, the overall majority of the arrested members belonged to the rank of knight. This was because this island was situated in the war territory of the Templars.

As reported in the previous Chapter, it regularly occurred that a great deal of the Orders' army were killed by the Muslims. The Order could quite easily bring the armies from the preceptories in Western Europe up to the mark again. The number of knights was in fact restricted by the financial possibilities of the Templars. After all, it did cost a fortune to maintain a knight, including horses, accommodation, armour and subordinate personnel. The historian Fossier (1988) calculated how expensive it was to completely kit out a knight. In 1180 a knight from Burgundy needed the income from thirty 'manses' (roughly three hundred hectares) in order to operate as a cavalryman. Eighty years later that was five times as much, which was mainly due to the fact that the price of horses during this period had increased six fold.

The function of castles

Castles were of an essential significance during the Western occupation of the Middle East. They served partly as compensation for the scarce amount of Westerners who permanently resided in the Middle East. The purpose of these buildings was twofold: in peace times they dominated the circumjacent territory and they prevented plundering trips by the Muslims. In war time the castles were refuges for the Franks. All castles also had a superb water and food supply. With regard to this, it is known that various strongholds could survive a siege for five years. The fortifications were not really suitable for the closure of country borders, because a large Muslim army could easily pass a castle without being bothered by the garrison.

The fortresses not only had a military function, but they were used especially to control and exploit the area. A regular part of a Templars castle was, of course, a chapel, in many instances, large in size. The one of Chastel Blanc was 23 metres long, ten metres wide and thirteen metres high. The church was dedicated to the archangel, Michael, who slaughtered the devil and his accomplices. From the chronicles, we know that these churches were not only for internal use.

The maintenance of a castle was very expensive and required a gigantic investment of capital and personnel. The colonists managed without the money and flow of supplies from Western Europe, which the orders surely had available. Since the second half of the twelfth century, the leaders of the country handed over the control of the castles successively to the Orders. The pronouncement of King Thoros of Armenia is characteristic. When he visited King Baldwin III of the Kingdom of Jerusalem in 1165, he said the following to the host:

> *When I came to your country and inquired as to whom the castles belonged, I sometimes received the answer: 'This belongs to the Templars'.' Elsewhere I heard: 'It belongs to the Hospitallers'.' Except for three, I had found no castle or city whereof it was said that it was your possession.*

After the battle of Hattin in 1187, nearly all of the castles came into the complete possession of the Order of the Temple, the Hospitallers and a few the Teutonic Knights. All Crusaders originally built a compact and rectangular castle, without a courtyard. The Orders furthermore, took the typical monastery quarters, such as chapel and refectory, as a starting point. In the thirteenth century they altered this shape, adapting it to contend with the improved attack techniques of the Muslims.

Besides, the castles were not the only places where the Templars lodged. In each of the Christian possessions they had a least one building, furthermore they owned many farms and large pieces of land. Historians guess, that around 1150, roughly 18 percent of the domain of the Latin States was in the hands of the Orders and that this percentage amounted to 35 shortly before the battle of Hattin. In the thirteenth century they undoubtedly possessed an even larger part of the Christian area. Practically all castles, therefore the administrative centre, were then in the hands of the Templars, the Hospitallers or (in a few cases) the Teutonic Knights. How many there were, we do not know, however the archives of the Hospitallers give us an indication. During their stay in the Middle East these knights had control over 56 fortifications in total. This amount changed during the two centuries: a few castles were momentarily in the hands of the Christians.

The Order of the Temple would not have had fewer strongholds than the Hospitallers. The number fluctuated just as with their colleague's Order. Jacob's Fort, for example, was in the hands of the Templars for not much longer than eighteen months.

'Atlit was never conquered by the Muslims. On 14 August 1291, the Templars left the castle and returned to Cyprus.

THE BATTLE FOR A STRONGHOLD

The conquering of a castle or a city demanded accurate preparations. A large army was needed in order to surround it, they had to take sufficient food with them and they had to have siege materials available (such as wood, iron and projectiles). It was no use waiting until the inhabitants of the castle were lacking in food and drink. From the chronicles, it is clear that the attackers were the first to have a shortage of provisions. At the conquering of Jerusalem in 1099, the Egyptians had destroyed or poisoned all the water sources in the immediate area. This forced the besiegers to undertake distant and dangerous journeys in order to fetch water for the men and animals. Apparently, the Crusaders thought that the Lord himself would hand over the city to them, for they had no siege material with them. Because there was no wood available in the vicinity, the besiegers did not stand a chance. The arrival of a fleet from Genoa, which had just landed at Jaffa, altered the situation. The Italians dismantled the ships and used these to build a number of large wooden towers. These were placed against the wall and with the use of a springboard the Crusaders could take the city.

The use of ladders or towers was the simplest way of entering a stronghold. Due to the condition of the terrain, that was not always possible. It also had the disadvantage of bringing the attackers into the reach of the defence. It was for this reason that the besiegers preferred to remain at a distance from the walls. This was possible with the use of the mangonel, the petraria and the trebuchet, with which stones and other projectiles could be fired. The mangonel and the petraria worked on the principle of torsion: that is to say that one would turn a rope so that when it was released, an object could be launched with force. The trebuchet was developed later, this, with the assistance of a counterbalance, catapulted projectiles. The trebuchet was more accurate than both of the other old machines and could launch heavier stones. From a distance of two hundred metres, round stones of approximately two hundred kilo's could be hurled. An arrow from a heavy bow did not reach much further than 140 metres, so the attackers could continue use the trebuchet undisturbed.

If the wall was sufficiently damaged, the army entered at the weakest point of the fortress. Whenever possible, the battering ram was used to destroy the last bits of the wall. In the chronicles, there is very little mention made of this weapon of attack: the writers apparently thought that the battering rams obviously spoke for themselves, so it was therefore not necessary to describe them. Of course the attackers made use of shields and small wooden houses to protect themselves from pitches, stones and arrows. The defence also operated catapults, which were mounted on platforms on top of the wall. The Muslims did not only use stones with these weapons of attack; they had knowledge of the Greek fire, which could not be extinguished with water.

Another method of weakening the castle was the undermining of a section of the structure. A tunnel was dug until it reached under the walls, in which wooden planks propped up the corridor. They filled the bottom of the pathway with straw and set this on fire. The tunnel then collapsed and that mostly happened along with the wall. A breach would appear, on which the attackers would concentrate. When this method became fashionable, the builders of the castles took this into account. In so far as it was possible, the Franks built a castle on rocks or old pillars were horizontally incorporated into the foundations. Once, the defenders undermined the tunnel of the attackers and hoped that they would subsequently collapse before the wall. This undermining took a lot of manpower: something which the defence did not always have.

The architects considerably altered, on the basis of the improved techniques of attack, the construction of a castle in the thirteenth century. At the beginning of the twelfth century, a castle with one outer wall could still hold out for a while. The castles which were built later, all had a double defence ring. If it was possible, the men built a castle on a spot where the attacker found it difficult to set up his artillery. There were towers built into the walls so that the men could fire a bow and arrow past the wall. The Templars preferred rectangular towers, but round towers were common.

The sortie was another defence possibility, but that was not always sensible. The defence could not withstand the chance of losing men, which went along with this. In the thirteenth century, special openings were made in the wall. It had already occurred on a few occasions that a sortie army was chased by the besiegers whilst the main entrances were closed.

Over a period of time, a castle occupied by the Franks could not be salvaged. The Muslims were pre-eminently skilled in the development of artillery. The most effective was a relief army, because an attacker could hardly fight a two fronted war. From the examples of the twelfth century, it is evident that the threat of a disrupting army alone was enough to abandon an attempt at capturing a castle. In the thirteenth century, the Christians could not muster up such an army. There were too few soldiers and the mutual discord had in the meantime, become too great.

The Castles of the Templars

The Kingdom of Jerusalem
The Kingdom of Jerusalem was by far, the biggest and most prosperous section of the Latin States. It originally consisted of only the city of Jerusalem, but Baldwin I and II considerably extended it during the first thirty years of the twelfth century. The Kingdom then linked not only Palestine, between the valley of the Jordan and the Mediterranean Sea, but also the costal area of the present day Lebanon, up to and including Beirut. Trans-Jordania, East of the Dead Sea and up to the Gulf of Aqaba was just as much a part of the Kingdom.

The Hospitallers had approximately three hundred possessions here. Included in these were castles, villages, farms, vineyards, mills, orchards and estates; in addition, they had a monastery in practically all of the cities. At least that is what appears in the archives of this Order, which is stored in Malta. In can be no other way other than that the Templars had a similar number of possessions. They were just as prominently present as their colleagues in the chronicles of that time.

The authors of these writings were actually war correspondents, because of which, we are better informed about their castles than about their other belongings (see the map on page 207). Our knowledge about the number and the nature of the Templars' castles in the Kingdom of Jerusalem is nevertheless fragmentary. What we do know, is that their castles were mostly built on the roads along which the pilgrims journeyed. This is in comparison to the Hospitallers, who established their castles nearer to the centre of the territories.

About 1149-1150, the Order of the Temple received permission to rebuild a castle in the ruin city of Gaza, from King Baldwin III. Gaza was situated to the South of the Kingdom, about fifteen kilometres to the South of the harbour city of Ascalon. The castle of the Templars was part of a ring of castles around the harbour city, the last bulwark of the Egyptians in the Kingdom. The idea was to withstand raids from Ascalon and to isolate the city from inland. When Ascalon was conquered in 1153 (see Chapter IV), the castle of Gaza was used by the Templars to control the surroundings.

In September 1187 the intact fort came into the possession of Saladin. The then Grand Master, Gerard of Ridefort, was taken a prisoner of war after the battle of Hattin and he demanded of his subordinates that they leave the castle. In exchange for this, he was released by Saladin. In 1192 the stronghold was recaptured during the Third Crusade and given back to the Templars by Richard I. As part of the treaty between Saladin and Richard, they had to leave again shortly thereafter. In 1240, Richard Plantagenet captured the castle, fortified it and donated it to the Kingdom of Jerusalem. The previously cited Matthew Paris wrote that he refused to give it to the Templars because they, according to Richard, were too proud. A short time afterwards it came into the possession of the Hospitallers, who conclusively lost it to the Egyptians in 1247.

The Templars also manifested themselves in Trans-Jordania. The Lord of Nablus, one of the most important men in the Kingdom, became a member of the Order in 1166. He gifted large segments of his land, situated on the other side of the river Jordan, to them. On one of these stood the castle of Ahamant (Amman), which was destroyed by the army of Noer-ad-Din a year later. Subsequently, the Templars would never return as rulers of the other side of the Jordan. Negotiations with the Muslims pertaining to this, in the thirteenth century, amounted to nothing.

About 1166, the Templars took over the castle of Safad from a local Christian baron. Hugh of St. Omer, a relative of Godfrey of Bouillon, according to an Arabian source, had it built in 1101-1102. King Amalric paid most of the costs for the renovation. Safad stood on an isolated hill and therefore had a strategic position. In 1189, Saladin captured the castle, but in 1240 the Templars were again able to retake it.

In Chapter VII the reconstruction is described. It was built on the remains of a mosque and a synagogue, indicating that Christianity had triumphed over both of the other religions. The building costs amounted to at least 1100 thousand bezants: in those days that was equivalent to about eighty percent of the annual income of the domains of the English King. Safad was even larger than the existing castle of the Hospitallers, Krak des Chevalliers (perimeter of 750 metres).

The harbour city of Arsuf was about the same size as Safad; approximately three football pitches in total. In 1266, the Egyptian Sultan, Baybars, made three unsuccessful attempts to conquer Safad, thereafter the castle still fell due to betrayal. The fall of the largest castle that the Franks had ever owned would have influenced Louis' decision to go on a crusade again. Ibn 'Abd al-Zahir, the biographer of Baybars, recounted how the conquerors of Safad went to work. Baybars had artilleries made in the region of Damascus and Acre. These were transported to the area by camels and the weapons had to be carried by the soldiers and even the emir, along the last stretch.

The catapults had little effect on the walls and Baybars looked for other methods of resource. He employed mining engineers who were surprised by the undermining of the defenders. Under the ground, the Muslims and the Templars had scuffles with each other. Because too many Muslims, for Baybars' liking, died, he practiced a ruse. He promised the native defenders a free passage, whereupon they could successfully leave the castle. Templar brother, Leon Cazelier, of Syrian origin, was sent to Baybars by the Templars to negotiate the conditions of surrender. The Templars wanted the Christians to be able to leave the castle unharmed. Baybars gave Leon to understand that he would slay all Templars: he promised to spare Leons life if he could convince the Templars to give up the battle. When the Templars opened the entrances, the women and children were taken prisoner and then sold at the slave market. The 150 Templars were all killed. According to another Arabian chronicler, Baybars spared the life of a Hospitaller, so that he could take the news of the fall of the castle to Acre. Leon saved his own life by converting to Islam. His betrayal was depicted forty years later, by the chronicler of the Templars of Tyre. The siege of Safad lasted six weeks.

Twelve kilometres to the North of Safad stood the castle of Chastellet, which was built in 1178 by Baldwin IV. It was known as Jacob's Fort because the daughters of Jacob had crossed the river Jordan there, centuries earlier. Although

THE MILITARY ROLE OF THE ORDER OF THE TEMPLE

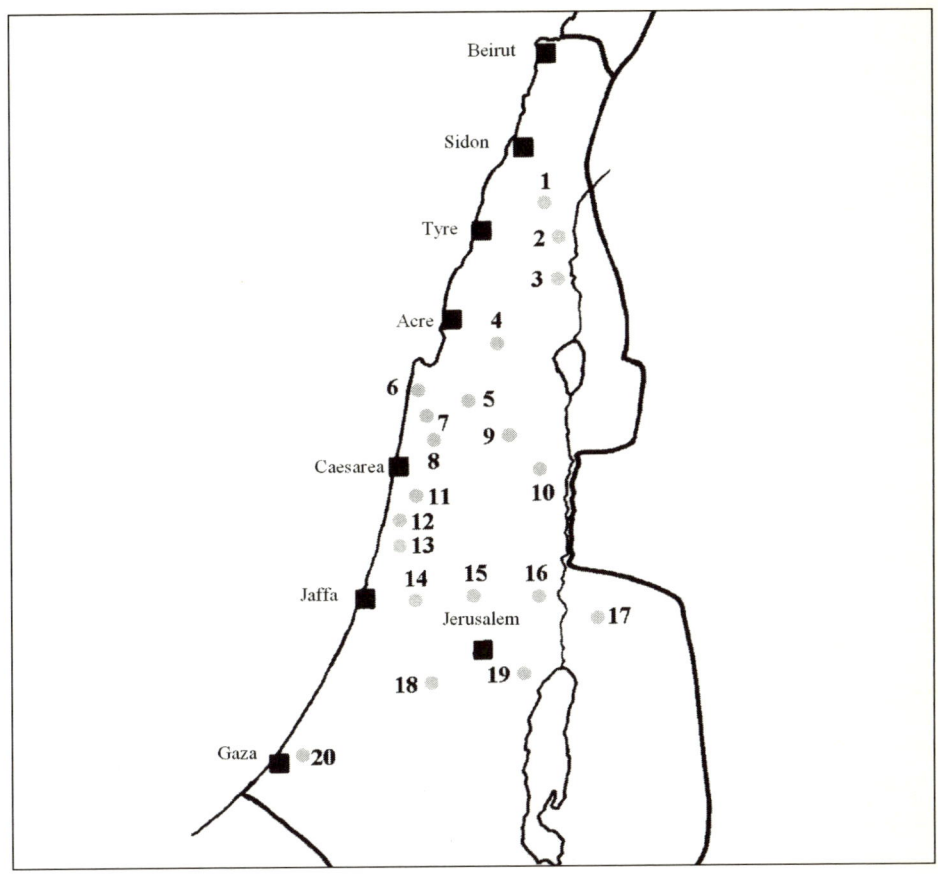

Map of the castles in the Kingdom of Jerusalem.

1   Beaufort (1260-1268)
2   Chastellet (1178-1179)
3   Safad (1166-1266)
4   Saffran (1172-1291)
5   Destroit (113?-1217)
6   'Athlit (1218-1291)
7   Merle (1187-1265)
8   Cafarlet (1255-1265)
9   La Feve (1172-1187)
10 Le Petit Gerin (1184-?)
11 Caco (1187-1265)
12 Tour Rouge (1236-?)
13 Montdidier (1236-?)
14 Casal des Plaines (1187-?)
15 Castel Arnaldi (1150-1188)
16 Quarantene (1170-?)
17 Amman (1166-1167)
18 Toron of the Knights (1172-1188)
19 Maldoim (1172-1187)
20 Gaza (1149-1187)

In addition, the Templars had fortifications in all Christian cities (such as Jaffa), or walled living areas (including Acre).

207

the Franks did not like the idea very much, Baldwin yielded to the pressure of the Templars to build a castle on this place. After the construction, which took six months, the King handed it over to the Templars. This new castle, an rectangular, massive building with a tower at every corner, stood on the banks of the river Jordan and was of huge strategic value. The secretary of Saladin, al-Fadil, described the castle.

> *The wall was more than six and a half metres thick; it was built from enormous stone blocks, each with a diameter of about five metres. The total amount of blocks was more than twenty thousand, and every block placed in the wall cost no less than four dinars and maybe more.*

It controlled the northerly entrance roads to the Kingdom of Jerusalem. Saladin realised the great importance of the castle and offered Baldwin IV a hundred thousand dinars if he would dismantle it. Because the King refused to do so, Saladin had to destroy it himself. In June 1179, he made his first attempt. Saladin defeated a relief army, but he could not conquer the castle. The Muslims took this occasion to take the Grand Master, Odo of Saint-Armand-les-Eaux, prisoner.

In August of the same year, Saladin succeeded in taking Jacob's Fort. As a result of undermining, one of the towers collapsed. Afterwards, the fort went up in flames. It was the first time that the Muslims had managed to capture a large castle from the Christians in this manner. The tunnel was fifteen metres long and a metre and a half wide. A large number of Templars died during the battle and Saladin took seven hundred men prisoner. The garrison commander, a Templar, set himself on fire when he saw that the battle was lost: he died rather than be taken prisoner.

The castle of La Fève stood in the centre of the Kingdom, which according to a German pilgrim, was built by the Templars before 1172. Another source suggests that the Order received it from the monastery of the Tabor Mountain, in about 1146. La Fèvre was more or less square, with a perimeter of about 420 metres. It stood at the crossroads of two important roads and was also a storage place for weapons, food and equipment. There were at least fifty to sixty knights co-located, 10 percent of the entire knight army of the Templars. It was used twice in 1183 as a gathering point of the Christian army. Gerard of Ridefort led his fateful attack of May 1187, on a Muslim army, at the spring in Cresson, from this castle.

La Fève also fell shortly after the battle of Hattin. An Islamic chronicler was very impressed with the fort:

> *Al-Fula* [La Fève] *was the best castle and the most fortified, the fullest of men and munitions and the best provided. It was for the Templars a very powerful fortress, a strong place and a reliable pillar. They had there an inaccessible fountain, an excellent pasture place, and a firm base; and there they spent winter and summer. It was a place where they met and received people, a place where they guarded their horses, a place where the torrents of their man flowed, a meeting place of their brethren, the residence of their devil and the place of their crosses, where their masses and their fire was kindled.*

He further wrote that there were not any knights in the fort when Saladin besieged it. These would have been all been slain at the battle of Cresson. The squires and the other craftsmen left the castle in exchange for their lives. The Hospitallers conquered a large convoy, with weapons and provisions from the dismantled castle, shortly thereafter. In 1240-1241, thanks to the Crusade of Richard Plantagenet, La Fève came back into the possession of the Order. It is unclear as to whether they repaired it and we also do not know when it was re-captured by the Muslims. However it was in the hands of the Egyptians in 1285; the Templars were probably driven out by Baybars in the 1260's. The remains of the castle are buried under the land and buildings of a kibbutz.

Close to La Fève, six kilometres to the East, stood the castle of Caco; it was not mentioned in any documents before 1187. Presumably, Caco was built by a vassal of King Baldwin at the beginning of the twelfth century and it was taken over by the Templars in the third quarter of that same century. The garrison of this small castle, existing of thirty knights, went with Ridefort to Cresson.

This fortress also fell shortly after the disaster at Hattin. In the beginning of the thirteenth century, the Templars had this under their control again, but it was definitively conquered by the Muslims in 1265. In 1271 the Templars, together with Crown Prince Edward, made a futile attempt to retake Caco. The large number of knights that were stationed in La Fève and Caco indicated that they found this area to be of great importance.

A number of other Templars' castles were also especially intended for the protection of the pilgrims. Casal des Plains stood on the outskirts of Jaffa, on the road to Lydda. On the most important road from the coast to Jerusalem, stood Castel Arnaldi and Casal des Plaines. Castel Arnaldi was built by the archbishop and the citizens of Jerusalem in 1132. The pilgrims frequently used the road from Jerusalem to Jaffa and they had to be protected against the Islamic highwaymen. William of Tyre described the building and ended the fragment with:

Thus, by the grace of God and also because of this fortress, the road became much safer and the journey of pilgrims to or from Jerusalem was rendered less perilous.

Castel Arnaldi stood on a spur in the mountains, between two fertile valleys. The ruins have never been excavated, but it appears that Arnaldi was also an rectangular castle with one defence tower in the Western wall. Around 1150 it was transferred to the Templars.

It is unclear as to who built the castle of Toron of the Knights, but the Order of the Temple took it over; in order to protect the pilgrim routes. Because it stood on an isolated mountain summit, it was difficult to reach. The oldest part was a tower, which was later encompassed by a rectangular enclosure of 72 by 55 metres, with domed quarters along the inside of the walls. Around it was an outside wall along the contours of the hills. One of the square towers of this wall is still visible. Saladin destroyed Castel Arnaldi and Toron of the Knights in 1188, and even though the Templars re-took both castles in the thirteenth century, it appears that they never rebuilt the forts.

Pilgrims, who arrived in Haifa or Tyre, mostly took the coastal route to the South and then came along Mount Carmel, which was protected since 1103 by the fort of Destroit. Somewhere in the 1130's, the Templars became responsible for this castle. It stood on the important trade road to Jerusalem and the Templars undoubtedly used it as a toll house for passing convoys. Destroit could house a garrison of approximately twenty mounted soldiers and was replaced by 'Atlit in 1217. This castle was built on the initiative of, and in cooperation with, the pilgrims, hence the name Chateau Pèlerin. In his chronicles, the bishop named in Chapter V, Oliver of Paderborn, describes that the Templars decided to build Chateau Pèlerin not only for military strategical reasons. They wanted to withdraw from, what they considerd to be, the sinful city of Acre. The castle was surrounded by the sea on three sides and deemed as impregnable. The stronghold had enormous stores, its own water supply and even a number of gardens. The outer wall was six metres thick and sixteen metres high, with a circumference of about four hundred metres. Towers, thirty metres in height, were built into the inner wall. An ingenious passageway system ensured that the soldiers could easily reach the various defence lines. The castle had a round church situated internally, with a diameter of more than thirty metres. It would have been a determind imitation of the Holy Sepulchre. By the way, the round form of a church was not an exclusive characteristic of a Templars church. Other orders also had circular churches, while most chapels of the Templars had a rectangular form. Due to the good relationship that Louis IX had with the Templars, it often occurred that the royalty lodged at this castle. Louis' wife gave birth to her son there. According to Oliver of Paderborn, there was a palace in the courtyard, whilst the remains of a Turkish bath were discovered during excavations. All large castles had luxurious accommodations, so that the Templars could adequately receive their important guests. Finally, Château Pèlerin was the most important prison of the Templars, so as mentioned earlier in Chapter III.

When the castle was nearing completion in 1220, it was raided by the leader of Damascus. He wanted to profit from the fact that most of the Franks army fought in the Nile Delta during the Fifth Crusade. The besiegers made use of seven large catapults. The Templars sent reinforcements from Damietta, Acre, Beirut, Tripoli and Cyprus. One witness, Oliver of Paderborn, described how the Order fed a garrison of four thousand men, while the other defenders had to arrange for their own food. According to Paderborn, the defenders managed to destroy the Muslim artillery with the help of the trebuchet, the mangonel and the petraria. When the Sultan of Damascus heard that there was a Christian liberation army on the way, he stopped the encirclement after a month. Château Pèlerin never fell due to a siege; even Baybars left it alone when he flattened the area to the ground in 1265. Castles which stood on the coast had the advantage of being able to be defend attacks from the water. The Christians were in fact Lord and Master of the sea during the whole of the Eastern occupation of the Holy Land. In 1291, the extremely decimated garrison left the castle of its own accord and journeyed to Cyprus. Further to the South, the Order possessed another castle on the coast, Merle (Dor). It is unclear as to when they managed to own this, but it is mentioned for the first time in 1187. It fell into the hands of the Muslims in 1265.

Near to the coastal city of Habonim, the Templars received the castle of Cafarlet from the Hospitallers in 1255, presumably in the framework of a land exchange. The castle, which originated from the eighth century, was built by the Muslims. In 1265 it was completely destroyed by Baybars. The Templars were extremely powerful in that area, after they had bought the village of Arames, in 1232. Arames had a strategic position, because it controlled the entrance to the pass to the Jezreel Valley at Mount Carmel. The Templars must have had more possessions in this area. In a treaty with the Muslims, from 1283, it is written about Château Pèlerin that it amounted in total to sixteen independent fortifications, including grounds. The Order of the Temple undoubtedly earned plenty of money here. The region was rich in fish, salt, olive oil, grapes, grain and fruit.

The flow of pilgrims between Jerusalem and the Jordan was bustling; after bathing in the river, many went to the 'Mountain of Temptation,' where Jesus was tempted by the Devil. Halfway, the Templars possessed the castle of Maldoim (Red Sistern). Maldoim stood on the busy pilgrim route, between Jerusalem and Jericho and was a rectangular castle of approximately fifty by sixty metres. It was protected by chiselled out pieces of rock. Inside the walls there stood a castle tower and various domed structures, including stables. On the top of a mountain, near to Jericho, there also stood a Templars fort, which served as a food and weapons storage place. Both fortifications, built before 1172, were destroyed by Saladin, and never rebuilt. According to a German pilgrim, who visited the Holy Land between 1169 and 1174, there was an oasis at the foot of the mountain near Jericho. This was known as the Garden of Abraham, which was protected by the Templars and the Hospitallers. The Templars also had a castle at the place where Jesus was baptised by John the Baptist. A pilgrim made reference to it, but did not mention the name of the fortress.

In the South of the present day Lebanon, stood the castle of Beaufort, which was captured by King Fulk in 1139. It was possessed by the Muslims in 1190 and returned into Christian hands in 1240, together with the fortified cavern of Tyron. This stood on a mountain with a fantastic over view of Sidon. Both strongholds were sold to the Templars in 1260 and they renovated the castle of Beaufort. In 1268, it was conquered by Sultan Baybars after an eleven day siege. He used at least 26 heavy artilleries. These caused a breach in the outer wall, whereupon the defenders retreated into the citadel. The Templars managed to send a messenger to Acre. The Muslim courier, who was sent back by the city, proved to be a traitor and gave the answer to Baybars. He falsified the message, shortly thereafter the garrison surrendered. The women and children were permitted to leave to go to Tyre, whilst the 480 defenders, including 24 Templars, were taken prisoner.

In 1260, the Templars had possession of the city of Sidon and the appertaining castle. This occurred after the Mongolians had plundered the city, but they did not succeed in conquering the castle. The owner, Julian of Sidon, was not in a position to repair the damage to the city and sold it to the Templars. Thereafter he entered into the Order of the Temple. The stronghold of the city of Sidon was built by the pilgrims, on an island directly on the coast, thirty years earlier. It was a small castle, but it was very resistant to an attack from the land. After the fall of Acre in 1291, some Templars escaped to this castle and chose the successor to the fallen Grand Master. A couple of months later, the remaining knights realised that it was useless to stay in the Holy Land any longer, left the castle and went to Cyprus.

The above mentioned castles were described by various eye witnesses, but we know that the Templars also possessed an unknown number of isolated turrets. Maybe Le Petit Gerin, Saffra, Montdidier and Tour Rouge belonged to them. They were modest buildings, which could not withstand a large-scale siege. In 1236, the Templars received Tour Rouge and Montdidier from a monastery order, with the agreement that they had to yield it to the Hospitallers. We can, to a certain extent, track down their remaining assets because of the various arguments with the Hospitallers. At least insofar as it is written in the archive of the Hospitallers. In the North of the Kingdom, at Doc, not far from Acre, the Templars owned a number of water mills. Upstream, the Hospitallers had water mills in operation. Back and forth, the Orders annoyed each other. In 1235, the Pope interfered in this conflict and threatened excommunication if violence continued to be used.

Tripoli
The county of Tripoli arose in 1109, when the First Crusaders conquered an identically named city from the Muslims. This Latin State was not much more than a small coastal strip of approximately sixty kilometres, the hinterland of the harbour cities of Tripoli and Tortosa, as it were. It was a little state, but relatively rich with fertile soil: olives and grapevines grew there in abundance. The region of the city of Tripoli was therefore an attractive object of attack to the Muslims, more so because it had no natural defences. The advantage of the military orders was mainly, that they could just as easily carry out plundering raids in the bordering Muslim territory.

From the information in the archives of the Hospitallers, it is evident that they owned about eighty estates and structures. We know even less about the possessions of the Templars in this county than of those in the Kingdom of Jerusalem. The chroniclers thought that the events in this state were of more importance. Tripoli is in fact hardly mentioned at all in the Bible and that made this region less interesting to the pilgrims (see map on page 216). Unlike in the Kingdom of Jerusalem and the principality of Antioch, the First Crusaders came across many castles there. The Byzantines had built these in the tenth and eleventh century in order to defend Antioch.

Around 1150, the Templars had the control over the first castles in the county of Tripoli. In 1152, they received a plot of land, from the bishop of the harbour city of Tortosa, on which they could build a new castle. The old one had been destroyed by Noer-ad-Din and the owner had no money to rebuild it. The Templars did have, and they made a strong fort there, part of the defence of the city. When Saladin conquered the city of Tortosa in 1188, he did not manage to take the castle. In 1202, the structure was damaged by an earthquake; hereafter it was rebuilt and extended. The castle of Tortosa stood on the coast and had use of a water gate; in the middle stood a castle tower of 35 square metres. The castle had two concentric defence walls, with a total of eleven towers. The inside wall was 25 metres high. After the fall of Acre, in May 1291, the Templars left their castle on the 3rd August 1291. It was one of the last bulwarks of the Order in the Holy Land.

From the deed of the bishop about the castle of Tortosa, it is clear that the Templars had the castle of Chastel-Blanc in their possession in 1171. They received it from the Count of Tripoli after Noer-ad-Din had destroyed it and an earthquake had annihilated the remains. It was situated a little to the South East of the city of Tortosa. The castle tower was rebuilt at least twice, after the earthquakes of 1170 and 1202. Even now the tower, with a floor area of 31 by eighteen metres and a height of 27 metres, makes a huge impression. Saladin probably did not feel strong enough to make an assault on it in 1188. An Arabian source records that Louis IX, during his stay in the Holy Land (from 1250-1254), fortified it. Chastel-Blanc fell in 1271, without any problems, into the hands of the Muslims; the seven hundred men of the garrison wanted to defend themselves, but the Commander of Tortosa ordered the army to surrender. The warriors did this in exchange for their lives.

A couple of kilometres to the North was their castle La Colée, of which we only know that it was in the possession of the Templars before 1243. Just to the South of Tortosa, near to the coast, the Templars castle of al-'Arimah was situated. It stood on a hilly ridge and gave a panoramic overview of the plains surrounding Tripoli and the sea. In the twelfth century it was alternately in the hands of the Christians and the Muslims, until the Templars had control over it in the thirteenth century. It was named in the 1285 treaty between the Order and the Muslims. It was probably lost at the conquering of Tripoli in 1289.

The ownership of these castles gave the Order important rights over the wide region, sixty kilometres inland to the river Orontes. The population was subordinate to the Order and the influence from the regular Church was minimal.

The Templars could exploit the land and above all, they had the right to close treaties with the surrounding Muslims. The Templars, together with the Hospitallers, were practically Lord and Master of the lands around Tripoli. Sometimes this led to reciprocal conflicts. The harbour city of Gibelet was gifted to both orders at the beginning of the thirteenth century. The Hospitallers received it from the Prince of Antioch and the Templars had Gibelet donated to them by the Count of Tripoli. It was then still in the hands of the Muslims, but both Orders nevertheless still argued about it. The city was worth discussing, because the clothing market alone already purveyed an annual fortune in taxes. The conflict was submitted to the Pope and, in 1221, he decided that the city should be equally shared. In 1231, they could actually exercise their joint control of the city, but a couple of weeks later it was recaptured by the Muslims. In 1261, both orders again possessed it and in 1266 the Templars permanently lost it. They gave, as part of the treaty with Sultan Baybars, their share of the city to the Muslims and left Gibelet. When the Muslims came to demand their rightful half of the city, the Hospitallers managed to hinder them and the whole city remained in their ownership.

Antioch
The principality of Antioch was, after Edessa, the second Frank city to be conquered during the First Crusade. Bohemond, a Norman originally from South Italy, received it in 1098 through a ruse. He deceived the Byzantines, the Muslims, and also the leaders who journeyed with him. Similar to Tripoli, this principality was not much more than a city on a small coastal slip, with the difference being that Antioch was much bigger than Tripoli. The Hospitallers had at least one hundred possessions there. In the 1130's, the Templars settled in the North of Antioch (see map on page 216). They probably did this at the request of, but anyway with the permission of, the leader of this principality.

The Order built five castles there; Baghras (the Order called it Gaston) was the largest and stood 26 kilometres to the North of the city of Antioch. The castle of Darbsak (Trapesak) was situated another fifteen kilometres to the North and yet further away was La Roche de Roussel and La Roche Guillaume. The fifth castle, Port Bonnel, stood on the coast between Antioch and Baghras. They formed a defence line for the principality, whereby the Templars functioned as autonomous land owners. Baghras and Dabsak were conquered by Saladin in 1188; the secretary and biographer of Saladin described them as 'formidable weapons of the protagonists of the infidels.' There were enough provisions, but the number of defenders was minimal. After all, in the previous

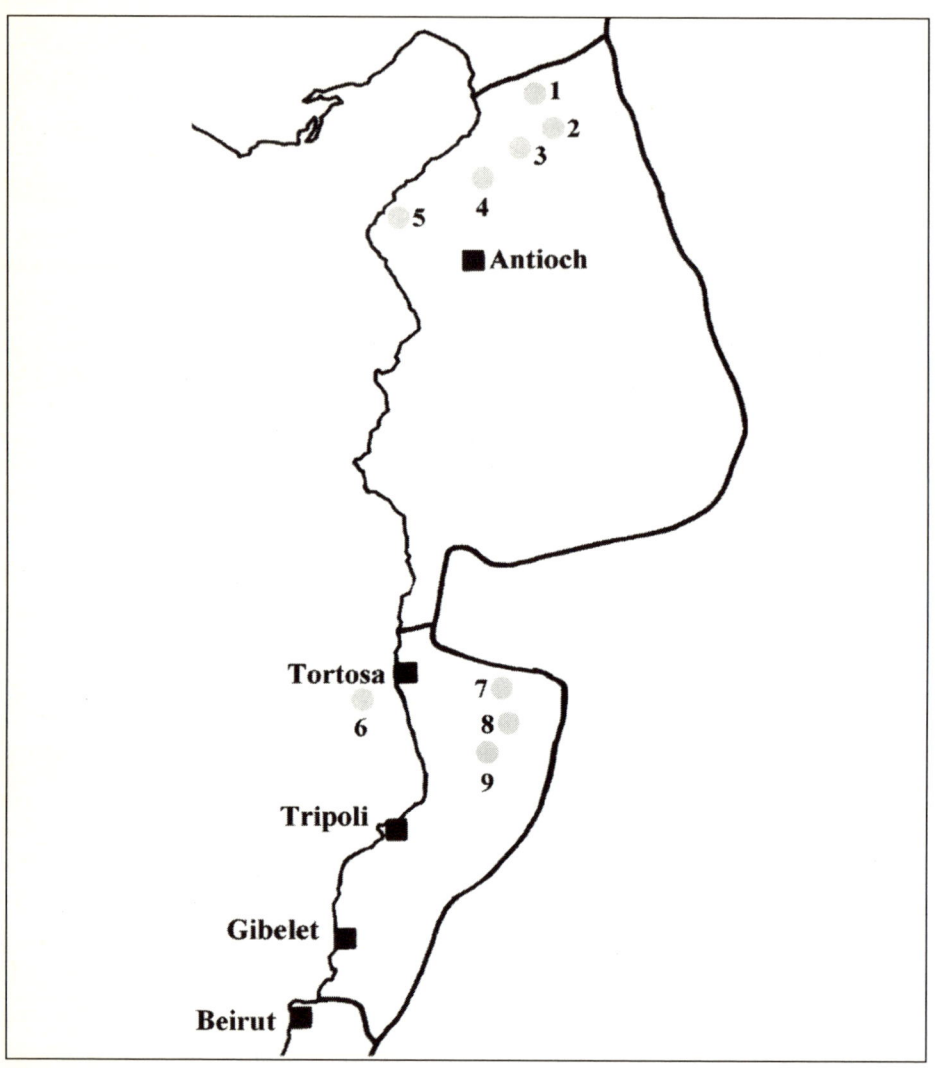

Map of the castles in Antioch and Tripoli.

Antioch
1 La Roche de Roussel (1136-1269)
2 La Roche Guillaume (1140-1266)
3 Darbsak (1136-1188)
4 Baghras (1130-1188 and 1216-1269)
5 Port Bonnel (1130-1269)

Tripoli
6 Ruad (1291-1303)
7 La Colee (1243-1289)
8 Chastel-Blanc (1171-1271)
9 Al-Arimah (1152-?)

Tortosa (1152-1291)
Gibelet (1210-1231 and 1261-1266)

year there were, more than three hundred Templars killed, before and during the battle of Hattin.

In 1191, Saladin wanted to flatten Baghras to the ground, but Prince Leo of the neighbouring Armenia had, in the meantime, captured the castle. Leo was actually a vassal of the principality of Antioch and the Templars regarded his possession of the castle as theft. After many discussions, a few squabbles and even the excommunication of Prince Leo by the Pope, they received Baghras back in 1216. In 1268 Antioch was conquered by the Muslims and a year later they left their castles of Baghras, La Roche de Roussel and Port Bonnel, of their own free will. Darbsak had already fallen in 1237, despite the stiff resistance of the Templars. Shortly before this, they had recaptured it from the Muslims. Only twenty of the 120 knights from the castle of Baghras, who tried to drive back the besiegers, survived the conflict at Darbsak that year.

THE FLEET OF THE TEMPLARS

In the Statutes of the Templars there is very little attention paid to their naval activities. It reads that the Commander of the shipyard in Acre is answerable to the Commander of the Kingdom of Jerusalem. There are no rules about the behaviour on board ships, the way of carrying out war at sea and suchlike. That was because their boats were only used for transport in the beginning.

Just after 1291, so the chroniclers suggest, warships were built in Cyprus. Thanks to the conflict between Western Europe and the Middle East, the reciprocal shipping traffic grew intensely. The large amount of goods from the Western dependencies, were transported rather quickly on their own boats. Acre was the most important import harbour, but the Templars were also established in other coastal cities, such as in Caesarea, Tyre, Sidon, Tripoli, Tortosa and Gibelet. The castle of Port Bonnel, in the North, also stood on the coast. The Templars also transported people: their own members and pilgrims. Italian merchants sometimes sold the pilgrims for the slave market, in Muslim places. The pilgrims trusted that the Templars did not involve themselves in these sorts of practices; above all the Templars ships sailed with an armed escort.

According to a contract from 1234, the Templars and the Hospitallers were not allowed to transport more than six thousand pilgrims a year from Marseille. This restriction was imposed by the other merchants. There was no duty charged on goods which were intended for the battle in the Holy Land. The Templars had possessed their own shipyard in Marseille since 1216. From the contracts that the Templars made with the English dynasty, the nature of trading between England and mainland Europe is apparent. From La Rochelle in France, wine was shipped to various harbour cities in England, including Plymouth. This was carried out by their ship the Templière. They transported the wool, which was produced on the English farms, to Flanders.

From various contracts, we also know a couple of names of the ships of the Templars: Bonne Aventure (1248), La Rose du Temple (1288-1290), Potta Johannis (1299) and La Bénite; the crew of this last ship numbered 33 hands. From some chronicles it appears that their merchant ships were used on different occasions for war activities, in 1188 near the city of Tyre and in 1219 at the conquering of the Egyptian town of Damietta. The most well know ship of the Order was the Falcon, which they purchased from Genoa. According to a chronicler, it was the largest ship of that time. In the days after Acre, the Falcon transported citizens for large sums of money to Château Pèlerin. Captain Roger of Flor, a non-knight member, handed the proceeds over to the Templars. There were rumours that he had held some money back and when the Grand Master wanted to talk to him about this, he sailed to Marseille. Roger left the ship behind, then exited the Order and entered into the service of the Byzantine Emperor. The Grand Master expelled him from the Order and told the Pope about him. After the fall of Acre in 1291, the Templars limited their hostilities chiefly to piracy. James of Molay, the last Grand Master, let write an essay to materialise in 1307, a new Crusade, in which he promised the Pope that he would make ships and men available.

Some people (Charpentier, Von Buttlar) believe that the Templars were the actual discoverers of America. They could have been responsible for a sudden large amount of silver, which was brought into Europe in the twelfth and thirteenth century. According to Charpentier this happened because the Templars had collected this from the silver mines of Mexico and North America. They could have copied the maps for these expeditions from the Muslims. In the chronicles, the Templars were not really known as extraordinary sailors. They possessed various wharfs, but they bought many of their ships from the Italian city-states. The Italians were Lord and Master of the Mediterranean Sea and were geared towards building their boats on this inland waterway. It is then very questionable as to whether these vessels were suitable for a journey across the ocean. In addition, the Italians had the best relationship of all the Christians with the Muslims, because of their many commercial treaties. If the Muslims had been in possession of maps of the Atlantic Ocean, the Italians (after the Muslims!) would have been the most suitable candidates for the discovering of

America. Here also, there is not one letter to be found in the archives about this.

Von Buttlar goes even one step further by alleging that the Portuguese, Henry the Navigator, could make his great discoveries thanks to the Templars. After the abolishment of the Order in 1312, the Order of Christ was established in Portugal seven years later. It was a continuation of the Templars and many ex-members joined the new military order. Vasco da Gama (1460-1524) was a member of this order and Henry the Navigator (1394-1460) was even Grand Master. Henry dedicated his life to sailing around the Cape of Good Hope. His structural approach in the field of navigation, cartography and ship building, later placed others in a position to navigate the seas of the world. With ups and downs, the subjects of Henry managed to sail along part of the West coast of Africa. First, Vasco da Gama was successful in going to India via South Africa in 1497, thanks to an Arabian pilot. There was about 180 years between the end of the Templars and the rounding of the Cape. From this, the conclusion still cannot be made that the Templars transferred secret information about the sailing, to the Order of Christ.

Columbus was married to the daughter of an former member of the Order of Christ and could, still according to Von Buttlar, thanks to the knowledge of the Templars, make his journey to America in 1492. If the Templars had already been to America in the thirteenth century, it is peculiar that their descendants took nearly two centuries to repeat this achievement. The argument of Charpentier and Von Buttlar is typical of the way that the Templars were involved in history. Columbus discovered America in 1492: because Columbus had relations with the Order of Christ and because this order recieved the previous Portuguese Templar possessions, in 1319 (seven years after the end of the Templars), it can be no other way than that the Templars were the first Europeans who went to America. Students from primary schools know that a horse is an animal, but that the turning around of this statement would be considered an absolute error.

JERUSALEM

The Temple platform is holy ground for Jews, Christians and Muslims. It is on Mount Moria, where according to the Old Testament Abraham wanted to sacrifice his son Isaac. Abraham is seen as a patriarch by the three large religions. Later, a thousand years before Christ, King Solomon built his temple on the Temple platform. In the beginning of the seventh century, the archangel Gabriel led the prophet Mohammed to this mountain to begin his ascension from the rocks. The Muslims built the Rock dome and the al-Aqsa mosque a couple of years later. They could do this undisturbed, because in 683 they had peacefully taken control of the city from the Byzantines.

In 1099, Jerusalem was conquered from the Egyptians by the Crusaders. That happened in a terrible manner; practically all the Jews and Muslims were murdered. Because of this, there were plenty of buildings available for the occupiers. Baldwin II provided shelter for Hugh of Payns and his comrades in a wing of his palace, previously the al-Aqsa mosque. Every Christian knows of the vanished Temple of Solomon and the Order did not need an advertising agency in order to choose a meaningful name: directly after this, the group named themselves the Order of the Temple.

Baldwin II moved home shortly thereafter and gave his residence, a number of outbuildings and the incorporated square, to the Templars. They extended their territory and added new buildings. Solomons Temple, as the al-Aqsa mosque became known, stood on a large square. The square was situated against the West city wall and the Templars were responsible for the defense of this part of the city. Near the entrance, encircled by a church, was the Mount of Olives and the garden of Gethsemane. In the middle of the square was the Templum Domini, nowadays this is called the Dome of the Rocks, with a golden cross on the top. In 1142, this building, thus originally a mosque, was dedicated to their church. Pilgrims were very impressed by the Templars complex, an administrative, financial, religious and military centre. A pilgrim claimed that there were at least ten thousand horses stalled inside the square. Another maintained that it was two thousand horses or fifteen hundred camels, but these amounts seem over exaggerated; five hundred is more likely. It remained the headquarters of the Order of the Temple until 1187. They had a number of gardens there and a cemetery. In other parts of Jerusalem, the Templars received and bought various other buildings, between 1150 and 1180. Thanks to Frederick II, Jerusalem was again in the hands of the Christians between 1229 and 1244, with the exception of the Temple platform. In 1243, the Templars again received the control of their original possession in and around the Temple platform. A year later they left this of their own free will; they would never return (see page 96).

Acre

King Baldwin conquered Acre in 1104, with the help of the fleet of Genoa and made it the most important harbour town in the Kingdom. Acre was accessible in practically all weathers. The Templars had various properties there. After the fall of Jerusalem, Saladin also drove the Christians out of Acre, but four years later the Christians returned again after a siege lasting two years. It was then the headquarters of the Order of the Temple, until Acre was recaptured in 1291 by the Egyptians. The Templar of Tyre described the possessions as follows:

> *The Temple was the strongest place of the city, largely situated along the sea-shore, like a castle. At its entrance it had a high and strong tower, the wall of which was twenty-eight feet thick. On each side of the tower was a smaller tower, and on each of these was a gilded lion passant, as large as an ox. Those four lions, together with the gold and the labour, cost 1.500 Saracen bezants, and were a noble sight to look upon. On the other side, near the Street of the Pisans, there was another tower, and near the Street of St Anne, was a large and noble palace, which was the Master's. In front of the house of the nuns of St Anne was another high tower, which had bells, and a very noble and high church. There was another ancient tower on the sea-shore, which Saladin had built one hundred years before, in which the Templars kept its treasure, and it was so close to the sea that the waves washed against it. Within the Temple area there were other beautiful and noble houses, which I shall not describe here.*

The Templars church in Acre had a special artefact. It was a cross that was made of material from a bath in which Christ had washed. On the request of the population, the brothers regularly carried it in a procession through the city.

It is said that the cross possessed healing qualities and ensured rain in times of drought. It attracted many extra pilgrims, therefore income, to the Templars church in Acre.

X. The image of the Templars

INTRODUCTION

It is not easy to gain a clear picture of the popularity of the Templars. We have various sources at our disposal, such as chronicles, deeds of transfer, prose and poetry. These writings do not always glow with impartiality. Matthew Paris was an admirer of Frederick II and it was therefore logical that he was critical of the Hospitallers and the Templars. At the same time he wrote about the fellow countrymen of the Emperor, the Teutonic Knights, with praise.

The texts in the transfer deeds are very positive about the Templars, but we do not know who formulated them. It could be that this was done by the Order itself and they would have taken their own concern into account. Minstrels from the Middle Ages sung what their customers wanted to hear. Besides, we know only a limited part of their repertoire.

An additional problem is that the opinion towards the military orders changed over time. Bernard of Clairvaux was very clear in his propaganda pamphlet *De Laude:* knights could be monks and with this receive absolution for their sins. In the thirteenth century the military orders had competition from the Mendicants, such as the Franciscans and the Dominicans. After the 1230's these monks gained many monasteries throughout Europe, which was undoubtedly connected to an altered vision towards Christianity.

In short, the picture is fragmentary and incomplete. Helen Nicholson (1995) performed detailed investigation into the image of the military orders in the twelfth and thirteenth century. On the basis of the chronicles, she determined the image of the Orders amongst 'citizens, farmers and outsiders.' She came to the following conclusion:

> *In 1291 the Templars and the other international military orders were well-established religious orders, indispensable to pope and kings, widely respected*

for their wealth and power, if not always their virtues. Christendom looked to them to spearhead the recapture of the Holy Land, after undergoing a few fundamental, necessary reforms to render them more efficient. The orders were not so corrupt that they could not be saved. The concept of the military order remained unquestioned, and abolition unthinkable; at least, no one appears to have thought of it.

It is determined that the rulers, including Kings and Popes, thought positively about the Templars. They enlisted them to carry out their financial household management and provided them with many privileges. Practically all monarchs and Church leaders used members of military orders for important public assignments. Even Philip IV, at whose instigation Order of the Temple was abolished in 1312, acted as their supporter for a long time.

The relationship between the Templars and the Muslims

One of the many theses about the Templars is that they had a peculiar relationship with the Muslims. Some authors go so far as to maintain that the Templars were pursued by Philip IV due to their positive opinion of the Muslims. The Order would have wanted, in a underhand way, to effectuate a symbiose between Christianity and Islam. They then cite from the chronicle of the Muslim Usāmah, who wrote in the period 1140 to 1185. In his autobiography, he went into detail about his experiences with the Franks, whom he had a low opinion about.

Usāmah was surprised by the fact that they found it acceptable for their women to have sexual relations with other men. The Muslim also spoke, with undisguised contempt, of the legal system of the Christians. Their method of submersing in water or the fighting of a duel to indicate a guilty party, he did not like at all. Usāmah regarded this manner of administrating justice inferior to that of the Muslims. The only positive thing about the Franks that he could say was that they were excellent fighters. The autobiographer was, besides this, impressed with their courage.

What does catch ones attention is Usāmah wrote about the Templars, that they were his friends:

> *Whenever I visited Jerusalem I always entered the Al-Aqsa mosque, beside which stood a small mosque which the Franks had converted into a church.*

> *When I used to enter the Al-Aqsa mosque, which was occupied by the Templars, who were my friends, the Templars would evacuate the little adjoining mosque so that I might pray in it.*

Also in the thirteenth century, some individual Templars had a good relationship with the Muslims. Grand Master William of Beaujeu received, at the end of the thirteenth century, for payment, information from a high ranking Muslim about the plans of the Egyptian Sultan.

On the whole this is true, but this is about exceptions to the rule. The Templars could kill Muslims without being punished and they took this very seriously. There are many examples of the putting of this mandate into practice. Contra wise, the Muslims paid back the Templars in the same way. Saladin was noble towards common knights, but he made an exception for the Hospitallers and the Templars. After the battle of Hattin in 1187, he had them killed in a ritual way. His successors, without exception, did this too; in addition to this, they had no compassion whatsoever for the Christians. At the end of the thirteenth century, the Muslims behaved in the same manner as the first crusaders had done two hundred years earlier. The Christian cities of Antioch (1268), Tripoli (1289) and Acre (1291) were flattened to the ground. The inhabitants were killed or (if they were young, strong and beautiful) traded on the slave market.

Another persistent misunderstanding is that the Templars gathered all sorts of knowledge from the Muslims. Architecture, alchemy and cartography are a few of the branches of knowledge that the Order has supposed to have learned from the Muslims. We do not come across a single example of this in any chronicle. Muslims made use of Greek fire, an extremely flammable mixture that could not be extinguished with water. It was an effective weapon in the battle against castles and a compact army. The Western Christians did not possess these means; at least no source has made reference to it. If the Templars were students of the Arabian scientists, then the producing of Greek fire would have been the subject of their first lesson. They were evidently not able to make Greek fire or to hire people to do so.

There is only one possible conclusion: other than a few exceptions, Muslims and Templars saw each other, vice versa, as enemies of their belief. In the Middle Ages the dissentients were all too quickly sentenced to death and both parties executed this verdict with passion and without any kind of trial.

The Western Monarchs

Up to the beginning of the fourteenth century, the Western European monarchs regarded it as a holy duty to take the cross. Only a few converted this wish into concrete actions. The monarchs, who did undertake a journey to the Middle East, relied heavily on the military orders during their pilgrimage. They played an important role in the collecting of taxes in order to pay for the journeys and were the most important military advisors.

The French royal house

The French King, Louis VII (1137-1180) was convinced that without the Templars his Crusade in 1148 would have failed. Out of gratitude, after his return, he gifted the Order the city of Savigny and an annual amount of money. From that moment on, the Templars were the most important bankers of the French royal house. The Kings saw to it that the bursar of the Parisian temple was appointed on intercession from them.

In 1160, a conflict arose between Louis VII and the Templars. He had entrusted three members of the Order with the guarding of a trio of castles in Vexin (see page 129). These stood in the then borderland between England and France. Under suspicious circumstances, the Templars relinquished the strongholds to the English King, Henry II. The three members of the Order of the Temple fled to England, where they were heartily welcomed by Henry. This event had no further influence on the relationship with the French royal house, because Louis bound no consequences to it.

Philip II August (1180-1223), participant in the Third Crusade of 1191, ordered that during his absence the revenues from his territories had to be paid to the Parisian Temple. He furnished the Templars and the Hospitallers with a fortune in 1222. With this money they had to keep three hundred knights, in addition to their normal contingent, in service for three years.

Louis IX, who reigned from 1226 to 1270, held just as much esteem for

Saint Louis.

the Templars; his son was born at Château Pèlerin in 1251. Between both of his Crusades he provided large sums of money to the Order for the defending of the Holy Land. They functioned not only as his bankers, but also that of his mother, brothers and sons.

The most well known brother of Louis, Charles of Anjou, became King of, amongst other countries, Sicily, Naples and Jerusalem. Charles financially supported the Order and in turn the Templars looked after the Kings interests in the Kingdom of Jerusalem.

The successors of Louis IX, Philip III and IV, forbad further extending of the Templars possessions. Actually, this was not unusual: the monarchy became more important and the sovereigns saw with envious eyes that ecclesiastical organisations controlled large parts of the Kingdom. In addition to the military orders, it also concerned the Franciscan and the Dominican brotherhoods. Philip IV, who became King of France in 1285, managed to considerably develop the authority of the monarchy. He nevertheless made use of the financial skills of the Templars in the first ten years of his reign.

The French historian Delisle gave a striking summary of this and he showed that the Templars were of service to the King in nine different ways. Included in this was the paying of justiciaries throughout the whole country, the financial commerce with the Jews from Auvergne, the costs of minting coins and the collecting of the tenths for the recent war with the Kingdom of Aragon.

The Templars were also financially responsible for the household management of the King and the Princes, and they arranged the pensions and the loans for many servants of the royal household. In 1295, some of these activities were taken over by a new royal organisation, but in 1306 the Templars still provided the outstanding payment of the soldiers who had been active in Picardy and Flanders (The Battle of the Golden Spurs of 1302).

The English monarchy
The Order of the Temple was a French orientated organisation. Nevertheless, they were popular in England and received many possessions there, though less than in France. The fact that they obtained a foothold in England was because the Crusade was a favourite activity and because French had been the language used in the higher circles since 1066 (William the Conqueror). Just as in France, the Templars in England were supported by the royal house. King Henry I (1100-1135) met Hugh of Payns in 1128 in Normandy. According to a chronicler 'the King received him with a lot of respect and gave Hugh many valuables, including gold and silver.' His successor, Stephen (1135-1154), added

icing to the cake and gave the Templars many estates. Both Stephen and his wife had family ties with various leaders of the First Crusade, like Godfrey of Boullion.

Henry II (1154-1189), due to his involvement in the murder of Cardinal Thomas Becket, placed a large amount of money at the disposal of the Templars and the Hospitallers. Shortly before the battle of Hattin, Gerard Ridefort paid for a mercenary army with this money, in spite of the agreements. Henry did not hold this against the Order, because a year later they played an important role in the collecting of the so called Saladin tenths. Henry's son, Richard I (1189-1199), was the first of the English monarchs who participated in a Crusade. His sympathy for the Templars is described in Chapter IV. A significant anecdote about Richard I and the Templars was circulating. The well known clergyman, Fulk Neuilly, advised the King to marry off his three daughters. When the King said that he did not have any daughters, the priest explained that he meant that figuratively. He thought of the three characteristics: 'Pride,' 'Avarice,' and 'Sensuality.' Richard would then have said that he could marry Pride with the Templars, Avarice with the Cistercian Order and Sensuality with the Church rulers. The members of the Templars were, just as those from the other military orders, definitely proud. It was a usual quality of knights: they had trust in their own capacities. Clerics thought of themselves as more Christian and better than other people. In this regard, the monk-soldiers were perhaps twice as proud as the commoners.

King John, the brother of Richard I, used the London Temple as a storage place for the Crown Jewels, but his son Henry III (1216-1272), thought that Paris was a more suitable place. In 1261 he allowed these jewels, due to his problems with the barons, be taken to the Parisian branch of the Templars. King John lent large sums of money from the Order of the Temple. In 1214, he deposited a huge amount of money in the French Templars house in La Rochelle.

The Templars must have subsidised his allies in Poitou with it. This did not put the Templars in a difficult position, although the French King could have quite easily taken this as a hostile deed. In the accusations against the Templars in 1308, there was no mention of high treason or espionage. This whilst large areas of France were still under the rule of the English. Despite the fact that the English and French Kings were regularly at war with each other, the Order managed, to a satisfactory degree, to keep the trust of both brawlers.

John was a suspicious person and had a very select party of advisors. The Master of the province of England, Aymmeric of Saint Maurer, was one of

Richard the Lion Heart.

them. Henry III also trusted the Order; they lent him lots of money and fulfilled all sorts of public functions to serve him. In 1227, Henry furnished the Order with extreme privileges, which were confirmed by Edward I in 1285. They gave the Order complete say over their English territories and the inhabitants. In 1237, Henry donated a large sum of money to the Templars, which was specifically intended for paying the ransom after the defeat at Darbsak.

When the English King visited Paris in 1254, he lodged in the French Templars building. It would have been the only place in Paris which was large enough to accommodate his entourage. He wanted to be buried in the Templars church in London, but after the restoration of Westminster Abbey, this became his last resting place. His regent, William Marshal (see Chapter III) was actually buried in the London temple.

Edward I (1272-1307), was the second English monarch who made the journey to the Holy Land. He did that in the years 1271 and 1272, when he was still Crown Prince. In order to pay for the trip, he lent a fortune from the English Templars. At the end of his life, in 1305, he informed the Grand Master that he wanted to go on a Crusade again.

The London fortress was not always so safe. In 1263, Edward I (then Crown Prince) pushed into the complex, despite opposition from the Templars, and broke a number of safes open. Inside was a large amount of money (ten thousand pounds), which the Order saved for different barons and merchants. His son, Edward II, followed in his fathers footsteps in July 1307, therefore shortly before the arrests of the Templars. He took approximately fifty thousand pounds in money and jewels out of the treasury of the Order. This had nothing to do with negative conduct in regard to the Order. The King just needed money and thought that this was a legitimate action. During the trial against the Templars, he carried out the instructions of the Pope with great reluctance. At the same time, he opposed the plans of his father-in-law Philip IV, to torture the English Templars.

The other rulers
The Order had comparatively few possessions in the German Empire. That was mainly due to the rivalry with the Teutonic Knights. The only monarch who had problems with the Templars was the German Emperor, Frederick II (1211-1250). Together with the Hospitallers, the Templars resisted his presence in the Middle East. Both military orders did this at the command of the Pope, who had in fact excommunicated Frederick II in 1229. The discord between

Frederick and the Orders actually dated back to before then. In 1220, the German Emperor had specified that the military orders did not have permission to, amongst other things, simply extend their territory. He was afraid that they would have total possession of Sicily in the very near future. Frederick was well aware of the importance of this island to the Templars.

During the early stages of his rule, he had donated various plots of land to the Order, and in 1223 he instituted the privileges that his forefathers had given to the Templars. That did not prevent him from sending a hundred Muslim slaves, who had worked for the Hospitallers and the Templars on Sicily, home in 1227 without compensation. Only after his death did Frederick II, via his will, give the Order all their possessions back.

When Manfred, partly thanks to the Master of South Italy, succeeded his half brother in 1258, better times dawned for the Order in this part of the German Empire. In 1262, he forbad the interference of his vassals in the territories of the Templars and he placed the Order under his protection. Charles of Anjou, the brother of the French King, overthrew Manfred in 1266 and succeeded him as ruler of Sicily and Naples. This had a favourable effect on the position of the Templars. They received extensive rights to export numerous goods from the harbours to the Holy Land.

The rulers of the Iberian Peninsula were constantly at war with the Muslims during the existence of the Order of the Temple. They could then also make good use of the help of the Templars. In Spain in particular, at least five other local military orders operated, besides the Templars and the Hospitallers. These were actively supported by the Kings, because they saw that the Templars and the Hospitallers placed their first priority in the Middle East. Once they were reproached for this, and Papal pressure was necessary to move the large Orders into being more active on the Iberian Peninsula.

The Hungarian King Andrew II (1205-1235), supported the Templars to the same extent and gave them various possessions. His son, who reigned from 1235 to 1270, annulled all these gifts. He did this with all the military orders, beginning with the Teutonic Knights: these were too influential for his liking. He confiscated the possessions of the Hospitallers, the Templars and the Order of Saint Lazarus because of the plundering of the Mongolians. Bela IV needed the wealth of the military orders to please his subjects.

There were no mighty Kings in the remaining territories of Europe. Italy consisted of city-states without these having a national influence. The fact that the Order had dozens of assets here, says enough about their popularity.

THE LOWER ECHELON

The Templars owned at least a thousand preceptories, spread throughout Europe. Each of the monasteries had many possessions in the immediate surroundings. The Order received, over a period of time, innumerable gifts from Counts, landowners, Bishops, Cardinals and from common people. All of them presumed that with such a gift they served God and inherited eternal life. In this respect, the military orders did not differ from the other monastic orders. Of course there were differences of opinion about their rights: numerous Papal pronouncements gave testimony to this to a great extent. This was really no different with similar institutions. The image of the Order in the eyes of the lower echelon, did not deviate from that of the secular and ecclesiastical leaders.

THE POPES

Between Urban II, the instigator of the First Crusade, and Clement V, who abolished the Order of the Temple, there were no less then 35 Popes in power. The various counter Popes are not included in this number. Some official Popes ruled for less than a couple of years and therefore they could barely present themselves. All the remaining Church leaders considered the Holy Land as Western territory and stimulated the Crusade whole heartedly. To them, the Muslims were heathens and they should be fought with the sword and the military orders were the ones who had to carry out this task for the Holy Chair. Only one or two gave out critical Bulls about the military orders, but, without exception, the Popes thought positively about the phenomennon of monk-soldiers and therefore supported them.

Paschal II (1099-1118) gave the Order of Saint John (the Hospitallers) a number of important rights in 1113. He sanctioned all (future) gifts, gave them permission to collect tenths on their properties and ordained the obedience of the European territories to the Grand Master. They could appoint their own leader and were only answerable to the Pope. At that time there was no mention of soldier duties; it only involved caring for the pilgrims. With this, Paschal created a precedent from which the Templars would later profit.

Honorius II (1124-1130) gifted the Templars with similar rights via the Council of Troyes in 1129. The important Bull, *Omne datum optimum*, of 1139 originated from Pope Innocent II (1130-1143). It was an acknowledgement of all privileges, donations and tax dispensations which the Order had received so far. But the Pope added something to this. In flowery biblical language, Innocent sang the praises of the Order of the Temple and gave, amongst other things, the Order the right to appoint priests themselves. Their independency, with regard to the regular clergy, was complete from that moment on.

The Pope was also quite explicit in his Bull of 1139, with the clarification of the tenths. All leaseholders and owners of ground paid 10 percent of their assets and the harvest to the regular clergy. The clergymen thought that if the Templars received a donation, they had the right to this tax. The Bull, *Omne datum optimum*, instructed that, if the bishop of the area agreed, this 'ten' should go to the Templars. According to documents from this time, this became a conventional agreement between the Templars and the other ecclesiastical authorities. The fact that the Templars had priests themselves strengthened their position. They in fact now cared for the salvation of the souls of their parishioners and therewith the right to charge for this service. The Order of the Temple was also exempt from all ecclesiastical taxes and they could collect on a certain amount of days per year in some of their churches.

Innocent II was under the influence of the great protagonist of the Order, Bernard of Clairvaux. In 1135, at the Council of Pisa, the Pope had already gifted an important donation to the Templars and called upon his Bishops to do the same. Eugenius III (1145-1153) went one step further, and in 1145 he permitted the Templars to own their own churches and cemeteries. Due to the offertories and the Masses, this was a nice extra source of income. That was at the expense of the existing clergy, who regularly protested against this.

These privileges altered the position of the Order in society. In the first instance, the Templars had broken away from society; the Papal decisions brought them back to the normal world. Besides, with these liberties the Templars were not placed in a unique position: the monks of Cluny, Clairvaux and the other Orders possessed similar privileges.

Eugenius III managed to be one of the few Popes to participate in a Crusade from beginning to end. Together with Bernard of Clairvaux he formed the duo which propagandised the Second Crusade.

Alexander III (1159-1181) was the first Pope to make use of the financial network of the Templars. The Order provided him with large loans and collected sums of money for him. The Pope confirmed the Bull, *Omne datum optimum* from 1139, at least four times. Naturally he did this because the regular clergy were still having problems with the privileged position of the Order of the Temple. He gave out 88 Bulls in which he protected the privileges of the Order.

Innocent III.

On one occasion he admonished the Order by letter and he ordered them to respect the rights of a French monastery. Alexander III did not succeed in organising a Crusade and he compensated for that by supporting the Order of the Temple. He also opposed the military purpose of the Hospitallers. He was afraid that this would be at expense of their original objective: the caring of the poor and the sick. The Order did not really care about this. The Hospitallers had already been militarily active in the Holy Land since 1136 and they were apparently unstoppable.

During the papacy of Alexander, the Third Lateran Council took place in Rome in 1179. Under the leadership of William of Tyre, the famous chronicler and Archbishop, the clergy made a frontal attack on the privileges of the military orders. It in no way affected the position of the Templars. Alexander gave the impression that he appreciated the monk-soldiers more than the regular clergy.

His successors, Urban III (1183-1187) and Clement III (1187-1191), responsible for the Third Crusade, also issued the Bull of 1139 again.

More than the other Popes, Innocent III (1198-1216) wanted to strengthen the position of the Church. He thought that the Pope, as the representative of God, had the authority over every person. It was logical that he supported the military orders wherever he could. In his more than fifty Bulls about the Templars, he did not allow for any misunderstandings; they fell under the responsibility of the Pope. Innocent criticised the monk-soldiers a few times, but in most Bulls he upheld their rights. He institutionalised that the Grand Master reported to the Pope about the situation in the Holy Land. He was the first to enlist the military orders at the distribution of the Papal wealth in the Middle East. Innocent gave the Teutonic Knights the same rights as their colleagues and propagated the Crusades like no other. The Fourth and the Fifth were realised, thanks to his effort, and he was just as much responsible for the massacre of the Cathars.

Gregory IX (1227-1241) had a lot of trouble with Frederick II and, just like his predecessors, he regarded the military orders as his allies. He gave the later Grand Master, Reginald of Vichiers absolution for the committing of simony. The well-being of the Templars soul was close to Gregory's heart. In 1238, he issued a Bull in which he consented that priests from the Jacobean Church could give forgiveness, to the Templars who were taken prisoner by the Muslims, for their sins.

His successor, Innocent IV (1243-1254) was aware of the financial needs of the military orders. He safeguarded them from the payment of taxes for the Sixth Crusade, because according to him, they had already contributed to the conflict against the Muslims. In addition, Innocent forbad all ecclesiastical leaders from excommunicating the members of the Order. With this, he repeated a Bull from one of his predecessors. This evidently was a regular occurrence; that the bishops in conflict with the Order clutched to this powerful means.

All Popes were originally from Western Europe. None of them had ever visited the Holy Land whilst in duty. However, when the Archbishop of Jerusalem coincidentally visited the Italian city of Viterbo, such a Papal election was taking place. As usual, it was a complicated procedure, in which strangers, not necessarily Cardinals, were not always without a chance. The Archbishop of Jerusalem was chosen as Pope and took on the name of Urban IV (1261-1264). It goes without saying that he propagandised a Crusade, but without result.

Gregory X (1271-1276) was also committed to the destiny of the Franks and placed 'the mother of all journeys' on the agenda of the Council at Lyon. Before he was Pope, he had been in the Holy Land for two years and heard of his appointing when he was on Crusade with Crown Prince Edward. The leading Western barons promised to help the Pope, but they considered themselves to be discharged of their promise after his death.

THE BEGINNING OF THE END OF THE TEMPLARS

Just as his predecessors, Boniface VIII (1294-1303) was well-disposed towards the Templars. He issued four favourable Bulls for the Templars. Boniface tried to mediate in the disagreement between the King of Cyprus and the Templars. He asked King Edward I of England not to levy tax on the goods that were brought to Cyprus. From the outset, the Pope dreamt about another Crusade; all European monarchs should participate under his leadership. He joined with his predecessors and wanted to discuss the integration of the most important military orders. The perculiarism of the pontificate of Boniface, was that he came into conflict with the French King, Philip IV. Just as Innocent III a century earlier, Boniface considered the Pope as the mightiest ruler of the Church and the world. But society had in fact changed: royalty had evolved into an institute which did not tolerate any ecclesiastical interference into secular affairs any more.

The first conflict between the Pope and Philip IV blew over. In 1296, Boniface determined that every layman who, without the express permission of the Pope, obligated clergy to pay taxes would be excommunicated. Philip reacted to this with a ban on the export of money and valuables by seculars and clergymen. Foreigners were denied the right to stay in France. These prohibitions hindered the money collection of the Papal servants. Boniface changed his mind by declaring that the French King could tax the clergy only when in dire need. Upon this, the French King withdrew his restrictive legislation.

In 1300, the conflict escalated, because Philip had arrested a French bishop on the suspicion of high treason. The Pope did not accept this, and publicised a Bull in which he, in an arrogant manner, demanded a sort of 'pilgrimage to Canossa' from Philip. Philip took possession of the Bull and convened a meeting of his most important subjects. The gathering established the sovereignty in secular affairs of the French Kings in 1302. At the assembly, it was proposed that a council be held, which had to take measures for the well being of the Church. The Pope was quick to react and in a Bull from 1302, he let it be known that he was the boss:

> *We pronounce, declare, determine and call out to every creature that wants to save his soul, must defer to the Pope of Rome.*

Philip ultimately saw this as an undermining of his authority. He held a sort of trial in the Louvre in 1303, in which he accused the Pope of, amongst other things, heresy, idolatry, simony, sodomy and murder.

The Master of the Templars in France, Hugh of Pairaud, signed the petition of the King along with his colleague from the Hospitallers. Philip wanted to remove the Pope, hereafter Boniface in turn wanted to excommunicate Philip. William of Nogaret, advisor to the French King, left with a small army to go to Italy and threatened the Pope, in his own palace, with death. Boniface was released after a couple of days because of the pressure from the residents of Rome, but he only survived this brutal attack for a month. In a way, Philip IV was responsible for the death of Boniface. The 84 year old Pope was extremely shocked by the heartless treatment by a servant of the King. His successor reigned for less than a year and was decidedly different to Boniface: pious, worthy and forgiving. He reconciled with the French King and annulled all sanctions against Philip IV.

The conflict between Philip and Boniface VIII had far reaching consequences for the Templars. The monarch had learned his lesson: there could never again be a Pope who wanted to impair the power of the French King. In addition, it was evident from the quarrel with Boniface that Philip could allow himself to put the Pope under pressure and even treat him with contempt. He would use this experience in his attack on the Order of the Temple. In this regard, the Order became the victim of the conflict between the Church and the state. The death of Boniface marked the end of the pretensions of the Church; the leading role of Popes in the world was gone forever.

XI. Fighting a losing battle

THE LAST GRAND MASTERS

Theobald Gaudin (1291-1293)
Few Templars, after the fall of Acre, succeeded in escaping to Sidon, where Theobald Gaudin was chosen as Grand Master. He was Commander of the Kingdom of Jerusalem and at that moment the highest in rank. No regular election took place. Theobald came from Chartres in France and was a member for many years. In 1261 he was taken prisoner, together with William of Beaujeu, by the Muslims. After his release, Theobald became the Commander of Acre and Château Pèlerin.

In 1291, a meeting of the Chapter General was held in Nicosia on Cyprus. There were at least four hundred brothers present; the majority came from the West of course. Again, it appeared that the Order was heavily dependant on the overseas areas. On 17th April 1293 Theobald Gaudin died, without having performed any notable feats.

James of Molay (1293-1314)
For the first time a rumour was circulating about the electing of a new Grand Master. James of Molay, with the promise that he did not want to become the new leader, led the election as Grand Commander. When it appeared as though Hugh of Pairaud would be choosen, James proclaimed himself as Grand Master. A knight made this statement during the trial of the Templars. It is indeed outstanding that, three days after the death of Theobald, James of Molay was chosen as Grand Master. Such a hasty appointment had never happened before.

James of Molay was a son of a French nobleman who was liege to the English King. He was born around 1250 and, according to him, a member of the Templars since 1265. When he came to the Holy Land in the beginning of the 1270's, he was disappointed that there was very little fighting. Together with

James of Molay.

a number of other young members, he complained to William of Beaujeu and he criticised him because of the fact that the Grand Master had signed treaties with the Muslims. Later he saw that William had no other choice. James told this during one of his interrogations during the trial against the Templars. As far as we know, James of Molay had not previously fulfilled an important function in the Order.

Practically immediately after his electing, James left to go to Europe: he wanted support for a new attack on the mainland. James of Molay was, in December 1294, witness to the abdication of Pope Celestine V and the succession of Boniface VIII. He visited the Kings of England, France, Naples and Aragon. The monarchs were however, too busy: Edward I and Philip IV fought a mutual war, Charles II of Naples wanted to reconquer Sicily and James II of Aragon was concentrated on the battle against the Moors. After a stay in Western Europe of three years, James of Molay left in 1296 to go to Cyprus, the new headquarters of the Templars, having achieved nothing.

WHO WANTS ANOTHER CRUSADE?

Europe does not care
The fall of Acre in 1291 marked the beginning of the last episode of the history of the Templars. The Order of the Temple presumed that the people in Western Europe were just as fanatic about the ideal of the Crusades as they were in the past. They did not understand that the disaster of Saint Louis had dampened the zest of the population. The Lord himself did not even allow a religious monarch

such as Louis IX to drive the heathens out of the 'Christian areas.' Towards the end of the eleventh century the cry 'God wants it' was widely accepted, but two hundred years later, this made no impression whatsoever. In addition to this, the increasing growth of the economy was of benefit to the whole population. This was not particularly a stimulus for taking part in risky adventures. People preferred to stay at home in order to improve their own position there.

The important Kings said that they were interested in a new Crusade, but this was nothing more than an empty promise. King Edward I of England tried to conquer Scotland, and Philip IV (the Fair) of France was determined to break the power of the nobility in his country. The recovery of the French royalty was incompatible with years of absence of the King.

The Popes proclaimed, yet again, the conquering of the Holy Land, but their influence had declined with the growth of the power of the monarchy. The Italian city-states of Genoa, Venice and Pisa remained Lord and Master of the Mediterranean Sea. In the Egyptian coastal cities, they possessed large businesses and had no desire in jeopardising their commercial interests with a Crusade. If they fought, they did so against each other.

The Orders remained a powerful institute, but their status was based upon the past. Both rivals of the Templars, the Teutonic Knights and the Hospitallers, altered their policies. In the thirteenth century, the Teutonic Knights increasingly turned their attention to the conquering and the Christianisation of East Europe. The Hospitallers temporarily returned to Cyprus after the fall of Acre. With the help of Genoa, they conquered the island of Rhodes in 1309 after years of battling, where they founded an independent state. From there they remained focused on the reconquering of the Holy Land, but they were not capable of much more than piracy. Despite several large-scale Muslim attacks, they held the island until the sixteenth century. Shortly thereafter, Charles V donated the island of Malta to the Hospitallers. The Templars did not manage to make such a turn around; they continued to believe in a revival of the old times.

James was the only one

Looking back, it was a miracle that the Franks were able to occupy the Holy Land for so long. From the preceding, it has obviously been proven that this was not because of the feats of the colonists. If the Muslims had wanted, the Christians would have been driven out of the Middle East decades earlier. At the peak of the power of the Latin States, there were approximately 120 thousand Westerners in the Holy Land. They were surrounded by about 12 million

Muslims; only Syria and Egypt already numbered more than 5 million inhabitants.

From the chronicles of the time, it is evident that the Hospitallers and the Templars were respected for their past achievements. The Christians did not, on the whole, hold both military orders responsible for the loss of the Holy Land. People were fully aware of their efforts and the costs in money and human life. What was also remarkable in the West was their dissension, and it was therefore not by accident that the collaborating of both Orders was first discussed at the Council of Lyon in 1274. Pope Nicholas IV asked his archbishops to discuss this subject in 1291, at their provincial council. In addition to this, he asked the French King, Philip IV, for an opinion about a merger.

Pope Boniface VIII (1294-1303) continued the discussion and Grand Master, James of Molay wrote a memorandum to his successor Clement V, at the request of the Pope in 1305, about this subject. He was obviously absolutely against it and had many different deliberations about this. It wouldn't do to allow the two centuries old Orders, each with its own tradition, to disband to become an entirely new one. The gifts would decrease with the amalgamation of the military orders and the healthy competition, which there was now, would disappear. He compared the positions of the Franciscans and the Dominicans with those of the existing Orders. The Grand Master acknowledged the rivalry between both military orders, but accentuated the results which were recorded therewith. Very astutely, James ended his writing with a summing up of the benefits of a fusion. It would create a reduction in costs, because an efficient organisation would arise. The new Order would, so he wrote with a threatening undertone, be strong enough to adequately defend their rights.

Philip IV had his own thoughts about the unification of the Templars and the Hospitallers. According to the chronicle from 1308, Philip IV would have asked the Pope, in 1305, to unite both of the French orientated organisations under the name of the 'Order of Jerusalem.' This new Order had to be under the leadership of a son of the French monarchy. It is highly questionable as to whether the Templars were aware of these rumours, or judged the stories about the fusion on their true value. They were used to the hostilities in the Middle East and were deaf to the threats from the overseas areas. The blame fell upon James of Molay; he had not taken the criticisms about his Order seriously enough.

The Order on Cyprus

The Templars continued with their battle against the Muslims, but this time at sea. They bought, in 1293, to compliment their two warships, another six from Venice. In 1299, a Mongolian army supported by the Armenian troops, invaded Syria. During this battle, somewhere between Aleppo and Damascus, the Mongolian army commander wrote to the King of Cyprus, Henry II and the Grand Masters of the Templars and the Hospitallers and asked them to take part in the expedition. There was a conference to dicuss this request, but Henry and the Grand Masters of the Orders did not succeed in coming to a collective approach. A year later the Grand Masters spoke with each other again, together with Amalric, the brother of Henry II, and an ambassador of the Mongolians.

This time they did sign a treaty and in 1300, this led to several acts of piracy in the Egyptian and Syrian harbour cities. Riley-Smith (1967) recounts a remarkable raid by the Hospitallers. They plundered the Syrian city of Maraclea and, shortly thereafter, a Muslim army took them unaware. They had no problem in expelling the Hospitallers because these Christians were drunk. A knight and twenty Hospitallers soldiers died in this activity.

A couple of months later the Christians again carried out an attack on the mainland. An army of six hundred knights, half of the Hospitallers and Templars, and the rest of Cyprus, left to go to the island of Ruad. The warriors, from there out, possessed the city of Tortosa for a few days. The promised reinforcements from the Mongolians left them waiting. They came when the Christian army had withdrawn again.

The Templars left a sizeable army behind on the island of Ruad: 120 knights under the leadership of the Marshall, five hundred archers and four hundred supporting personnel. This was about half of the manpower of the castle of Safad. The Egyptians sent a fleet of sixteen warships from Tripoli in 1302 or 1303. The garrison strongly resisted, but was forced to negotiate a free passage. They were promised this, but the Muslims did not keep to their word. They took the Templars prisoner and transported them to Egypt. The mercenaries were beheaded. A rescue fleet from Cyprus came too late. The imprisoned Templars refused to renounce their faith and died in the dungeons of Cairo. Just as the other members of the Order, they did not want to know anything about the integration with Islam.

The Hospitallers and the Templars had established themselves on Cyprus, but King Henry II had mixed feelings about this. He had seen the Orders functioning on the mainland and was undoubtedly afraid that they wanted the same independent position as in the Holy Land. The Templars especially, did not behave like guests, but expressly interfered with the state business of the island. The King complained to Pope Boniface about the position of the Templars. Boniface tried to mediate by pointing out to Henry the role of the Templars in the Holy Land, and to the monk-soldiers the fact that they were received hospitably by the King. Henry curtailed the Order of their privileges by, amongst other things, stipulating that the extending of the territories on Cyprus would only be permitted if the Pope and the King found that acceptable.

The Templars and the Hospitallers, despite this, could not resist interfering with the governing of the island. Amalric, the brother of Henry, attempted a coup d'etat in 1306 and he was supported in this by the Templars. They would have lent him a large sum of money with which he could finance the coup. There was the threat of a civil war and the Grand Masters of the Templars and the Hospitallers acted as intermediaries. In 1307 an agreement was made, this was signed by the seals of Henry, Amalric and both of the Grand Masters. They confirmed the power of Amalric and ensured the dethroned King of an annual income, with the condition that he kept quiet. Henry definitely did not keep to his side of the bargain and started a rebellion against his brother. The Templars helped Amalric, and the Marshal of the Templars eventually managed to convince Henry to sign a new treaty. When the Marshal confirmed this agreement with his stamp, he appeared to have antagonised the ex-King with the words: 'Quod scripsi, scripsi.' This means: 'What I have written, that I have written.' These were the words which Pilatus spoke to the high priests when they insisted on replacing the text 'The King of the Jews' (INRI) with an inscription that Jesus had proclaimed that he was the King of the Jews. The Hospitallers were neutral at first, but later chose for Henry who, after the murder of Amalric in 1310, was reinstated into his old function. The Templars had yet again made the wrong choice.

James of Molay goes to Paris

In 1304 the Master of England, William de la More, received permission from King Edward I to go to Cyprus with his entourage. He could even take money with him, despite a general ban on the exporting of this. Edward wrote a letter to James of Molay shortly thereafter, in which he sounded the praises of William. He asked the Grand Master to send the English Master back as soon as possible. Edward, who had been in the Holy Land when he was Crown Prince, wanted to take part in a Crusade again. James had to fully inform the King of the situation in the Middle East via the Master. The King also wanted a plan of action for his pilgrimage.

At the request of Clement V, James of Molay put his thoughts about the new Crusade on paper. James said of himself, that he could not read, let alone write. He would have dictated the letter, composed in Latin, to his secretary. It was a well structured and explicit letter, right up his street. The Crusade had to become a large-scale operation of twelve to fifteen thousand knights and five thousand infantrymen. The Kings of France, England, Sicily and Spain had to be involved in this. James had concrete ideas about the possible landing spots, but he wanted to disclose these in a confidential meeting with the Pope. It was necessary for the Italian city-states to agree a truce and the trading with Alexandria had to be stopped immediately. The gathering place should be in Cyprus and the target Egypt. The Order of the Temple could make a fleet of ten war ships available. The Grand Master wanted to discuss further elaboration of his plans with the Pope during his visit to the West in 1307. James began his epistle as follows:

> *In the name of God, Amen. With the calling to undertake a great Crusade, with the collective Christendom, the destruction of the enemy of our faith and for the reconquering of the Holy Land drenched with the blood of Christ, I declare complete consent. And when it should please your Holiness and the Lord Cardinals, to begin discussions immediately and as quickly as possible, about such a Crusade with the Kings of France, England, Germany, Sicily, Aragon, Spain and with the other mighty and less mighty rulers, whose hearts God may enlighten for such a pious and commendable undertaking...*

It was a very unrealistic story: around this time about 3 million people lived in Egypt. A gigantic army would have been needed to be able to keep this country occupied. Let alone the fact that the neighbouring Muslim soldiers would not let it go, and undoubtedly would rush to the aid of Egypt. At the same time, James had totally underestimated the situation in Europe. The named Kings lived at odds with each other and it was naïve to imagine that they could collectively manage to complete a successful Crusade.

James of Molay concentrated on France. Philip IV was after all, the most powerful monarch of his time. Alas, the Grand Master was not always tactful. According to the chronicler of 'the Templar of Tyre' (who liked William of Beaujeu, but hated the last Grand Master), Philip was given the cold shoulder by the Grand Master. The treasurer of the Parisian Temple had lent Philip four hundred thousand gold florins, without the permission of the Grand Master. James threw the bursar out of the Order and, despite pressure from the Pope and the King, refused to reinstate him. He would have thrown a letter from the Pope with this request into the hearth. The grade of truth of this history should be doubted, because the treasurer of the French Order was still in service during the arrests in 1307. It genuinely indicated that the Order of the Temple had not lost any of its proud character, even in a period when the tide was turning.

The French King, Philip IV, gave the impression that he trusted the Order of the Temple. Hugh of Pairaud, the Visitor of the Order, had regular contact with him. He received a document from the King in 1304, in which the King promised to protect the Order. Philip found shelter inside the strong walls of the Templars complex in Paris, in 1306, when a rebellion broke out in the city. In March 1307, Philip attended a religious service, where a number of new members were admitted. The Rule forbad the presence of outsiders, but for high nobility an exception was made, which was understandable.

In May 1307, James of Molay arrived in Poitiers, where the Pope had established his headquarters in the meantime. James spoke with Clement V about the rumours that were circulating in the French court. He wanted an investigation into the accusations about the detrimental practices of the Order. Thereafter he visited King Philip IV and admitted that sometimes mistakes were made when confessions were taken. He still made the assumption that the Order would be enabled to punish the guilty, according the stipulations of the Rule. In June 1307, James was at the Chapter meeting of the Parisian Templars. Discussions would take place there about the rumours regarding the irregularities in the Order. Subsequently, he left again to go to Poitiers to talk with the Grand Master of the Hospitallers and the Pope about a new Crusade. Thereon, the leader of the Hospitallers left in August to go to Cyprus and James of Molay went to Paris, to face his ruination.

The inquisition

In the thirteenth century, the Crusades were begun by the Popes as a means to combat heresy. This took place in South France as well as in Germany. The Crusades against the Cathars, which lasted from 1209 to 1244, ended up as failures. Because the Cathar faith was not destroyed from root to tip, the papacy chose for another strategy. The newly founded Dominican Order had the task of converting the Cathars by preaching. The Dominicans lived just as poorly as the leaders of the Cathars. The intervening of the Dominicans was like a seed bearing no fruit, so harder measures were necessary to bring the Cathars on the right path.

During the thirteenth century a legal concept was therefore developed, in which the Church and the state both fulfilled a role: the inquisition. It was the Church that judged if people had a devious religious awareness, hereafter the state took care of the appurtenant punishments. These varied from the loss of property, to being burnt at the stake. For the determining of a heretic thought, the Dominican Order was mainly brought in. When someone was accused of unusual conceptions, then he had absolutely no chance. The suspect stood totally alone. It was dangerous to be a witness for a heretic, because you ran the risk of ending up in the dock. For the rest, the engaging of a solicitor in the Middle Ages did not conform to the basic rights of the individual. Furthermore, the inquisition bore a strong hierarchical character. It placed high nobility in a position where they could get rid of troublesome subjects and take over their possessions.

The legal system was set up in such a way that the Church was always right. Therefore, there was no point in denying the accusations. Sins could only be forgiven, if the suspect renounced his concepts. If the heretic went back on his confession, then there was only one suitable punishment: burning at the stake. Via a Papal Bull in 1252, torture was introduced; apparently it was necessary to improve the rules of the inquisition. The Dominicans, with their pursuit of the Cathars, learnt which way was the best to combat heresy. They would use these experiences during the trial against the Templars from 1307 to 1312.

The financial conduct of Philip IV

Contemporaries describe Philip IV as a blond, tall and handsome man, hence his nick-name 'the Fair.' He was a superb knight and huntsman. Philip descended from Hugh Capet, who became the French King in 987. Thanks to this long tradition and the image of his grandfather, Saint Louis, the nation regarded the French monarch as semi-religious. Philip IV stimulated his advisors to develop a theory to break the power of the Holy Chair. For them, the royal might was more important than that of the Church, because there were already Kings in France before Christianity. Philip IV was also of the opinion that the kingship was entrusted to him by God himself. The fact that he managed to have his grandfather declared a Saint in 1297, was also a feather in his cap. It is obvious that these conceptions brought the French monarch into conflict with the Church. Boniface was a Pope with outspoken ideas about the relationship between the Church and the state. In Chapter X, it is described how Philip had all his own way and managed to bring the papacy to its knees with stiff measures.

The government of Philip (1285-1314) was characterised by high military expenditures. Part of France was the property of England, however this land was formal liege of the French King. During the reign of Philip, on several occasions, armed and therefore expensive conflicts took place. Flanders was also a place of concern for the King. French troops were humiliated more than once by the Flemings striving to obtain independence. The most well known of these fights, is the 'Battle of the Golden Spurs' of 1302. The elite of the French knights were crushingly defeated by farmers and townspeople at this occurrence. In addition to this, Philip inherited a gigantic debt from his father. Philip III had held a Crusade, which was a total disaster, against Aragon and upon his death the loans were far from settled. In order to pay these expenses, high taxes were levied. The Church suffered especially from these: historians claim that the clergy, in comparison, donated the most to the treasury. During his reign, Philip demanded of all the clergy, at least 24 times, that they relinquish 10 percent of their income, legacies, or both to him. The conflict between Boniface and Philip IV certainly had a financial background. The population were also not forgotten by the French King. On a number of occasions, the monarch devalued the legal currency. That is why, in 1306, a great rebellion broke out and the King fled to the Templars complex! A couple of days later the French army restored the peace at the cost of many lives.

The Lombards, the traders and bankers of the Italian city-states were also treated harshly by the French King. In 1291, they were arrested and released again after paying large sums of money. Their profits were skimmed by the French administration in the years thereafter. In 1311, Philip IV confiscated all their belongings and money and arrested them again. The Jews suffered in the same manner. In July 1306, all Jewish possessions were confiscated and all Jews were, if they did not have themselves baptised, thrown out of the country, penniless.

AN APOCRYPHAL STORY

In the year 1305, the Christians were again ready for a new Pope. The conclave had already been together for a year in the Italian city of Perugia, deliberating about this. The population thought that the length of time it took was wearisome. The city had to entertain the choosing gentlemen like royalty, and the costs incurred because of this were shifted onto the citizens. One of the reasons that the conclave took so much time, would have been brought about by the fact that the two penultimate Popes had died of unnatural causes. Celestine V was killed by means of his successor Boniface, whilst Philip IV had a hand in the death of Boniface.

The chronicler, Villani, alleged that Bertrand de Got and Philip spoke with each other in great secrecy in the spring of 1305, somewhere in France. Bertrand was the Bishop of Bordeaux, therefore liege to the English King. Philip would have promised the Church leader that he would use all his influence to make sure that Bertrand became the next Pope. As compensation for this, Philip demanded that Bertrand, amongst other things, did the following: the Church of France had to relinquish 10 percent of the ecclesiastical contributions to the French throne throughout the next five years. Bertrand also had to declare his predecessor as a heretic and there should be ten new French Cardinals named. The sixth favour, Philip would not yet disclose: the new Pope would get to hear about this when the time was suitable. A number of years later the Pope would discover that Philip had his eye on the abolition of the Order of the Temple. We read about these events in the chronicles of the Florentine, Giovanni Villani, who wrote down what he heard during a business trip through France and the Netherlands. Villani's stories are to this day, seen as fantasies. They give in any case, an idea as to what the contemporaries thought about the power struggle between the Church and the state. Villani was convinced that the French attack on the Templars was a premeditated plan.

XII. The End

THE ARRESTS, 14 SEPTEMBER 1307 – 13 OCTOBER 1307

In a letter, dated 14th September 1307, Philip gave his sheriffs instructions to prepare for the arrests of all French members of the Templars. We still have a number of examples of the letter, a few in French and a couple in Latin. Obviously the vassals of the King knew which languages the different sheriffs understood. The epistle contained over 1900 words, approximately five pages from this book, and was well thougt out. The King wrote that he was filled with disbelief and abomination when he heard from trustworthy sources that the Order of the Temple appeared to be a heretic organisation. He didn't want to believe it at first, but Philip was nevertheless convinced that the Order was secretly performing and stimulating scandalous practices. The members denounced Christ, spit on his image and kissed each other all over their bodies. Above all, they were indulging repulsive mutual sexual relations and they worshipped an idol.

The King wrote in the letter, that he had consulted the Pope about this, he had spoken to his own advisors and, upon the request of the French inquisitor, he had enlisted the sheriffs to arrest all members of the Order. They had to be imprisoned and placed available to the inquisition, the ecclesiastical court. The French state had to confiscate all their possessions and to keep them until the charges were thoroughly investigated. The imputations of the King were not very original because Pope Boniface had been accused of the same offences a number of years before.

The arrests took place in the early morning of Friday 13th October. It could possibly be due to this occurrence that we say that "Friday the thirteenth' is an unlucky day. Given the logistical complexity of the operation, (France had at least eight hundred preceptories) the execution of the instruction was a great success. According to official sources, twelve members escaped, presumably there were at the most twice as many. Approximately two thousand members were secured, including the French leaders and the Grand Master of the Templars, James of Molay.

The head of the Order knew of the considerations of the French King. In consultation with James of Molay in August 1307, Clement V had informed the King that a Papal investigation would be arranged to look into the degree of truth in the negative stories about the Templars. But Philip IV did look before he leapt. Minister William of Plaisians alleged that the King had begun with his own investigation a number of years previously. He had commissioned twelve men to infiltrate the Order and to report their findings to him. The King would have done this after a number of members, who had lost their robe, had told him of the shady practices within the Order. The Pope claimed, in 1308, that during several conversations with Philip, he had told him that he attached no belief to the rumours about the Templars. Clement V and James of Molay must have thought that it would not be as bad as all that. But Philip was apparently in a rush: he was desperately short of money and the leaders of the Order were in France at that moment. Besides, he did not trust the Pope and he was undoubtedly afraid that the Church was intending to arrange for absolution for the Templars.

The combating of heresy was of course a matter for the Church, hence Philip emphasizing in his letter, that the arrests were carried out at the request of William d'Imbert (also called William of Paris). He was a French monk of the Dominican Order and in his capacity as inquisitor of France, in a sense, a sort of representative of the Holy Chair. William knew the King well, because he was his father confessor.

The first examinations, 14 October 1307 – 24 October 1307

The King and his advisors were aware that the evidence against the Templars was wafer thin: they needed confessions quickly. In anticipation of the hearings, the prison guards received instructions to intimidate and torture the Templars. It had to be explained to the members, that a confession would lead to forgiveness, whilst those who denied the accusations would be sentenced to death.

There are 138 preserved depositions from the Parisian hearings of October and November 1307, including that of the Grand Master and the other leaders. Only four members completely denied the indictments. The others admitted that the Order was guilty of (some of) the named heresy. Nearly all members declared that they were forced into carrying out these practices and that they had renounced Christ in word, but in their hearts they knew better. From the hearings in the provinces outside of Paris, 94 still remain which give the same impression as those from Paris. Here, we also come across few complete denials.

It is irrefutable that the vast majority of the prisoners were mentally and physically tortured. Exhaustion, intimidation, turning up the heat (literally), the hanging of weights from the testicles were the usual ways in France, to ensure that the administration of justice ran 'carefully and cleanly.' A member of the Order declared in 1310 that 25 Templars had died through torture; other members said that number was higher.

As far as is known, there were very few knights amongst those arrested: most were priests, sergeants or servants. It is logical really, because the conflict to liberate Palestine was carried out from Cyprus, which was their headquarters at that time. The Western possessions, with the exception of the Iberian Peninsula, in fact had to generate money and goods on behalf of the battle. Of the 138 people from the Parisian statements, we know the positions of 73 of them: fifteen knights, seventeen priests and 41 sergeants or servants. The fact that there were not many knights, made the work of the tortures even more straightforward. Knights would have probably acknowledged the accusations less easily.

From the Parisian statements it can be seen that 105 Templars admitted to denouncing Christ. 120 members confessed to spitting on the crucifix and on one or another image of Christ. Furthermore, there were 103 members that were kissed on the back, anus or navel and in 102 instances it was admitted that homosexual behaviour was encouraged. Only three said that they had actually carried out sexual relations with a male member of the Order. One maintained that he had made love with James of Molay three times in one night on Cyprus. Finally, nine arrestees mentioned the worshiping of idols, which was described in various ways. All confessions ended with the following formula:

> *Interrogated on the subject of his evidence which has been mixed with whatever falsehood or, that he by force, for fear of torture, imprisonment or whatever other reason, emotionally affected the truth by violence, he says under oath nay; on the contrary, for the well being of his soul, he has told the unadulterated truth.*

From declarations from those arrested in the period 1308 to 1311, we know for sure that this was far from the truth.

THE END

THE EXAMINATIONS OF THE LEADERS, 24 OCTOBER 1307 – 26 OCTOBER 1307

William d'Imbert, the French Inquisitor, interfered with the first 37 witness's statements in Paris. He did this, conforming with procedure, just after the torturers had finished their work. The leaders of the Order were personally heard by him. On October 24th 1307, the Grand Master gave in. He declared to William d'Imbert that the accusations were more or less true, but denied ever being guilty of committing sodomy. It is not clear if James of Molay was tortured. A witness described that the Grand Master, during a meeting, had shown burn wounds and cuts on his arms, legs, back and stomach to the public, but the grade of truth in this statement was doubted. In any case, his circumstances were terrible; his testimony was taken when he had been in prison for eleven days (see appendix).

Whatever is true, James of Molay was an old man who had held a high position in society for years. The day before his arrest he wore the slips from the shroud of the recently deceased sister-in-law of Philip. The abrupt and humiliating action of the King and his Church must have been a tremendous trauma, but it got worse for James. On 25th October, he appeared before an assembly of scientists, religious men and members of the nobility. He repeated his statement in front of these important people. It was an incomprehensible deed for the leader of the Templars. He did not realise the consequences of his confession and totally misjudged the situation. Maybe the Grand Master, who withdrew his confession a couple of months later, was made specific promises. A distressing detail to this is that this gathering took place in the Templars house in Paris, then one of the largest properties of the Order.

The next day 38 members, including the highest ranking leaders, standing before a similar group and also on their own terrain, endorsed the statement of the Grand Master. That was what Philip needed; the legitimate character of his order to arrest, thanks to a quick success, he could afterwards easily defend. Of course, he ensured that everyone from outside and within the Order heard the confessions. The statement of the Grand Master and the other leaders broke the resistance of the other members. Total obedience was after all, one of the pillars of the organisation. Undoubtedly, the torturers did not have to do as much overtime any more.

It looked like the action of Philip was a conclusive success and that the whole affair could still be concluded in the year 1307. The possessions of the French Templars were now in the control of the King. From official registrations of goods, it did not appear to be true that there were a lot of liquid assets confiscated, but that the value of the estates and the appurtenant buildings were more than a pretty penny. Besides that, it is unclear as to what happened to the treasures of the churches and the valuables given for safe keeping by the outsiders. It cannot be ruled out that this fortune was confiscated by Philip. We know of more than one preceptory which Philip sold or rented to local feudal lords. Clement V wrote a letter to the King in December 1310, in which the following passage is clear enough:

> *On the subject of the matter of the management of the possessions of the Templars in your Kingdom, the Pope is well aware that all is lost and misspent, something that he had envisaged when he was residing in Poitiers.*

The first reactions from abroad were very sceptical. It was generally known that the French King, from the beginning of his reign (1285), was in great financial difficulties. No one could fail to notice his conflict with the previous Pope, about the imposing of higher taxes on the clergy and the exploitation of the Jews and Italians in France.

The reaction of the Pope, 27 October 1307 – 23 December 1307

For Philip, the standpoints of the English monarch and the King of Aragon, who did not believe the accusations of the French monarch, were uninteresting. The attitude of the Pope, Clement V was more important: a Frenchman, named in 1305 with the assistance of the King. He was regularly ill and well known as a weak personality. To the surprise of the King and his advisors, the Pope was furious. In a letter from 27th October 1307, the Pope expressed, in no uncertain terms, that Philip had gone too far.

The Order of the Temple was an ecclesiastical organisation and therefore was the responsibility of the Holy Chair. He considered the action of Philip as an attack on the Church and the Pope. Clement sent two Cardinals to Paris to discuss the case of the Templars with the King. The members and the possessions of the Templars had to be handed over to these two clergies, so that the Church could decide what should be done with them. The Pope wanted to take charge, without having to undo the action of the French King. William d'Imbert, the representative of the Holy Chair was after all the one who gave the instruction for the arrests.

Naturally, the Pope was afraid of Philip; he was well aware of the fate of his predecessor, Boniface, who had to pay for his opposition to the King, with his life. Still he defied Philip IV and made sure that the trial would go on for years. In a Papal Bull of 22 November 1307, Clement V actually commissioned all Christian monarchs to arrest the Templars and place all the possessions available to the Church. The Pope explained that he had already heard rumours about the possible impurity of the Order in 1305. Although he refused to believe these, he could not ignore the results of the action of the French King; even more so, because the highest ranking leader of the Order of the Temple, had spontaneously admitted to some of the allegations before a large attendance in Paris. He also noted in the Bull that if the accusations turned out not to be true, that the honour of the Order would be reinstated. Clement V was apparently not convinced about the guilt of the Order.

THE IMPASSE, 24 DECEMBER 1307 – 26 MAY 1308

At the end of 1307, James of Molay appeared before the two Cardinals appointed by the Pope. The Grand Master withdrew his earlier confession: he would have done this out of fear of torture. Many other members from the Order also retracted their statements. This considerably delayed the demise of the Order. In the first six months of 1308, representatives of the King and the Pope negotiated over the progress of the trial. At the beginning of 1308, the Pope postponed the activities of the French inquisitors. He said that he would take responsibility for this himself.

Philip still did not relinquish his control over the members and the possessions, and sought support from the theologians of Sorbonne. He asked this respectable college seven questions, five of which were about the legitimacy of his action. The other two questions were concerning the possessions of the Order of the Temple. He wanted to know if these had to be handed over to the monarch of the country in which these assets were acquired, or to the Church. If they eventually had to be made available for the liberation of the Holy land, who had to then supervise them: the Church or the King? The answers from these experts must have disappointed Philip. In March 1308, a month after the request of the King, the scholars said that the Pope did indeed have the right to further lead the trial against the Templars, and that the possessions of the Templars should be used towards the liberating of Jerusalem.

But again Philip was not discouraged. During the first six months of 1308, all sorts of pamphlets appeared which were very negative about the Templars and above all, condemned the slowness of the Pope. On the grounds of the fact that Philip had already previously made use of such a method, historians are convinced that this slanderous campaign was led by the French Court. In addition, Philip invited Bishops, noblemen, representatives of cities and other important personage to a meeting of the French Parliament in May, in Tours. He undoubtedly made sure of a select company. We don't have a report of this meeting, but it can be no other way than that the high representatives of the King raked up the evil character of the Order of the Temple again. At that time, they also knew the power of a good propaganda campaign. Philip did everything to create a basis for his dealings.

THE NEGOTIATIONS BETWEEN CLEMENT V AND PHILIP IV, 26 MAY 1308 – 11 AUGUST 1308

At the end of May, the King and the Pope met with each other in Poitiers, at that time the temporary residence of the Pope. Philip was in the company of his closest advisors. A small army had come along with the King. The predecessor of the Pope, Boniface, was intimidated in a similar way in 1303 and, for that reason, had lost his life. On 29th May, the Pope held a meeting in the royal palace of Poitiers. Included in those present were, Cardinals, Bishops, members of the French Court and a number of other highly regarded men.

The French minister, William of Plaisians, was the spokesman. There are different versions of this speech available. All of them say that Plaisians, in the name of the King, explicitly explained to the Pope that the Order of the Temple had changed into a heretic organisation and had to be punished. The words of the French minister were endorsed by two Archbishops and a number of other speakers with a secular background.

The Pope was not impressed. He acknowledged that the King had spoken to him a number of times about the rumours, but that he did not believe the insinuations. He contradicted the French minister as if he had given the King permission to arrest the Templars. In addition, he emphasised that the Church wanted to initiate an investigation, and if it appeared that the accusations were founded, appropriate measures would be taken by him.

In a second gathering, fourteen days later, the French minister repeated his argument, this time in a grimmer tone. He concluded his oration with three demands: all Templars, including those outside of France, had to be arrested, the inquisition had to continue the hearings and the Order had to disappear from the face of the earth. Despite this, the Pope remained insistent that he could only accept a decision if the members and the possessions were assigned to the Church. The clergy-like monks could only be judged by the Church. At the same time, Clement was of the opinion, that even if the French Templars were heretics, he did not want to abolish the Order.

After Philip had listened to this, he announced that he wanted to deliberate over the development of the trial. He brought a new means of pressure into the conflict. At the end of June, a group of 72 members of the Order, transported to Poitiers, appeared before a gathering between the Pope and the Cardinals; first closed, later public hearings. It is known what 54 of them said; only one member, a priest, maintained that he knew nothing of the heretical practices in the Order. The others confirmed the drift of the hearings of October 1307. Obviously, the French government had carefully chosen the members. They were undoubtedly men who either had a grievance with the Order, or who were repeatedly threatened with torture. They all said that they had given their evidence of their own free will. High ranking Templars were absent, because, due to illness, they would not have been in a fit state to undertake the trip to Poitiers.

The Deciscion of the Pope, August 1308

The confessions from the members of the Order placed the Pope in a position where he was able to nuance his standpoint, without losing face. Behind the scenes a lot of discussions were held about this, by the representatives of the Pope and the King. Finally, in August 1308, the Pope published a number of Bulls about the conflict.

The individual members of the Order of the Temple were placed under ecclesiastical authority, but would be guarded by soldiers of the King. If the Church requested this, they had to be immediately placed at their disposal. Therefore the situation had not changed, because the King held complete say over the French Templars. Ordinary members would be judged by the provincial Archbishops from the entire Christian Empire, whilst the Pope would sentence the leaders.

The Pope then named a commission of eight people who would determine the guilt of the Order as such. They had to present the results to a specially convened council. This ecclesiastical assemby would begin on 1 October 1310 and was held in Vienne (south of Lyon). Besides the handling of the case of the

Templars, this council would also decide about a new Crusade and the reforming of the Church. The Pope now gave permission for the continuation of the proceedings of the French inquisition.

The possessions, in the event of the disappearance of the Order, would be beneficial to the Holy Land. The Pope named a curator in every district, who had to keep an eye on the goods. The Pope promised that the ongoing income would be used for the original aims of the Order of the Temple. Should the Order be innocent, then the Templars would get everything back. The King was in danger of losing sight of the goods. On 14 August, the Pope sent three Cardinals to Chinon for the questioning of the highest leaders of the Order. Two of them were Frenchmen, both were friendly with the King, the third was an Italian. All of the leaders again admitted to some of the charges and with that, they confirmed the statements of their subordinates in Poitiers a number of months previously.

The correspondence between the Pope and the King in the meantime, carried on as usual. The King, who hoped to have the whole affair wrapped up in 1308, complained about the slow movement of affairs, He wanted clarity about the continuing procedure on the subject of the Templars, who would not confess or who had withdrawn their earlier admission. Philip carried on hammering for a uniform court procedure and mainly directed this abroad. Again, Philip gave instructions about the way that the hearings must take place, with as the ultimate method, the use of torture instruments. Those who confessed received absolution, but remained prisoners. Again many were tortured and now it also helped. In that time bodily harm did not matter to the inquisition if it was to save a soul of a sinner. Eternal burning in hell was always worse than burning the earthly feet.

King Philip remained in control of the possessions, contrary to the understanding he had with the Pope. In some instances the proceeds from the Templar houses went directly into the royal treasure chest. At the same time he held the control over the hearings. Not only because his personnel guarded the Templars, but mainly because most of the high French clergymen were under his influence. Philip really wanted more. He wrote a letter to the Pope, in which were the names of the people, who in his opinion should take a seat in the commission of eight. He asked the Pope not to refuse his proposal.

The charges, 12 August 1308

On 12 August 1308, the Papal charges against the Order of the Temple were presented. The Bull consisted of 127 articles and was a repercussion of the examinations of October and November 1307, and from those of Poitiers. The Order of the Temple would be found guilty of the following heretic practices, amongst others:

1. they denied Christ, the crucifixion of Christ, Jesus, the Holy Virgin, and sometimes the saints of God, stimulated by the leaders who received them into the Order and thereafter;
2. the new members were obligated to spit, urinate and trample on the cross, even on Good Friday;
3. the Templars worshipped a cat, which sometimes appeared to them in their assembly;
4. they believed that their leaders could give them absolution;
5. upon entering, the brothers were kissed on the mouth, the navel, or on the bare stomach and on the buttocks, on the base of spine, and sometimes on the penis;
6. their entrance rituals were secret;
7. the brothers were encouraged to practice homosexuality;
8. they had idols in each province, namely heads, of which some had three faces, some one, and others had a human skull;
9. they believed the head could save them, it could then make riche, it made the trees flower and it made the land germinate;
10. prior activities were observed in the whole Order, were already long existing practices and were statutorily determined.

The Order of the Temple was not accused of the proverbial overwhelming alcohol abuse by the members, something that for a religious Order was extremely offensive. In the sixteenth century, Rabelais (1534) and Paradin (1552) wrote for the first time about the tavern saying, 'drink like a Templar'. Thirteen hundred years earlier, some Christians were made out to be 'wine drinkers,' whilst later the expression, 'drink like a Pope', became fashionable. Apparently all sorts of bad qualities of other people and groups were all of a sudden credited to the Templars.

In the Great Dictionary of the Dutch Language, the trial is referred to. Therein, it is wrongfully recorded that the Templars were accused of drunkenness during the trial.

The following lines of verse from a Dutch poet (beginning of the seventeenth century) are well known:

I have been there..., where drunkards sat, and drunk as Templars, and swore like Croats.

The charges ended with four articles, wherein it was said that the Grand Master, the Visitor and the Masters of the provinces of Cyprus, Normandy and Poitou and many others had admitted to the accusations: to those of the inquisition and many times in public. Some members (such as priests, knights and others) had acknowledged a majority of these impeachments in the presence of the Pope and the Cardinals.

The instruction of the commission of eight was the investigating of the 127 articles of the Papal charges.

The commission of eight, August 1309 – June 1311

Philip would have been satisfied with the formation of the Papal commission. The chairman had for many years now, been an important advisor to the King and two other members were regularly absent because they were carrying out a governmental order from Philip IV. There was just one member of whom it is not certain whether he had a close relationship with the French royal house. Philip IV added another two members on his own initiative. William of Nogarat and William of Plaisians were regularly present at the hearings and they emphatically interfered with the Court proceedings. It is also notable that the sessions were held in Paris and not in Avignon, the new residency of the Pope. Because the Templars were imprisoned in places throughout the country, there was no logistic reason to choose Paris as a gathering place.

The commission had to judge the Order and not individual members. In August 1309, they assembled together for the first time, a year after the Pope had initiated them. After defining the procedure, the commission decided that they would hear the defendants on 12 November.

It was not until the 22 November, therefore three months after they had been invited to attend, that the first members were presented, despite the fact that there were several hundred Templars imprisoned in Paris. Apparently the servants of the King wanted the members who were going to testify, to be well prepared for their statements. As to the manner of how that occurred, nothing is officially known, but in the past, Philip had 'won his spurs on this terrain.' The first who appeared wanted to defend themselves and were consequently sent back to their cell. Subsequently, Hugh of Pairaud, the Visitor of the overseas areas, was questioned. He wished only to give his statement to the Pope. The Grand Master, who was heard on a number of occasions in November 1309, made a confused and sick impression. He asked the commission for time to think about the question of how, and in which way he could defend the Order.

The members who came after him did better. Ponsard of Gizy, the Commander of Payns, told the commission that he knew of 36 Templars that had died in Paris due to being tortured. He then added that he had been informed that others had also been slain in other places. All the articles that were introduced against the Order were in his opinion, in conflict with the truth. Ponsard wished to defend the Order and wanted to pay the costs for this with the proceeds from the possession of the Order of the Temple. When questioned he declared that he was tortured:

> *...in the three month which elapsed before the confession made by him in the presence of the Lord Bishop of Paris, he was placed in a pit, his hands having been tied behind him so tightly that the blood ran to his nails. If he was again tortured he would deny everything he was now saying and say whatever anyone wished.*

He named the names of two priests who could aid him in his defence, Renaud of Provins and Pierre of Bologna. In a proceeding session, it was apparent that these men were adequately juridically competent to be able to defend the Order. That did no apply for Ponsard, but his resistance was the first indication that the commission would face worse predicaments. James of Molay was heard for the second time, but he limited himself to testimony of his belief in God. William of Nogarat, regularly present at the assemblies of the commission, impressed upon the Grand Master that Saladin had already accused the Order of sodomy and heresy. James said, entirely rightfully, that he had not heard this story. He reacted inadequately and told the following: together with other young members, he had reproached William of Beaujeu for signing a peace treaty with the Muslims after the Crusade of Edward I.

Only later did he realise that this was a wise decision. Subsequently he asked the commission if he could hold some church services with his priests, which was honoured. The Grand Master had again behaved as an incompetent leader of the Order.

At the end of November 1309, the commission ended the first sitting and announced the re-opening of the sitting in February. The Cardinals wrote a letter, in which they called upon the Bishops to co-operate fully, by ensuring the availability of the Templars who wanted to defend the Order. The letter had a wonderful effect. When the proceedings began again, 532 members came forward for the defence; at the end of March there were nearly 600. They originated from Cahors, Toulouse, Tours, Nimes, in short, from different areas of the Kingdom. In the same month, James of Molay appeared again, but instead of defending the Order, he demanded a meeting with the Pope. The other high ranking leaders sided with his standpoint shortly thereafter.

The defence, March 1310 – May 1310

At the end of March the commission, in a mass assembly, saw about 550 Templars. All of whom had sat in the French dungeons for approximately two and a half years, in by no means optimal circumstances. After the intentions were explained to the audience, the 127 articles of the complaint were read out. As is well known, these were composed by the Pope and the King in August 1308, after the meeting in Poitiers.

The reading took place in Latin, a language that only a few of those present could understand. When asked, the Templars had said that there was no need for the commission to read out the articles in the vernacular. They refused to listen to this ungodliness any longer, because they considered the accusations to be false.

The commission wanted, for an efficient process, the Templars to name a number of solicitors. Pierre of Bologna, the representative of the Order to the Papal Court, and Renaud of Provins, Commander of Orleans, stepped forward. They were both priests and were described in the documents as literary men. They made a number of demands regarding their living conditions, named two names of the Templars who had to assist them and required regular contact with the Grand Master and the French leaders. Due to the hierarchical character of the Order, the latter was an essential point. The commission reminded the Templars however, that they had refused to defend the Order, and insisted upon urgency because the council would begin in about six months time. Notaries were named, who would record the statements of the members in the ensuing times. In the month of April, the number of defendants grew to about six hundred members.

The defence, besides Pierre of Bologna and Renaud of Provins, was made up of William of Chambonnet, Bertrand of Sartiges (both knights) and Robert Vigier (on behalf of the servants). In November 1307, Pierre of Bologna still admitted that some of the accusations were correct. Now he retracted this, because at that time he had been tortured. Renaud of Provins had more or less made a confession, but he now declared that the accusations were unfounded. From their arguments in the documents, it is evident that both priests were juridically educated. Both knights had never made a confession. They were valuable for the defence, because they had already been members of the Order for more than thirty years, of which a number of years were in active service in the Holy Land.

Obviously, the defence explicitly brought forward that the confessions were of no value whatsoever, because these were gained trough torture; Pierre of Bologna pointed out that this violence was still occurring. Subsequently, he frequently asked himself, how it was possible that up until just before the arrests, new members from important families were entering the Order. If the Order was a heretic organisation, then surely these families would have kicked up a fuss? Other members yielded statements about the role of the Order in the Holy Land and emphasised the trust that many monarchs had in the Templars.

At the same time, a juridical document appeared, more than likely coming from the circles of the court. According to the author of this piece, the defence was unlawful. It was absolutely clear that the Order was a heretical organisation: King Philip IV was not the prosecutor of the Order, but the defender of the Church. The existence of a defence suggests the possibility that the Order could have been innocent. An English Templar really hit the nail on the head when in 1308, he declared that the inquisition

> *did not intend to bring the truth to light, but from an accused make a guilty person.*

The patience of Philip IV was heavily tested. In October 1307 he had all the members arrested and in April 1310, the end of the trial was still not in sight. Even worse, the Pope, at the beginning of 1310, postponed the Council of Vienna for a year due to the long duration of the investigation.

The defence put aside, May 1310

The Papal Bull of August 1308 gave the King the chance to bring a definitive blow to the Templars. This Bull had in fact left the judging of the individual members to the leaders of the Church. The Archbishop of the province of Sens, Philippe of Marigny, could help him in speeding up the process. Philippe was a brother of the French minister of Finances and he was, on recommendation of the King in 1309, appointed by the Pope as the Archbishop of the province of Sens. The diocese of Paris belonged to the province of Sens and that suited Philip IV. Philippe called a meeting together in May 1310 in Paris, to judge the individual Templars. When the defence heard about this, it was immediately clear to them what was going to happen. The defence managed to arrange an extra meeting on Sunday 10 May. Pierre of Bologna insisted that the commission should stop the Archbishop of Sens and demanded that all Templars that wanted to defend the Order were placed under the Papal authority. He wanted to speak to the Archbishop of Sens in the presence of the commission. The chairman, who had close ties with the royal house, listened to the appeal of Pierre and apologised because he had to attend Mass.

The other members of the commission announced to the defenders that they wanted to deliberate internally at the request of the defence. They gave their decisive answer the same evening; the commission could formally do nothing because the Archbishop was acting in accordance to the Papal Bull of August 1308. The following Friday, the commission discovered that Philip was on the brink of taking 54 Templars to be burnt at the stake. They were members who wanted to defend the Order and they had confessed in 1307, but now belonged to the group which said that these confessions had been given under torture. According to Philippe of Marigny the retraction of the statements made them heretics. Two employees of the commission were immediately sent on their way. They had an audience with Philippe, to whom they explained that the 'warming' of the 54 members would interfere with the work of the commission. At the same time, the duo informed the Archbishop of the request of the four defendants from the previous Sunday. Philippe of Marigny listened to them and explained that they did not have a signed request with them.

The same day, the 54 members were incinerated just outside Paris. Eye witnesses declared that they all professed their innocence. A couple of days later, four others suffered the same fate. Philippe went thoroughly to work, because the skeletal remains of the former treasurer of the Parisian Temple were exhumed, and this Templar still underwent a cremation. Shortly thereafter, another nine followed from the province of Reims. Those who retracted their original statement at any time deserved, according to the law of the inquisition, to be burnt at the stake without any form of trial. Other ecclesiastical laws could be explained in the way, that during the investigation the defenders must not be punished. The solicitors of the Templars were too short of time to be able to ask for attention to be paid to this. It was not accidental that the Archbishop acted quickly: he completely cracked the defence.

A couple of days later it appeared to be the turn of Renaud of Provins. This defender of the Order came from Sens and had to appear as an individual before the archiepiscopal court. Now the commission did intervene and they managed to keep Reanud as a defender of the Templars. That failed with Pierre of Bologna. He was unfindable from that moment on and he suddenly disappeared from the process reports. 44 Templars did appear and they told the commission that they had changed their minds: they abandoned any further defending of the Order.

The commission of eight is finished, June 1311

The commission subsequently postponed their proceedings until the beginning of November 1310. From the defence, it appeared that only two knights were left, William of Chambonnet and Bertrand of Sartiges. They were told that Pierre of Bologna and Renaud of Provins had declared, of their own free will, that their original confessions were true after all and that they had shirked the defence. Pierre of Bologna would have escaped from prison after his declaration. The commission further explained that Renaud had been thrown out of the priesthood by the Council of Sens, therefore he could no longer take part in the defence. Both knights had neither the knowledge nor the courage to continue the defence. They were not named in the trial documents any more.

The commission subsequently gathered in June 1311 and heard another 215 witnesses. Few had the courage to defend the Order: obviously Philip continued to conduct the selecting of the Templars. Only 87 of the original 597 defenders turned up. There were 84 of them who re-confirmed their statements made when they were arrested. A number of them even denied that they belonged to the group of nearly six hundred, despite the fact that the group had been registered in March. The confessions followed the same pattern as the hearings of October and November 1307. The 'heretics' maintained afresh that it was the fault of the Order and that they had committed these sins against their will. It was not necessary for many outsiders of the Templars to testify against the Order. The Templars dug their own grave, although it was unmistakably under the threat of torture. Only fourteen courageous people insisted that the accusations were untrue.

The commission finished its work on 5 June 1311; on that day they gave the King of France a report over the last two years. The report even went by special courier to the Pope. In the meantime, the French Archbishops carried on with the judging of individual members. On 5 March 1311, six Templars from the province of Sens were sentenced to life long imprisonment; including Renaud of Provins.

The Pursuits in Other Countries

The Low Lands
It is known that the Flemish Templars went to Paris as prisoners to defend their Order. They declared that they had lived as honourable Templars, practiced charitas and were hospitable, that they humbly wore the red cross on their robe and that they held fair Chapter Meetings, without abuse and conformed to the Christian faith. Included in them was Gossin of Bruges, the last Master of Flanders. It is unknown what happened to them afterwards.

The Duke of Brabant, Jan II informed the French King by letter that he had carried out his request to arrest the Templars in November 1307. In the chronicles of the trial, no Brabant's names really appear. Theobald of Bar, the Bishop of Liège, wrote to Philip that the Templars had few possessions in his diocese.

Two years later, in his diocese, a commission was named which had to investigate the accusations against the Templars, but we do not know the results. In 1311, the legal rights of possession for the Templars of Alphen (Noord-Brabant) were assessed. According to the report, this happened in the absence of the Templars, without this further being declared.

Britain
Edward II succeeded his father, indeed Edward I, in the summer of 1307. Just as with the French royal house, the Kingdom of England had gone through expensive times. Edward I had been at war with France and Scotland, without much success, and the royal house had not made itself popular with the English nobility. Although there were relatively few Templars living in England, they

possessed about forty preceptories. Since 1129, lots of money and goods were sent annually to the headquarters of the Order of the Temple. Edward II, the future son-in-law of Philip, was capable of withstanding the temptation. In the beginning, he left the possessions of the Templars alone.

Edward wrote a letter to his future father-in-law, at the end of October, with therein the message that he did not believe the accusations addressing the Templars. At the beginning of December 1307, he sent a letter to the Kings of Aragon, Castile, Naples and Portugal in which he defended the Order. Shortly afterwards he mentioned in writing to the Pope that he should consider them innocent. Just as in France, the Templars had carried out military and financial services for the royal house. On 14 December 1307, Edward received the Papal Bull of 22 November, in which the King was asked to arrest all Templars. This left the King with very little choice. On 26 December the King sent word that this was set to take place on 10 January 1308.

This happened in a completely different manner than in France. Approximately 150 members were arrested and an unknown number managed to get away scot-free. A historian mentioned that as being a few hundred, but gave no explanation for this high number. After two years, there were as yet nine fugitive members arrested. The King subsequently confiscated the possessions of the Order. Most Templars could continue to live in their preceptories, some even until September 1309 when the Papal interrogation commenced in England. The Master of the province of England, William de la More, was imprisoned in Canterbury on 9 January 1308, but was treated with respect. In May, he was released and in November 1308, again taken prisoner. Only then did the King command the guards to intensely watch over the Templars.

On 13 September 1309, therefore two years after the arrests in France and shortly before the beginning of the commission of eight, who had to determine the judgement of the Order of the Temple, the inquisition visited England. They consisted, self-evidently, of two Frenchmen who were assisted by English priests, including the Archbishop of York and the Bishops of London and Lincoln. All Templars were moved to the prisons in London, York and Lincoln. Edward II wrote to his governors in Eire and Scotland, that the Templars in these countries had to be imprisoned. Between 20 October and 18 November 1309, the inquisition questioned, in the presence of the Bishop of London, 43 members of the Order. This took place in the Church of the Holy Trinity in London. They were suspected of 87 infringements, so a part of the 127 determined by the Pope together with Philip in August 1308. These were in association with those sections of the charges which concerned individual members. Nobody confessed, whilst the questioning of external witnesses also produced nothing more. At the beginning of December 1309, the inquisitors asked the King for permission for the interrogations to continue to conform to the ecclesiastical rules. The English legal system was not familiar with using torturing practices and in contrast to France, an inquisition did not exist. This phenomenon was already accepted early in the thirteenth century in France and became a standard instrument of the monarchy. The Templars were re-heard, whereby torturing on a modest scale was allowed, and again the inquisitors had no success.

In June 1310, one month after the executions of the 54 Templars in France, the inquisitors wrote a letter of complaint to the Archbishop of Canterbury. They could not find anybody who could suitably handle the instrument of torture. They also expressed to the Bishop that the French procedure should be followed. The inquisitors added a number of proposals, of which the most far reaching, was that the English Templars should be brought over to France. They also suggested that the confessions of the French Templars should be circulated in England, in order to prevent potential protests. The letter helped somewhat, because the King repeated a couple of times, that the ecclesiastical procedures must be followed. In September 1310, the provincial Council of Canterbury took the decision that the Templars from London and Lincoln had to be separated. If the worst came to the worst, they approved the use of torture. These acts of violence should not lead to permanent injury and no blood was allowed to flow. Apparently this seed bore no fruit, because in December 1310, the Pope offered Edward II forgiveness for all sins and Gods everlasting mercy if the hearings could be continued in France.

The inquisitors finally had success in June 1311. Three members admitted to some of the charges; just before the Council of Vienne, they received absolution. William de la More, the English Commander, remained stubbornly denying all the accusations. The claim that he had given the ordinary members absolution, he strenuously denied. William was then taken to the Tower to await a Papal judgement, where he died in February 1313. The other Templars agreed with a statement that the Order had been so seriously scandalised that they wanted to submit themselves to atonement. They were again reconciled with the Church, where after they spent their last years in different monasteries.

The investigations in Eire and Scotland provided hardly anything. In Scotland, two Templars were questioned and in Eire fourteen, but without any confessions worth mentioning. The difference with France was enormous. This was mainly because tortures only started being practiced for the first time halfway through 1311. Another difference between England and France was the number of external witnesses: 145 in the British Isles and six in France. It was noticeable that a number of Templars thought that the Commander could give them absolution from small sins. He was not qualified for this religious act, but it undoubtedly had to do with the fact that not all Templars saw a difference between absolution from a priest, and the forgiveness that the men received from the Commander when they had broken the Order rules.

The Iberian Peninsula
Since the founding of the Order, the Templars fought in the present day Spain and Portugal against the Moors. Some of their possessions were received via inheritances, but most of them through battle. During a large part of the twelfth century they could keep 20 percent of the territories they conquered, with the permission of the men in power. In contrast to the Western European countries, the Order in this area, in addition to preceptories, possessed castles (seventeen and strategically placed), so there were a large number of knights. The Kings of Aragon, Castile and Portugal were at least as suspicious as Edward II. They had, like no other Western country, experienced which role the Order of the Temple played in the battle against the Muslims. In October 1307, King James II of Aragon informed the Pope that, to his horror, he had heard of the actions of the French King, and he only wanted to take measures after the Pope had informed him of the truth.

However, the King intervened in December 1307, nearly two months before he received the Papal Bull of 22 November. He did that out of the fear that the Order of the Temple would have the time and the sense to militarily defend themselves during the trial. The Order knew of the French actions and it was rumoured that they withdrew to their castles. Of course, James II was captivated with the fact that Philip had seemed to extend his possessions in a simple manner. At the end of December 1307, he reported to the Pope that if the Order was abolished, certain possessions should be transferred to the monastery where his daughter lived. In February 1308, he instructed his representative at the Papal Curia, to come to an agreement with the Pope. James II wanted to reward the two nephews of the Pope, who lived in James's domain, if he should receive the control over the possessions of the Order of the Temple. The King was not planning on relinquishing the goods to the Church, not even if a new Order was established. The castles on the coast and the border in particular, were extremely important to him.

In January 1308, James II conquered the most important and richest possessions of the Templars in Valencia, without much resistance. Many knights were taken prisoner, including the Master of Aragon. In the other areas that proceeded with less speed; the Templars were warned and entrenched themselves in their seven remaining castles. Ramon Sa Guardia became their new leader and he tried to reach a solution through diplomacy. He asked the Queen to mediate and he wrote a letter to James II. Herein, he directed attention to the struggle against the Muslims of the previous centuries, and referred to the very recent battles in which many Templars died for the sake of Aragon. In addition to taking part in the war, the Order gave many charities not so long ago, to 26 thousand poor people during an epidemic. He asked the King to release the Master and the other members and wanted justice and a fair trial. The answer from the King was short, and boiled down to the fact that he would follow the decisions of the Pope. Ramon continued writing and like Pierre of Bologna in France, he asked his readers how it was possible, that for almost two hundred years already, members from refined and noble families gave years of their lives to an Order which could be guilty of heresy.

On 1 February 1308, the army of James II began with the besieging of castles, whilst the discussions continued. The King remained fixed on the standpoint that he had to obey the Pope, who was after all, the substitute of God and therefore ruled over everyone. Between August and November 1308 most castles surrendered. In May 1309, the last but one fell into the hands of the King by means of betrayal. After a siege of one and a half years, the governments' army conquered the last castle of the Templars in July 1309. All members were now imprisoned, but under the circumstances they received proper treatment.

The Bulls of the Pope from August 1308 could now be carried out. Just as in England, in Aragon torture was not part of the usual law and despite the insistence of the Pope, there were few members tortured in Aragon. No one confessed, only a few outsiders declared that they knew of the worshipping of a head and secret entry procedures. In November 1312, the last individual Templars were judged and acquitted of all accusations, conforming to the Papal Bull.

On Majorca, in Portugal, and in Castile, things proceeded similarly to in Aragon, but without any attempt to resist. On Majorca, the members of the Order were arrested at the end of 1307, but the hearings did not begin until 1310. In the Kingdoms of Portugal and Castile, the arrests probably began just at the beginning of 1308, but the Templars here, also admitted to none of the accusations. There are historians who presume that the rulers of the Iberian Peninsula had no interest in the conviction of the Order of the Temple, because if that was the case, the Pope could lay claim to the possessions. When the Kings realised that they had nothing to be afraid of, they returned to being against the Order.

Italy

There had already been possessions of the Order of the Temple in Italy since 1138, though not as many as in France or on the Iberian Peninsula. Furthermore, Italy consisted of different independent areas and that gave a varied impression of the persecutions. There were seven Papal and provincial commissions established, which subjected relatively few Templars to a hearing. Only in the Kingdom of Naples, where a relative of Philip reigned, it does appears that torture was used on a large scale. Between October 1309 and July 1310, a commission visited about ten cities in the Papal domain. They recorded hardly any result. A couple of members admitted to one or two of the charges after being tortured. In Florence, the inquiry for the province of Tuscany took place in September 1311. Of the thirteen Templars questioned, six admitted to some of the charges, including the Commander of San Gimignano. The remaining seven denied all accusations, even after being tortured.

The commission did not record their statements in the documents, because they were given by members who had just entered into the Order or by service personnel. The commission in Lombardy was favourable to the Order of the Temple. Halfway through 1311, the last meeting of the investigation commission took place in Ravenna. Seven members of the Order denied the accusations, whereby a proposal to torture them was rejected. The commission finally decided to release the members and pronounced that if the majority of the Order was innocent, the Order of the Temple had to be preserved.

Germany

Just as in Italy, this territory consisted of various separate states which reacted differently to the calling of the Pope. It is estimated that there where probably 36 preceptories established in Germany. In the summer of 1308, nearly a year after the events in France, the Archbishop of Magdenburg took a number of Templars prisoners. The Master of the province of Germany was one of them. The Bishop of Halberstadt felt that he had been overlooked, and excommunicated the Archbishop, which was declared null and void by Clement V in September 1310.

In the Rhine region in 1310 and 1311, a number of provincial commission meetings took place. In Trier, situated in the Rhine Region, the Archbishop interrogated a number of members and declared the Order free. In Mainz, the commission received a sudden visit from 21 armed Templars on 14 May 1310. Their leader strongly denied all the accusations and stressed that the Order had not received a fair trial. The Archbishop promised to ask the Pope for advice. A month and a half later, the commission reconvened and heard 49 witnesses, including 37 members, three Counts and a monk. They praised the merits of the Order and the Archbishop joined them in his concluding judgement. This decision was annulled by Clement V, because such a verdict could only be passed by the Pope.

Cyprus
The only important action outside Western Europe took place on Cyprus, where the headquarters of the Order of the Temple was established. The political situation was complicated in those days and in 1306, with the help of the Order of the Temple, King Henry II was dethroned by his brother Amalric. The Templars had trouble with the policies of Henry II, whom they considered as an opponent to the obtaining of a base on the mainland of Palestine. Amalric proclaimed himself as the Governor of the island.

The Papal Bull of 22 November 1307, in which the Christian leaders were commissioned to arrest the members of the Order, reached Cyprus on 6 May 1308. On 12 May, an emissary of Governor Amalric went with the Papal Bull to Limassol, where the highest ranking leaders resided. Ayme d'Oselier, the Marshal, could agree to give most of the possessions into custody, but did not want to relinquish neither the weapons nor the liquid assets. He suggested that all members should withdraw to a few castles and, pending further Papal notices, that these could be besieged by the royal army.

Governor Amalric could not agree with that and sent a new emissary, a monk called Baldwin, who communicated to the Templars, that by refusing they faced the threat of the death penalty and total destruction. After further negotiating, they reached an agreement. The leaders, on behalf of the 83 knights and 35 servants, made a public statement in Nicosia about their innocence. Baldwin translated this into French for them and added that the Templars were good Christians.

But Amalric proved to be untrustworthy. The following day, his soldiers began with the inventorying of the possessions of the Order in Limassol, Paphos and Famagusta. In Limassol, they found many weapons such as, 930 hauberks, 970 crossbows and 604 helmets. The Templars decided not to just give up. On 1 June 1308, their last resistance was broken in Limassol. All members were arrested and secured. The inventorying carried on; in liquid assets, they found a large sum of money. It goes without saying that there is a story that says that the rest of the money was hidden.

The leaders formed a conspiracy to flee from the isle, using a Genoese warship. It was discovered and the guard on the Templars was subsequently strengthened. The first hearings were in May 1310, nearly two years after the arrests. First of all, 21 external witnesses appeared, a majority of which were positive about the Order. Many inhabitants of Cyprus could remember only too well that they, thanks to the heroic behaviour of the Templars during the fall of Acre, were able to escape to Cyprus. The week after, 76 members were heard, including at least 38 knights. Not one of them admitted to any of the accusations. A month later, 35 outsiders made similar statements.

During these last rounds of sittings Governor Amalric was murdered, most probably by a follower of his brother. It meant the return of King Henry II, in August 1310. A year later, in August 1311, the King received a letter from the Pope, in which he asked for a new trial, but this time with the use of torture. Undoubtedly, this was music to Henry II's ears, who had definitely not forgotten the role of the Templars at the coup of his brother.

There is nothing to find of these trials in the chronicles, but a historian does later make reference to the death of Ayme d'Oselier and many other Templars in the dungeons of the castle of Kerynia.

The other countries
In addition the Order of the Temple had other possessions in Austria, Bohemia, Hungary, Slovenia, Poland and Greece (see Chapter V). There is nothing known of the pursuits in these states. In Bohemia members of the nobility misappropriated the possessions of the Order. Included in these were the Templars who took private control of estates.

THE END OF THE ORDER OF THE TEMPLE

On Saturday 16 October 1311, Clement V opened the council in the Cathedral of Vienne, near to Lyon. On the agenda was: the Order of the Temple, a new Crusade and the reforming of the Church. There were ecclesiastical representatives from all over the Roman Catholic areas; from Eire to Hungary and from Scandinavia to South Italy. The Kings were all invited, but only Philip was present during some of the council. It is obvious which point on the agenda Philip was interested in. The other monarchs sent diplomatic representatives.

The arrests of the Templars. It is clear to see from the clothes that these are not knights, but sergeants.

In the months prior to the council, the Pope was kept busy with the evidence against the Order of the Temple. In August 1311, Clement V sent other instructions to get confessions by means of torture to Castile, Aragon, Portugal, Tuscany, Lombardy, Cyprus and Greece. He wanted to involve these in the formation of judgements of the council. Together with a number of confidants, he studied the evidence and he prepared the final charges.

The Pope had also formally invited the Order of the Temple, in August 1308, to defend themselves. According to his letters he was extremely surprised that at the end of October, nine Templars did indeed show up. They wanted to defend the Order and said that there were between fifteen hundred and two thousand followers gathered in the region of Lyon to give the defence strength. Clement V had the nine arrested, in the hope that the assembly would quickly make a decision about the abolishment of the Order. Nothing more was heard about the followers.

Directly after the commencement of the council, the Pope appointed a commission which had to make a proposal to the gathering. During the first months of the council, it became clear that the overall majority of the Bishops present thought that the Order had to be able to defend itself. Even most of the French representatives supported this idea. Also on the subject of the dividing of the possession of the Order of the Temple, things did not go according to the wishes of Clement V. He wanted to give the possessions to the Hospitallers, whilst the King of Spanish Aragon was in favour of donating them to his own Order of Calatrava. Philip advocated the founding of a new Order, under the leadership of a member of the French royal house. The council wanted to establish a totally new international Order, with the purpose being the reconquering of the Holy Land.

To put power into his words, Philip appeared in Vienne in 1312: his two brothers, his three sons and a large army were emphatically present. That made an impression on the Pope. On 22 March, he gathered with the preparation committee and on 3 April, in the presence of the French royal house, he announced that he had decided to abolish the Order of the Temple; this without pronouncing a judgement on the accusations. Clement V would still deliberate the question as to what should be done with its possessions and its members, The Bull which abolishes the Order is called the Vox in excelso and was dated 22 March 1312.

> *...It is true that the previously mentioned Order, on the grounds of trials against it, operated as a heretic organisation, can not be judged by a definitive proclamation... therefore we abolish, not without bitterness and soul suffering, not through a judicial proclamation, but out of fatherly concern and apostolic defectiveness, the named Order of the Temple together with all its establishments, stipulations and names, for ever with the permission of the Holy Council...*

The Pope negotiated with diplomats from France and Aragon about the possessions of the Templars. On 2 May he dictated his decision to the council. All possessions of the Order of the Temple should be transferred to the

Hospitallers, with the exception of those in Aragon, Portugal, Castile and Majorca. These areas would be deliberated about. The leaders who did not co-operate were excommunicated.

In August 1313, Philip wrote in a letter to the Pope that he agreed with the decision, with the condition that the Hospitallers should be completely reformed. This stipulation has caused various historians to think that the French King intended the destruction of not only the Order of the Temple, but also the Hospitallers, from the beginning. The long duration of the trial against the Order of the Temple and the death of the King in 1314 would have interfered with the carrying out of his original plan. The decision of the Pope resulted in the already long discussed fusion between both of the largest military orders, but in a different way than James of Molay had ever thought possible.

Despite the threat of excommunication, the transferring of the possessions of the Templars did not proceed without a hitch. In France, the Hospitallers had to pay a large amount of money to the King to cover the trial costs, a couple of years later this payment was considerably increased. In other countries the new owner had to also negotiate for a long time before they could obtain the possessions of the Order of the Temple. In 1323, the largest share was actually transferred and given the complex situation and the quantity of property, this happened in a relatively short space of time.

In England in 1308, an inventory of the goods of the Order was made. It counted 36 pounds in liquid assets in the forty preceptories. Perkins (1910) estimated that King Edward II received fifteen hundred pounds net annually from the assets of the Templars in the period 1308-1313. It seems peculiar that in 1308, only 36 pounds was found in the preceptories. With this amount, we do not have to immediately think about the hiding of a treasure. It could be that the English Templars had just sent all the liquid surpluses to Cyprus. Furthermore, the making of an inventory of another man's credits was not a fraud-proof activity. That was even more so if it involved an organisation suspected of criminal activities. Maybe individual Templars hid certain amounts of money. Such a treasure would not have been very big; the Order had high outgoings and sent its money regularly to the headquarters on Cyprus. The English King was slow in handing over the Templars goods to the Hospitallers. In 1337 or 1338, they received the control over the New Temple of London.

The successor of Clement V, John XXII, rounded off the negotiations of the Temple possessions on the Iberian Peninsula. The Kings of this area were afraid that with handing over of goods of the Order of the Temple to the Hospitallers, a Papal power might arise in their country, which they would not have a grip on.

THE END

Council of Vienne.

In 1274, the council, for this reason, had already spoken out against a fusion of both Orders. Because the Peninsula was still partly in the hands of the Moors (in 1492 Granada was conquered), the position of both Orders was different from that of other monastic orders in the rest of Europe. The possessions were comparatively much larger, they were military locations and the Templars and Hospitallers, in comparison to the other countries, had many more soldiers than civilian functionaries. Eventually the Hospitallers received a limited number of preceptories, whilst the rest of the earlier assets of the Templars, for the most part, were donated to new military orders. In Portugal the possessions were transferred to the Order of Christ. This Order was officially recognised by the Pope in 1319 and was in a sense a continuation of the Portuguese branch of the Templars.

The convictions of the members ran comparatively smoothly. The common members, who were innocent or had deferred to the Church, were allowed to enter into a monastery or spend their last days in their previous Templar property. They all received a good pension as long as they continued to behave like clergymen. From various reports, it appears that not everyone held to his stipulation. There were those who married and lost this pension because of it. During the third decade of the fourteenth century, the attention paid to most of these people weakened and they disappeared out of the chronicles. A notable event occurred in Palestine around 1340. A German pilgrim came across two older men, near to the Dead Sea, who told him that they were members of the Order of the Temple. They had been taken prisoner by the Muslims after the fall of Acre in 1291. Then they entered into service of a Sultan and had started a family. The events in Europe had totally eluded them. A little while later, they went to Europe, were taken into the Papal court and spent their last years with their families in France.

The highest members of the Templars were deferred to the Papal court of law, but the Pope was not in a hurry with the adjudicating of the four leaders. It was not until 22 December 1313 that he appointed a special committee of three Cardinals to conclude the remnants of the whole process against the Order of the Temple. On 18 March 1314, the four leaders appeared at a public session of the court in Paris. To the dismay of the audience, James of Molay and Geoffroi of Charney, the Preceptor of the Temple in Normandy, declared that the Order was absolutely innocent and they publicly retracted their earlier confessions. When Philip the Fair got wind of this he immediately reacted. After a short discussion with his jurors and a shallow consultation with the Papal committee, he had the two men put to death by burning them at the stake, the same day. This occurred on the island near to the Ile-de-la-Cité, where a memorial is now a reminder of this happening. The other two leaders spent their last years in prison.

According to legend, James of Molay was supposed to have put a curse on the Pope and the King, shortly before the fire killed him. He predicted that within in a year, they would have to take responsibility for their actions before a heavenly court of law. Actually, both leading men died that very same year.

The degree of truth of the accusations

The trial documents, drafted by representatives of Clement V and Philip, are practically the only writings which give us an insight into the nature of the charges against the Order of the Temple. These charges were not original: they formed a collective of heretic practices, such as those which have regularly emerged in the chronicles since the eleventh century. The accusations against the

Cathars, in the South of France at the beginning of the thirteenth century, belong to the most well known. A very important difference between the Cathars and the Templars was that not one single Templar wanted to die for his 'heretic faith.' This is in contrast to the Cathars who had many martyrs.

In the conflict between Boniface and Philip, Philip made use of similar impeachments. Generally, the opinion is that the advisors to Philip IV based these complaints against the Templars, in a sly manner, upon those heresies well known to the French folk. They were helped with this by the members of the Order, who apparently were not able to withstand the torturing and consequently readily admitted the accusations held in front of them.

With the reading of the confessions, one cannot get away from the impression that the Templars fanatically fantasized. It was as if they wanted to please their audience with strange stories about the practices in the Order. The descriptions of the kissing ritual are characteristic. The Templars kissed, or were kissed on their clothing or the bare body, the mouth, navel, chest, between the shoulder blades, back, shoulder, anus, thighs, between the thighs, the nipple, the neck, stomach and ankles. Such a variety surely, cannot be taken seriously. Anyway, it could be that this kissing ritual has become proverbial. A less well know saying is: watch out for the kiss of a Templar. Apparently it was dangerous to be kissed by a Templar.

The same diversity concerns the worshipping of idols and the mentioning of secret rules. Despite desperate attempts from the servants of the King, there were no traces to be found of these practices. After the trial, many historians searched for documents with a mysterious character, without result. A servant of the Order declared that he had heard that an important Templar had left just before the arrests in Paris, with eighteen ships. This testimony, for many people, gives reason to presume that the Templars took their treasure to safety. Of course, this is nonsense. This statement was undoubtedly made under (the threat of) torture. Besides, it is highly questionable as to whether the Order owned so many ships. If they did have eighteen ships, they were stationed at Cyprus to fight against the Muslims there, by way of piracy.

The giving of such strange statements is not unique: later cases from history demonstrate that people are prepared to let their fantasies run away with them under extreme torture. It was not any different then. Pierre of Bologna managed to put it nicely into words when, in April 1310, he stated that

> ...*the brothers of the Order in the Kingdom of France were suddenly arrested with a destructive frenzy and led like sheep to the slaughter house, in one blow*

James of Molay and Geoffroi of Charney, the Commander of Normandy, die by burning at the stake.

> they were robbed of their possessions and all other affairs, handed over to a strict imprisonment, and were innumerably tortured in a variety of ways, whereby many died, many were permanently handicapped, and because of this, many were forced to lie about themselves and the Order.

It goes without saying that sodomy occurred in the Order; it is with good reason that the Rule paid attention to this. At the court, in monastic orders and within the Roman Catholic clergy, there were for sure men who were guilty of this mortal sin. By the way, the Western Europeans thought that homosexuality was a frequently occurring phenomenon with the Muslims. Christian merchants were involved in the selling of young boys to various Muslim leaders. Because the perfects, the leaders of the Cathars, always travelled in pairs, it seems obvious that male erotica was practiced. We cannot draw the conclusion from this, that there were therefore special relationships between the Templars and the Muslims or the Cathars.

Entry into the Order and the Chapter meetings were closed and the disclosure of what happened there, had as a consequence, exclusion from the Order. This shroud of mystery was not understood by everyone, inside or outside the Order. On the other hand, this procedure was nothing special; all monastic orders had internal gatherings.

It seems as though corruption and licentiousness was a second nature of the clergy. The rise of the Mendicant Orders in the thirteenth century was, without a doubt, a reaction to the luxurious lifestyles of many ecclesiastical leaders. The large amount of possessions of the Templars was definitely striking, but on the whole nothing special within the ecclesiastical organisation. There were rumours flying around about all sections of the Church and the manner of how they, rightfully or wrongfully, came into their possession. The accusations aimed at the Templars were therefore not unique.

The veneration of artefacts had been a firm part of the Christian belief since the fourth century. People believed that the remains of God fearing people were the medium to God, and a respectful approach, such as worship and osculation were a normal ritual. In the first instance the local Saints were especially popular and, after the fall of Jerusalem, the Western market was inundated with the body parts of people who figured in the Bible. The Order of the Temple also owned a great amount of artefacts; after all, they were close to the source. In addition, many relics were used for the securing of a loan to the secular leaders. The Templars honoured their remnants as holy, just as everyone else in the Middle Ages.

More than one member of the Order described the worshipping of a head. Later it was suggested that this could have been the skull of Hugh of Payns, the first Grand Master. For this time, that was not an unusual phenomenon: every self respecting parish owned a body part of a Saint in order to stimulate the pilgrimage and therefore their income. A divine service in the darkness, with a veneration of relics included, conjured up a mystical sphere. Whoever has experienced that, knows that it has a mysterious character.

Those who take the confessions of the Templars during the trial seriously, fail to appreciate the nature of the process. Philip IV and his advisors began the trial with a charge, consisted of a collection of centuries old heresies. The martyrs were forced into admitting these, so there should be no value attached to their statements. All the more so, because from other sources, it appears that the Order of the Temple was never suspected of heresy. Those who give the Order of the Temple an important place in the history of the Turin Shroud for instance, and suspect that the Order worshipped this robe, are completely off the mark. This accusation was an invention of Philip IV, based upon the knowledge that every Christian organisation honoured relics. There was nothing peculiar about it, unless you make a cat or a mysterious object out of it.

Conclusions

The Hospitallers played no role whatsoever in the trial against their fellow Order. They concentrated themselves on the conquering of Rhodes from 1306, but one can be certain than that they kept a close eye on what happened to the Templars. Historians differ in opinion with the question of which Order was the richest; the majority estimate that the Order of the Temple had the most money. According to the thirteenth century chronicler, Matthew Paris, the Templars possessed nine thousand and the Hospitallers nineteen thousand preceptories. Every preceptory, according to Matthew, could supply a completely armed knight for the Holy Land. It is unclear as to how Matthew came by his figures. It is a recognised fact that he exaggerated terribly, but the Hospitallers did have more possessions. The bank activities of the Hospitallers, compared to those of the Templars, did not amount to anything. Their preceptory in the city of Paris was noticeably smaller than the Templars property in the French capital.

Supposing that Philip IV was intending to lighten his financial worries, it was logical that he chose the Templars as his target. He saw the gigantic Templars complex in his city and he had experience of the banking activities of the Order. It was very obvious that he overlooked the humble Hospitallers in this regard.

Subsequently, it has to be determined that the Order of the Temple stood absolutely no chance. Philip decided to destroy the Order in about 1306, and he had the power to do so. The Pope and many high clergymen were appointed upon his intercession and were hardly prepared, or in a position to speak out against the King. In addition, he had sufficient secular influence at his disposal to completely instigate the necessary implementations. On the other hand, the Order of the Temple seemed more powerful than it actually was. They had many possessions and were independent, but that is precisely what made them a vulnerable and favourite subject.

In the second instance, the Kings of England and Aragon understood all too well that they could, thanks to Philip, get rid of a state within a state. Besides, the concept of the Crusade was no longer popular with the general public at the beginning of the fourteenth century. The fall of Acre in 1291, was the last disappointment from a series of many. Actually, only the first Crusade was a success; all the other seven were failed undertakings. Without the Crusades, the Order of the Temple was an empty organisation and that made it very vulnerable.

Together with the Hospitallers, the Order of the Temple was the figurehead of the conquering of the Holy Land. This aim seemed further away than ever in 1305. It was obvious that they were no longer considered to be in a position to return to Palestine. Whilst both of the other military orders found new targets (the Teutonic Knights in East Europe and the Hospitallers on Rhodes), the Order of the Temple remained stuck in the past. In 1307, James of Molay had just come up with a plan of action for the reconquering of the Holy Land.

Philip played it cleverly. He ensured, even if sometimes on the borderline, that the proper formal procedures were followed. He knew to mobilise the resistance at the suitable moment, and to eliminate the defenders. The calling in of Philippe de Marigny, in all its slyness, was particularly a stroke of mastery. The Pope had after all, transferred the convicting of the individual members of the Order to the Archbishops. Philippe was more or less well within his rights when he sent 54 of the most assertive Templars to the stake at the peak of the defence. Subsequently, it did not take much effort to let the most important defender, Pierre de Bologna, disappear. Clement V had not protested when Philip suggested to him that he should guard the Templars on behalf of the Church. It was the highlight of the devils game of Philip, the rest was the finishing touche.

James of Molay was no match for the intrigues of Philip. He did not know what was going on. He insufficiently realised that the Order of the Temple was a hierarchical organisation, and without his leadership, practically operated with a broken wing. Undoubtedly, in the direct conflict with the Muslims, he was an exemplary leader. He did not know the first thing about governmental and social strategies. Only at the end of his life did he manfully stand his ground and that led directly to his cremation.

Lots of books have been written about the motives of Philip. Officially, nothing is known of his standpoint because he let others do the talking. In the meantime, historians are convinced that he was a powerful leader, who inspired his ministers and other advisors. From the manner in which he practised his administration from 1285, it is easy to deduce why he wrung the neck of the Order of the Temple. He was after its wealth: possessions, exploitation results and liquid assets. His period of reign was distinguished by financial problems and complications: the Church, the Jews and the Lombards were his first victims.

Of course there were additional arguments. The Order of the Temple fell directly under the Pope, whereby Clement V could himself decide if they deserved to be abolished. A secular ruler could not be definitely sure if a Pope would come who would bring his military order into action during a conflict between the Church and the state. And, this in a time when the royal houses were developing themselves more and more into a form which gave them absolute power over the whole country. Some historians think that Philip considered himself to be the guardian of the Church, and that he was seriously of the opinion that this was threatened by the heresy of the Order of the Temple. Given the fact that there is not one known letter from Philip containing his personal considerations, every contention about his motives could be true.

The action of Philip was a clever piece of propaganda, relationship management, strategic and targeted acting: not for the sake of the ecclesiastical salvation, but because of self profit.

XIII. The Templars are dead, long live the myths

INTRODUCTION

The Order of the Temple was definitely not an underground operating organisation. The Templars needed money and manpower and they never made a secret of these facts. Not everybody was just as lucky with their unconcealed begging. The rights and privileges that the Templars received from the ecclesiastical and secular institutes were after all at the expense of others, in many cases the clergies of the parish churches and they had a big problem with that. The many Bulls which the Popes released had a recurrent theme every time: the settling of differences of opinions over territories, (ecclesiastical) taxes and other financial matters between ordinary clergy and the Templars.

In the period between 1120 and 1307, the Order was never suspected of breaking the Roman Catholic rules of faith. Their opponents would have done their utmost to look for ways to discredit the Templars. Should there have been heretic practices taking place then they would have definitely attracted attention. The critic of William of Tyre, who knew the Order from close up, went on about their (supposed) financial greed and their independent position pertaining to the Archbishop of Jerusalem. Other chroniclers agreed with him, but they were also not referring to lack of trust in the faith.

In addition to this, the youngest sons of families throughout Europe, sometimes generations in succession, became members of the Order. Some of them were famous, but in general the members belonged to the lower nobility. These people were of old Roman Catholic houses and not prepared to die for a heretic organisation. The Order of the Temple was far from a closed club because they needed constant new warriors. They could not permit a ballot committee and the demands for entry were therefore never set highly. The keeping of a secret of whatever nature, would have definitely been impossible in such an open club. On close examination, the Order of the Temple was not a 'real' Roman Catholic organisation. They did not interfere with religious business which occurred outside of the Order at all. It is therefore understandable that they, not like the Dominicans for example, played absolutely no role in the conflict of the Popes against the heretic movements. The members were first and foremost knights, who found an ideal way of putting their military training into practice, in the aims of the Order of the Temple. Their extra reward was that they went to heaven after indulging in their hobby. In the Middle Ages, that was the best that one could achieve.

The myths about the Templars

The Renaissance, black magic

Writings regularly appeared in the years after the fall of the Templars, in which the guilt of the Order was questioned. Authors, especially the Italians (Dante, Boccaccio), Germans and to a lesser degree, the English, were convinced of the innocence of the Templars. The Order would have been the victim of the greed of Philip IV. The French on the whole defended their King and the first Papal historians went on about the scandalous blasphemy of the Templars. With airing all these conceptions, the Papal historians do not provoke the impression that they have conducted thorough investigations.

In 1531, a book was released by the famous German humanitarian scholar, Agrippa von Nettesheim, *De Occulta Philisophia*. Goethe had this man in mind when he wrote *Faust*. Agrippa published his work in a period when the ridding of black magic and witches was the order of the day. The German gave two examples of this form of heresy: the Bogomils and the Templars. The Bogomils formed a heretic movement (the so called Gnostics) in Greece in the eleventh century. The Byzantine chroniclers, Psellus and Anna Commena, made reference to this Christian sect. Anna mentioned their heretical beliefs and Psellus described the secret rituals. The Bogomils were supposed to have devoted themselves to orgies so that they could subsequently offer the babies that were a result of these. The ashes of the infant were cooked in bread and then eaten. According to Agrippa, the Templars were guilty of such activities too.

He suggested, in addition to this, that there was a connection between the witchcraft of older women, and the practices of the Templars. *De Occulta Philosphia* was the most popular book about magic, during the Renaissance. A few decades later, the French writer Paradin agreed, with Agrippa: new members of the Templars had to worship a figure when they joined the Order. The image was covered with a human skin and had two glowing carbuncles for the face. The forthcoming members had to renounce Christ and scorn the cross. Afterwards an orgy took place with the women that were present. If a child was born, it was passed around the brothers in a circle until it was dead. The baby was then cooked and an ointment was made from the remains, which was then smeared into the idol. Psellus (again: from the eleventh century and referring to the Bogomils) was Paradins source and he described this ritual in detail. Paradin knew of another practice of the Templars: the ashes of a dead member of the Order were mixed into a drink and consumed by the brothers. So as described in Chapter XII, Paradin reported that *drink like a Templar* is a tavern saying, originating from the drinking bouts of the Templars.

The Frenchman Bodin, also an author of the Renaissance, appears to have a more realistic vision of the oppressions of the Templars. He blamed the powerful of the earth for the suppression of the minorities, for their own benefit. The Jews, the first Christians, Gnostics and the Templars were, for him, classic examples. He cited German scholars who, according to him, had sufficiently proved the innocence of the Order of the Temple. Philip IV invented the accusations in order to be able to confiscate their money and estates. Bodin was the first publicist who put the fall of the Templars in a broader scope.

A Flemish Jesuit, Del-Rio, wrote a manual on the pursuance of witchcraft. He came to the same conclusion as Bodin: the Templars were innocent.

The French brothers Dupuy were the first historians to investigate and publish part of the trial documents. Their book from 1654 served a political purpose: Cardinal Richelieu, the most important minister of all of the French monarchy, wanted to prove the power that the royal house had over the French Church. The trial against the Templars was an excellent example of this. The Dupuy brothers did not have the Papal archives at their disposal and their choice out of the other archives was very selective. Their conclusion was obvious: Philip IV was completely within his rights and had good grounds for destroying the Order.

In the nineteenth century, historians had access to the whole archive for the first time, including the Papal documents.

Chivalry
After the Renaissance a new element appeared in the discussions about the monk-soldiers. The medieval knight was idealised and Italian and English authors chose the Templars as the noblest example of the past. They were Knights of Christ, prepared to die for the honour of God and the defending of

the Holy Land. In the following decades, the knighthood became synonymous with noble, courteous, brave, and all sorts of 'chivalrous' associations arose. This was all related to the rise of citizenry; the new realms, just as the nobility centuries before, wanted to belong to an exclusive organisation. The Freemasonry, originated in the eighteenth century, was an important example of this. The Scot Ramsay, domiciled in France, was the first Freemason who made the connection with the Crusade and the Hospitallers. He did not mention the Templars during his speech in 1736. There are those who insist that he did not dare to do so because this Order was subtly thought about in France. The Freemason was searching for standards and values and expressed these on account of the traditions and metaphors from the past.

The secrets
The German branch of the Freemasonry was the first to establish a relationship with the Templars, and the Scot Johnson completed the story in 1760. The conflict of the Templars in the Holy Land was the fifth phase in world history; the sixth began after the death of James of Molay. The Grand Masters were in the possession of particular knowledge about the Essenes, a Jewish sect from the beginning of our era. This was passed on to them by the Canons of the Holy Sepulchre in Jerusalem.

James of Molay was given the name Hiram by the authors, the murdered builder of the Temple of Solomon. During the night before his execution, 'Hiram' told the Count of Beaujeu the secret of the Grand Masters. James sent the Count to the Parisian Temple and he came back with the shroud of the Grand Master. In the folds the following was hidden: a silver case with the secrets of the Order, the crown of the Kingdom of Jerusalem, the seven armed candlestick from the Temple of Solomon and the four golden images of the evangelists from the Holy Sepulchre. James also told the Count of Beaujeu the secret hiding place of the treasure of the Templars.

The Order was continued in 1314 in Scotland, so Johnson knew. He wrote with authority, because he was, according to him, 'Knight of the Grand Lion of the High Order of Lords of the Temple of Jerusalem.' It is unclear if the conceptions of Johnson have anything in common with those of the Freemasonry.

In itself, it seems peculiar, in a time when the Age of Reason was declared as being of the highest importance, that these kinds of ideas were expressed on a large scale. The Roman Catholic Church no longer had influence on the sciences and Newton managed to bring a system to the world. With the progress in science, the need for romance increased and just as in the Renaissance, this was searched for in the past. It is a logical reaction to the rationalisation of society. In the following centuries, in connection with the Freemasons or not, different variations about the role of the Templars were still published. The historian Partner (1990) gives a detailed analysis. It seems as though our knowledge about the Templars has become greater over the centuries. In the first instance they were judged as being heretics. They were the culprits of black magic and later holders of another secret, without any new information being available. It is reassuring to know that this secret is preserved by a respectable organisation such as the Freemasons.

The Hiram Key

The Freemasons, Knight and Lomas, are convinced that their brotherhood dates from way before our era. Moses passed on the principle, originally from Egypt, of this association over to the Jews. The royal house of David was continued conforming to the rituals of the Freemasons. Jesus, as a descendant of David, was a leading figure in this organisation. The Templars discovered secret rolls about the first Christian community in Jerusalem, under the Temple. This was during the leadership of James, the brother of Jesus. The Templars, with the aid of the old scripts, became the founders of the Freemasons.

In their book *The Hiram Key* they founded this theory. Knight and Lomas claim that there are three possible explanations for the starting of the Freemasons.
1. They are just as old as the rituals claim. The Order does indeed stem from the events around the building of the Temple of King Solomon, and handed over to us in an unknown manner.
2. The Freemasons emanate from the medieval masons- or stonemasons' guild, whereby the practical skills of the stonemasons were translated into the so called 'speculative' freemasonry knowledge about lifting the morals.
3. Their ritual directly derives from the 'Order of the Poor Soldiers of Christ and the Temple of Solomon,' better known as the Templars.

They keep silent about a fourth more likely option: in the eighteenth century a number of creative minds founded the Freemasons and completed them, in a highly inventive way, with a large amount of rituals.

Knight and Lomas begin their search with an overall history of the Templars,

and immediately go astray. One error follows the other. An incomplete anthology:
1. Jerusalem was not conquered on the 14th June, but the 15th July 1099 by the Western Europeans.
2. The Pope recognised the Hospitallers in 1113 and not five years later, as the authors claim.
3. Regarding Baldwin II, the King of Jerusalem, they write the following: 'All of a sudden something altered in their original plans. In October 1126, Baldwin died and it was probably not coincidental that Hugh of Pays travelled to the West for the first time to look for new recruits, a few months after the death of their benefactor. Did they go through all of their money and food before they had completed the search? Or had they purposely awaited the death of Baldwin so that he could not share in the proceeds of the treasure?'
Baldwin was very much alive in 1126, and actually died on 21 August 1131.
4. Of the First Grand Master, Hugh of Payns, Knight and Lomas say that he (after the Council of Troyes in 1129) remained married to a Catherine of St. Clair, a Scottish lady of Norman descent. All the historians agree that Hugh, in 1129, had already been a widower for dozens of years. Apart from that, it is inconceivable that a leader of a monastic organisation was married. Not one single Pope, let alone Bernard of Clairvaux, would have accepted that.

Both Freemasons dealt with practically the whole of the world's history in their book: the Sumerians, the Egyptians, the Jews, the Life of Jesus and James, and suchlike. If they have compiled these just as carefully as those about the Templars, then that says enough about the value of the truth attached to their theories.

According to Knight and Lomas the Templars excavated on Mount Moria, under the remains of the Jewish Temple. They indicate this by writing that, "there is in fact proof that they have performed detailed excavations there." A British archaeologist is believed to have found objects in the mountain, at the beginning of the twentieth century, which 'without a doubt, belonged to the Templars.' Supposing that they were indeed possessions of the Templars, then the question remains as to who put these things there and when.

In addition, in their book they regularly claim that they have previously proved that the Templars have done excavations. A fine construction: you

Angels hand over the Grail to a couple of people.

present a hypothesis, provide no proof whatsoever and state that it is true. Hence, quicksand.

It is evident that there have been excavations under the Temple remains. Empress Helena excavated there in the fourth century and the First Crusaders followed her example in 1099, twenty years before the Templars had the control over the Temple platform.

The authors go totally too far when they deal with the Turin Shroud. They conclude that James of Molay was crucified during his interrogation, on the basis of a frieze in a Scottish church. Under the leadership of the inquisitor of France, William d'Imbert, the Grand Master was nailed to the cross in the same way as Jesus. James was removed from the cross and wrapped in a shroud: the same one that the Templars used for their secret, and therefore absolutely unknown, entry rituals. Thanks to the good care of the family of Geoffroi of Charney, James of Molay survived the torturing.

Parzival

Since the fourth quarter of the twelfth century, novels (prose and poetry) have been released, in which the military orders fulfilled a role. In these stories, the Templars were mentioned more often than the Hospitallers. This has nothing to do with the popularity of the Templars, but rather the difference between both Orders. The Hospitallers were a combination of knights and charitas, while the purest form of the monastic soldier was the Templar. It is obvious that the authors of romances of chivalry took the Order of the Temple as an example. The military orders played a supporting role in all of these stories; they helped the hero (not a member of the Order) in his battle against evil. If there was a conception of spirituality, then this was introduced by others, mostly hermits. In the novels, the military orders were seen as soldiers of Christ and not as monks with a religious message. In that regard, this was in unison with the chronicles of that time.

An unusual category of these fictitious stories is the Grail romance. Chrétien of Troyes (died 1188) was the first with *Le Roman de Perceval* or *Le Conte du Graal*. Directly after these, various other Grail novels appeared; to this day, many are inspired by this topic.

Wolfram von Eschenbach was the only medieval author who connected the Grail with the Templars. Wolfram was a subordinate of Hermann, the Landgrave of Thüringen in Bayern. Hermann was well known as a patron of poets and artists and was one of the founders of the Teutonic Knights. Wolfram lived from about 1170 until shortly before 1220 and knew the gentlemen of Walldürn, the inhabitants of the castle of Wildenberc. It is not unimaginable that Wolfram went on a Crusade with his feudal lord, Hermann, in 1198. That would explain his great knowledge of the Eastern culture. He was an educated layman, had a thorough command of the German and French language, knew a lot about the Middle East, but he did not hold a high ranking position. The story of Chrétien was well known to him, but according to his postscript, Wolfram thought that the Frenchman had done an injustice to the original story. Around 1210, he wrote his most famous work: *Parzival.*

The main character, Parzival, grew up in the forest, because his mother did not want him to become a knight. This still happened though, and after all kinds of adventures he joined the Round Table of King Arthur. On his first visit to the Grail stronghold (Munsalvaesche), he did not know precisely which question to ask.

When he later realises, he goes in search of the Grail. After a number of exciting adventures he finds it, and it turns out that Parzival appears to be the heir to the Grail stronghold. At the same time, the book describes the adventures of Gawain, the best knight of the Round Table. Parzival can be read on a number of levels: it is an exciting knight story, telling of the development of people, it handles the choice between good and evil and it is about the spiritual (Parzival) and the material man (Gawain).

Wolfram employs a symbolic use of language, which is in fact explained in many ways. He could have done that in order to hide a secret, or to prevent the inquisition at that time, from accusing him of heresy. These statements are not obvious. Medieval religious men, authors and artists were continually looking for a current translation of the biblical conceptions. In that time, a numerical theory arose for instance, with a religious basis. So the use of the number zero was inhibited for years by the Church, because it was discovered by the devil.

Wolfram spoke about the 'Templeise' as the guards (that is something different to supervisors!) of the castle where the Grail was kept. The Templeise are not identical to the Templars: indeed, they serve to pay a penance for their sins, protect the Holy places and have to remain chaste. But they do not live under the Rule of a military order and they could marry if they were sent out to govern a country. Their emblem is the turtle dove, the symbol for chastity, and not a cross. Although the Templeise are allowed to look at Holy affairs, they do not function as ecclesiastical advisors of the Holy places. Here also, a hermit fulfils this role. It could have been that Wolfram had the Templars in mind when he devised the Templeise. In his book he often makes use of the many occurring phenomena of the Middle Ages.

And the Grail: Wolfram is completely unclear what sort of object it was. If Parzival sees the Grail for the first time, it is in a condition to provide a lot of people with warm and cold provisions. Wolfram describes it so:

> ...*the highest heavenly filling which was root and branch at the same time. It was a thing called the Grail, and it surpassed all earthly perfection. She who wears the Grail is called Repanse de Schoye. The nature of the Grail was such that who ever wanted to appropriately take care of it had to correctly preserve his chastity, and avoid all deceit.*

The object was left on this earth by a bevy that rose high above the stars. It could only have been woven by someone who is known in heaven and is destined to be there. A hermit (the uncle of Parzival) gave a further description: a stone, called lapsis exillis, which provides nourishment and has a healing property. A man, even though he was very ill, could not die in the first week after he saw the stone. 'Though he beheld the stone for two hundred years, only his hair became grey.' On every Good Friday, a dove appeared which flew down from heaven and it placed a Host upon the stone. The stone was a source of nutrition, whose power maintained the knightly brethren (the guardians). The supervisors of the Grail could be boys as well as girls. The Grail was cared for by virgins and was only visible to Christians. On the edge of the stone a text once appeared. Thus, it foretold who was designated by heaven to be the guardian of the Grail. Finally, Wolfram stressed that many knew of the existence of the Grail, without knowing anything much else about it.

There are some authors who, in their own way, have let their fantasies run away with them with this story. The castle of Musalvaesche would in reality have been the Cathars castle of Montsalvat of Montségur and, because of this the Cathars were called upon to be the supervisors of the Grail. That is rather far fetched. It is more obvious that Wolfram had the castle of Wildenberc in mind (Monsalvaesche-Mont sauvage-Mons silvaticus-Wildenberc).

For the rest, also partly on the grounds of other Grail novels, the Grail has been made out to be everything and more besides: a goblet, a dish in which the blood of Jesus was collected, a meteor, a grape vine, an aura, the Stone of Wisdom, the Ark of the Covenant, the Turin Shroud, a floating chessboard, a holy book and a sculptured head of Jesus. Baigent and his fellow writers have a different explanation in their book, *The Holy Blood and the Holy Grail*, the

Holy Grail was called the Sangraal or Sangreal, in various documents. That produces a pleasant word game: Sangreal became Sang Royal, meaning royal blood. And that has to be the blood of Christ, that is to say, his descendants.

Wolfram von Eschenbach described the Templeise as the guards of the Grail. The supervisors were boys or girls, but surely not templeise. Nobody could capture the Grail, because it was decided from heaven as to who would be named the guardian of the Grail. Up to the present day, there are people who firmly maintain that the Templars possessed the Grail, on the basis of the book, *Parzival*. The most probable reasoning is that Wolfram enjoyed, without further ulterior motives, to tell this chivalrous story in a symbolic language. If only he knew what he had done.

THE ARK OF MOSES

In his book, *The Sign and the Seal: the quest for the lost Ark of the Covenant*, the journalist, Hancock, describes his search for the Ark of the Covenant. Long ago, after the departure of the Jews out of Egypt, Moses made the Ark of the Covenant on the instruction of God. Shortly thereafter, he received the stone tablets on which the Ten Commandments were written and the Jews stored these in the Ark. During the centuries thereafter, the Ark played a crucial role in all the battles which the Jews delivered. At a certain moment in time, the Jews, whispered to by God, deemed it necessary to choose a permanent place for the Ark. In the tenth century before Christ, King Solomon therefore built his Temple in Jerusalem, especially for the Ark.

Solomon procreated a child with the Queen of Sheba, who according to Hancock, originated from Ethiopia, around the same period. She adopted the Jewish religion and went back to her own country, where the child of Solomon was born. At the age of 20, this offspring went to Jerusalem and, with the help of some priests, stole this Holy object. Since then, the Ark has been stored in a chapel in Axum, a place in the North of Ethiopia.

This legend was put into writing in the Ethiopian chronicle, *Kebra Nagast* (from the thirteenth century). This coincides with the fact that the Ark is the most important artefact of the Orthodox-Christian Ethiopian Church. People have stored a replica of the Ark in all of the approximately twenty thousand churches, since the fourth century. It is an exceptional artefact of Ethiopian Christianity, which is closely affiliated with the Greek-Orthodox Church.

The history from the *Kebra Nagast* is not at all in line with the readings of the Bible. Indeed, Moses made the Ark of the Covenant and Solomon built the Temple as the storehouse of the Ark. The Queen of Sheba went to visit Solomon, stayed in Jerusalem for a while and returned to her own country. In the Bible it does not make reference to her conversion or the impregnation of the Queen by Solomon. In addition to this, according to Bible scholars, Sheba was a place in Yemen and not in Ethiopia. The Bible also suggests that the Ark was still in the Temple of Solomon in the seventh century before Christ:

> *Hezekiah received the letter from the hand of the messengers and read it; then Hezekiah went up to the house of the LORD and spread it before the LORD. And Hezekiah prayed before the LORD, and said: O LORD the God of Israel, who are enthroned above the cherubim...*

This is in II Kings, Chapter 19 verse 14-15; the cherubim stood on the lid of the Ark. After this, the Ark is not mentioned in the Bible any more. That is peculiar, because it was an extremely important object to the Jews. It is unclear what has happened to the Ark of the Covenant.

Hancock is well informed and claims that the Templars were too, and that they hid this knowledge in two important cultural objects; the Cathedral of Chartres and the book *Parzival*. The builders of the Cathedral of Chartres and the author of *Parzival* (Wolfram von Eschenbach) knew of the chronicle *Kebra Nagast*. They were aware of where the Ark of the Covenants was and made a treasure map from the book and the church. Only initiates could understand the code and there was only one medieval organisation that was qualified: the Templars. They were responsible for ensuring that this code was assimilated into the church and the book.

Hugh of Payns would have had one goal in mind when he founded the military order: to find the Ark of the Covenant. Hugh, during one of his first pilgrimages, had learned about this from old Jewish documents. He discovered that the Jews had hidden the Ark in the Temple platform, shortly before the destruction of Jerusalem, in the sixth century before Christ. The Templars, in the first years of their existence, excavated the mountain, but found nothing. The fact that the Ark was not brought triumphantly to Europe, underlined these suppositions. The Order did find the plans to the building of the original Temple and they slyly handed these to Bernard of Clairvaux. Shortly afterwards, the Order found out where the Ark really was and they instructed that this information had to be hidden in the church and a book. Hancock considered

On the most Southerly point of Athos, the famous Greek peninsula, a Templars cross is depicted on a fountain. The fountain has been there since 1996.

the Templars to be master builders and claims that it was thanks to them that the Gothic style was introduced into Europe.

The story of Hancock's is shaky from every angle. He has noticed that there is a great similarity between the Cathedral of Chartres and *Parzival*. Both are symbolic, but that was nothing special: pre-eminently, symbolism is the distinguishing quality of the means of communication in the Middle Ages. Huizinga gives numerous good examples of this in his book *The Waning of the Middle Ages*. There are countless messages assimilated into the church of Chartres. The ornaments and the stained-glass windows symbolise observations of human nature, the past and the prophetic meaning of the Bible. The builders wanted to make a Christian encyclopaedia of limestone and glass, from the

Cathedral. Solomon, the Queen of Sheba and the Ark, are obviously all featured. That is surely true, because there are already more than eighteen hundred images incorporated into the church.

Hancock further claims that the Grail in *Parzival* is nothing other than the Ark of the Covenant. Wolfram described the Grail so vaguely that many things fit the description. In this Chapter, there is a detailed overview given of this. Hancock goes too far when he speculates about the nature of the Ark. Moses knew the secrets of the Egyptian knowledge and he put these into the Ark of the Covenant. Maybe it was a sort of nuclear reactor and capable of performing miracles.

Gothic architecture was definitely not brought into Europe by the Templars. The art historian, Janson, states that not one previous style can be so accurately originally determined as that of Gothic. The Templars had nothing to do with it. Finally, it remains incomprehensible to presume that the Templars wanted to keep their knowledge of the Ethiopian Ark, if they had any, secret. From the fourth century, there was already contact between the Church of Rome and Ethiopia. The Ethiopians did not hide the fact that they had the Ark of the Covenant. There was no point in hiding this information in a secret treasure map. Above all, why would the Templars hide secret information in publicly accessible objects? Especially if the 'secret' was a very simple message. They could have sufficed with 'Kebra Nagast' or 'Ethiopia and the Ark.'

Hancock writes that the Templars were present in Ethiopia for years and he based this supposition on two things. According to the legend, white men had been in Ethiopia in the twelfth century, and the journalist saw crosses which looked suspiciously like those of the Templars in a number of churches. That white men visited Ethiopia in the twelfth century, is more than probable. At the beginning of the thirteenth century, several travel guides had already been circulating in the Middle East, about Ethiopia. Ali ibn-Abi-Bakr, died in 1215, wrote a book for pilgrims about Ethiopia, amongst others. Of course the Western adventurers knew of these documents and they went on a quest. Marco Polo was definitely not the first white explorer.

We know for sure that the Templars had a red cross on their chest. It stands to reason that these followers of Christ chose for this symbol. The cross was the sign of the participants in the First Crusade in 1095. To think that the symbol of the cross was discovered by the Christians remains an example of Western arrogance. The cross, in many variations, is the most universal of the simple symbolic signs, and in no way limited to Christianity. In lots of cultures and long before Jesus lived, people depicted the cross. In the African culture, the cross marked an intersection between the paths of life and death. In the South American culture, it is also a very old, cosmic conception. In a later book (*Fingerprint of the Gods*); the journalist himself indicates that the Mexicans, centuries before the Crusades, frequently display the cross of the Templars on their pyramids.

Hancock knows how to get all of this across beautifully; the tales of the Brothers Grimm really have a higher grade of validity than the fantasies of Hancock.

Postscript

THE TRAIL STILL GOES ON

The glass can be raised again, as the quest is over. Without a doubt, it has been demonstrated that the Templars belonged to a Roman Catholic organization with a military purpose. The main difference between the Order of the Temple on one side, and the Hospitallers and the Teutonic Knights on the other, was because of the fact that they were the victims of the impulsive actions of a monarch eager for wealth. The author has few illusions: in the future, fabrications will continue to be published about 'his' Order.

Initially, it has to be admitted, the apocryphal books were the nicest to read. *The Holy Blood and the Holy Grail* especially, came across as an exciting boy's book. However, as the knowledge grows, the irritation of the notorious nonsense and speculations increases. Anyway, the medieval chroniclers made similar use of prose. It was mostly the monks who saw a divine intervention in nearly every event. The religious man had little other choice, because people in those times were all too quickly accused of heretical thoughts. Furthermore, objective chronicling was dangerous for another reason. The powerful ones on this earth, and their successors, were also reading over the shoulder of the author. These were to judge and to punish, if necessary, the authors and their families according to their own norms and standards. With this in mind, the studying of the Middle Age works becomes much more interesting.

The chronicling about the Templars radically changed after the trial of 1307-1312. The fact that the Church and the French monarchy had earmarked the Order as a heretical movement, gave later authors a free range of play. They could accuse the Templars of all sorts of everything, without restriction, and go unpunished. These authors supported the Church and the French monarchy in this way: yet afterwards they were right.

POSTSCRIPT

The persecution of the Order of the Temple, after the death of James of Molay in 1314, was not over: later accusers, up to the present day, carried on with the trial and pulled out all the stops. With this, they were not impeded by a great deal of knowledge. It was only during the nineteenth century when scientist began with responsible investigations of the Crusades, and with it, that of the Templars. It was then discovered for example, that it was not Peter the Hermit who instigated the Crusades, but that he only reacted to the calling of Pope Urban II. Up until then, the historians had given Peter a pivotal place in the beginning of the European journey to the Holy Land. Due to the fact that the investigation into the Crusades mostly took place in France, it had a propagandist background. The French, including Madelin, wanted to demonstrate that their country was the founder of European expansionism. Because France possessed great parts of the Middle East in the twelfth and thirteenth centuries, various French historians, after World War One, were of the opinion that their country could claim the rule over Lebanon and Syria: objective historical writing!

The documents from the trial against the Templars (repeated again: written by the accusers) were completely investigated and published at the end of the nineteenth century. It was only then that it became clear that Philip IV had carried out a very clever strategy. Then, the damage had already been done. Too many authors had surrounded the Templars in a shroud of secrecy.

In a way, the authors of apocryphal books about the Order of the Temple had behaved just like Philip IV. They go off prejudices, lard these with suggestive facts and judge the Templars again and again. Also, in another regard, there is a similarity with the French King: he was after the possessions of the Order, whilst the authors, with their best sellers, want to fill their bank accounts at the expense of the Templars. And, just as during the trial at the beginning of the fourteenth century, the Order does not stand a chance. The accusations against them are, by definition, the same as the judicial verdict.

May this book be a contribution to the defending of the Order of the Temple.

Appendices

APPENDIX A

Inventory of the goods from the house of Baugy (13 October 1307)

Introduction

In the letter of 14 September 1307, Philip VI ordered his sheriffs to make a summary of all the possessions of the preceptories of the Templars. This document is one of the few remaining inventories.

The Templars monastery of Baugy was situated 24 kilometres to the South East of Bayeaux, in Normandy. After the abolishment of the Templars, it was transferred to the Hospitallers. During the Hundred Year War (1337-1453) between England and France it was partially destroyed, and it was restored by the Hospitallers at the end of the fifteenth century. Part of the church and the foundations of the monastery of the Templars buildings remain.

The report was originally in the Old French Language.

Text

Inventory of the goods from the house of Baugy, made by Jean of Verretot, sheriff of Caen, on the Friday after the holi day of Saint Dennis, in the year of our Lord, 1307, along with Lord Richard of Bretteville, knight, and in the presence of brother Aubin, Commander of the aforesaid house, brother Raoul and brother William, his associates, Nicole de Bois, Richier of Tombeur, Ranouf Gourdet, Bertin of Coisel, William Hamon, justiciaries of our ruler the King.

First, fourteen milking cows, full with milk; also, three young cows of more than a year old; also, a young ox; also, seven calves that were born in the preceding year; also, two large oxen; also, a small cow which is still suckling; also, three cattle;

Also, a hundred sheep; also, 180 ewes and lambs.

Also, pigs as well as sows, 98 items; also, in the house of the Temple a sow with eight suckling piglets; also, a pig of more than a year old, males as well as female; also, four suckling foals of a year; also, the horse of the Commander and a pack horse; also, four cart horses.

Also, a grain shed in Saon (near to Baueux), of which the value by the Commander is estimated to be 120 livres tournois.

Also, there is, next to the shed of Baugy, about nine hectares of ground, some with wheat and some with rye; also, twelve hectares with barley and butter beans; also, seven and a half hectares with oats; also, seven hectares with split peas; also, three hectares with beans, of which they have used a quarter since the middle of August, according to what the Commander says and the word of the witnesses from the personnel of the house.

Also, during hay making time, they have transported eight cart loads of hay to the house, of which they have eaten and used quarter, which is the testimony of the Commander and the personnel of the house.

Also, the yields of the wheat which is still to be received in the periods from the last holy day of Saint Michael, there are about five hectolitres, to the measurements of those of Bayeaux, hence the Commander.

Also, the yield of the barley that still has to be harvested after the previously mentioned Saint Michael, about four hectolitres according to the Bayeaux measurements, hence the Commander.

Also, from the hemp which is estimated as being a hundred pennies or there abouts.

Also, bacon and beef to more or less consume.

Also, five well used carts, mostly in good condition; also, three ploughs with the appertaining harnesses.

Also, half a barrel of wine;

Also, a small amount of barley beer for the servants and the tradesmen;

Also, baked bread for the servants and the tradesmen of the house;

Also, in the kitchen, a large copper pot a five cups; also, an iron stove; also, a hearth; also, a small water kettle, a tripod, a fire iron; a set of irons, a grate, three large caldrons and a small one and a fireplace to cook water.

Also, geese and poultry inside the house; also, sixteen empty barrels;

Also, in the chapel, four pairs of complete church vestments; also, a chalice; also, the church books and the blankets and the ornaments from the altar.

Also, in the room of the Commander, three solid silver goblets, two large and one small; also, a small silver oxidized drinking cup on a pedestal; also, two oxidized and in poor condition beakers on a pedestal and another small wooden goblet.

There was no money and the Commander said that the men would be paid in kind.

Also, in the room of the Commander, two pairs of bed sheets, a piece of rough linen, a blanket for the bed of the aforesaid Commander, one indigo coloured blanket, of which the Commander says that he had bought for one of his brothers; also, three overcoats lined with fur, a robe, four pairs of work trousers, three robes and a rain cape for the Commander; also, in a chest, a light blue overcoat, belonging to the wife of Lord Roger des Planes and is a pledge, so as Commander and Bertin de Coisel said; also, an overcoat, a robe which belongs to Jean Hervieu; also, an overcoat, which belongs to Guillot Gagnebied; also a cushion.

Also, there is a sleeping hall and somewhere else a guest quarters with twenty feather beds;

Also, tablecloths as well as towels for the inhabitants of the house, fourteen pieces;

Also, two bowls and tow other wash basins for the cleaning of the house;

Also, the necessary materials for the making of beer for the present house;

Also, there are thirty striped sheets found, which still have to be cut;

Also, properties of the house, according to the Commander, a mill and a tenth of the value of a hundred livres, which were given by various parties in rent, of which the aforesaid Commander said that he had partially received these.

The above mentioned concerns, in the name of the King, were entrusted under careful watch of Robert Burnouf of Planqery, Samson of Canchy, Robert Soupire and William Hune of Castillon. The command shall be carried out by Bertin of Coisel, resident servant, who will make sure that the house will be well operated.

A summary of the household personnel and the subordinates who were in service at the house of Baugy and they said that one had to still pay their wages and that their duration is fixed until the holi day of Saint Martin, the forthcoming winter.

Reverend William Duredent, chaplain of the church of the house.
Herouart of Roi, clerk of the house concerned.
Phillipe Alain, cow herder.
Jean Goiet, shepherd.

Denis of Boulanger, herder of the foals.

Thomas of Ballery and Thomas Vaque, who keep a watchful eye on the plough and the harnesses;

Pierre of Roi and Robert Tison, who have the plough and the harnesses under their watchful eyes;

Jean Quentin and William Drouet, who have the plough and the harnesses under their watchful eyes;

Geoffrey of Semilly, doorkeeper of the house.

Robin of Queu, brewer and cook.

Jean Leveque and Jourdin Liart, servants of the guesthouse.

William of Fort, under vassal, forester of the house.

In the dairy there are three servants.

Jean Osber, pig herdsman.

William of Gausel; helps Jean with tending to the pigs.

Mathieu of Quemin, Jean Chouquet and his wife, have been maintaining the house for a long time.

The Commanders servant.

The herdsman who tends to the geese.

Finally

There were four members of the Order present in the Templars complex of Baugy; three sergeants and a chaplain. That could, given the fact that there were a thousand preceptories at the most, in France, be in line with the total number of arrests of around two thousand. Furthermore, there were 26 farmhands, including a married woman. The monastery was a mixed farm and it also possessed a mill. There was of course, hardly any money, and weapons were not mentioned in the summary. The last would be correct: after all there were no knights at the monastery of Baugy.

APPENDIX B

WHAT JAMES OF MOLAY SAID

Introduction

Part of the trial document is a report of the hearing of the last Grand Master of the Templars, James of Molay. It is originally in Latin and dates from 24 October 1307. On 26 November and 28 November 1309, and 2 March 1310, the leader appeared before the Commission of Eight. The reports of this are saved and can also be found in the book of Lizerand, *Le Dossier de Affaire des Templiers*.

The hearing of James of Molay, Grand Master of the Order of the Temple (24 October 1307)

In the name of Christ, Amen. It is crystal clear to all, from the deed present, that in the year of Our Lord 1307, sixth indictie [ecclesiastical year], in the month of October, the 24th day of the month, the second year of the Pontificate of the very Holy Father the honourable Lord Clement V, Pope through the divine providence, representative of the apostolic authority in the Kingdom of France, in the house of the brethren of the Temple in Paris, a judicial investigation will be opened against certain people who find themselves in this location and are accused of heretical crimes.

Also present is a governmental notary and the undersigned, brother James of Molay, Grand Master of the brethren of the Temple. He has sworn on the saints of the gospels, which are held before him and touched by him, of himself and others, in a trial regarding the faith, to tell the pure, unadulterated and complete truth.

When asked for the point of time and the manner of his acceding, he declares under oath that he was received into the Order 42 years ago, in Beaunne, in the district of Autun, by brother Humbert of Pairaud,[1] knight, in the presence of brother Aumaury de la Roche[2] and various other brothers, the names of which he no longer remembers.

---

[1] The brother of the father of Hugh of Pairaud, who was the Commander of England until 1270. Hugh was the Visitor of France during the trial.

[2] Aumaury de la Roche was Commander of France in 1264.

He also says under oath that, after he had made various promises concerning the rules and statutes of the Order, they laid the robe on his shoulder. Those who admitted him brought him a bronze crucifix, with a portrait of Christ on it and they said and forced him to renounce the image of Christ. And he did so, albeit against his will; and when those who admitted him compelled him to spit on the cross, he spat on the floor. If he is exhaustively asked about how many times he had spat, he says under oath that he had only done it once; and he remembered it well.

When questioned, given the fact that he had taken an oath of chastity, as to whether he had participated in carnal relations with his brothers, he says under oath that he has never done such a thing.

Upon the request to declare, under oath, if the other brothers were received in this manner, he says that he believes that they did not treat him any differently to the others; he added to this as a matter of fact, that he had admitted very few Templars. Nevertheless, he says under oath that after he had received the new members, that he instructed those who assisted to do what they had to do. He also says under oath that he had intention that the men would receive them in the same way as it happened with him.

When questioned as to whether he had combined his testimony with any deceit at all, or whether he had stretched the truth due to duress, fear of torture, imprisonment or any other reason whatsoever, he says under oath nay; on the contrary, for the sake of his sole, he has told the unadulterated truth.

Finally
The denial of James of Molay, that he was being threatened also appears in the other reports from the hearings. It does not say anything about what really happened. On the contrary, you could say that it suggests that there was at least a measure of intimidation. In addition, James of Molay had already been in custody for twelve days, undoubtedly in uncomfortable circumstances. Although James could not read, he must have known what was in the document: the following day he in fact confirmed his confession in front of a large public.

The last sentence is very important; in the presence of the inquisitor, James of Molay unburdened his conscience. Now nothing stood in the way of the entrance to heaven. He undoubtedly supposed that that was the end of that. Maybe he was promised that after his declaration, he and the Order would be left in peace.

A letter exists from November 1307, in which it says that Philip IV offered James of Molay the possibility of escape. He would have refused to do so because according to him, the Order was without sins. The story is third hand and it must be pure nonsense. Philip IV intended on destroying the Order from the very beginning and he could not allow himself to lose the control over the ultimate man of the Templars. James himself, according to his activities during the last years of his life, was not sharp enough to organise resistance from abroad. Philip would have realised the risk, that his advisors had induced James to a better strategy, was too great.

APPENDIX C

Dan Brown, The Da Vinci Code

The best seller *The Da Vinci Code*, by Dan Brown, is an undoubtedly wonderfully written exciting thriller, centered on the theme of the Holy Grail. The book falls under the category of fiction and this is the case for not only the plot, but also for most of the 'historical facts' which are presented by Brown. Godfrey of Bouillon was for instance not a Frenchman, but a Flemish Duke and he was definitely not King of Jerusalem. He was, at his own request, called the Advocate of the Holy Sepulcher, whilst his successor assumed the title of King. The fact that the Templars were in the Holy Land during the Second Crusade and that they told King Baldwin II that they wanted to protect the Christian pilgrims is, in chronological terms, a miracle. The Second Crusade took place in 1148 and Baldwin died seventeen years earlier. Brown claims that the Templars took nine years to find the treasure in the Temple and that they were given unlimited power by Pope Innocent II directly thereafter. The Order was founded in around 1120 and in 1139 Pope Innocent II proclaimed the bull, *Omne datum optimum*, for the first time, in which they, just as all the other Roman Catholic Orders, only had to be answerable to the Pope.

Brown makes things polychromatic with his claims that Pope Clement V was asked by God to cleanse the earth by seizing all the Templars and torturing them until they confessed all their sins to God. It was actually the French King, Philip IV, who had the French division of the Order of the Temple arrested en masse in 1307. The reason that the following trial took five years to complete, is because Pope Clement fought tooth and nail against what he saw as an illegal action. Only when placed under great pressure from the King, was the Pope finally prepared to dissolve the Order at a council held in France, in the presence of the King and part of his army. Moreover, without ever declaring them guilty of the accusations, which were made by the King. What is strange is that Brown, had he really studied the history of the Templars instead of twiddling his thumbs, could have stage-managed this Order, without deviating from his plot.

The fact that Brown accuses the Templars of secretive tasks is not a surprise, because as been written in this book, he is not the first. According to various authors they were the ones to discover America, to have found the body of Jesus, which they hid in South France (unfortunately the authorities will not give permission for exhumation), control The Knowledge of all Knowledge (which could not prevent their downfall), to have searched for the Ark of the Covenant (first of all in Egypt and then in Ethiopia), or that they were protecting the descendants of Jesus. These kinds of impeachments are based on half-truths and facts taken out of context, which moreover were mostly introduced in tensively written books.

To say that the Bible was composed by Constantine the Great is contrary to the truth. The Roman Emperor (272-337) worked, just as many as his predecessors did, on the principle of, *One God, one State, one Emperor,* and conscientiously chose for the Christian religion. During the Great Persecution (303-312), he saw first hand the vigor that Christianity possessed. His intervention in the Council of Nicea (325) was only intended to bring about peace in the Roman Empire; theological matters did not interest him (Ter Veen, 2004). The so called canonical books, our present Bible, were first named by Anthansius in 367 in his Easter Letter. His vision was sanctioned by a number of councils within fifty years, where after the other Gospels, including very legitimate, were burnt on a large scale.

It is clear to Brown what the Grail represents:

> *The Grail is a person, Mary Magdalene, who was supposed to continue the Christian Church for Jesus. She was the vessel in which the regal blood of Jesus Christ was carried; she was the womb from where the descendants would continue, and the tendril on which the holy fruit sprouts.*

He is in agreement here with Margaret Starbird, who in her book, *The Woman with the Alabaster Jar,* defended this theory. Brown has also adopted the hexagram and the appurtenant philosophies from her. Unlike the thriller writer claims in his book, Starbird is a voice in the distance. The reason that scientists disagree with her on this, is that Mary Magdalene does not appear in any medieval Grail novel whatsoever. On top of which, she bases herself on *The Holy Blood and the Holy Grail* and controls the style of discourse of her work in the same way as the authors. Substantiations are not necessary here and historical facts are turned around or incompletely told, in such a way that she creates a new reality.

That is called fiction, a métier which Brown indeed has mastered excellently.

APPENDIX D

List of Grand Masters

Hugo of Payns	1120-1136
Robert of Craon	1137-1149
Everard des Barres	1150-1152
Bernard of Tremelay	1152-1153
Andrew of Montbard	1153-1156
Bertrand of Blancfort	1156-1169
Philip of Nablus	1169-1170
Odo of Saint-Amand-les Eaux	1170-1179
Arnold of Torroja	1179-1184
Gerard of Ridefort	1184-1189
Robert of Sablé	1191-1193
Gilbert Erail	1194-1200
Philip of Plessis	1201-1209
William of Chartres	1210-1219
Peter of Montaigu	1219-1232
Armand of Périgord	1232-1244
William of Sonnac	1247-1250
Reginald of Vichiers	1250-1256
Thomas Bérard	1256-1273
Willem of Beaujeu	1273-1291
Theobald Gaudin	1291-1293
James of Molay	1293-1314

Illustrations

MAPS
The Four Latin States	30
Israel anno 2000	30
The Temple mountain	96
The Christian erea anno 1244	162
Acre	182
Castles in the Kingdom of Jerusalem	207
Castles in Antioch and Tripoli	216
(all made by TS ter Veen)	

PHOTO'S
The Council of Clermont. *Bibliothèque Nationale, Paris.*	16
Map of the world from the thirteenth century. *The British Library.*	20
Peoples' army of Peter of Amiens. *Bibliothèque Nationale, Paris.*	22
Taking Jerusalem. *Vienna, Österreichische Nationalbibliothek.*	23
Heaven and hell. *Bibliothèque de Strasbourg.*	24
Bernard of Clairvaux. *Bodleian Library, Oxford.*	35
Hospitallers. *Royal Malta Library.*	39
Plan of Jerusalem. *Royal Dutch Library, The Hague.*	44
Transport ships. *Louvre.*	50/51
Mounted Templars. *Bodleian Library, Oxford.*	53
Templar. *Fresco from the church of Blanzac.*	84
Louis VII takes up the cross. *Bibliothèque Nationale, Paris.*	88

Deliberation at Acre. *Bibliothèque Municipale, Lyon.*	91
Saladin. *Vigne, Paris.*	100
Battle of Hattin. *Corpus Christi College, Cambridge.*	105
Saladin. *The British Library/Bridgeman Art Library.*	107
Duel. *The British Library/Bridgeman Art Library.*	112/113
Zierikzee. *MJ ter Veen.*	123
Frederik II. *Biblioteca Apostolica Vaticana.*	158
Sint Joris. *Byzantine Museum, Athene.*	170
Saint Louis in Egypt. *The British Library.*	179
Crusade scene. *Antwerp.*	194
Templar. *Fresco from the church of Blanzac.*	198
Saint Louis. *Bibliothèque Nationale, Paris.*	225
Richard the Lionheart. *The British Library/Bridgeman Art Library.*	228
Innocent III. *Fresco in the Church of Subiaco.*	233
James of Molay. *James of Molay, Parijs, 1912.*	238
Arrest. *British Museum.*	272
Council of Vienne *Sixteenth century fresco from the Vatican.*	275
The last Grand Master burning at the stake. *British Museum.*	278
The Grail. *Bibliothèque Nationale, Paris.*	289

Cover
Returning from the Crusade.
Painting by K.F.Lessing, nineteenth century.

Brief bibliography

Allegro, J.M., *The Treasure of the Copper Scroll*, New York, 1960
Andrews, R. en Schellenberger, P., *The tomb of god*, London, 1996
Armstrong, K., *Jerusalem: One City, Three Faiths*, London, 1996
Baigent, M., Leigh, R., Lincoln, H., *The Holy Blood and the Holy Grail*, London, 1982
Barber, M., *The Templars and the Turin Shroud*, The Catholic Historical Review, 68 (1982), 206-225
Barber, M., *The trial of the templars*, Cambridge, 1978
Barber, M., *The new knighthood*, Cambridge 1994
Bennet, M., '*La Règle du Temple*' *as a Military Manual*, Studies in Medieval History presented to R. Allen Broen, Woodbridge, 1989, 7-19
Birks, W. en Gilbert, R.A., *The treasure of Montsegur: a study of the Cathar Heresy and the nature of the Cathar secret*, London, 1987
Boorstin, D., *The Discoverers*, New York, 1983
Brown, P., *The rise of Western Christendom/Triumph and Diversity*, Oxford, 1996
Bulst-Thiele, M. L., *Der Prozess gegen den Templerorden*. Die Geistlichen Ritterorden Europas, Sigmaringen, 1980
Bulst-Thiele, M.L., *Sacrae domus militiae templi hierosolymitani magistri*, Göttingen, 1974
Burman, E., *The Templars, Knights of God*, Rochester, 1986
Busken Huet, Cd., *Het land van Rembrandt*, Den Haag, 1974
Buttlar, Joh. von, *Die Wächter von Eden*. München, 1993
Comnena, A., *The Alexiad*, Penguin, 1969
Curzon, H. du., *La maison du temple de Paris Histoire et description*, Parijs 1888
Dailliez, L., *Guide de la France templière*, Parijs, 1992
Demurger A., *Vie et mort de l'ordre du Temple, 1118-1314*, Paris, 1991
Deslile, L., *Mémoire sur les Opérations Financières des Templiers*, Parijs, 1889
Duby, G., *Guillaume le Maréchal ou le meilleur chevalier du monde*, Paris, 1984

Duby, G., *Les trois ordres ou l'imaginaire du féodalisme*, Paris, 1978
Durbec, J-A., *Introduction a une liste des biens du Temple saisis en 1308 dans la region des Alpes-Matitimes*, Nice Historique, 54 (1954), 45-52
Durbec, J-A., *Les Templiers en Provence. Formation des Commanderies et réperation géographique de leurs biens*, Provence Historique, 9 (1959), 3-37, 97-132
Edbury, P.W. en Rowe, J.G., *William of Tyre, Historian of the Latin East*, Cambridge, 1988
Fleckenstein, J., *Die Rechtfertigung der geistlichen Ritterorden nach der Schrift 'De laude novae militiae' Bernards Clairvaux.* Die geistlichen Ritterorden Europas, Sigmaringen, 1980
Finke, H., *Papsttum und Untergang des Templerordens I und II*, Munster, 1907
Forey, A., *The military Orders, from the Twelfth to the Early Fourteenth Centuries*, Macmillan, 1992
Fossier, R., *Peasant Life in the Medieval West*, Oxford, 1988
Hancock, G., *The sign and the seal: the quest for the lost Ark of the Covenant*, London, 1992
Hardenberg, H., *De Nederlanden en de Kruistochten*, Amsterdam, 1944
Hendrikx, P.A., *De oudste bedelordekloosters in het graafschap Holland en Zeeland*, Dordrecht 1977
Hiestand, R., *Papsturkunden fur Templer und Johanniter*, Gottingen, 1972
Hitti, P.K., *An Arab-Syrian Gentleman and Warrior in the period of the Crusades*, reprint London, 1987
Honour, H. and Flemming, J., *A World History of Art*, London, 1982
Huig, M., Lunsingh Scheurleer jr., D.F., *De Middeleeuwen*, Aulapocket, 1994
Huizinga, J., *The waning of the Middle Ages*, London, 2001
Huygens, R.B.C., *De constructione castri Saphet*, North-Holland Publishing Company, 1981
Jansen, H.P.H., *Geschiedenis van de Middeleeuwen*, Aulapocket, 1993
Janson, H.W., *History of Art*, New York, 1986
Joinville, J. de, *The Life of Saint Louis*, Penguin, 1993
Kedar, B.Z. en Pringle, D., *La Fève: a Crusader Castle in the Jezreel Valley*, Israel Exploration Journal, 1984
Kennedy, H., *Crusaders Castles*, Cambridge, 1994
Kersten, H. en Gruber, E.R., *Das Jesus-Komplott: die Wahrheit über das Turiner Grabtuch*, Munich, 1992
Knight, C. en Lomas, R., *The Hiram Key*, London, 1996
Krück von Poturzyn, M.J., *Der Prozess gegen die Templer*, Stuttgart, 1983
Lane-Poole, S., *Saladin and the Fall of the Kingdom of Jeruzalem*, Beirut, 1964

Lizerand, G., *Le Dossier de l'affaire des Templiers*, Paris, 1964
Maalouf, A., Rovers, *Les croisades vue par les Arabes*, Paris, 1984
Madelin, l., *L'Expansion francaise*, Paris, 1918
Marshall, C., *Warfare in the Latin East*, 1192-1291, Cambridge, 1992
Mathieu-Rosay, J., *La véritable histoire des papes*, Paris, 1991
Meer, T. van der, *De wesentlijke sonde van sodomie en andere vuyligheeden*, Amsterdam, 1984
Melville, M., *Les Débuts de l'ordre du Temple*, Die Geistlichen Ritterorden Europas, Sigmaringen, 1980
Molin, K., *The non-military functions of crusader fortifications*, 1187-circa 1380, Journal of Medieval History, Vol 23, No 4 (1997)
Mollat, G., *Dipersion définitive des templiers après leur suppression, Comptes Rendus des Séances de l'Académie des Inscriptions et Belles-Lettres*, Parijs, 1952, 376-380
Müller, W., *Die heilige Stadt*, Stuttgart 1961
Nicholson, H., *Templars, Hospitallers and Teutonic Knights*, Leicester University press, 1995
Norwich, J.J., *Byzantium, The Early Centuries*, Penguin
Norwich, J.J., *Byzantium, The Apogee*, Penguin
Norwich, J.J., *Byzantium, Decline and Fall*, Penguin, 1996
Norwich, J.J., *The Normans in Sicily*, Penguin, 1970
Parker, W., *The Knights Templars in England*, Tuczon Arizona, 1963
Partner, P., *The Knights Templar and their Myth*, Rochester, 1990
Perkins, C., *The Wealth of the Knights Templars in England*, American Historical Review, XV (1910), pp. 252-263
Pernoud, R., *The Crusades*, London, 1962
Phillips, G., *The search for the Grail*, Londen, 1995
Picknett, L. & Prince, C., *The Templar Revelation*, Londen, 1997
Prawer, J., *Military Orders and Crusader Politics in the second half of the XIIth Century*, Die Geistlichen Ritterorden Europas, Sigmaringen, 1980
Pringle, D., *Reconstruction the castle of Safad*, Palestine Exploration Quarterly (1985), 141-149
Ramakers, E., *Tempeliers in Maastricht?*, De Maasgouw, tijdschrift voor Limburgse geschiedenis en oudheidkunde, Jaargang 109, 1990
Richard, J., *Les Templiers et les Hospitaliers en Bourgogne et en Champagne méridionale*, Die Geistlichen Ritterorden Europas, Sigmaringen, 1980
Riley-Smith J., *The Knights of St. John in Jerusalem and Cyprus 1050-1310*, London, 1967

Roggé, P., *Tempelridders*, Kultureel jaarboek Provincie Vlaanderen, 1972
Runciman, S., *A History of the Crusades I, the First Crusade*, Pinguin, 1991
Runciman, S., *A History of the Crusaders II, the Kingdom of Jerusalem*, Pinguin, 1991
Runciman, S., *A History of the Crusades III, the Kingdom of Acre*, Pinguin, 1991
Runciman, S., *The Sicilian Vespers*, Cambridge, 1992
Schoengen, M., *Monasticon Batavum*, Amsterdam, 1941-1942
Setton, K.M., *A History of the Crusades I, the First hundred years*, The University of Wisconsin Press, 1969
Setton, K.M., *A History of the Crusades II, the later Crusades 1189-1311*, The University of Wisconsin Press, 1969
Setton, K.M., *A History of the Crusades III, the Fourteenth and Fifteenth Centuries*, The University of Wisconsin Press, 1975
Setton, K.M., *A History of the Crusades IV, the Art and Architecture of the Crusader States*, The University of Wisconsin Press, 1977
Setton, K.M., *A History of the Crusades V, the Impact of the Crusades on the Near East*, The University of Wisconsin Press, 1985
Setton, K.M., *A History of the Crusades VI, the Impact of the Crusades on Europe*, The University of Wisconsin Press, 1989
Smail, R.C., *Crusading Warfare, 1097-1193*, Cambridge, 1995
Streefland, A.A., *Tempeliers in Brabant, de commanderij Ter Brake bij Alphen*, Jaarboek Geschiedkunde en Oudheid te Breda, 1979/1980
Upton-Ward, J.M., *The rule of the Templars*, Woodbridge, 1992
Villhardouin, G. de., *The Conquest of Constantinopel*, Pinguin, 1993
Willemart, P., *Pour Jérusalem: croissade et djihâd*, Paris, 1988
Wolfram von Eschenbach, *Parzival*. Uitgeverij Vrij Geestesleven, 1986

Index

Aachen 120, 138, 154
Abraham 212, 219
Acre 10, 38, 48, 52, 53, 56, 60, 63, 70, 71, 73, 89, 109, 111, 113-115, 118-120, 127, 142, 143, 148, 150, 152-159, 161, 163, 165-167, 169, 172, 175, 176, 181, 183, 184, 186-189, 206, 210, 212-214, 217, 218, 221, 224, 237-239, 241, 276, 281
Adhémar of Le Puy 19, 21,28
Agrippa von Nettesheim 284
Ahamant, Templar castle 97, 205
Al-'Arimah, Templar castle 214
Al-Aqsa mosque 31, 46, 75, 108, 220, 223, 224
al-Fadil, Arabian chronicler 208
al-Fakhri, Templar spy 187, 188
Albania 186
Alcazar 119
Aleppo 102, 141, 158, 241
Alexander III, Pope (1159-1181) 232, 233
Alexander IV, Pope 69
Alexius I, Byzantine Emperor 15
Alfonso-Jordan 85
Allegro 139
Alphen 122, 124, 130, 264
Amalfi 38
Amalric, Governor of Cyprus 270, 271

Amalric, King of Jerusalem 32, 82, 95-99, 102, 151, 189, 205, 241, 242, 270, 271
Amman, Templar castle 97, 205
Andrew II, King of Hungary 119, 149, 230
Andrew of Montbard, Grand Master 92-94, 127
Andrews 42, 43, 45, 46
Anglia 129, 130
Anjou 33, 34, 43, 85, 134, 185, 186, 226, 230
Anna Commena, chronicler 284
Antioch 21, 28, 54, 58, 61, 70, 72, 83, 85, 86, 89, 92, 97, 108, 109, 118, 141, 155, 158, 177, 183, 185, 190, 192, 197, 213, 215, 217, 224
Apulia 53, 113
Aragon 53, 54, 82, 102, 115, 116, 128, 142, 181, 186, 226, 238, 243, 246, 252, 265, 267, 268, 272-274, 281
Arames 211
Archambaud of Saint-Armand 129
Armand of Périgord, Grand Master 157, 166, 176, 177
Armenia 61, 86, 141, 190, 201, 217, 241
Arnold Bouchart, Templar on Cyprus 110
Arnold of Torroja, Grand Master 82, 102, 103
Arsuf 113, 206

317

Ascalon 87, 92-95, 97, 159, 160, 164, 176, 205
Athens 134
'Athlit, see Château Pèlerin
St. Augustine 36
Austria 114, 131, 135, 149, 271
Auvergne 151, 226
Avignon 258
Axum 293
Ayme d'Oselier, Marshal of Cyprus 270, 271
Aymmeric of Saint Maurer 131, 229

Baghras (Gaston), Templar castle 72, 86, 87, 141, 158, 160, 215, 217
Baghdad 83, 178
Baigent 38, 40, 43, 46, 95
Baldwin I of Bouillon, King of Jerusalem 28, 45, 147, 204
Baldwin II of Bouillon, King of Jerusalem 28, 31-34, 45, 46, 85, 204, 220, 288, 307
Baldwin III, King of Jerusalem 89, 92, 95, 97, 103, 201, 205
Baldwin IV, King of Jerusalem 99, 101-103, 206, 208
Baldwin V, King of Jerusalem 102, 103
Baldwin IX, Count of Flanders 129, 146
Barber 27, 32, 67, 125, 156, 177
Barbonne 33
Barcelona 115, 128
Baroche, Master of Lombardy 146, 147
Bartholomew of Neocastro, chronicler 155
Baugy 300-303
Baybars 174, 184, 185, 187, 191, 206, 209, 211, 212, 215
Beaufort, Templar castle 140, 160, 184-186, 212

Beirut 204, 211
Bela IV, King of Hungary 136, 230
Benoît d'Alignan, Bishop of Marseille (1229-1267) 163
Bérenger Saunière 42
Bernard of Clairvaux 34, 36, 37, 49, 65, 71, 86, 87, 89, 92, 93, 118, 127, 163, 222, 232, 288, 294
Bernard of Tremelay, Grand Master 92, 93
Bertrand de Got, bishop 247
Bertrand of Blancfort, Grand Master 94, 97, 98
Bertrand of Sartiges 261, 263
St. Bertin 44, 46
Bertrand of St. Gilles 21
Bethsaida 173
Bevignate, church 137, 175
Boccaccio 284
Bodin 285
Bohemia 271
Bohemond 19, 21, 215
Bohemond V, prince of Antioch 158
Boniface 119, 235, 236, 238, 240, 242, 246-248, 253, 254, 277
Boniface VIII, Pope (1294-1303) 235, 236, 238, 240
Bonne Aventure, Templar ship 218
Borkum 120
Bosporus 19, 145
Breda 122, 124
Brindisi 118
Bristol 131
Bruges 129, 130, 264
Bulgaria 14
Burgundy 85, 126, 127, 164, 166, 200
Buttlar von 46, 47, 218, 219
Byzantium 13, 14, 129, 145

INDEX

Caco, Templar castle 104, 209
Caesarea 150, 159, 183, 217
Cafarlet, Templar castle 211
Cahors 78, 260
Cairo 83, 153, 157, 161, 176, 178, 184, 188, 241
Cambridgeshire 67, 132
Cana 150, 173
Canterbury 265, 266
Capernaum 173
Carmel 210, 211
Casal des Plaines, Templar castle 209
Castel Arnaldi, Templar castle 209, 210
Castel Blanc, Templar castle 155, 185
Castile 265, 267, 268, 272, 274
Catalonia 129
Celestine V, Pope 238
Champagne 32-34, 40, 46, 126-128, 159, 163, 164, 181
Charles I of Anjou, King of Sicily 134, 185 187, 226, 230
Charles II, King of Naples 238
Charles V 239
Charlemagne 138
Charles Martel 115
Charpentier 218, 219
Chartres 15, 28, 31, 33, 40, 45, 46, 148, 237, 294, 295
Chastel-Blanc, Templar castle 92, 143, 148, 160, 177, 200, 214
Chastellet, Templar castle 206
Château Pèlerin, Templar castle 71, 73, 140, 150, 152, 154, 158, 160, 182, 184, 189, 211, 212, 218, 226, 237
Chinon 256
Chrétien of Troyes 290
Cathars 95, 119, 148, 149, 234, 244, 245, 277, 279, 292

Clement III, Pope (1187-1191) 110, 233
Clement IV, Pope 184
Clement V, Pope 124, 231, 240, 243, 244, 247, 249, 252-254, 260, 270-274, 276, 281, 282, 304, 307
Clermont 15, 18
Cluny 15, 115, 232
Cologne 119, 124, 135
Columbus 219
Conrad of Montferrat 109, 112
Cresson 104, 192, 208, 209
Conrad III 89
Constantine, Roman Emperor 13, 27, 41, 138, 308
Constantinople 13, 14, 19, 21, 82, 97, 134, 135, 145-148, 185
Croatia 134, 150
Cyprus 48, 52, 53, 56, 73, 110, 111, 125, 178, 181, 183, 186, 189, 199, 200, 211, 213, 217, 235, 237-239, 241, 242-244, 250, 258, 270-272, 274, 277

Dailliez, historian 33, 125
Dalmatia 134, 148
Damascus 33, 83-85, 89-91, 97, 101, 150, 152, 157-161, 163, 165-167, 169, 172-178, 181, 182, 184, 206, 211, 241
Dante 284
Darbsak (Trapesak), Templar castle 108, 158, 215, 217, 229
David 40, 287
De Laude 34, 36, 37, 71, 163, 222
Delisle, historian 226
Demurger, historian 32
Denney 67
Destroit, Templar castle 210
Dirk VI, Count of Holland 118
Dokkum 119, 120

Dor (Merle), Templar castle 211
Dowaai 33
Durbec, historian 127

Eagle 67
Edessa 21, 28, 83, 87, 146, 215
Edgar, King of England 125
Edward I, King of England (1272-1307)
   132, 229, 235, 238, 239, 242, 259
Edward II, King of England (1307-1327)
   264-266, 274
Egmond 93, 118
Egypt 10, 14, 83, 87, 90, 92-99, 101, 104,
   119, 144, 145, 150-155, 159-161, 173-
   178, 180-182, 185, 187, 189, 240, 241,
   243, 287, 293, 308
Eight Crusade 161
Eire 53, 130, 132, 265, 266, 271
Ely 132
England 26, 34, 53, 67, 79,,80, 82, 102,
   110, 114, 118, 119, 125, 129-132, 136,
   154, 159, 164, 176, 183, 185, 186,
   218, 225, 226, 229, 235, 238, 239,
   242, 243, 246-266, 268, 274, 281, 300
Ethiopia 10, 293, 294, 296, 308
Eugenius III, Pope (1145-1153) 89, 232
Eustachius Canis, Master of France 129
Everard des Barres, Grand Master 82, 89,
   91, 92

Falcon, Templar ship 218
Famagusta 270
Fickettscroft 131
Fifth Crusade 119, 148, 149, 151, 153,
   180, 211
Flanders 34, 98, 117, 129, 130, 147, 186,
   218, 226, 246, 264
Fleet Street 131

Florence 133, 269
Floris III, Count of Holland 118
Fossier, historian 200
Fourth Crusade 129, 144-146, 149
France 15, 18, 19, 21, 23, 33, 34, 42, 43,
   45, 48, 53, 69, 78, 80, 86, 87, 89, 91,
   92, 94, 102, 110, 112, 113, 119, 124-
   129, 131, 136, 147-149, 151, 154, 159,
   161, 178, 181, 183-186, 199, 200,
   218, 225-227, 235-239, 243-250, 252,
   254, 264-269, 273, 274, 276, 286, 290,
   299, 300, 303, 304, 307
Francis of Assisi 151
Freemasonry 41, 287, 288
Frederick II, German Emperor 120, 121,
   153-157, 159, 161, 175, 176, 190, 220,
   222, 229, 230, 254
Frederick Barbarossa, German Emperor
   110, 118, 121
Fulcher of Chartres 15, 28, 31, 33, 45, 46
Fulk, Count of Anjou 33, 34, 85, 87, 89,
   118, 212, 226
Fulk Neuilly 227

Gaza 87, 101, 109, 159, 160, 176, 192,
   199, 205
Galilee 160, 163, 169, 171, 173, 184
Gaston (Baghras), Templar castle
Gelre 117, 118
Genghis Khan 157
Genoa 28, 147, 156, 161, 183, 187, 202,
   218, 221, 239
Geoffroy of Charney, Master of Normandy
   147
Geoffroi of Charny 147
Geoffroy of Villehardouin, chronicler 145
St. George 46
Gerard of Ridefort, Grand Master 82, 103,

INDEX

104, 106, 107, 109, 111, 129, 205, 208
Germany 13, 19, 26, 87, 89, 102, 111, 118, 120, 131, 135, 150, 184, 243, 244, 269
Ghent 130
Gibelet (Jabala) 158
Gideon 104
Gilbert Erail, Grand Master 142, 143
Gilbert of Lacey 95
Gisors, castle 129
Godfrey of Bouillon 19, 21, 28, 40, 117, 129, 205, 307
Godfrey of Sint-Omaars 129
Goethe 284
Gossin of Bruges, Master of Flandriae 264
Granada 116, 275
Grayana, Templar castle 115
Gregory VII, Pope 17
Gregory IX, Pope (1127-1241) 144, 155, 156, 234
Gregory X, Pope (1271-1276) 234
Groningen 117-120, 150
Gruber 146
Guy of Lusignan, King of Jerusalem 102, 103, 106, 108, 109, 111, 112, 186, 190

Haarlem 122
Hadrian IV, pope 95
Haifa 150, 183, 210
Halberstadt 135, 269
Hancock 46, 293-297
Hattin 104, 106, 109, 110, 112, 141, 150, 176, 192, 193, 201, 205, 209, 217, 224, 227
Hayo of Wolvega 119
Hebron 85, 175
Helena 27, 41, 138, 290
Hiestand 34, 48
Helen Nicholson, historian 222

Henry I, King of England (1100-1135) 135, 226
Henry II, King of England (1154-1189) 79, 105, 129, 132, 136, 225, 227
Henry III, King of England (1216-1272) 126, 156, 227, 229
Henry II, King of Cyprus 241, 270, 271
Henry the Navigator 219
Henry the Younger 80
Heraclius, patriarch of Jerusalem 108, 131
High Holborn 130
Hiram 286, 287
Holborn 130
Holland 117-121, 125, 150
Holy Sepulchre 27, 28, 41, 138, 149, 156, 211, 286
Honorius III, Pope (1124-1130) 120
Hugh, Count of Champagne 32
Hugh, Count of Vermandois 19
Hugh of Bourbonne 127
Hugh of Jouy, Marshal 181
Hugh of Payns, Grand Master 32-34, 46, 84-86, 127, 220, 226, 279, 288, 294
Hugh of Pairaud 82, 236, 237, 244, 259
Hugh of St. Omer 205
Hungary 19, 53, 134, 136, 149, 150, 186, 271
Huizinga 26, 295

Ibn 'Abd al-Zahir, Arabian chronicler 206
Ibn al-Athir, Arabian chronicler 108
Ibn-al-Furat, Arabian chronicler 173
Ibn Shahhad, Arabian chronicler 108, 109
'Imad-ad-Din, Arabian chronicler 107
India 219
Innocent II, Pope (1130-1143) 231, 232, 307
Innocent III, Pope (1198-1216) 119, 134,

141-144, 147, 234, 235
Innocent IV, Pope (1243-1254) 234
Istanbul 13, 146

Jabala (Gibelet) 158
Jacob's Fort, Templar castle 94, 101, 201, 206, 208
Jan II, Duke of Brabant 264
Jaffa 113, 120, 158, 164, 175, 183, 202, 209, 210
James II, King of Aragon 238, 267, 268
James of Molay, Grand Master 57, 75, 82, 218, 237, 238, 240, 242-244, 249-251, 253, 259, 260, 274, 276, 281, 286, 290, 299, 304, 305
James of Vitry, Bishop of Acre 153, 154, 163
Janson 296
Jericho 212
St. Jerom 19
Jesus 10, 18, 27, 29, 38, 40-45, 57, 65, 76, 81, 137, 138, 146, 150, 168, 170-173, 212, 242, 257, 287-292, 296, 307, 308
Jezreel Valley 211
John, King of England 87, 131, 148, 227
John II, Byzantine emperor 86
John XXII, Pope 274
John of Brienne, King of Jerusalem 148, 156
John of Joinville 180, 181
John the Baptist 38, 69, 212
Johnson 286
Jordan 27, 60, 61, 97, 98, 101, 118, 150, 159, 169, 171, 172, 204-206, 208, 212
Julian of Sidon 212
Justinian, Roman Emperor 72

Kalavun 187, 188

Kerak 159, 160, 175-177
Kersten 146, 147
Khorezmian Turks 157, 176
Knight, Freemason 11, 41, 286-288
Krak des Chevalliers, castle of the Hospitallers 206

La Bénite, Templar ship 218
La Colée, Templar castle 214
La Fève, Templar castle 208, 209
La Forbie 175-178, 192
La Motte-Palayson 33, 128
La Roche Guilllaume, Templar castle 215, 217, 218, 304
La Roche de Roussel, Templar castle 215, 217
La Rose du Temple, Templar ship 218
Lauwerszee 119
Lazarus, Order of Saint 38, 69, 122, 230
Le Petit Gerin, Saffran, Montdidier en Tour Rouge, Templar castle 213
Leigh 38
Leo, King of Armenia 61, 141, 217
Leon 184, 185, 206
Leonardo da Vinci 148
Leopold, Duke of Austria 114
Liège 122, 264
Limassol 270
Limburg 118, 122
Lincoln 38, 265, 266
Lincolnshire 67, 131, 132
Lisbon 118, 119, 150
Lomas, Freemason 138, 287, 288
Lombardy 53, 133, 135, 146, 269, 272
London 53, 62, 80, 108, 130, 131, 136, 137, 227, 229, 265, 266, 274
Lotharingen 43
Louis VII, King of France 82, 86, 89, 91,

97, 125, 129, 225
Louis IX, King of France 73, 82, 120, 177, 181, 183, 211, 214, 225, 226, 229
Louis XVI, King of England 126
Lucca 133
Lydda 209
Lyon 186, 234, 240, 255, 271, 273
Maastricht 118, 122
Magdalon 173
Magdenburg 269
Magna Charta 131
Mainz 269
Majorca 268, 274
Maldoim (Red Sistern), Templar castle 212
Malta 11, 204, 239
Manfred, King of Sicily 230
Mansurah 178, 180
Marco Polo 296
Marseille 40, 53, 120, 129, 149, 160, 163, 165-167, 181, 217, 218
Mary Magdalene 40, 173, 308
Massada 46
Matthew Paris 54, 126, 155, 177, 205, 222, 280
Mecklenburg 118
Merle (Dor), Templar castle 211
Mexico 218
Mohammed 14, 272, 220
Mongolians 135, 136, 157, 168, 178, 184, 187, 212, 230, 241
Montdidier, Templar castle 213
Montfort, castle of the Teutonic Knights 164, 184
Moria 219, 288
Mount Tabor 173
Moses 10, 293, 294, 296
Munich 135

Nablus (Sichem) 82, 97, 175, 205
Naples 43, 68, 226, 230, 238, 265, 269
Navarre 115, 116, 159, 164, 166
Nazareth 104, 155, 173
Néaufle, castle 129
Neuchâtel, castle 129
New Temple 131, 274
Newton 286
Nice 127, 128
Nicholas IV, Pope 240
Nicosia 111, 237, 270
Nimes 260
Normandy 26, 34, 147, 226, 258, 276, 300
Norway 93
Noer-ad-Din 87, 89, 90, 92, 95-99, 205, 214

Odo of Deuil 89
Odo of Saint-Amand, Grand Master 82, 97, 103
Oliver of Paderborn 119, 120, 210, 211
Omne datum optimum 65, 86, 143, 231, 232, 307
Orleans 260
Orontes 214
Otto I, Count of Gelre 118
Otto II, bishop of Utrecht 119
Overijssel 117

Palestine 9, 14, 15, 18, 27, 32, 41, 157, 204, 250, 270, 276, 281
Paphos 270
Paradin 257, 284, 285
Paris 62, 89, 126, 129, 130, 135, 136, 149, 163, 227, 229, 242, 244, 246, 249-253, 258, 259, 262, 264, 276, 277, 280, 304
Parker 132
Parzival 290-296

Paschal II, Pope (1099-1118) 231
Payen of Montdidier 213
Pelagius 151-153
Perkins, historian 274
Peter of Montaigu, Grand Master 151-153, 157
Perugia 137, 175, 247
Peter of Amiens (the Hermit) 18, 19, 117
Philip of Nablus, Grand Master 82, 97
Philip of Plessis, Grand Master 143, 148
Philip II Augustus, King of France 80, 110, 113, 225
Philip III 226, 246
Philip IV 10, 11, 130, 189, 223, 226, 229, 235, 236, 238-249, 253, 254, 258, 261, 277, 279, 280, 284, 285, 299, 305, 306, 307
Philippe of Marigny 262
Picardy 226
Picknett 148
Pierre of Bologna 259-263, 268, 277
Pisa 28, 49, 133, 161, 183, 187, 221, 232, 239
Poitiers 115, 128, 177, 244, 252, 254-257, 260
Poitou 53, 227, 258
Poland 135, 136, 157, 271
Ponsard of Gizy 259
Port Bonnel, Templar castle 215, 217
Portugal 33, 53, 54, 115, 116, 118, 136, 219, 265, 267, 268, 272, 274, 275
Potta Johannis, Templar ship 218
Poussin 43
Provence 128, 129, 142, 151
Psellus, chronicler 284, 285

Qumran 46, 138

Rabelais 257
Rainhardus of Caro, castellan of Safad 165
Ramakers 122
Ramon Sa Guardia 268
Ramsay 11, 286
Ravenna 138, 269
Raymond Berenguer III, Count of Barcelona 115, 128

Raymond of St. Gilles, Count of Toulouse 21
Red Sistern (Maldoim), Templar castle 212
Reginald of Vichiers, Grand Master (1250 1256) 180, 181, 234
Reims 80, 263
Renaud of Provins 259-261, 263, 264
Rene of Anjou 43
Rennes-le-Château 42, 43
Rhodes 111, 239, 280, 281
Richard I, King of England (1189-1199) 82, 110, 161, 205, 227
Richard of Bures Grand Master (1244-1247) 177
Richard of Cornwall 156
Richard Plantagenet 161, 162, 176, 205, 209
Riley-Smith, historian 241
Robert of Craon, Grand Master 85, 86, 89, 91, 112
Robert of Sablé, Grand Master 111, 112, 142
Robert Vigier 261
La Rochelle 53, 86, 136, 218, 227
Roger of Flor, sergeant 218
Rolduc 118
Rome 13, 14, 18, 19, 33, 41, 70, 102, 110, 119, 133, 137, 138, 141, 233, 236, 296
Rotterdam 117

INDEX

Ruad 241
Rudolf van Seppenrode 118
Rijnsburg 118

Safad, Templar castle 95, 140, 160, 163-173, 184, 205, 206, 241
Saffran, Templar castle 207
Saforia 104, 108
Saida (Sidon) 143
Saladin 87, 96-114, 141, 150, 153, 163, 176, 178, 184, 191, 205, 206, 208, 210, 212, 214, 215, 217, 221, 224, 227, 259
Salerno 68
San Gimignano 133, 269
Savigny 225
Schellenberger 42, 43, 45
Scotland 34, 53, 130, 132, 239, 264-266, 286
Second Crusade 33, 76, 83, 87-92, 118, 149, 195, 232, 307
Sens 262-264
Seventh Crusade 177, 186, 192
Sibt Ibn al-Jauzi, Arabian chronicler 155
Sichem (Nablus) 175
Sicily 26, 43, 53, 110, 120, 133, 134, 136, 154, 156, 157, 185, 186, 224, 230, 238, 243
Sidon (Saida) 142, 183, 189, 212, 217, 237
Siena 133
Simon Magus 66
Sixth Crusade 120, 121, 154, 156, 234
Slovenia 134, 271
Sodomy 10, 71, 72, 235, 251, 259, 278
Solomon 9, 31, 40, 63, 76, 138, 219, 220, 286, 287, 293, 294, 296
Somerset 74
Sorbonne 253

Soure 33, 115
Spain 82, 102, 115, 116, 131, 136, 142, 151, 181, 184, 230, 243, 267
Split 150
Stephen, King of England (1135-1154) 67, 149, 150, 227
Stephen of Sissey, Marshal 184
Streefland, historian 121, 122

Syria 14, 21, 80, 83, 150, 159, 173, 183 185, 206, 240, 241, 299

Tagus 116
Tartus 92
Temple Brurer 131
Templecombe 74
Templière, Templar ship 218
Terricus, Grand Commander 109, 141
Texel 117
Thames 131
Thebes 134
Thessalonica 134
Theobald of Bar, bishop 264
Theobald Gaugin, Grand Master 1291-1293 184, 189, 237
Theodosius, Roman Emperor 36
Third Crusade 110, 114, 118, 120, 142, 205, 225, 233
Thomas Aquinas 37
Thomas Becket 38, 105, 227
Thomas Bérard, Grand Master (1256-1273) 183, 184
Thoros, King of Armenia 201
Tiberias 104-106, 143, 163, 169, 173
Titus 42, 138, 139
Toron of the Knights, Templar castle 210
Tortosa 92, 108, 140, 155, 160, 187, 189, 213, 214, 217, 241

Toulouse 19, 85, 128, 260
Tour Rouge, Templar castle 213
Tours 254, 260
Tower 210, 266
Trapesak (Darbsak), Templar castle 215
Trier 135, 269
Tripoli 21, 45, 53, 54, 58, 61, 67, 70, 83, 85, 92, 95, 98, 99, 102-104, 109, 141, 143, 155, 183, 186, 187, 190, 192, 211, 213-215, 217, 224, 241
Troyes 32, 34, 49, 53, 57, 127, 128, 130, 144, 146, 231, 288, 290
Tunis 120, 185
Tunesia 185
Turin Shroud 146, 148, 279, 290, 292
Tuscany 53, 133, 269, 272

Urban II, Pope 15, 17, 36, 115, 117, 231, 299
Urban, Pope (1183-1187) 18, 21
Urban IV, Pope (1261-1264) 184, 234
Usāmah 27, 67, 95, 223
Utrecht 117-119

Valencia 267
Vasco da Gama 219
Venice 28, 48, 53, 144, 145, 161, 183, 239, 241
Verona 103
Vexin 225
Vienne 255, 266, 271, 273
Villani 247
Viterbo 234
Vlaardingen 117, 119
Von Buttlar 46, 47, 218, 219

Walcheren 118
Wales 132

Walter Sans-Avoir 18, 19
Westminster Abbey 229
Willem I, Count of Holland 119
Willem II, Count of Holland 120
William of Beaujeu, Grand Master (1273-1291) 184, 186-188, 224, 237, 238, 243, 259
William of Chambonnet 261, 263

William of Chartres, Grand Master 148, 150, 151
William the Conquerer 26, 74, 226
William d'Imbert (William of Paris) 249, 251, 252, 290
William de la More, Master of England 242, 265, 266
William Marshal 79, 259
William of Nogaret 236
William of Plaisians, minister of Philip IV 249, 254, 258
William of Sonnac, Grand Master 177, 178, 180, 309
Wolfram von Eschenbach 290, 293, 294
Wilson 40

York 131, 265
Yorkshire 131

Zara 144
Zengi 85, 87, 90
Zierikzee 121, 122

INDEX